CLEARING THE LAST HURDLE
Mapping Success on the Bar Exam

CLEARING THE LAST HURDLE
Mapping Success on the Bar Exam

Wanda M. Temm

Clinical Professor of Law
Director of Bar Services
University of Missouri-Kansas City School of Law

Wolters Kluwer
Law & Business

To contact Customer Service, e-mail customer.service@wolterskluwer.com, call 1-800-234-1660, fax 1-800-901-9075, or mail correspondence to:

Wolters Kluwer Law & Business
Attn: Order Department
PO Box 990
Frederick, MD 21705

3 4 5 6 7 8 9 0

ISBN 978-1-4548-5002-1

Temm, Wanda M., author.
   Clearing the last hurdle : mapping success on the bar exam / Wanda M. Temm, Clinical Professor of Law, Director of Bar Services, University of Missouri-Kansas City School of Law.
      pages cm
   Includes bibliographical references and index.
   ISBN 978-1-4548-5002-1 (alk. paper)
1. Bar examinations—United States. 2. Law examinations—United States. I. Title.

KF303.T46 2014
349.73076—dc23
                                        2014028298

SUSTAINABLE FORESTRY INITIATIVE   Certified Sourcing
www.sfiprogram.org
SFI-00756

About Wolters Kluwer Law & Business

Wolters Kluwer Law & Business is a leading global provider of intelligent information and digital solutions for legal and business professionals in key specialty areas, and respected educational resources for professors and law students. Wolters Kluwer Law & Business connects legal and business professionals as well as those in the education market with timely, specialized authoritative content and information-enabled solutions to support success through productivity, accuracy, and mobility.

Serving customers worldwide, Wolters Kluwer Law & Business products include those under the Aspen Publishers, CCH, Kluwer Law International, Loislaw, ftwilliam.com, and MediRegs family of products.

CCH products have been a trusted resource since 1913, and they are highly regarded resources for legal, securities, antitrust and trade regulation, government contracting, banking, pension, payroll, employment and labor, and healthcare reimbursement and compliance professionals.

Aspen Publishers products provide essential information to attorneys, business professionals, and law students. Written by preeminent authorities, the product line offers analytical and practical information in a range of specialty practice areas from securities law and intellectual property to mergers and acquisitions and pension/benefits. Aspen's trusted legal education resources provide professors and students with high-quality, up-to-date, and effective resources for successful instruction and study in all areas of the law.

Kluwer Law International products provide the global business community with reliable international legal information in English. Legal practitioners, corporate counsel, and business executives around the world rely on Kluwer Law journals, looseleafs, books, and electronic products for comprehensive information in many areas of international legal practice.

Loislaw is a comprehensive online legal research product providing legal content to law firm practitioners of various specializations. Loislaw provides attorneys with the ability to quickly and efficiently find the necessary legal information they need, when and where they need it, by facilitating access to primary law as well as state-specific law, records, forms, and treatises.

ftwilliam.com offers employee benefits professionals the highest-quality plan documents (retirement, welfare, and non-qualified) and government forms (5500/PBGC, 1099, and IRS) software at highly competitive prices.

MediRegs products provide integrated health care compliance content and software solutions for professionals in healthcare, higher education, and life sciences, including professionals in accounting, law, and consulting.

Wolters Kluwer Law & Business, a division of Wolters Kluwer, is headquartered in New York. Wolters Kluwer is a market-leading global information services company focused on professionals.

For Katie, Carrie, and Keith—
the loves of my life,

and

For the students at the University of Missouri-Kansas City
School of Law, this is for you.

—WMT

Summary of Contents

Contents

CHAPTER 4
Building Essay-Writing Skills   33

CHAPTER 5
Building Multistate Performance Test Skills   51

CHAPTER 6
Building Multistate Bar Examination Skills   79

Preface and Acknowledgments

Scope

This book will guide you through all of the tasks involved in bar preparation and show you how to effectively structure your study. In addition, you will improve your skills by working through practice questions that include all three types of bar exam components—multiple choice questions, essay questions, and performance tests. The book's score sheets are designed to help you structure your answers to score well.

Content

After an introductory chapter on putting the pieces together for bar preparation, the book focuses on understanding how memory works. The bottom line of bar preparation is memorizing rules so that you can recall and use the rules applied to new hypotheticals. Chapter 2 not only describes how memory works, but it offers specific suggestions for how to encode information for later recall.

Chapter 3 focuses on establishing a game plan for bar preparation study, reviewing what a bar prep student should be doing the first few weeks of study, the next weeks, and the final weeks. Most bar prep students flounder their first few weeks because they are unsure of what exactly they should be doing. This book will guide you in how to structure your study. Chapters 4 through 6 focus on the three main parts of the bar exam in most states: essay skills, MBE skills, and performance test skills. Each chapter offers guidance on improving skills in each area, showing you how to use practice questions and score sheets to the greatest advantage.

Chapter 7 focuses on building confidence. The bar exam is a high-stakes exam—often the first high-stakes exam a bar prep student has taken. As a result, anxiety runs high. This chapter will give you specific guidance on how to handle nerves and maintain sanity during the bar preparation time period.

The following chapters then focus on each topic tested by the Multistate Essay Exam (MEE) and Multistate Bar Examination (MBE). Applicants in states that do not use the MEE will find that the skill-building suggestions and strategies work just as well in any topic area. States that do not use the MEE still test most of the same topics. I have used these materials for Missouri, a Uniform Bar Examination state, and for Kansas, a state-specific essay state, as well as for other states. Each chapter includes starter mind maps.

How to Use This Book

This book was designed to be used in a for-credit bar review course in law school. This book may also be used as a supplemental text during your bar preparation shortly before the bar examination. In a for-credit course, your professor will likely choose to cover only some of the chapters according to his goals for the course. Use the remaining chapters to supplement any commercial provider's materials during your bar preparation.

The book does not provide complete, detailed outlines of the substantive law of each topic. It does provide an initial outline of each topic that can form your initial steps in preparing your own memorization materials. As explained in Chapter 3, reviewing prepared outlines is only the first step in preparing your study materials; you will continue to supplement your materials with rules that you have missed in your practice multiple choice and essay questions.

Author

Professor Wanda M. Temm joined the UMKC School of Law faculty in 1991 as a full-time legal writing faculty member. In the early 2000s, the UMKC School of Law faculty began studying why previous excellent bar results had taken a significant fall to 67-72%—slightly below the state average. A faculty committee ultimately concluded that a variety of factors influenced bar passage. Professor Temm co-founded the UMKC Bar Prep Program and moved the program from a few practice essays to a program that provides study strategies and tactics for all aspects of bar preparation. UMKC's current bar passage rate for students actively participating in the program is above 95%, reaching 100% on several occasions.

Acknowledgments

This book is the product of materials developed for the University of Missouri-Kansas City Bar Prep Program. Many thanks go to the faculty who have taught in the program throughout the years, including Barbara Wilson, Judith Popper, Aaron House, and Leo Salinger, and to administrative assistants Elizabeth Couzens and Norma Karn, who have seen this manuscript in its various forms too many times. Their support has been unending and their contributions too numerous for words.

Special recognition goes to Rachel Wickstrum, the creator of the cartoons featured throughout the book. Her creativity and flair have resulted in visual representations of legal concepts that have helped many students to remember those concepts on the exam. Special thanks to research assistants Kelly Thompson and Jay Wheeler. Kelly's research on memory and her work on the essay score sheets were priceless. Jay's work creating the mind maps for the Teachers Manual was more detailed than I could have imagined. This book is better for their assistance.

Thanks as well to Dean Ellen Suni, the UMKC administration, and the UMKC law faculty and staff for their support of the UMKC Bar Prep Program over the years. That support has allowed us to provide our students a top-notch program using innovative teaching methods. This book would not have been created without their support.

Special thanks to the National Conference of Bar Examiners for working with me to ensure that bar applicants had access to authentic MBE, MEE, and MPT questions in this book. This book is better because of the NCBE's cooperation. In addition, the Mind Maps were created with iMindMap software. Mind Map is a registered trademark of the Buzan Organisation Limited 1990, www.thinkbuzan.com.

Lastly, special thanks to Professor Emeritus Edwin Hood. His request to "grade a few essays" started me down this path, helping me find my passion.

WMT
July 2014

CLEARING THE LAST HURDLE
Mapping Success on the Bar Exam

CHAPTER 1

Putting the Pieces Together

I. FIRST THINGS FIRST

You are rounding the corner. The end of your law school education is in sight. But "it" is out there. Waiting for you. The bar exam. The last hurdle. The last obstacle to surpass to reach your goal of practicing law. The horror stories and rumors are everywhere. Students studying eighty hours a week and still failing. The top student in the class who failed. Students needing to take the exam multiple times to pass. How can you ever do this?

Relax. Take a deep breath. You can do this. You have either graduated or will soon graduate from law school. You were selected by your law school for your aptitude to succeed. Your law school received many other applications, but it chose you. You have been preparing for this exam since law school orientation. Since that day you have been developing the exact skills you need to succeed on the bar exam. That is what your law school education was all about: preparing you to be a lawyer. Law schools do that differently, and few argue that law schools do not need to improve. The bottom line of any legal education is learning how to analyze law and how to apply that law to a new set of facts—the very skills the bar exam is assessing.

What you don't have and need to have to pass the exam are two things—a game plan and confidence. Your game plan includes the tasks that you complete to prepare to take the exam. Confidence includes confidence in your own abilities, trust in your preparation, and appreciating that you do not have to know everything to pass the bar exam.

A word about advice. Everyone will give it. Your fellow students, attorneys you know, your family, your friends—everyone has advice on taking the bar exam. Most of it will have some value. Even your parents' advice to get more sleep is good advice. For those that have actually taken the exam and succeeded, their advice to you probably helped them and may help you. But it may not be right for you. You may not learn the same way. You may not memorize the same way. So, listen to the advice and understand that it may or may not work for you.

II. DEVELOPING YOUR GAME PLAN

Many students head into bar exam preparation assuming that completing the commercial bar course they purchased is all they need to do. They go to class or watch the video lectures. They fill in the lecture handout blanks. They do a few practice questions. They continue working. They take vacations. They think nothing of missing a week of lectures, as they can catch up later.

Well, later comes sooner than you think. And when it comes, it hits you that you just wasted a month doing not much of anything of the real work of bar prep.

What is the real work? First, you must learn the law you did not learn in law school. From courses you did not take to concepts you did not understand, bar prep is the time to get it done. Understand the subject matter and it goes without saying that you are on your way to succeed.

Secondly, you must commit that law to memory. The bar exam is not open book. In some jurisdictions, you walk in the room with nothing—not even your own pen. You may be counting on being able to recognize the correct answer on the multiple choice questions, but you have to write something down on the essay questions. Indeed, memorizing the law is actually the key to doing well on the multiple choice questions as well.

Lastly, you need to be able to keep all the law you memorized fresh to be recalled on those two critical days.

How are you going to get this done? You should plan on approximately five hundred hours of study. That includes the time spent in your commercial bar preparation class and the time you spend on your own. That also means that you will not have much free time. If you try to work while you are preparing, you will not spend the same amount of time as those who are focusing only on bar prep.

The biggest problem with working is fatigue. It's hard to put in an eight- or nine-hour work day and then spend four to six hours studying. It can be done, but it will definitely drain your energy. This book will guide you in how to spend your study time to put you in the best situation to succeed, whether working or not.

Almost every commercial bar preparation course includes materials with fill-in-the-blank sentences or spaces for short answers. You follow along filling in the blanks while the lecturer speaks. The purpose of these types of materials is to keep you engaged with the material as it is being presented. Just listening to lectures does not activate your brain in the fashion needed in order to remember the material in the long term. Likewise, just reading the materials is not enough. Engaging with the materials enables your brain to retain the information. This book includes many suggestions on how to engage with the material and how to transfer that material into your long-term memory, the essence of any game plan.

Just reading practice questions and their answers results in an insufficient engagement with the material. You should not wait to do practice questions until you have "everything" memorized. You need to use the questions as a means to help learn the level of detail you need in your rule, the level of detail you need in your application, the organization of the analysis, and the style of questions in each subject area. For example, you will find that questions testing proximate cause tend to follow similar fact patterns and similar calls of the question.

This book assists you with using practice questions as a means to ensure that you are studying the law in enough detail, that you are applying the law in enough detail in your answers, and that you are organizing your answers well. This book includes practice essay questions and score sheets that show you how a sample answer is broken down into the components of a written analysis. Yes, your first year legal writing course is on the bar exam! The written analysis on essays and on performance tests boils down to organizing by a series of analyses, each organized by Conclusion or Issue, Rule, Application, and Discussion. CRAC/IRAC lives on!

This book includes a starter "mind map" on every topic tested on the Multistate Essay Exam. Most states test the same topics or alter the list slightly. But, what is a mind map? A mind map is a way of thinking about a topic matter, working step-by-step through a topic to be sure that you have identified issues. Mind maps also help you take the entire subject matter and boil it down to the essential part of the topic that you must know to pass the question.

Having a game plan structures your time so that you are not spinning your wheels and the time you spend is put to its best worth. Chapter 3 will give you more definite guidelines for how to spend your time during each part of bar preparation.

III. BUILDING CONFIDENCE WITH KNOWLEDGE

Knowledge is empowering and reassuring. The more you know and understand the task ahead of you, the more directed your preparation can be and the more confidence you have because you are facing a known entity rather than an unknown one.

A. Licensing Requirements

Your license to practice law is not a national license. Each state outlines its own requirements to obtain a license in that state. You will be licensed in just that state. States have different regulations regarding whether they will acknowledge and accept a license to practice law obtained in another state. That acknowledgement is called "reciprocity." One of your first tasks then is to understand the licensing rules for your state and for any other state in which you might wish to practice law.

Most licensing requirements have two major components: a determination of character and fitness to practice law and the passage of that state's bar examination. Character and fitness also includes passing the Multistate Professional Responsibility Exam. Some states require new admittees to take a mandatory professionalism continuing legal education course[1] and/or a basic skills course.[2] Some states that have adopted the Uniform Bar Examination add the successful completion of a state-specific law examination to their licensing requirements.[3]

One resource to locate information about your specific jurisdiction's licensing requirements is the National Conference of Bar Examiners' (NCBE) website—www.ncbex.org. You will find links to every jurisdiction's licensing authority's website. Be sure to bookmark both the NCBE website and the website for your jurisdiction as these will be frequent reference sources for you.

---

1. Ariz. R. 34(N)(1) (Arizona); C.R.C.P. 201.14(4) (Colorado).
2. West's F.S.A. Bar R. 6-12.3 (Florida); ILCS S. Ct. R. 793(C)(1) (Illinois); I.C.A. R. 41.12 (Iowa).
3. Missouri requires a mandatory open book test entitled the "Missouri Educational Component Test." Mo. Sup. Ct. R. 8.08(c). Arizona requires applicants to complete a course on Arizona law. Ariz. R. 34(j).

Another invaluable resource is your law school's academic success faculty. These faculty usually have the information critical to your jurisdiction. The career services staff or student affairs staff are often the "go-to" folks to assist students with bar exam questions.

Take a minute and research the licensing requirements in your chosen jurisdiction. Complete this checklist to keep the requirements handy.

Licensing Requirements Checklist[4]

Jurisdiction:

Educational requirements:

Law student registration required?

Due date for application to take bar examination:

Fees to take the bar examination and for character and fitness determination:

Location of bar examination:

Dates of examination:

Multistate Professional Responsibility Test passing score:

Any jurisdiction-specific additional requirements such as mandatory Continuing Legal Education (CLE) hours or passage of a state-specific exam:

Topics tested:

B. Character and Fitness

As an attorney, you will represent clients and owe those clients a fiduciary duty. You will also be an officer of the court. The goal of a character and fitness determination is "to assure the protection of the public and safeguard the justice system."[5] To do that, the Board of Bar Examiners in each jurisdiction determines an applicant's character and fitness through an investigation.

Each jurisdiction will define "character and fitness" for itself. A typical definition is that an applicant must possess the "traits, including honesty, trustworthiness, diligence and reliability that are relevant to and have a rational

---

4. Denise Riebe and Michael Hunter Schwartz, *Pass the Bar!* 59-60 (Carolina Acad. Press 2006).
5. Mont. R. Pro. on Comm'n on Character and Fitness (available at http://www.montanabar .org/associations/7121/files/2012_Final_CAF_Rules%20of%20Procedure.pdf.).

connection with the applicant's present fitness to practice law."[6] Boards of bar examiners are concerned the most with an applicant's criminal record, untreated mental illness and substance abuse, lack of candor, and irresponsibility.[7] Each board will have its own guidelines on each of these concerns. Your academic success faculty and perhaps your professional responsibility faculty may be able to answer your questions concerning personal issues.

C. The Bar Examination

The actual exam is typically two or three days. Each state determines for itself how its examination is constructed. Typical components include multiple choice questions, essay questions, and performance tests.

1. Multistate Bar Examination

All states except Louisiana include multiple choice questions developed by the NCBE. In addition, Guam, Northern Mariana Islands, Palau, and the Virgin Islands have adopted these multiple choice questions. These questions are given on the same two dates across the nation in every adopting jurisdiction—the last Wednesday of February and July. This part of the bar examination is called the Multistate Bar Examination (MBE).

The MBE consists of 100 multiple choice questions in a 3-hour time period in the morning and another 100 multiple choice questions in a 3-hour time period in the afternoon. If you are down to the last five minutes and haven't answered every question, fill in the rest of the answer grid and then go back and correct if you have time. Ten of the questions are being evaluated for future use. Be sure to answer all 200 questions as you will not know which questions are the test questions. There is no penalty for incorrect answers.

The subjects include federal Constitutional Law; Contracts, including the common law and the Uniform Commercial Code Article 2; Criminal Law and Procedure; Evidence (testing the Federal Rules of Evidence); Federal Civil Procedure; Real Property; and Torts. The NCBE provides subject matter outlines for each subject to help applicants direct their study.

The MBE is scored by the NCBE on a nation-wide basis. The ten test questions are not included in the score. The raw score is thus determined by your correct answers to 190 of the questions minus any questions that the NCBE decides are not "good" questions. Why would a question be tossed out? Questions are tossed out when the nation-wide results show the question was ambiguous or that there truly was more than one correct answer. Your raw score is then scaled to reflect the difficulty of the exam vis-à-vis prior exams. It is that scaled score that is then used by the jurisdictions. Each jurisdiction decides how much weight to give that score. Uniform Bar Examination states weigh the MBE scaled score at 50%.

---

6. Minn. R. for Admission to the Bar 2A(6).
7. Lori E. Shaw, *What Does it Take to Satisfy Character & Fitness Requirements?*, 37 Student Lawyer, October 2008 (available at http://www.americanbar.org/publications/syllabus_home/volume_44_2012-2013/winter_2012-2013/professionalism_whatdoesittaketosatisfychracterandfitness require.html>).

Chapter 6 will assist you in developing your strategy for studying for the MBE and in how to attack the questions to improve your chances of selecting the correct response.

2. Essay Questions

No matter who drafts the essay questions or what law is applied, essays require analyzing a set of facts, recalling the rule from memory, applying that law, and then communicating your analysis in written form. Whether the question is 30 minutes or 60 minutes, contains one major issue or a dozen issues, or covers one topic or three topics, the analysis is what counts in the end.

a. Multistate Essay Exam

The Multistate Essay Exam (MEE) is written by the NCBE. Thirty jurisdictions currently utilize MEE questions. Six 30-minute questions are offered for each administration of the exam. Jurisdictions may decide which of the questions they use. Uniform Bar Examination states must use all six. Jurisdictions also decide the relative weight given to the MEE and other scores. Uniform Bar Examination jurisdictions weight the MEE component 30%.

The NCBE considers "[t]he purpose of the MEE is to test the examinee's ability to

- identify legal issues raised by a hypothetical factual situation;
- separate material which is relevant from that which is not;
- present a reasoned analysis of the relevant issues in a clear, concise, and well-organized composition; and
- demonstrate an understanding of the fundamental legal principles relevant to the probable solution of the issues raised by the factual situation."[8]

The MEE covers the topics included in the MBE and additional topics. The following table lists these topics. Some of these topics are actually two separate topics. For example, Criminal Law has quite a different focus than Criminal Procedure. One focuses on the elements of crime, mens rea, and defenses while the other focuses on the constitutional protections afforded criminal defendants.

Most questions focus on only one area of law. Some questions may include more than one area of law. For example, Conflicts of Law is always paired with another topic such as Federal Civil Procedure or Family Law.

MEE questions are scored by each jurisdiction and not by the NCBE. Any questions about scoring should be directed to that jurisdiction. The raw scores are then sent to the NCBE, which takes the raw score and employs any weighting required by the jurisdiction. The NCBE determines the scaled score and returns it to the jurisdiction.

b. State-Drafted Essays

State-drafted essays are used in jurisdictions that do not use the MEE in whole. These jurisdictions may use a combination of MEE questions and state-drafted questions or rely solely on state-drafted questions. These questions are typically drafted by the members of the Board of Law Examiners themselves or by committees appointed by the board.

---

8. http://www.ncbex.org/about-ncbe-exams/mee/.

MEE TOPICS
Agency and Partnership
Conflict of Laws
Constitutional Law (Federal)
Contracts (including UCC Article 2 Sales)
Corporations and Limited Liability Companies
Criminal Law and Procedure
Decedent's Estates
Evidence
Family Law
Federal Civil Procedure
Real Property
Torts
Trusts and Future Interests
Uniform Commercial Code: Secured Transactions

State-drafted essays may focus on specific aspects of that jurisdiction's law or may focus on the same topics covered in the MEE. Texas, for example, tests consumer rights, including insurance, oil and gas, and bankruptcy. North Carolina includes legal ethics and taxation. Be sure to research the topics your state's bar examination covers.

State-drafted questions are scored by that jurisdiction. Different jurisdictions grade on different scales, such as 5 points, 6 points, 10 points, or 100 points. Those raw scores are then sent to the NCBE to be scaled to the same scale as the MBE with the jurisdiction's required weighting. Then, just like the MEE, that scaled score is sent back to the jurisdiction.

Chapter 4 focuses exclusively on building essay-writing skills. That chapter's focus on skill building works for MEE and for state-drafted essays. Using these specific strategies can help you have your structure set so that you can drop the rule in and apply it and keep your focus on getting enough detail in your answer.

3. Performance Tests

a. Multistate Performance Test

The Multistate Performance Test (MPT) adds another dimension to the skills tested on the bar examination. Just like the MBE and essay questions, the MPT is designed to test your analysis skills. The MPT is an assessment of "an examinee's ability to use fundamental lawyering skills in a realistic situation."[9] This is

---

9. http://www.ncbex.org/about-ncbe-exams/mpt/.

accomplished by giving the applicant a drafting "task that a beginning lawyer should be able to accomplish."[10]

Good news! The MPT does not require that you have law memorized. Instead, it gives you the law to analyze and asks you to apply that law to a set of facts. The facts are contained in a "File," which can include letters, deposition transcripts, witness interviews, invoices—basically anything that an attorney uses to gather facts. Sometimes facts are missing and part of the applicant's task is to identify those missing facts. Other facts are ambiguous or irrelevant. Your job is to recognize those situations and identify sources of additional facts.

The law is contained in a "Library." This Library includes all the law you are to analyze—statutes, excerpts from cases, administrative regulations, or rules. You are not to support your analysis with other law that you know. You analyze what is given to you.

The MPT includes a memo from a partner at your firm or from a supervising district attorney requesting that you draft a particular document. The NCBE lists the different kinds of documents that have been included in past MPTs. Most of the time, the MPT is a letter, a memo, or a brief.

MPTs are graded by the jurisdiction, usually on the same scale as an essay question. That score is then sent to the NCBE who scales it according to each jurisdiction's policies.

What is most challenging about the MPT is the time constraint. Each MPT is 90 minutes. Virtually every applicant will be time-pressured to complete the task. Time management is an essential strategy to perform well on the MPT. Chapter 5 will give you specific suggestions for developing a game plan to do well on your MPTs.

b. State Performance Tests

Some jurisdictions add their own performance tests. California, for example, requires that you pass two of its performance tests. They are similar to the style of the MPT, but focus on California law.

D. Uniform Bar Examination

In February 2011, Missouri and North Dakota were the first jurisdictions to administer the Uniform Bar Examination (UBE) developed by the National Conference of Bar Examiners. As of the July 2014 administration, 14 jurisdictions have adopted the examination.[11] The UBE allows your score on the bar examination to be transferred to another state, allowing licensure in more than one state without taking a second bar examination. Applicants frequently must choose a jurisdiction before they have secured employment. Once employed, they discover they are required to be licensed in a different jurisdiction. If both states have adopted the UBE, the first state's score is transferred to the second state. Thus, the applicant does not have to take two bar examinations! This increased mobility of your examination score should be more economical for an applicant as the fee to become licensed in the second jurisdiction by

---

10. *Id.*

11. Alabama, Alaska, Arizona, Colorado, Idaho, Minnesota, Missouri, Montana, Nebraska, New Hampshire, North Dakota, Utah, Washington, and Wyoming. http://www.ncbex.org/about-ncbe-exams/ube/.

transferring a UBE score may be less[12] and the applicant will not have to miss work and give up weekends to study for a second bar exam.

The NCBE's philosophy is that "an individual who performs to an acceptable level on a high-quality licensing test has attained valuable currency that should be accepted by other jurisdictions."[13] Each jurisdiction determines its own character and fitness requirements, sets its own passing scores, and determines how long incoming UBE scores will be accepted, among other decisions. A jurisdiction may require applicants to complete a jurisdiction-specific educational component or pass a test on jurisdiction-specific law in addition to passing the UBE.

The UBE starts with two MPT questions in the morning of the first day. The afternoon includes six 30-minute MEE questions. The second day is the MBE. The MBE is weighted 50%, the MEE 30%, and the MPT 20%. All parts of the examination are prepared by the NCBE. Jurisdictions continue to score the MEE and MPT questions themselves.

IV. MAINTAINING YOUR SANITY

No doubt about it, the bar preparation months and examination days are a stressful time in your life. The bar examination is a high-stakes test. Failing to pass the bar exam means that you cannot practice law. While there are many things that you can do with a law degree, most graduates wish to practice law in some fashion. Additionally, most applicants either do not have employment secured following graduation or their employment requires passage of the exam. That only increases the stress.

Stress has a physical impact on your body, on your mental state, and on your thinking. If you are constantly worried and thinking about what happens after the exam, you cannot be as focused on engaging with the material and memorizing the material. Chapter 7 will give you specific suggestions for managing your stress and building your confidence in your abilities and your preparation—a key component in lessening your stress.

V. THE NEXT STEP

Now that you have a better idea about what the bar examination actually entails, it's time to get started. Our first step is to understand how memory works. Our goal is to have as many of each bar examination topic's rules in our long-term memory as possible. How are we going to accomplish that task? Chapter 2 focuses exclusively on memory and using mind maps.

Next, you need to develop your game plan for studying and build your skills in writing essays, answering MBE questions, and writing MPTs. Chapters 4 through 6 give specific suggestions for building skills. Chapters 9 through 20 focus on

---

12. As of September 2013, North Dakota's fee for a transferred UBE score was $775 while the fee to take the exam was $825 to $975. Compare http://www.ndcourts.gov/court/committees/barbd/julybarinst.pdf with http://www.ndcourts.gov/court/committees/barbd/instscore.pdf.

13. http://www.ncbex.org/assets/media_files/UBE/NALP-Bulletin-Article-by-EM-March-2010.pdf.

specific topics and the strategies unique to each topic. Starter mind maps are included with each topic as well as practice questions and score sheets.

Lastly, you need to build your confidence. This entire book is designed to do that. Chapter 7 offers specific suggestions to build confidence. Chapter 8 focuses on specific suggestions for those repeating the exam.

Keep one thing on your mind while you prepare, whether this is your first exam or whether you have taken the exam before: You can do this!

Finish Line

CHAPTER 2

Understanding Memory and Mind Maps

Believe it or not, you already have some of the law you need for the bar exam in your long-term memory. This law was not there prior to law school. Did you know what a tort was? What did you know about negligence prior to law school? Had you ever heard the phrase "proximate cause," much less known what it meant? At a minimum, you now know that to hold a defendant liable for a negligent act the defendant must have had a duty to the plaintiff and must have breached that duty. That breach must have then caused the plaintiff's damages; both actual causation and proximate causation are required. Somehow over the last three years, that information was transferred into your long-term memory. Information you did not already know. And, more importantly, you also now have the ability to recall that information effortlessly.

The more we understand about how memory works the better our chances of staying focused on encoding techniques to transfer as much information about bar-tested topics into our long-term memory.

I. MEMORY: WHAT IS IT AND HOW DOES IT WORK?

In essence, memory is the "ability to retain information over time."[1] Our focus is on three different types of memory: sensory, short-term, and long-term. Understanding these different types of memory help us understand how they function together.

When perceived, information first enters the **sensory memory**. Our mind stores information there for very brief periods of time. Information in sensory memory will be quickly forgotten if you do not actively pay attention to it. The role of the sensory memory is two-fold: it helps filter various stimuli and prevents us from becoming overwhelmed; it provides the opportunity to decide whether the incoming information is important. Attending to the information held in sensory memory then transfers that information to short-term memory.

Short-term memory, or working memory, also holds information for short periods of time. Much like sensory memory, short-term memory will dispel information quickly if you do not pay attention to it. Short-term memory goes

---

1. Rod Plotnik, *Introduction to Psychology* 239 (6th ed. 2002).

through cycles—allowing new information in, retaining it, then erasing that information and beginning again with new information.

This type of memory is characterized by two limiting features. The first is limited duration, which refers to the short period of time information remains in short-term memory—usually less than thirty seconds. Entering information quickly over-writes existing information, whether verbal or visual stimuli. Secondly , short-term memory can only hold about seven items simultaneously in its verbal function. Four stimuli can be held in the visual function of short-term memory at the same time as the seven verbal stimuli. Thus, "the visual function of working memory expands the number of items that students can simultaneously focus on while learning the law."[2]

Certain techniques may help overcome these limiting functions, such as maintenance rehearsal and chunking. Maintenance rehearsal refers to the act of repeating certain information in order to keep it in short-term memory for a longer period of time. Chunking aims at improving short-term memory by increasing the number of items it can hold at one time. This process consists of grouping individual pieces of information together in a larger unit to remember, called a chunk. Chunking verbal stimuli and visual stimuli together increases the number of both kinds of stimuli that can be remembered. Moreover, chunking visual and verbal stimuli leads to a better understanding and retention of the concepts than either individually.[3]

While short-term memory allows us to concentrate on relevant information, the information must be encoded in order to become permanently stored. If we do not engage the information in our short-term memory, it slips away and is forgotten. On the other hand, paying attention to the information held in short-term memory, bolstered by rehearsal techniques, allows the information to be encoded for storage in long-term memory.

Long-term memory is the process of storing information for extended periods of time, with the possibility of retrieving that information in the future. Information reaches long-term memory after being transferred from short-term memory through the encoding process. There are two kinds of long-term memory. Procedural, also called nondeclarative, long-term memory "involves memories for motor skills (playing tennis), some cognitive skills (learning to read), and emotional behaviors learned through classical conditioning (fear of spiders)."[4] Procedural memories are not among those we have the ability to recall. We can, however, recall and retrieve declarative memories. Declarative long-term memory "involves memories for facts or events, such as scenes, stories, words, conversations, faces, or daily events."[5] Declarative memory also consists of two different types: semantic and episodic. Semantic declarative memory refers to the knowledge of facts and concepts, while episodic declarative memory comprises knowledge of activities, personal experience, and events.

Information stored in long-term memory remains there on a relatively permanent basis. Ideally, the information will be available for recall at a later

---

2. Hillary Burgess, *Deepening the Discourse Using the Legal Mind's Eye: Lessons from Neuroscience and Psychology that Optimize Law School Learning*, 29 Quinnipiac L. Rev. 1, 27 (2011).

3. *See id.* at 29 (citing Slava Kalyuga, Paul Chandler, & John Sweller, *Managing Split-Attention and Redundancy in Multimedia Instruction*, 13 Applied Cognitive Psychol. 353, 362 (1999)).

4. *Id.*at 246.

5. *Id.*

TYPES OF MEMORY			
	Storage	Length of time	Attributes
SENSORY	Involuntary.	Very brief; can be less than a second.	Helps us sort stimuli so as not to be overwhelmed. Vanishes unless we pay attention to it.
SHORT-TERM OR WORKING MEMORY	Focused attention moves information from sensory memory.	Short periods of time, less than 30 seconds.	Stimuli cycles in and out. Capacity is limited: 7 verbal and 4 visual stimuli. Must encode information for retention in long-term memory.
LONG-TERM MEMORY	Effortful encoding moves information from short-term memory.	Extended periods of time, often permanent.	Stores information for lengthy time periods with the possibility of retrieving the information in the future.

time. Exactly what and how much we are able to recall or retrieve from long-term memory depends largely on how the information was encoded and other factors such as interference. Remember that memories are not complete and accurate copies. Our goal in bar preparation is to transfer as much information about bar-tested topics into our long-term memory through encoding to recall it in as much detail as we can.

II. IMPORTANCE OF ENCODING

Encoding plays a central role in the ability to retrieve and recall information. The encoding process involves transferring new information from short-term memory into long-term memory by changing that information into neural codes. Two kinds of encoding can occur. Automatic encoding involves the transfer of information to long-term memory without effort. Information about personal events, skills, or habits is encoded automatically. Conversely, effortful encoding involves hard work and concentration. Usually, factual or complex information requires effort to encode. The two primary methods of effortful encoding are rehearsing/repeating the information and making associations.

When it comes to encoding information, mere rehearsal proves less effective than the alternative method of forming associations. Repetitive rehearsal does not form a location in our memory to allow us to recall the information easily. Meanwhile, elaborative rehearsal "involves using effort to actively make meaningful associations between new information that you wish to remember and old or familiar information that is already stored in long-term memory."[6] This method of encoding provides cues as to the location of

---

6. *Id.* at 249.

the newly stored information, thus making it more beneficial. Encoding information is much like saving information on a computer—it is necessary to have a solid system in place for labeling and filing information, otherwise retrieval will be difficult or impossible.

According to the Network or Connectionist Theory, "we store related ideas in separate categories, or files, called nodes. As we make new associations among information, we create links among thousands of nodes, which make up a gigantic interconnected network of files for storing and retrieving information."[7] Forming new associations essentially creates "mental roads" between nodes.

Another way to think about memory is to compare it to a warehouse. Better warehouse organization leads to easier recall. The most important memory improvement technique while studying is to think about what you are reading, instead of simply looking at the material—stop and reflect along the way. Echoing the significance of forming connections between new and old information, remember that "[w]hen you think about the material, you connect it to your existing knowledge, and these connections make it easier to later retrieve the material."[8]

Ultimately, remembering information often boils down to how that information was encoded. The strongest system for encoding information is elaborative rehearsal, if associations are formed. Under the levels-of-processing theory, "[i]f you encode by paying attention only to basic features . . . information is encoded at a shallow level and results in poor recall. If you encode by making new associations, this information will be encoded at a deeper level, which results in better recall."[9]

Doing practice bar questions is one way you will encode bar-tested topics into your long-term memory. Simply trying to answer hundreds of questions without doing something with the information you receive is an example of merely rehearsing the information. You hope by being as familiar as you can with the information that you will be able to recognize the correct answer on the exam. In essence, the information is stored on a shallow level leaving it unreliable for recall.

Better storage requires that you make associations with that information, not just be familiar with the material. Encoding through making associations means that you must take the commercial provider's outlines and turn them into your own memorization materials—your library. In Chapter 3, Developing Your Game Plan, we will focus on specific techniques to help you make associations and build your library while you practice questions and review information.

III. FORGETTING

Forgetting is the "inability to retrieve, recall, or recognize information" stored in long-term memory.[10] Interference and poor (or changed) retrieval cues are among the most common problems when it comes to remembering.

"Retrieval . . . is initiated by the presentation of one or more retrieval cues, and the amount retrieved depends on the similarity of this retrieval cue to the stimuli present during encoding."[11] Retrieval cues are essentially mental

---

7. *Id.* at 262.
8. David A. Lieberman, *Learning and Memory: An Integrative Approach* 453 (2004).
9. Plotnik, *supra* note 1, at 249.
10. *Id.* at 265.
11. Lieberman, *supra* note 6, at 425.

reminders that we generate by forming associations or mental images. Such cues might be contextual or other cues that stimulate the senses. Even if the information is stored, a missing cue may render the information irretrievable.

Interference occurs when the recall of some information is blocked by other information. "New material tends to interfere with old materials."[12] The greater the similarity between previously learned information and the information currently being learned, the greater the likelihood of confusion. Mental overcrowding is another example of interference. Other common memory problems include a negative self-concept, under-learning, disuse and lack of attention, and effort. Time can also hinder memory.

The first step to avoid forgetting is actively engaging with the material and intending to remember. Overlearning, talking about the material out loud, daily review, and practice tests are valuable tools to combat the threat of forgetting. In addition, constructing connections between ideas and getting a feel for the big picture can be quite useful. A technique called the "spacing effect" helps to prevent memory decay. The spacing effect requires eliminating cramming sessions and restructuring study habits to include studying for shorter periods over the course of several days and studying across subjects. Your game plan will take advantage of this effect by reviewing several topics a week and then going back over previously encoded topics.

IV. CONCENTRATION

Common barriers to building concentration include fatigue, distractions, and hunger. Take care of your physical needs for sleep and food. Then, quite simply, the main solution is to build an interest in the material. Setting goals and studying in a place designated only for that purpose are also effective concentration boosters. In addition, varying the study activity, setting a time frame to study, relating learning, organizing the task, and pacing comprise several other concentration tools.

V. DOES WRITING IMPACT OUR ABILITY TO REMEMBER?

Taking notes, writing down what we do not want to forget, seems like good common sense. But does it make a difference? At the very least, writing gives us the opportunity to clarify our thoughts. Different regions of the brain come into play. Each region of the brain processes different types of information, such as visual, auditory, or verbal communication. While each region has its own process, each communicates with the others. Writing creates spatial relationships in terms of the information being written and these spatial relationships engage different regions of the brain. Such links between regions of the brain help strengthen the process of information storage. The writer must also filter information and make decisions about which information is the most relevant or significant. Writing involves actively thinking about how to evaluate and order

---

12. Academic Resource Center Idea Sheet, *Forgetting*, Utah State University 1 (2006), http://www.usu.edu/arc/idea_sheets/pdf/forgetting.pdf.

incoming information. This process, as opposed to the actual notes taken, is critical and helps fix ideas more firmly in our minds. The end product of what you write is far less important than the process of thinking about and analyzing the material. The thinking and analysis is the encoding.

In terms of biology, another specific area of the brain might play a key role. "Writing stimulates a bunch of cells at the base of the brain called the reticular activating system (RAS)."[13] The RAS is the "automatic mechanism inside [the] brain that brings relevant information to your attention."[14] Thus, the RAS acts as a filter—placing greater importance on what you are actively concentrating on. The physical act of writing, then, brings it to the forefront.

VI. IMPROVING YOUR MEMORY

In terms of study time, set specific goals. Identify what you need to accomplish in the time you have available. Keep your work space organized, clean, and free from distractions like your cell phone or TV. During your study session, take breaks to refocus your attention. When you complete your study session, evaluate it—identify what you can change to make the next session more productive. A wide variety of study strategies can assist you during your study session. However, some activities are more beneficial than others. Consider which methods have worked for you before and consider using other methods such as creating summaries or visual organizers.

VII. MIND MAPS AS A MEMORY TOOL

The technique of mind mapping was developed during the 1960s. With an extensive volume of written work in the areas of learning, memory improvement, and maximizing one's mental skills; Tony Buzan is credited with, at the very least, popularizing and promoting the use of mind mapping. A mind map is essentially a diagram, or a "two-dimensional drawing or representation . . . of the critical information and concepts being discussed."[15] This type of visual diagram illustrates ideas in a "relational context, with the main topic at the center of the map, major subtopics on branches radiating from the main topic, and sub-subtopics around each subtopic," and so forth.[16] All maps start with a core idea or concept and branch outward. These maps allow us to "rapidly generate, structure, classify and visualize ideas."[17]

Mind mapping offers a variety of benefits and advantages. As opposed to traditional note-taking, the design of mind maps helps keep the big picture in mind. This technique is also more flexible than traditional outlining because it

---

13. Melanie Pinola, *Why You Learn More Effectively by Writing Than Typing*, Lifehacker (2011). Available at http://lifehacker.com/5738093/why-you-learn-more-effectively-by-writing-than-typing.

14. *The Reticular Activating System: Your Automatic Goal Seeking Mechanism*, Make-Your-Goals-Happen.com (date unknown) (exploring the role of RAS in the context of goal setting), http://www.make-your-goals-happen.com/reticular-activating-system.html.

15. Nerino J. Petro, Jr., *Hate Taking Notes? Try Mind Mapping*, 27 No. 4 GPSolo 20, 21 (Feature, June 2010) (Westlaw Lawprac Index).

16. Diane Murley, *Technology for Everyone . . . Mind Mapping Complex Information*, 99 Law Libr. J. 175 (2007).

17. Dave Maxfield & Michael Deutch, *Mind Mapping for Lawyers*, 21 S.C. Law 18, 19 (Sept. 2009).

allows information to be captured and easily rearranged and enables us to step away from and return to the map without losing our place. Along the same lines, a mind map is often easier to comprehend, thus saving time and allowing us to be more productive. Because less writing is typically required to generate a mind map, reviewing the map proves much faster.

Perhaps the most significant advantage of mind mapping is the ability to see concepts in relation to each other. Because traditional, hierarchical note-taking often takes the form of listing, it is difficult to demonstrate relationships between concepts. Mind mapping provides the opportunity to "differentiate between different ideas and concepts using shapes, colors, and images" and allows us to group concepts together and show relationships between them.[18] In this sense, mind mapping engages both the creative and analytical hemispheres of the brain. The promotion of visualization plays a key role in the success of mind maps. It is often said that we think and learn in three primary ways: auditory, kinesthetic, and visual. While we each prefer one method, we use all three. "Regardless of [your] preferred learning and thinking style, visualization can simplify complex ideas, show the relationship between those ideas and help organize thoughts."[19] Mind mapping allows us to see ideas and concepts in a non-linear fashion, breaking away from more rigid forms of note-taking. Mind mapping takes advantage of our ability to hold seven stimuli in our verbal function and four stimuli in our visual function of short-term memory. Integrating these stimuli in a mind map, we are chunking the information in a manner that should lead to easier recall and open space for more integration of stimuli.

There is no one right way to create a mind map. Each is unique to the creator and for the creator's needs. It encapsulates how you envision the topic. What are its components? Are there subcomponents? Are there definitions or dates that are relevant? Numerous types of mind-mapping software are available, frequently at no cost. This listing is just a few sources that are available.

- www.thinkbuzan.com
- www.mindjet.com
- www.xmind.net
- www.mindnode.com
- www.novamind.com

There is a learning curve with any new software. Spend some time learning how to use the software before you delve into creating your maps.

VIII. CREATING A MIND MAP

Let's create a mind map to give you an idea of how to take the mind map starters provided in each topical chapter of this book and expand them to cover what you need to know for the bar exam on that topic.

For our example, let's use a science topic in elementary school that requires understanding the different types of animals. Your goal is to understand the characteristics of each type of animal so that you can classify different animals because you understand and have memorized each animal type's characteristics.

---

18. Petro, *supra* note 13, at 22.
19. Maxfield and Deutch, *supra* note 15 at 20.

The starter mind map would place each type of animal on a branch.[20]

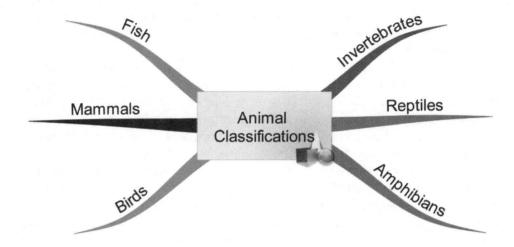

Then, based on the information you need to understand and memorize, you branch off each main component with the subcomponents. These subcomponents could be the same for each main branch. Thus, each animal type would have a branch for origins, a branch for characteristics, a branch for habitat, and a branch for food. But, they don't have to be. This mind map is for you. It doesn't have to be perfectly balanced. One animal type might need only three of the four or maybe four completely different subcomponents. It is up to you and what you need to memorize.

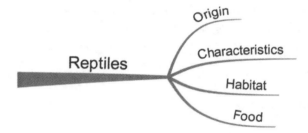

For some branches, use a text box to give a definition or explanation.

---

20. Laura Klappenbach, "The Basic Animal Groups," http://animals.about.com/od/animal-facts/tp/animal-groups.htm.

For others, use more branches for differentiation of the concepts.

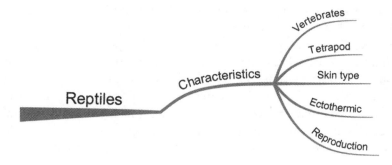

Then add more text boxes or branches as needed.

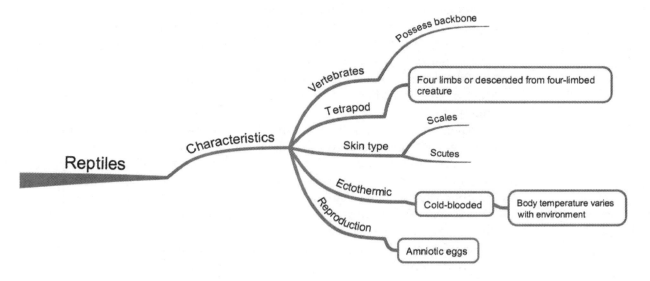

Your mind map has now grown in detail. Let's see how this branch of the map fits into the overall map.

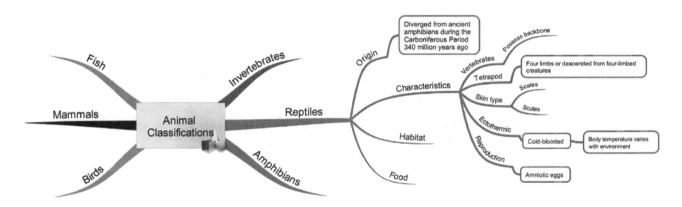

Picture doing the same thing with each branch. A mind map is not something you read left to right. Start in the middle and go out on each branch on which you are working. Then, step back and see the big picture. You will see the association between the details of the branch and the big picture.

What has been happening in your brain while you have prepared this map? While you have been sorting the information and deciding what goes where and how it should be memorialized, you have been encoding the information into your memory. This effortful encoding involves hard work and concentration and makes up a key component of the "real work" of bar preparation. You are learning the material and storing it in your mind in such a way that you will be able to recall that information when you need it on the exam. You are making associations between concepts. Now when you review the physical embodiment of your mind map before the exam, you are rehearsing and repeating the information drawing on the associations you created in the map. As an end result, the information is stored in your long-term memory and you are able to recall it when you need it.

In this book, mind mapping for the bar exam includes the visual diagramming and also serves as a method to organize your thinking about bar topics. Creating a bar topic mind map requires you to sort and prioritize information about the rules, thus analyzing and organizing the information. But you can also use the mind map on the exam itself—obviously not your written mind map, but your visualization of it. When stumped, begin at the center point of your map and follow the branches through the topics until it triggers the issue and its rule. Most of the time that will do the trick and the issue and rule will become apparent.

When should you make your mind maps? Each student will create mind maps at different times during their preparation. Some will immediately begin their mind maps as they conceptualize the overall topic. Others will wait until they have spent some time in the topic and feel more ready to tackle it. Either way, try to have your mind maps at least partially complete by the start of your second month of bar prep. Then, you can finish them for your needs during those last few weeks.

Remember that your ability to store rules in your long-term memory is necessary to perform well on both multiple choice questions and on the essay portions of the bar exam. This real work of bar prep takes the most significant and critical portion of your bar preparation time.

CHAPTER 3

Developing Your Game Plan

Your bar preparation has three phases. First, you must learn the law. Next, you must memorize the law. Lastly, you must refresh your recollection of the law in the last two weeks to be sure all the rules are fresh. How much time will this take? Approximately 500 hours. That includes time you spend in your commercial bar prep course, time you spend reviewing material, time you spend memorizing or preparing outlines, time you spend doing practice questions, even time reading this book!

I. THE STARTING GATE

When do you start your preparation? In one sense, it started your first day of law school as you began gaining the skills you need and began learning the substance of bar topics. At the end of law school, the time is ripe to prepare for the bar exam directly.

A word of caution: Your law school may allow you to finish graduation requirements after your commencement ceremony and still certify you to take the bar exam if the jurisdiction allows it. Do not be tempted to do that. Finishing class requirements on top of starting bar prep is a recipe for failure. Just get your work done during the semester and avoid the double-work that happens if you wait.

A. First-Time Takers

1. For-credit Courses

For first-time bar exam takers, the time to start depends upon several factors. If you are fortunate to be at a law school that offers a for-credit class in bar prep skills, that course is your best time to start. A for-credit course is frequently offered in the last semester of law school. It will help you in developing your game plan, trying out your game plan, making adjustments to your game plan as you go, reinforcing the skills you have, and attaining the skills you need.

2. Taking a Commercial Bar Preparation Course

If you are not able to take a for-credit course, are graduating law school right before the exam, and are taking a commercial bar preparation course, you need to consider when your law school holds graduation and when your commercial bar preparation course begins. If possible, take some time off after graduation. Relax. Do things you enjoy. Spend time with family and friends. You just got through your finals and submitted your last papers. Bar prep can wait until your commercial bar prep course begins. That does not mean to take the first few weeks of bar prep off in order to vacation! Every week of bar prep has a purpose. If you enter bar prep planning to take a week or so off, then you need to start your bar preparation *before* the commercial prep course begins. Do not wait until you get back from vacation.

3. Self-Study Approach

If this is your first time taking the bar exam and you do not intend to take a commercial bar prep course, you need to consider whether you want to work at the same time. If you do not plan to work, you can still take some time off after graduation. You can begin at the same time that the commercial bar preparation courses begin. If you plan to work and study with a self-study approach, then you really do not have time for a couple of weeks off. Taking a self-study approach does not mean you can jam it all in in less time. Those 500 hours hold true for you, too. As most of your day is spent working, you will have fewer hours to devote to bar study each day. It will be necessary to start earlier and spread your study over a longer period of time.

B. Repeat Takers

If this is not your first time taking the bar exam, the answer to when you should start is different. First, you may have significant time between the results and the next exam. You need some time to adjust to the results you received. Once the initial adjustment is over, take all that emotion and turn it around to motivate you to show the bar examiners that they should have passed you the first time!

Secondly, most repeat takers are employed by the time they are taking the exam again. Working 40 or more hours a week while preparing for the exam can be done, but you will be fatigued and will have little down time. If you did not do a commercial bar prep course the first time, seriously consider taking one this time. It will help you stay on track. It is a large expenditure, to be sure, but worth it.

If you did complete a commercial course the first time, you should generally start your study six to eight weeks before the first-time takers start. If you did not make your own flash cards, outlines, or flow charts the first time around, start making those for every topic. Start with the "Big Seven"—the topics tested on the MBE: Constitutional Law, Contracts, Criminal Law and Procedure, Evidence, Federal Civil Procedure,[1] Real Property, and Torts. Do one topic a week. Once the first-time takers begin, switch to the essay topics.

If you did make your own outlines or flash cards, two possible things happened. First, you may not have put enough detail into the rules you were memorizing. Or, you put too much detail into your rule such that you could not memorize much of it or it kept you from focusing on what is critical. Thus,

---

1. Starting with the February 2015 exam.

you need to supplement or cull appropriately. Chapter 8 gives repeat takers more guidance in preparing to retake the bar exam.

Whether you are taking the bar exam for the first time or retaking the exam or you are taking a commercial bar prep course or taking a self-study approach, or you are working or are spending 100% of your time on bar study, your game plan starts in the same place—learn the law.

II. THE GAME PLAN

A. Phase One—Learn the Law

Most commercial bar prep courses begin with the Big Seven. It makes sense to start with the Big Seven as you know they are worth half of your points in most jurisdictions. In UBE or MEE states, it also makes the most sense as you will likely have essays on the Big Seven as well.

Most law schools require these courses in the first or second year of law school, thus, they are all familiar to you. Some of the concepts you may have learned very well when you took the course, and this review will just be refreshing your recollection. Other concepts you may not have fully grasped or your professor may not have introduced in your particular course.

If you had difficulty with a course, it is tempting to save it for last. Starting with something familiar is comforting when you are under the stress of this challenge. And facing that bear of a course can be discouraging. But you do have to face it. You cannot skip a topic—particularly one of the Big Seven.

Before a lecture in your commercial bar prep course, skim the outline for that topic. You are seeking to get a big picture of the topic—how everything fits together. Start to become familiar with the buzz words or key concepts. Do not read the outline for complete understanding at this point. Just refamiliarize yourself with the topic. If you did not take a course in a particular topic, do not wait until the lecture to start learning the topic. Those are the topics in which you need to read the outline in more depth, rather than skimming the material.

During the lecture, keep engaged with the materials by filling in the blanks or doing the short answer problems. No need to bring your laptop or tablet to the lectures. Keep your phone off and out of the way. This is not the time to text friends or answer email. Facebook and Twitter really can wait. Tell your family and friends not to expect immediate responses to their texts and emails during lecture. If at home, set up your environment to avoid distractions as much as you can. If possible, plan a lecture spot away from home. Take your laptop and earphones and view the lecture at your favorite coffee spot. You are less likely to be distracted by the call of undone chores.

After the lecture, review your notes. Now, you are just checking to see if you missed anything. If you did miss a concept in the lecture, ask a friend for clarification that day. Yes, that day! Even a few days later, you will forget to ask or forget why you needed to know.

A word about study groups: If you have worked with a study group in law school and found it beneficial to you, then keep working with the group during bar preparation. You can ask your questions about the law in a nonthreatening environment. Your group will support each other, even if it is just commiserating about the work involved. Study groups are a great way to learn from each other.

Someone in your group may have taken a course that you did not take and can further explain concepts after the lecture if you don't understand them.

1. Building Your Library

Now your work truly begins. In Chapter 2, we discussed the importance of memory and we discussed techniques to improve your memory. But Phase One is not about memorizing. It's about getting ready to memorize. The process of getting ready is actually a part of memorizing, but for our purposes it's easier to think about as first getting ready to memorize and then second actually memorizing.

Your first step is to gather your study materials and organize them in the manner in which you best memorize. How do you know what is the best manner? How have you memorized before the bar exam? Think back over your approximately 20 years of education. How did you memorize multiplication factors? You used a combination of materials from flash cards to one-minute drills. How did you memorize American history? Perhaps you made your own outline of dates and events or you read the material many times hoping the information would stick in your head. In undergraduate courses, your exams required you to show your understanding of the theories and public policies involved in historical events in an essay or a research paper, rather than memorize dates and facts.

So, which method should you use for the bar exam?

* Flash cards or note cards
* Flash card app on smartphone/tablet/computer
* Outline
* Flow chart
* PowerPoint
* Mind map

Another method may work for you. Choose the method you have had success with in the past. Some topics may work better with one method while other topics work better with a different method. Allow yourself to explore and experience different methods.

If you are not sure where to begin, start with definitions. Move to elements of causes of action and crimes. Then add detail by adding the rules for each element. Then add defenses to the causes of actions and crimes and off you go!

How much should you write on a flash card or a PowerPoint slide? For memory encoding, including full sentences may result in stimulus overload such that the key points are lost in the text. Writing out full sentences on flash cards is just showing your full outline on short pieces of paper. Instead, on one side of the card put the concept: for example, battery. On the back of the card, list the trigger phrases for the elements of that intentional tort.

BATTERY	• Harmful or offensive contact • Intent • Causation

Then, make another flash card to set out more detail on one element.

Harmful or Offensive Contact	• Reasonable person standard • Includes anything connected to the person ("purse") • No consent • Apprehension ≠ required

Continue with each element as needed.

You might be thinking, "Why bother"? The commercial bar preparation provider provided flash cards or shortened outlines for me to use. Those materials are fine as a back-up. But it is the process of thinking and organizing the material yourself that starts the memorization process—encoding that information into your long-term memory. Reading someone else's work does not provide the same kind of encoding. Making your own library enables you to actually learn the material while you are building your own materials to memorize from in phase two.

Should each member of your study group make materials on a subject for you to share? That is not a wise choice. That method may have worked well for you for a final when you could rely mainly on your short-term memory. But the bar exam requires that those materials be in your long-term memory. Encoding the material over time and working with the material yourself is really the best method.

Now, how do you start building your library of materials? Do you include everything? Use the content in this book or your lecture handouts as the basis of your library. You will add to this basis throughout your bar preparation, particularly as you autopsy your answers to practice questions.

2. Using Practice Questions to Learn the Law

Taking practice questions is an excellent way to learn material. Yes, to learn it. At this point, you are not trying to assess your memory. Instead, you are using the essays to learn the details of the rules and how they work together. As you learn the law more comprehensively, you will better understand it and it will be easier to memorize.

At this point, take practice questions open book. Spend as much time as you need. Remember, the point is to learn the material, not to assess your memory. You may wonder if spending 90 minutes doing a practice essay is worth it. It absolutely is! Those 90 minutes mean you understand that part of the law in a way that you would never have understood it if you had taken the question closed book in a limited time. Then, your answer would have been sketchy, at best. You would read the answer, but it wouldn't sink in. By practicing questions open book and with unlimited time, you are giving yourself the opportunity to really delve into the subject.

3. Finding the Answer

What happens if you still don't get it? Do you give up and pray that the topic does not appear on an essay or in a multiple choice question? No. Just ask. Ask

EXAM TIP
Do not include every single detail of the rules that are contained in the long outlines of each topic in your library. Your goal is to have 75% of the topic down cold. Chapter 7 explains this strategy.

for help. Dig into the substantive outline. If that doesn't do it, email or talk with the commercial bar preparation lecturer or general office. The office will find out for you. Or, email or talk with a professor at your law school.

This is the phase to work on learning as much as you can. Don't give up on anything.

B. Phase Two—Memorize the Law

Five weeks before the exam is the time to really start memorizing. You should have a substantial part of your library built with just a few remaining topics to complete. Start with the Big Seven. Your commercial bar prep provider will offer at least one full-day practice MBE exam. Start memorizing shortly before that exam. At the beginning of this phase, most of your time will be spent finishing your library, but adding in an hour or two of memorization per day is the way to go. As you move to the end of this phase, half of your time will be spent memorizing and half of your time will be spent on practice questions.

1. Memory Techniques

At this stage, the time is ripe to take your substantive material and apply memory techniques to aid your recall. By building your own library, you have already spent significant time memorizing—time well-spent encoding the information into your memory. Now we want to make more new associations to achieve a deeper level of encoding.

Using various mnemonic devices can assist in making those deeper associations. Acronyms, acrostics, rhythm and song, chunking, and method of loci help to encode information by forming new associations. **Acronyms** are formed by using the first letter of each word and are particularly useful when remembering words in a specific order. Indeed, some acronyms are used more frequently than the words themselves, such as NFL (National Football League), BTUs (British Thermal Units), and Scuba (Self-Contained Underwater Breathing Apparatus).

An example for use in bar study is "A FLIP," which can assist you in remembering the four types of invasion of privacy causes of action.

A Flip
* **A**ppropriation of likeness
* **F**alse **L**ight
* **I**ntrusion of seclusion
* **P**ublication of private facts

Acrostics are similar to acronyms in that you use the first letter of each word, but you create a sentence or phrase instead of a single word. For example, the lines of a musical staff are remembered by, "Every Good Boy Does Fine." "My Dear Aunt Sally" is used to remember the mathematical order of operations— multiple and divide before you add or subtract. To remember the Dormant Commerce Clause requirements that limit state action, think:

Nonresident Statutes are Rude.[2]
* **N**ondiscriminatory intent, construction, and application
* **S**ubstantial nexus between state interest and burden on non-resident

---

2. www.cram.com/cards/bar-exam-mnemonics-and-acrostics-mbe-and-mbee-984740.

- **A**pportioned between residents and nonresidents that reflects fundamental fairness
- **R**elated to state services or resources

Rhymes and **songs** have been used for decades to remember information. Have you ever been in the midst of alphabetizing something and had the ABC Song float into your head? Why is that? You encoded the information through song. Indeed, for centuries rhyme, rhythm, and repetition have helped storytellers to remember a tribe's history or to remember Homer's *Odyssey*.

If you like to create, this can be a powerful tool to aid your memory. It draws upon auditory memory more than the others. A former colleague teaching Wills and Trusts began each class with her students singing parts of the intestacy rules to familiar tunes.[3] Needless to say, the students had these rules solidly memorized.

We use **chunking** regularly without thinking about it. Chunking refers to grouping information in a meaningful way to reduce the amount you need to store in your memory; thus, making it easier to remember. Telephone numbers are not a long series of numbers for a reason. The grouping of 3-3-4 is easier to remember. We can even chunk our acronyms.

Oil Cans are self-authenticating (self-authenticating documents).[4]
- **O**fficial publications issued by public authority
- **I**nstruments—negotiable and commercial paper
- **L**abel, tag, or trademark affixed on item in regular course of business
- **C**ertified public documents (by clerk of agency or court that had custody)
- **A**cknowledged documents signed before notary, sworn to truth, content, and execution (except wills)
- **N**ewspapers and periodicals with reasonably wide circulation
- **S**ealed documents (government certified)

Method of loci was also used by ancient storytellers and orators. It requires organization, visual memory, and association. Start by identifying a common path that you walk or use the set-up of a room. As you visualize your walk or the room, picture the landmarks along the way such as the door to the room or the bottom of the steps as you leave for your walk. As you picture the landmark, associate the first concept you wish to remember with that landmark. For example, defamation requires (1) defamatory language on the part of the defendant; (2) the defamatory language is of or concerning the plaintiff; (3) publication of the defamatory language to a third person; and (4) damage to the plaintiff's reputation.

Visualize "defamatory language about the plaintiff" by thinking of the word "liar" spray painted on the door (defamatory language). Then, move to the next landmark, such as the bottom of the steps leading outside. Picture the words "John is a liar" spray painted there (of or concerning the plaintiff). Then, at the next landmark picture a person whispering in the ear of another (publication to a third person). Then, picture a group of people laughing about another

---

3. Professor Julia Belian's intestacy songs are available on www.YouTube.com.
4. www.cram.com/cards/bar-exam-mnemonics-and-acrostics-mbe-and-mbee-984740.

person (damage to reputation). At each landmark, associate the concept with the landmark. Consider how to visualize the concept with the landmark.

The best of these memory techniques are the ones you create yourself. Just by going through the process of trying to create one helps encode the information into your memory.

2. Seek Support

Now is the time to bring out your stack of flash cards or outlines or flowcharts and ask others to quiz you as a check on your memorization. This is a great way for the significant people in your life to help you as they all want to do. Plus, for the reluctant significant other that does not quite understand why you still can't do all the chores you used to do, it helps them see the enormity of the task you are trying to accomplish.

A 2006 family film demonstrates the power of support in learning to memorize. *Akeelah and the Bee* follows a young girl as she prepares for the National Spelling Bee. She gets her family, her friends, and her neighborhood to assist her. While you don't need to go that far and ask the cashier at your local grocery store to quiz you, enlisting others to help you not only gives you emotional support but also helps you assess your memorization status.

3. Using Practice Questions to Assess Your Memorization

At this point, you want to use practice questions to assess your memory of the law. If you have already written out 20 essays or more, then bullet-outline your answer. You are checking to see if you have properly identified the issues and stated the rules in enough detail. If you are still struggling with recall of the rules, dig back into straight up repetition to encode those rules a bit deeper. If you have not written out very many essays, then continue to do that in this phase. Half the points are in the application and half are in the rules.

Here, study groups can be immensely helpful. Take a practice question and have each person write out an answer. Compare your answers to the model answer and discuss why some identified certain issues and others did not. Clear up any misunderstandings of the rules. Determine why one member's rule statements worked better than yours. All of this discussion is further encoding the material into your long-term memory.

C. Phase Three—Keep it Fresh

The last two weeks is the final push. Your goals are to continue your memorization of rules, to continue to use practice questions to assess your memory, and to keep what you have already memorized fresh to be able to recall easily. Thus, keeping track of where you are with each topic is essential. Plan these last two weeks very carefully.

One approach for the final two weeks is to review one of the Big Seven and one essay topic each day the first week. Each day, assess where you are with the previous day's topic by doing 50 MBE questions on that topic and bullet-outlining the rules for at least five essays on that topic. Still missing some of the rules? Continue to add them to your library. Continue your review of rules through the next week.

The second week, you need to review the remaining essay topics but continue with daily MBE questions. Switch the 50 MBE questions to mixed topics. With mixed-topic question sets, you do not know the topic of each question ahead of time. This will keep you on track heading into the exam. Any additional time is spent on the topics that need more work. Then, begin reducing the number of MBE questions you do every day to avoid fatigue.

Avoid the temptation of giving up on a topic. Giving up on a Big Seven topic is shooting yourself in the foot. Those topics will be tested. You know they will. The math simply does not work to give up on one of these topics. Not only are they a set percentage of the MBE questions, but they are also potential essay questions.

BAR PREP CALENDAR	
Week One	Phase One-Learn the Law
Week Two	Phase One-Learn the Law
Week Three	Phase One-Learn the Law
Week Four	Phase One/Two-Learn/Memorize the Law
Week Five	Phase Two-Memorize the Law
Week Six	Phase Two-Memorize the Law
Week Seven	Phase Three-Memorize the Law/Keep It Fresh
Week Eight	Phase Three-Memorize the Law/Keep It Fresh
Exam Week	No Cramming!

SAMPLE SCHEDULE FOR PHASE THREE						
Sunday	Monday	Tuesday	Wednesday	Thursday	Friday	Saturday
Finish outlines/ flash cards. MBE 50Q. on a trouble topic. Review Const. Law.	MBE Const. Law 50Q. Review Contracts, Sales, Agency/ Partnership.	MBE Contracts 50Q. Review Criminal Law/Crim. Procedure, and Corps.	MBE Criminal 50Q. Review Evidence & Secured Transactions.	MBE Evidence 50Q. Review Torts & Comm'l Paper.	MBE Torts 50Q. Review Property & MPT samples for format.	MBE Real Property 50Q. Review Federal Civil Procedure.
MBE Fed. Civ. Pro. 50Q. Review Family Law & all MBE topics.	MBE Mixed 50Q. Review Wills & Trusts.	MBE Mixed 34Q. Review any trouble topics.	MBE Mixed 34Q. Review any trouble topics.	MBE Mixed 34Q. Review all topics.	MBE Mixed 34Q. Review all topics.	MBE Mixed 34Q. Review all topics.
MBE Mixed 34Q. Review all topics.	Travel to exam site. Locate testing room, restrooms, etc. Get a good night's sleep! Avoid cramming.	BAR EXAM— MPTs & Essays	BAR EXAM— Multistate Bar Exam	You Did It!!! WHEW!!!		

That topic could also be part of the MPT question. One student "never got" Constitutional Law and gave up on it early. His bar exam included the standard number of multiple choice questions, an essay question, and the MPT—all on Constitutional Law. Without question, it was a poor judgment call to give up on that topic!

At this point in time, many students start weighing the chances of a topic appearing on an essay question to decide whether they should spend additional study time on that topic (hoping that the topics they are skipping will not be tested), or continue to study all topics. If a student decides to stop studying three topics because they never really understood them and those three topics are essay questions, they have just guaranteed a poor performance on the essay portion. Because the essay questions are worth 30% of the exam on the UBE and more in other jurisdictions, that student is risking lopping off 15% of the points or more on the exam before they start. Thus, they must perform at a high level on the rest of the exam. If one of the skipped topics is an MBE topic, they are lopping off even more.

Some students bank on excelling in one topic to make up for a poorer performance in another topic. Be careful of such an approach. Excelling on a topic at a high enough level to balance out a poor performance is very difficult to do. Reaching a high score on essay questions is difficult and usually not a mathematically sufficient margin to overcome poor performance on another question or two.

The last weekend should be an easing off. First, you want to get plenty of sleep. The more rested your brain, the better you will perform. Secondly, we know that cramming does not result in long-term memory storage. And, there's too much information to keep in short-term memory to be of much good. You are better off skimming your outlines and flash cards and hitting the hay.

D. The Exam Days

Spend the Monday before the exam traveling to the exam site. Look around and locate your testing room, the seating setup, and the restrooms. Lay off the caffeine in the evening. Set out exactly what you must and can bring into the exam including your photo identification. Get some good sleep. Set as many alarms as you can—from a hotel wake-up call, to family and friends calling you, to your travel clock, to your tablet, to your cell phone, and to the hotel's alarm clock. This is the exam you do not want to start late.

Eat breakfast with protein. Skip the donuts from the vending machine. Arrive before the exam's starting time to register and locate your seat. Once in the exam room, do not be tempted to look at your notes on your computer while you are waiting. That may result in your expulsion from the exam. Be sure to take a real break at lunch. Avoid cramming for the afternoon. Take a brief walk. Do not load up on carbohydrates. You don't want a sugar low in the middle of the afternoon.

Hopefully, on Tuesday evening some of the weight will be off your shoulders. Tuesday has the most possible topics. Tuesday evening you know the next day is only the Big Seven and that you will be tested on all of them. Spend some time after the exam doing something to help you relieve stress—go on a run or walk, have a pedicure or massage, go to a movie, go work out in a gym—something that is designed to help you relax. Avoid alcohol. Have a decent dinner and then spend the rest of the evening relaxing, skimming the Big Seven, and getting a

Eat Breakfast!

good night's rest. Again, set out what you need to take into the exam. Set all your alarms, once again.

If you have noticed that you are a slow starter on multiple choice questions—that is, that you need to get warmed up—then do fifteen questions that morning for warm up. Then, you'll be in the groove for the actual exam. Again, take a break for lunch. The fatigue will be starting to hit. Take a walk around the block to clear your head. No cramming.

And, at last, it's over. After the exam, drive home safely. At some point, you will second guess your answers. Everyone does that; it's hard to avoid. To the extent that you can, have the attitude that you did the best you could and you could not have asked for more of yourself.

A recent successful bar taker's mother went with her to the exam site. Her mom drove, took care of setting alarms, and had lunch waiting in their room. The bar taker didn't have to think about where she was going to eat or how long the line would be. She didn't have to be around bar takers that love to talk about the questions immediately after the exam. She had someone else to talk with about other things—someone who did not put any pressure on her, but offered tons of positive support. The last day of the exam, she didn't need to worry about getting up early to pack her things to check out of the hotel on time. She slept some more. Her mom took care of packing and checking out after the bar taker started her exam. If you have a loved one who can provide practical and emotional support without pressuring you to talk or suggesting "don't you want to study more?"—then bring them along!

The wait for the results will seem interminable. Try to keep in mind that worrying and ruminating about the results will do you no good. Your scores are out of your control at that point. If you already have a job, it is tempting to jump in and get started. If you can, take a long break or vacation. Read the book you set aside when bar prep started. Play a lot of golf. Spend time with your family and friends. Just refresh and rejuvenate before you start working.

Let's Celebrate!

E. Getting Your Results

Jurisdictions differ on when they release results and how they release results. Some jurisdictions will post your individual result to an online account and others will mail letters. Some will post successful exam numbers on its website and some will post names of successful applicants. Be knowledgeable about the requirements for having your number or name posted. Some jurisdictions require that all of your character and fitness requirements are met before your name is posted, including passing the MPRE. You will have a sleepless night or two not knowing if it is character and fitness determination holding you up or if you actually failed the exam. Prevent that from happening by being sure you have all your ducks in a row for the character and fitness requirement long before the results come out.

The results are in and now you know. Celebrate sensibly. Thank your support system for all they did. Your hard work paid off!

If you were unsuccessful, it will at first seem like the end of the world. It really is not. It just means that some of your plans will be on hold until the next exam cycle. You are not the first person to be unsuccessful, nor will you be the last. Chapter 8 gives specific suggestions for those taking the exam an additional time.

CHAPTER 4

Building Essay-Writing Skills

I. TYPE OR HANDWRITE?

Most jurisdictions give applicants a choice to type or handwrite their essay and MPT answers. Examiners agree that typed answers are most certainly easier to read than handwritten answers because no deciphering is required. The problem with handwriting is legibility. Bar examiners will make every effort to decode handwriting because they do not want to punish an applicant based upon poor handwriting. Yet, an irritated bar examiner is not a good thing.

Typists tend to write too much. The speed of their keyboarding skills and the ability to cut-and-paste blocks of text often means language is unnecessarily repeated, transitions are lengthy, and language is wordy. Typists' organization is often more haphazard as their ability to quickly write words means they often do not stop and think first about what they are writing. Handwritten essays tend to be shorter and more focused on the issue, resulting in better organization of the answer.

In the end, whether you type or handwrite does not affect your score on either an MPT or an essay. Both have advantages and disadvantages that may impact your score, but one does not outweigh the other as a general rule.

II. SCORING

Essays are graded by the board of bar examiners in your state and often with the help of additional attorneys appointed for that purpose. Remember that these are busy folks. They volunteer for these positions and usually are maintaining an active law practice. As such, they appreciate the well thought-out answer that is organized and well written.

Different jurisdictions use different scoring scales. Whether your jurisdiction uses a 5-point scale or a 100-point scale, everyone in your jurisdiction is graded along the same scale. Jurisdictions have various safeguards in place to ensure reliability of their scores. Some jurisdictions calibrate scores by more than one examiner grading the same question and the examiners exchanging exams with the other person grading the same question after a set number of answers. For example, after every 30 questions graded, they exchange their last five graded essays and grade them again to see if they receive the same score. If they don't, then they can discuss the issue and reach a decision on how to score. Jurisdictions do their reliability check in different ways, but all attempt to ensure their grading is equitable for all examinees.

Once a jurisdiction completes its essay grading, including the MPT, the raw scores are sent to the NCBE. The NCBE then scales the scores to match the 200-point scale used on the multiple choice questions.

Each jurisdiction decides its own cut-off score; that is, the score required to pass the exam. After the NCBE completes the scaled scores, each individual jurisdiction then receives a report of all their test-takers with their scaled scores on each part of the exam and their total scaled score.

When results are released, you may or may not receive your actual score. Jurisdictions differ as to how much information they reveal to their examinees when results are available. Some jurisdictions only reveal the pass/fail result. Others reveal all information given to them by the NCBE.

III. THINK FIRST!

Begin your approach to each essay with a plan of attack. The first one-third of your time should be spent reading and planning your answer. What will you read first? What will begin your answer? How should your answer be structured?

Be sure to keep track of your time. Do *not* go over the allotted time. Each question is worth the same number of points. Perfect scores are rare, and there is no extra credit for particularly brilliant answers. Thus, deciding to spend 60 minutes on a 30-minute question is not a good idea. Even spending ten extra minutes on the first three 30-minute questions means you will have no time for the sixth question. You will not earn enough points in those extra minutes to outweigh the zero you will receive on the unanswered question.

Your plan of attack begins with **reading the call of the question**. The call of the question is a treasure trove of information. Usually, you will at least be able to determine the topic being tested. Sometimes, you will be able to narrow your focus to the more specific issue being tested. For example, the call could be as explicit as: Did Testator execute a valid will? This call not only tells us the overall topic—Wills—but also tells us the specific subtopic—formation and execution of a will. With just reading the call of the question first, you know to diligently read the facts pertaining to execution. If you read the facts first and then read the call of the question, you would need to go back and reread the facts related to execution.

Once you have determined the topic, you can let your thoughts focus on only the rules for that topic and ignore all other topics. If you are also able to identify the sub-issue, you can immediately call to mind the rule for the subtopic. You can go ahead and bullet-outline the rule.

Reading the call of the question first also prevents you from putting the analysis for part three of the question under your part one answer. You will already know how the examiners have separated the issues and how they want you to structure your answer. If you do put your answer for part three under part one, then, if handwriting, draw a simple arrow to indicate where it does belong. If typing, cut and paste the text appropriately.

Let's try this out. Read the call of the question first.

Call of the Question[1]

1. Was Benjamin and Susan's business relationship a general partnership, a limited partnership, or neither? Explain.
2. Does Susan have the right to end her business relationship with Benjamin? Explain.
3. Assuming Susan has the right to end the business relationship, how should Benjamin's claims be resolved? Explain.

What does the call of the question tell us? We immediately know that this question deals with partnership. We also know that the first issue involves whether this is a partnership and what kind of partnership it is. The second and third questions deal with how the relationship ended.

Bullet-outline the rules for the creation of a partnership for part one of your answer. Bullet-outline the rules for ending a partnership for part two and maybe part three of your answer. Do we need to be concerned at this point about the difference between questions two and three? Not really. The facts should help us determine the distinction.

Bullet Outline of Rules

1. P-ship = assn of two or more persons carrying on a business as co-owners for profit.
   • General p-ship—no formalities/writing.
   • Limited p-ship—writing needed. File w/sec'y of state.
2. Can always end relationship.
   • No reason required.
   • If breaches p-ship agrmt, then liable for damages.
   • If p-ship agrmt doesn't state a specific term, then no breach.
3. Distribution of assets:
   • Costs of sale
   • Outside creditors
   • Inside creditors
   • Capital returned
   • Profits/losses split

Now, read the facts. As you read the facts, confirm the subject matter. Identify the legal relationship of the parties. Are you dealing with a buyer and seller, a tortfeasor and victim, a husband and wife? For the Wills question, is it the executor and beneficiary or two beneficiaries in the dispute? Be sure to underline

---

1. The Multistate Bar Examination ("MBE®") questions, the Multistate Essay Examination ("MEE®") questions, and excerpts from the Multistate Performance Tests ("MPT®") have been reprinted by permission from the NCBE®. Copyright© by the National Conference of Bar Examiners. All rights reserved.

any dates. Dates are given only when relevant. Rarely is a date given that is not relevant. Look for the ways any actors differ from each other. If the question is whether A is liable to B and C, look at how B and C are different. If they were the same, there would be no reason to have the call of the question ask about both. Therefore, the examiners have a reason to ask you about liability for each.

As you go through the facts, you can jot down and align the relevant facts with the parts of the rule you previously bullet-outlined. If you had not read the call of the question first, you would read all the facts then the call of the question, then determine the rule, and then probably need to reread the facts as you were not reading them with the rule for the sub-issue in mind. By reading the call of the question first, you have saved an enormous amount of time. Time is your most precious commodity in taking an exam—time that you can now spend on improving the depth and organization of your analysis.

Read the facts a second time to be sure you did not miss any legally significant facts on your first reading. Fill in your outline and prepare to write. Now that we know the facts, we can expand our outline of the rules to differentiate parts two and three. Part two deals with the dissolution of the partnership and part three deals with the distribution of the assets. Moreover, we can identify that Benjamin's claims require us to determine if the property is a partnership asset.

Place each legally significant fact under the rule to which it applies. Now, we are ready to write our answer.

Facts for Sample Question

Susan is a talented furniture restorer. Benjamin is a wealthy furniture collector who enjoys buying and selling furniture. Benjamin and Susan agreed to form what they called a "limited partnership." Benjamin would be the limited partner, would contribute $50,000 for working capital, and would contribute an additional $100,000, if needed. Susan would be the general partner, with full authority to buy, restore, and sell furniture, using her own well-equipped workshop and custom tools. They would split the profits as follows: 70% to Benjamin and 30% to Susan until Benjamin received an amount equal to his $50,000 capital contribution plus interest at 11%. Thereafter, the profits would be split 50%-50%.

Benjamin and Susan did not put their agreement in writing or take any other action to formalize it. Benjamin gave Susan $50,000 for the business, and Susan purchased, restored, and sold furniture. After six months of allocating distributions under the 70%-30% formula, Benjamin was repaid his total $50,000 capital contribution and accrued interest. Thereafter, profits were split 50%-50%.

The business has now become so successful that Susan will not need any additional capital from Benjamin. The business has $8,500 in its bank account and has no outstanding debts.

Susan has told Benjamin that she wants to end their business relationship. Benjamin claims that Susan has no right to dissolve the business just as it begins to produce profits. He further claims that if Susan does end the relationship, she must pay him 50% of the cash in the bank account, his share of the goodwill, and an amount equal to 50% of the value of her tools. The tools, which were Susan's before she entered into the agreement with Benjamin, are worth $50,000, and Benjamin asserts that they are assets of the business. Susan denies that Benjamin is entitled to a share of the goodwill, if any, or to 50% of the value of the tools.

Preparing to Write

Susan is a talented furniture restorer. Benjamin is a wealthy furniture collector who enjoys buying and selling furniture. Benjamin and Susan agreed to form what they called a "limited partnership." Benjamin would be the limited partner, would contribute $50,000 for working capital, and would contribute an additional $100,000 if needed. Susan would be the general partner, with full authority to buy, restore, and sell furniture, using her own well-equipped workshop and custom tools. They would split the profits as follows: 70% to Benjamin and 30% to Susan until Benjamin received an amount equal to his $50,000 capital contribution plus interest at 11%. Thereafter, the profits would be split 50%-50%.

Benjamin and Susan did not put their agreement in writing or take any other action to formalize it. Benjamin gave Susan $50,000 for the business, and Susan purchased, restored, and sold furniture. After six months of allocating distributions under the 70%-30% formula, Benjamin was repaid his total $50,000 capital contribution and accrued interest. Thereafter, profits were split 50%-50%.

The business has now become so successful that Susan will not need any additional capital from Benjamin. The business has $8,500 in its bank account and has no outstanding debts.

Susan has told Benjamin that she wants to end their business relationship. Benjamin claims that Susan has no right to dissolve the business just as it begins to produce profits. He further claims that if Susan does end the relationship, she must pay him 50% of the cash in the bank account, his share of the goodwill, and an amount equal to 50% of the value of her tools. The tools, which were Susan's before she entered into the agreement with Benjamin, are worth $50,000, and Benjamin asserts that they are assets of the business. Susan denies that Benjamin is entitled to a share of the goodwill, if any, or to 50% of the value of the tools.

1. Pship = assn of 2 or more persons carrying on a business as co-owners for profit
   - General p-shp — no formalties/ writing
   - Limited p-shp — Writing needed. File w/sec'y of state
     – called themselves a limited p-shp
     – no writing
     – profits 70/30 til capital returned, then 50/50

2. Can always end relationship
   - No reason required
   - If breaches p-shp agrmt, then liable for damages.
   - If p-shp agrmt doesn't state a specific term, then no breach
     – **no written agmt**
     – **S wants to end**

3. Claims?
   a. Bank account
   - Rule: Distribution of assets
     – Costs of sale
     – Outside creditors
     – Inside creditors
       no outstanding debts.
     – Capital returned
       Benjamin was repaid his total $50,000 capital contribution and accrued interest.
     – Profits/losses split
       split 50%-50%.
       $8,500 in bank account.

   b. Tools
   - Rule: ??
     – Susan's prior to agrmt. Used in business

   c. Goodwill
   - Rule: ??

Sample Answer

1. Susan and Benjamin formed a general partnership, not a limited partnership. **Under** partnership law, a partnership is an association of two or more persons to carry on as co-owners a business for profit. No written formalities are required. A limited partnership is not formed unless a certificate is filed with the secretary of state.

   Here, Susan and Benjamin had an agreement to form a furniture restoration business. They agreed to share profits. Although they did not put their agreement in writing, they still formed a general partnership, as no writing is required. As they did not file a certificate of limited partnership with the secretary of state, it would not be a limited partnership. **Therefore**, Susan and Benjamin formed a general partnership.

2. Susan had the right to end the partnership. **Under** partnership law, a partnership can be dissolved by a partner's refusal to carry on in the business together. If leaving violates any terms of the partnership agreement, the departing partner is in breach of the agreement and may be liable for damages.

   Here, the agreement is not for a set term and does not have a definite end. **Therefore**, Susan had the power and right to end the partnership and is not in violation of their agreement.

3. Benjamin is entitled to one-half of the bank account, but is not entitled to half the value of the tools. If goodwill is present, he would be entitled to half. **Under** partnership law, partnership assets are reduced to cash upon dissolution of the partnership. The proceeds are distributed first to the costs of the sale of the assets, then to outside creditors, and then to inside creditors. Capital is returned next, and any remaining funds/profits are split per the agreement.

   Here, the business has no debt and Benjamin's capital has already been returned with interest per their agreement. **Therefore**, any remaining assets are split 50/50.

   Cash: The $8,500 account will be split in half.

   Tools: **Under** partnership law, partnership assets are those purchased by the partnership or given to the partnership. **Here**, Susan used her own tools, but did not give them to the partnership. Even if she had, it would be her capital contribution and she would be entitled to their return. **Therefore**, Benjamin is not entitled to half of the tools' value.

   Goodwill: **Under** partnership law, goodwill is the going concern value of the business. If a value cannot be placed upon it, then it is questionable if it even exists. **Here**, it is doubtful goodwill exists as it cannot be valued. It's just Susan doing good work.

   Therefore, Benjamin is entitled to half of the bank account, but that is all, unless the goodwill can be valued.

IV. PROPER FORMAT

Legal readers expect legal analysis to be written and presented in a certain manner. Bar examiners are legal readers and thus expect to read legal analysis in that same manner.

First, **use the basic structure of setting out a legal analysis in a rote manner.** Law professors use various acronyms to describe this structure—IRAC, IREAC, CRAC, CREAC, etc. Your analysis becomes a series of these structures: CRAC,

CRAC, CRAC, CRAC, CRAC, etc.; one for each issue or sub-issue. Each structure has the same underlying doctrine as its basis—it requires the drafter to set forth the rule that governs the issue before applying that rule to the facts. Rule before application. If you don't have time for the complete CRAC structure on each sub-issue when writing a particular analysis, at least do RAC, RAC, RAC, RAC; or RA, RA, RA, RA.

Order of Analysis

Business Records Exception to Hearsay
Rule = Hearsay is inadmissible without an exception.
Definition: Hearsay is an out-of-court statement offered for the truth of the matter.
Apply hearsay definition to facts.
Conclude: Hearsay?
Rule for business records exception.
Apply business records exception to facts.
Conclude: Business records exception apply?
If yes, then evidence is admissible.
If no, then evidence is inadmissible.

Next, start a new paragraph to start your **application** section. Don't overlook application. Just stating the rule and a conclusion will not garner the points you need. Look at any sample answer to a bar essay—half the points are in the rule and half the points are in the application. Even assuming you received every single point for every rule, that would not be enough to be successful. The key to scoring well lies within the application.

The application is not a place to retell the story or just restate the facts. It is the place where the writer connects specific legally significant facts to the specific language of the rule, often called the "phrase-that-pays" or "critical language." For example, one part of the business records exception is that the record must have been made "in the course of a regularly conducted activity of a business."[2] That phrase—"course of a regularly conducted activity of a business"—**is** the phrase that pays. That is the key language of this element of the rule that you must connect to the facts of the hypothetical.

Suppose an essay question has you representing a defendant who was sued by a plaintiff injured in a motor vehicle collision with one of your client's delivery trucks, driven by an employee. One of the claims is that the defendant did not properly maintain the truck. Because the defendant owns a fleet of delivery trucks, the defendant has its own maintenance department. You want to admit into evidence the maintenance records that are kept in a folder for each vehicle. You need to show that the maintenance records were made in the course of the regular activity of the business. The hypothetical states that the mechanic performing the maintenance must keep track of what service she performed, the date, and the time the work was completed. The mechanic must then sign the form.

---

2. FED. R. EVID. 803(e).

How would you apply the rule to these facts? It would not be enough to just state that the defendant's maintenance records were kept in the course of a regularly conducted activity of a business. That is just a conclusion. You have to insert the legally significant facts and tie them to the phrase that pays to reach your conclusion.

> Defendant's maintenance records were kept in the course of a regularly conducted activity of a business as defendant had its own maintenance department and each mechanic indicated the service she performed on the maintenance folder every time maintenance was done on the vehicle.

This tying together of the legally significant facts with the phrase that pays is the heart of application and is what will garner you major points. Do this with each and every rule.

Think of application like the proof of a math problem. You need to show the examiner how you reached your answer. When you made a minor misstep in a math problem like a calculation error, the teacher would still give you partial credit. It's the same thing on the bar exam. You need to show the examiners your work—your proof of the analysis. If you make a misstep, you will get credit for the part you did do correctly. If you just state the rule and state the *incorrect* conclusion, you get no credit for the part of the application that you got correct because it stayed in your head and did not get put down on the exam. Put every step of the process you do in your head down on the paper, going step-by-step from the rule, through the application, to the conclusion for each issue. The examiner will not give you points for what they think you probably thought. They will only give you points for what you actually state.

Next, **use signposts**. When we drive, a signpost tells us where we are or what direction we should go. A reader needs signposts to keep track of where they are and where they are going. As the writer, it is your responsibility to make the reader's job effortless. Signposts help you do that. Moreover, ritualistically using signposts helps you keep track of where you are and what you need to do next.

The first signpost to use is **UNDER**. "Under" begins the sentence where you state a rule. Follow "under" with the general source of the rule. "Under the Uniform Commercial Code. . . ." "Under the Federal Rules of Civil Procedure. . . ." "Under Torts law. . . ." This signpost immediately tells the reader that this sentence will be the rule. It helps you to be sure that you state the source of the rule and that you clearly separate the rule from the application and conclusion sections.

The signpost that signals the reader that the writer has moved to application is **HERE** or **IN THIS CASE**. "Here, the husband supported the wife throughout law school." "In this case, the plaintiff filed its complaint on. . . ." "Here, the directors held a meeting without giving notice to. . . ." Using "here" cues your reader that you are starting the application. It is also your clue that you need to make those connections between the facts and the critical language o.

THEREFORE signals the reader that you are now concluding this part of the analysis. There should be a conclusion—a "therefore" sentence—at the end of each sub-issue and then again at the end of each answer to a call of the question. "Therefore, the maintenance records are admissible under the business records exception to the hearsay rule." "Therefore, the petition was filed out-of-time under the statute of limitations," etc.

If thinking about your analysis using an IRAC or CRAC doesn't come easily, then always do **Under-Here-Therefore; Under-Here-Therefore; Under-Here-Therefore, etc.**, and you won't go wrong!

Next, if the question has **multiple parts**, your answer should have the same number of parts and be in the same order. Do not be tempted to collapse the parts into one analysis or analyze the parts in a different order. Remember, the examiners designed the question to have multiple parts and had a reason to do so. The examiners are addressing different issues in each part of the question. If you can't identify the separate issues, then look carefully at how the actors differ such that the analysis differs.

Use headings to separate the different parts. If you do not like to use headings, leave a space between each part, at a minimum. If there is only one call of the question, there will still be multiple parts. Bar essay questions usually contain more than one issue. If it does appear to be only one issue, it will still have multiple sub-issues. Be sure to analyze each issue and sub-issue separately.

Next, **discuss any general rules before you discuss any exceptions**. It may be clear that the call of the question is asking about an exception. But you need to lay the foundation of the general rule before you reach the exception. For example, a question involving the business records exception to the hearsay requirement may be clear-cut from the call of the question. But before you address the particulars of the rule for the business records exception, the examiner needs to first know that it actually is hearsay. Thus, analyze the general rule about hearsay before you discuss the business records exception.

Finally, **use definitions** immediately after your rule for any parts of the rule that are at issue. Don't assume the reader knows what you are talking about. Explain the rule as you would to a client, not to someone whom you believe knows the rule. For example, stating the rule that hearsay is inadmissible without an exception[3] is not enough. Hearsay must be defined—an out-of-court statement offered for the truth of the matter.[4] Then, apply that rule to your facts and conclude whether the evidence is hearsay and thus inadmissible. Then, give the rule for the business records exception and apply it to the facts. Only then have you given the examiners a complete analysis of the call of the question. Note that you do not give the rule for hearsay and its exception at the same time to create one large rule. They are separate sub-issues that must be analyzed separately.

Check the table of the Order of Analysis for the Business Records Exception discussed previously to see how definitions fit into rule statements, how the general rule is analyzed before the exception, and how each sub-issue—is this hearsay and is this admissible under the business records exception—is set out with separate CRACs.

---

3. FED. R. EVID. 802.
4. FED. R. EVID. 801(c).

V. AUTOPSY YOUR PRACTICE ANSWERS

An integral part of your game plan is doing practice essay questions. During Phase One, you are using your practice to help learn the law. In Phase Two, the goal is to assess your memorization of the law. Under either phase, doing an autopsy of your practice answer is critical to your game plan's success.

Only you are in your head when you write the essay answer. Only you know why you did or did not state something. Did you not know that rule? Did you not remember the rule, although you did know it? Did you not see that issue? Did you do a cursory application? Did you misread the facts? Only you can determine the underlying reasons why your answer was incomplete or inaccurate.

Examining or performing an autopsy of your answer includes looking at everything you wrote and classifying it as rule, application, or conclusion. Then, analyze the practice answer and identify the rules, applications, and conclusions. The score sheets utilized in this text already do that for you.

Lay them side-by-side. What was in the model answer, but not in your answer? Was it a rule? If yes, then add that rule to your flash cards/outlines/flowcharts you are making on each topic. Was that rule already in your flash cards/outlines/flowcharts? Then, highlight it. The next time you review your materials your brain will pause on the highlighted area and that will remind you that you missed it once before, and pausing will also encode that rule deeper into your long-term memory. Was it application? Take note of how the examiners tie the facts to the critical language or phrase that pays of the rule for each issue. As you do more practice essays, strive to include the same level of application in your answers.

Also, check your organization. Did you lay out the rule before you applied it to the facts? Did you lump all the rules together and then try one big application? Note how the sample answer has a conclusion-rule-application-conclusion for each and every issue and sub-issue. Did your organization follow the same pattern? Take note of the order that the examiners laid out the different issues and sub-issues. Are your issues in a similar order? Consider why you did not lay them out in the same order.

Be brutally honest in assessing your answer. Your rule needs to match the stated rule with the same level of detail. Do the critical language, phrase that pays, or buzz words match? While some variation is allowed in sentence structure, the gist must be the same. For example, your answer states that hearsay is a statement made by someone not at the trial. The rule is both that hearsay is an out-of-court statement offered for the truth of the matter and that hearsay is inadmissible without an exception. You cheat yourself if you see those two statements as the same.

Consider this autopsy as a part of your learning and memorization process. Each review of the law encodes it into your memory. Merely reading the answer does not encode the rules at a deep enough level. The tough autopsy does that.

Let's work through an autopsy by analyzing the model answer to identify rule-application-conclusion on each issue. Then, we want to lay our answer beside it to see what we missed and what we could articulate in a clearer manner. Highlight the model answer with what you missed. Then, to pinpoint the areas we need to improve, use a score sheet that you can incorporate into your flash cards or outline. Lastly, add what was missing to your outline or flash cards. If that rule is already there, then highlight it. Remember, while you are doing this autopsy, you are actually encoding the rules further into your long-term memory. Thus, it is time well-spent.

Highlight the portions of the Model Answer that are not in the Sample Answer. Then, do the same thing with the score sheet.

Now check your outline/flash cards/etc. to be sure these rules missing in your answer are there and in the same detail. Add them or highlight them to help you remember the next time.

SAMPLE ANSWER

1. Susan and Benjamin formed a general partnership, not a limited partnership. **Under** partnership law, a partnership is an association of two or more persons to carry on as co-owners a business for profit. No written formalities are required. A limited partnership is not formed unless a certificate is filed with the secretary of state.

   Here, Susan and Benjamin had an agreement to form a furniture restoration business. They agreed to share profits. Although they did not put their agreement in writing, they still formed a general partnership as no writing is required. As they did not file a certificate of limited partnership with the secretary of state, it would not be a limited partnership. **Therefore**, Susan and Benjamin formed a general partnership.

2. Susan had the right to end the partnership. **Under** partnership law, a partnership can be dissolved by a partner's refusal to carry on in the business together. If leaving violates any terms of the partnership agreement, the departing partner is in breach of the agreement and may be liable for damages.

   Here, the agreement is not for a set term and does not have a definite end. **Therefore**, Susan had the power and right to end the partnership and is not in violation of their agreement.

3. Benjamin is entitled to one-half of the bank account, but is not entitled to half the value of the tools. If goodwill is present, he would be entitled to half. **Under** partnership law, partnership assets are reduced to cash upon dissolution of the partnership. The proceeds are distributed first to the costs of the sale of the assets, then to outside creditors, and then to inside creditors. Capital is returned next, and any remaining funds/profits are split per the agreement.

   Here, the business has no debt and Benjamin's capital has already been returned with interest per their agreement. **Therefore**, any remaining assets are split 50/50.

   Cash: The $8,500 account will be split in half.

   Tools: **Under** partnership law, partnership assets are those purchased by the partnership or given to the partnership. **Here**, Susan used her own tools, but did not give them to the partnership. Even if she had, it would be her capital contribution and she would be entitled to their return. **Therefore**, Benjamin is not entitled to half of the tools' value.

   Goodwill: **Under** partnership law, goodwill is the going concern value of the business. If a value cannot be placed upon it, then it is questionable if it even exists. **Here**, it is doubtful goodwill exists as it cannot be valued. It's just Susan doing good work.

   Therefore, Benjamin is entitled to half of the bank account, but that is all, unless the goodwill can be valued.

Model Answer

1. The business relationship between Benjamin and Susan was a general partnership. Although Benjamin and Susan agreed to form a limited partnership, a limited partnership was not created because a limited partnership may only be created under specific statutory authority. The Revised Uniform Limited Partnership Act requires, among other things, that a certificate of limited partnership be filed with the secretary of state. Here, the facts indicate that Benjamin and Susan did not put their agreement in writing or take any other action to formalize it. Thus, Benjamin and Susan's relationship was not a limited partnership.

   Notwithstanding the fact that Benjamin and Susan did not create a limited partnership, they did create a general partnership. A partnership is an association of two or more persons to carry on as co-owners a business for profit. No formal agreement is required to create a partnership, and it is generally not necessary for a partnership agreement to be in writing. In this case, it is clear that Benjamin and Susan created a partnership, although they did not evidence such a relationship in writing. Benjamin and Susan agreed to operate a furniture business with Benjamin providing the working capital and Susan having full authority to operate the business. They further agreed that they would split the profits of the business. The Uniform Partnership Act provides that the receipt by a person of a share of the profits is prima facie evidence that he is a partner in the business (and under the Revised Uniform Partnership Act, a person who receives a share of the profits is presumed to be a partner). Here, the profits would initially be split 70% to Benjamin and 30% to Susan until Benjamin was repaid his capital contribution, and later they would be split 50%-50%. Consequently, a partnership was established between Benjamin and Susan.

2. Susan has the right to end the business relationship with Benjamin. As noted above, the relationship between Benjamin and Susan was a partnership. When no definite term or particular undertaking is specified for a partnership, a partnership at will is created. A partnership at will may be dissolved by the express will of any partner at any time without penalty to the partner dissolving the partnership. Because Benjamin and Susan did not specify a term or particular undertaking for their partnership, Susan has the right to end the business relationship.

3. Benjamin is entitled to 50% of the cash in the bank account and may be entitled to his share of the goodwill of the business, but he is not entitled to 50% of the value of Susan's tools. Dissolution gives to each partner the right to have the business wound up and her share of the surplus paid in cash. Here, Susan has rightfully terminated the partnership and is entitled to have the business liquidated. Because there are no partnership liabilities and Benjamin has been repaid his capital contribution, Benjamin and Susan will split the partnership assets equally per their agreement.

   Benjamin is not, however, entitled to receive 50% of the value of Susan's tools because the tools are not partnership property. The controlling factor in determining if property is partnership property is the intent of the partners. Although Benjamin and Susan agreed that Susan would use her tools in conducting partnership business, they did not agree that Susan would make a contribution of the tools to the partnership. . . .

SCORE SHEET

Stated	Implied	
		1. Creation (40%-50%)
_√_	_____	**Conclusion/Issue:** Benjamin and Susan formed a general partnership, not a limited partnership.
_____	_√_	**Rule:** Under the uniform acts regarding partnership law,
_√_	_____	Creation of a partnership is function of the intent of the putative partners to establish "an association of two or more persons to carry on as co-owners a business for profit."
_____	_____	Receipt of a share of the profits is prima facie evidence of partnership.
_√_	_____	No writing requirement needed for a general partnership.
_√_	_____	To form a limited p-ship, a written certificate of limited p-ship must be executed and filed with the secretary of state.
_____	_____	Subjective belief of the parties is not relevant.
_√_	_____	**Application:** Here,
_√_	_____	B & S intended to operate their furniture restoration business as co-owners for profit, even though they were legally mistaken in calling the venture a limited p-ship.
_____	_____	Profits first divided 70%-30% then 50%-50%.
_√_	_____	Relationship was not memorialized in writing of any kind and there was no filing with the secretary of state.
_√_	_____	**Conclusion:** Therefore, Benjamin and Susan formed a general partnership.
		2. Dissolution (5%-10%)
_√_	_____	**Conclusion:** Susan has the legal right to terminate the partnership.
_____	_√_	**Rule:** A partner always has the right to dissolve the p-ship.
_____	_____	Partner is not required to have a reason to dissolve.
_√_	_____	Partner is liable for damages if the dissolution contravenes the partnership agreement.
_____	_√_	Where partnership agreement does not specify a definite term or objective for the p-shp to achieve, then dissolution does not contravene the partnership agreement.
_√_	_____	**Application:** Here,
_√_	_____	Agreement does not specify any term.
_____	_____	Purpose of p-ship is to restore and sell furniture, which is a continuous activity that does not constitute a particular undertaking.
_____	_√_	**Conclusion:** Thus, this is a partnership at will and Susan has the power and the legal right to dissolve the partnership.
		3. Winding Up (40%-50%)
_√_	_____	**Conclusion:** Benjamin is entitled to one-half of the cash and one-half of any goodwill (if it exists).

continued on next page

Stated	Implied	
_____	__√__	**Rule dividing assets:** When not a wrongful dissolution, p-ship property is applied to discharge the p-ship's liabilities, and the surplus is paid to the partners.
_____	_____	If no contrary agreement of the parties, surplus split 50%-50%.
__√__	_____	**Application:** Here,
__√__	_____	No liabilities. No outside or inside creditors as B has already been paid. Need only to split up partnership property.
__√__	_____	**Rule on partnership property:** All property brought into the partnership or subsequently acquired is p-ship property.
__√__	_____	**Application:** Here,
__√__	_____	Cash on hand is p-ship asset.
__√__	_____	Facts state S "would use her own" well-equipped workshop and custom tools for the p-ship's operations.
__√__	_____	S did not contribute ownership of tools to p-ship, but made them available for use by the p-ship.
__√__	_____	Somewhat like B's $50,000 contribution as of equivalent amounts.
_____	_____	Although not like $50,000 as B was repaid with interest and no similar provision for the tools.
_____	_____	No evidence that the parties treated tools as p-ship property.
__√__	_____	**Conclusion:** Probably not p-ship property.
__√__	_____	Even if tools considered p-ship property, their contribution was a "capital contribution" by S.
_____	__√__	She is entitled to return of capital contribution prior to distribution of profits.
__√__	_____	Goodwill is the "going concern" value.
__√__	_____	**Application:** Here,
_____	__√__	S will argue that because she is a professional there is no goodwill attributable to business, but instead her personal reputation and individual skill. Thus, no goodwill to divide.
_____	__√__	**Conclusion:** As no wrongful dissolution, good will is valued and divided, if recognized.
__√__	_____	**Overall conclusion:** B entitled to receive one-half of the $8,500 bank account and one-half of any goodwill, if recognized.

VI. COMMON WAYS TO LOSE POINTS

A. Mismanaging Time

Multistate Essay Examination questions are 30 minutes each. You will have six of them in a three-hour period in an MEE or UBE jurisdiction and you must keep track of your own time. Other jurisdictions' essays have longer or shorter time periods. Some jurisdictions prohibit watches, and all prohibit cell phones. As soon as you are registered and locate your seat, make note of each clock in the room so you can look up quickly. Limit yourself to to the time limit for each question. Even if you feel just 10 more minutes would push your score to new heights, avoid the temptation. The numbers just don't work for that to happen. Rarely is that time worth it, because it means 10 minutes must be taken off another question. Do that on the first three 30 minute questions and you now have 60 minutes for the three remaining questions that need 90 minutes. They are worth the same number of points as the ones you spent more time on, and you just short-circuited the number of points you could possibly receive.

B. Wasting Time Answering a Question Different from the Question Asked

Every hypothetical raises several issues. If the call of the question is very general, such as "discuss" or "explain the causes of action," then you are free to discuss them all. More likely, however, the call of the question will not be that broad and will focus on two or more issues or one issue that has several sub-issues.

You may be tempted to show the examiner how much you know by addressing other possible issues. Indeed, one of those issues may be so appealing to you that you decide to focus most of your time on it. But then, that is not what the examiner asked. Indeed, that is exactly what the examiner chose not to ask. The points are assigned to the questions asked; no bonus points are left over. Thus, failing to analyze the questions asked and answering something else is not a strong strategy. Indeed, no matter how brilliant that other answer is, it cannot make up for the points lost by not answering the questions asked.

C. Not "Showing Your Work"

The examiner does not get to speculate. He may only give you points for what is written down. He cannot guess at what you meant to put down or what you thought about before you began writing. Your written answer must stand on its own. Thus, show every step of your analysis for every issue—rule, including definitions; application; and conclusion. Lead the examiner step-by-step through your thinking process so that there is no doubt that your analysis is proven. When you make a mistake in that analysis and reach the wrong conclusion, the examiner can still give you points for how you got there. The examiner can only do that if you show your work.

D. Assuming the Grader Knows the Law and Not Referencing Specific Tests/Elements

As a law student, you are accustomed to writing final exam essays that you know will be read and graded by your professor. You may use a shorthand method of referring to certain rules that your professor used in class. You know the professor knows the rule, so you may feel no need to explain it.

Your bar essays are to be written to your client. Not another lawyer, a client. You must assume that your reader knows nothing about the rules. You must explain everything to the reader. Define every term of art. Lay out every element of a rule and then define each. Apply every single element. Don't skip a single step of the process.

Remember, your goal is not to tell the examiners every single thing you know about a topic. The examiners only want to know about the specific issues in the call of the question. Thus, don't spend time discussing how to create a partnership when the facts explicitly state that the partners entered into a valid partnership agreement. Likewise, don't list all possible hearsay exceptions when only one or two are at issue.

Likewise, don't repeat all the facts. The examiner already knows them. Stick to CRAC with all discussion of the facts tied to the critical language of the "phrase that pays" of the rule.

E. Writing Lengthy Sentences and Paragraphs with Grammar Issues

Listen up, typists. The "Enter" key is your friend. Use it. There is nothing worse as a grader than getting a wall of typed words without a single paragraph to break it up. It's reading a stream of consciousness rather than an organized analysis. Separate issues deserve separate paragraphs. Indeed, in a lengthy issue, put the rule and application in separate paragraphs.

Everyone needs to use periods. Frequently. Short sentences serve you better. Your analysis will be easier to read and to understand. In a lengthy sentence, your main point may be buried in the middle or saved until the end when the reader has given up trying to understand what you were trying to say. Now, you don't have to go the route of "See Jane. Run Jane. Look Jane." Shorter sentences do not mean you must be laconic in your writing. Just don't make them 50 words long! As a rule of thumb, avoid having a sentence that runs more than three lines of typed text.

Avoid using the shorthand abbreviations you use to take notes. Use only recognized abbreviations after you have first identified them. Thus, the first time state "Uniform Commercial Code (UCC)," and the next time you can just state UCC.

Do your best to use correct spelling and proper grammar. Some errors will be overlooked, but an essay riddled with errors will not impress an examiner and make her want to bring you into the fold. That's not to say you need polished, perfect writing. You don't. But constant sentence fragments and misspelled words make the examiner doubt your ability.

F. And, the Biggest Point Loser—Skimming All of the Questions First!

It's so tempting. You are handed the essay questions in a group and are given the signal to begin. You just want to take a peek at them to make sure that your dreaded topic isn't there and that your favorite topic is there. Going through each question enough to be sure about their topics takes time. Doing that with all of the questions takes a significant amount of time. And, what's the end result? Peace of mind? Nope. Panic.

You'll see that your favorite topic is not there and your least favorite topic is there instead. You begin to dread what is coming up. You can't focus on the first question, because you know number two is the worst topic. All you can think about is number two. You end up doing poorly on the first question even though it is a topic that you are fairly comfortable with. You skip number two and move on to three, another comfortable topic. Except, now you are still thinking about number two and how on earth you are ever going to be able to answer it. And, on it goes.

Avoid this temptation. Answer each question in the order that it is given to you. Spend the allotted time and then move on. If you don't spend all of the time on a topic, then you'll have time to go back later. You have to attempt the dreaded topics when they come. Apply your mind map and do your best. Then move on. If something comes to you later, you can go back and add it. This approach helps to avoid the panic that sets in when you skim them all first.

VII. AVOID PANIC

One common fear of applicants is having a question that they will have no idea how to answer. Let's put that fear at ease right now. You will. You will have a question that you do not immediately have any idea how to answer. So, no need to panic that it might happen, as we know it will happen.

What are you going to do when that happens? Hyperventilate? You might have if you didn't know that it was actually going to happen. Because you do know, you can plan what to do. Pull out your mind map of how to tackle questions in that topic area. Go through the topic step-by-step and it will come to you.

What if nothing comes to you? Your mind is a complete blank. Then, guess. Yes, guess. It's an educated guess, but making a guess may garner you a point while leaving it blank is worth zero points.

For example, a groom demands his bride sign a pre-nuptial agreement the morning of their wedding without talking about it beforehand. It states that she agrees to no property provision if they divorce within five years. One year later, the couple is now divorcing and she discovers that he had hidden assets, is worth several million dollars, and is not a penniless law student after all.

The issue is whether the pre-nuptial agreement is valid. You did not take Family Law in law school and you did not study it very much in your bar preparation. First, take a deep breath. Get as much oxygen flowing to your brain as you can. Then, pause and consider—what do you know? An "agreement" indicates it's a contract. You do know about contracts. That means there must be mutual assent. Did the bride assent? Could she fully assent when it was given to her that morning? Could she fully assent when she didn't have all the facts? What would you guess? The groom should have fully disclosed his assets and given her more time to consider. Craft a rule, put it down, apply it, and move on. If the rule comes to you later, go back and redo.

Your mind-set entering the exam needs to be "I can do this," because you can do this. Have confidence in yourself. You will have studied hard for the bar exam, probably harder than anything else you have done. Take a deep breath. You will be fine.

CHAPTER 5

Building Multistate Performance Test Skills

I. SKILLS TESTED

Each component of the bar exam is designed to assess your ability to apply fundamental legal principles and legal reasoning to a given fact pattern. It asks, can you identify the issues raised by a fact pattern, understand what is relevant, demonstrate an understanding of the legal principles involved, and apply the rules to the facts? The MEE does this through 30-minute essay questions. The MBE does this with 200 multiple choice questions. In both components, you must be able to recall the law on your own in a closed-book fashion.

The Multistate Performance Test (MPT) is quite different. It is designed to test the same skills, but in a more realistic situation: Can you complete a task that a beginning lawyer should be able to accomplish? "The MPT requires examinees to

- sort detailed factual materials and separate relevant from irrelevant facts;
- analyze statutory, case, and administrative materials for applicable principles of law;
- apply the relevant law to the relevant facts in a manner likely to resolve a client's problem;
- identify and resolve ethical dilemmas, when present;
- communicate effectively in writing; and
- complete a lawyering task within time constraints."[1]

The skills being assessed include the:

- ability to develop and evaluate strategies for solving a problem or accomplishing an objective, including the ability to:
  - identify and diagnose the problem;
  - generate alternative solutions and strategies;
  - develop a plan of action;
  - implement a plan of action; and
  - keep the planning process open to new information and new ideas.

---

1. www.ncbex.org/about-ncbe-exams/mpt/overview-of-the-mpt/.

- ability to analyze and apply legal rules and principles, including the ability to:
  - identify and formulate legal issues;
  - identify relevant legal rules within a given set of legal materials;
  - formulate relevant legal theories;
  - elaborate on legal theories;
  - evaluate legal theories; and
  - criticize and synthesize legal arguments.
- ability to analyze and use facts and to plan and direct factual investigation, including the ability to:
  - identify relevant facts within a given set of factual materials;
  - determine the need for factual investigation;
  - plan a factual investigation;
  - memorialize and organize information in an accessible form;
  - decide whether to conclude the process of fact gathering; and
  - evaluate the information that has been gathered.
- ability to communicate effectively in writing, including the ability to:
  - assess the perspective of the recipient of the communication; and
  - organize and express ideas with precision, clarity, logic, and economy.
- ability to organize and manage a legal task, including the ability to:
  - allocate time, effort, and resources efficiently; and
  - perform and complete tasks within time constraints.
- ability to represent a client consistently with applicable ethical standards, including:
  - knowledge of the nature and sources of ethical standards;
  - knowledge of the means by which ethical standards are enforced; and
  - ability to recognize and resolve ethical dilemmas.[2]

For the MPT, the examiners give you the instructions, a File, and a Library. In the past, the instructions have been identical for all MPT questions. That's not guaranteed. So, one step is to verify that the instructions have not been changed from the instructions you read during your practice questions. Just a quick skim should do it.

The File consists of documents, including a memo from the assigning attorney spelling out the task you are to accomplish. Frequently, another memorandum is included that spells out the format for the document. Read this carefully. Specific guidelines are included for specific format issues, such as headings. Note that these memos not only instruct you as to format, but also as to whether to use an objective or persuasive tone.

Other parts of the File include fact documents such as deposition transcripts, notes from a witness interview, an invoice, a receipt, a purchase order, a contract, medical records, police reports, and letters. These are the sources for the facts, which are not summarized for you. You must extract the relevant facts from these source documents.

The Library contains the law that you are to analyze. You are not to include any law that you already know, but are to analyze only what is given in the Library. The law is set in the fictitious jurisdiction of Franklin, although the law may mirror regulations or uniform acts that you already know such as

---

2. www.ncbex.org/assets/media_files/Information-Booklets/MPTIB2014.pdf.

the Uniform Commercial Code. The law may include statutes, regulations, court rules, model rules, and excerpts from cases. Not all may be relevant to the issues raised. Thus, you must pull from the Library the relevant law that you will then apply to the facts.

Instead of presenting your analysis in an essay response or by answering multiple choice questions, you are to prepare a specific document. Examples include a predictive memorandum to your supervising attorney, a client letter, a persuasive brief, a statement of facts for a persuasive brief, a contract provision, a will, a proposal for settlement, a witness examination plan, a discovery plan, or a closing argument. The three documents used the most are a predictive memorandum; a letter; and a persuasive brief that may include a statement of facts, point headings, and the argument. Those are not guaranteed, of course. You should be prepared to draft any of the documents listed.

Scoring the MPT is virtually identical to scoring an essay question. The same scale is used. Just like an essay question, different issues on the MPT may be worth a different number of points. Issue one may be 60% and issue two may be 40% of the total available points. Each jurisdiction decides how much weight to give the overall MPT score. Uniform Bar Examination jurisdictions weight the MPT at 20%.

II. GAME PLAN FOR THE MPT

Your game plan for the essays and multiple choice questions has consisted of making your own materials for memorization and then using practice questions to both learn the law and memorize the law. Your game plan for the MPT is much simpler. No memorization is necessary. The examiners give you the law you need! Your preparation is twofold: practice MPT questions and reviewing formats.

Completing practice MPT questions is critical to your success. They cannot be taken for granted just because no memorization is involved. In many respects, they are like a closed-research writing assignment from your first year of law school; the difference is that there will be more irrelevant facts and irrelevant law. In addition, professional responsibility issues may arise. Sometimes you are asked what additional facts you need. While the format may be something with which you are very comfortable, it may not be. And, the biggest reason to do practice questions—time pressure.

No doubt about it, the MPT is a time-pressured assessment. While 90 minutes sounds like a lot of time, you will find the length of the materials you must read and analyze far exceeds the comparable time spent reading an essay question. The facts are not organized in any particular fashion.

Two schools of thought exist as to how to approach the reading. You should do sufficient practice to decide which method works best for you. The first school of thought focuses on the Library first:

- Verify that the instructions are the same as they were for the practice questions.
- Read the memo from the supervising attorney to understand the task.
- Read the memo regarding format, if included.
- Read the Library.
- Analyze the law in the Library and make an outline.

> **EXAM TIP**
> Drafting a statement of facts is more difficult than it may seem. Remember to focus on the facts relevant to that motion and not on everything that happened in the case. The examiners want to see if you know the difference!

- Read the File and insert the relevant facts into your outline.
- Verify the facts by a second read of the File.
- Draft the document.

The rationale behind this approach is that you will have a better analysis and save time by understanding the law before you read the facts. By understanding the law, you will more quickly see which facts are relevant. By outlining the law first, you have a jump start on the organization of the analysis. This approach is recommended for at-risk students.

The second school of thought focuses on the File first:

- Verify that the instructions are the same as they were for the practice questions.
- Read the memo from the supervising attorney to understand the task.
- Read the memo regarding format, if included.
- Read the File to better understand what happened.
- Read the Library.
- Analyze the law in the Library and make an outline.
- Read the facts a second time to identify relevant facts.
- Insert the relevant facts into your outline.
- Verify the facts by a third read of the File.
- Draft the document.

Some applicants find they must read the facts several times when they read the File first. The first time they read to understand what happened. The second time they read to identify the relevant facts. They then read a third time to verify the facts.

You will need to decide which method works best for you. The only way to do that is to do enough practice questions to know. Because this is time-pressured, you must gauge what you currently can do in that time frame. Thus, unlike your first sets of essay practice questions, you must keep to the strict time limit of 90 minutes. Then, as you practice, autopsy your answer. Your ability to analyze and draft a better document will improve.

Just like essay questions, spend your initial time reading and thinking about the issues and rules. Forty-five minutes of the 90 minutes should be spent reading and thinking. Then, the next 45 minutes are spent drafting and revising the document. Do that with each MPT if your jurisdiction requires more than one.

The Uniform Bar Examination includes two MPT questions. They are back-to-back, the first morning of the exam. You are given both MPT questions at the same time, and time is not called on the first MPT after 90 minutes. You must keep track of your own time. Spending too much time on the first question means you will be short on time on the second MPT. Both MPTs are worth the same numbers of points. You gain no advantage by spending more time on one than on the other. Practice taking two MPTs back-to-back in three hours in order to see how necessary it is to keep to the time limits. Do not read both MPTs together to decide which one to do first. You have to do both any way. Start with the first one and, at 90 minutes, switch to the second one, even if the first one is not as complete as you would like.

Just as with essay and MBE questions, reviewing your practice answer is where you will learn the most. Each MPT comes with a Point Sheet from the NCBE. This Point Sheet outlines in detail what is expected on that MPT. Most of the time what is on the Point Sheet is more than anyone could write in

90 minutes. It is meant as a guide for the local state bar examiners to decide how to grade that MPT. It is still worth reviewing so that you can see if you properly identified all of the issues, properly synthesized the rules, organized the analysis appropriately, provided sufficient application, used the correct tone (whether objective or persuasive), and properly addressed the task recognizing any professional responsibility issues that arose.

Reviewing the bar examiners' Point Sheet also informs you about how the points are allocated. Sometimes the Point Sheet allows the grader to give credit for tangential issues not raised by the actual File and Library, for example, the canon of construction that hand-written words prevail over typewritten words in a contract. Most of the time, however, those issues are not worth the time, particularly if you focus on them to the exclusion of the main issues raised by the Library given to you. If you go off too much on a tangent, you need to learn what the bar examiners are really looking for to sharpen your issue-spotting skills.

III. PROPER FORMAT

Your document needs to be in the proper format, both in substance, in form, and in tone. You can keep the form fairly basic, but it should not be in the style of an essay answer to the question. A letter should look like a letter. A brief should look like a brief. Bluebook citation format is not required, although you need to include some kind of attribution of authority. Just the case name, *Smith*, or the statute number, § 65-210, is sufficient.

MEMO FORMAT

MEMORANDUM

To: Partner
From: Associate
Date: July 30, 2014
Re: *Popper v. Wilson*—Intentional Interference with Contract, Jurisdiction Issues
          File No. 14-1234

Our client, Bonnie Wilson, was served with a complaint alleging intentional interference with contract. This dispute arises from. . . . The firm needs to decide whether to file a motion to dismiss for lack of jurisdiction.

First . . . .

[Read the memos from the partner carefully. The firm may have an established format regarding memos including the use of headings. Headings are appropriate in predictive memoranda even if not required by the supervising attorney.]

[Include your analysis here.]

LETTER FORMAT

July 30, 2014

Dear Mr. House:

This letter is in response to your inquiry regarding the legal issues involved in establishing your business as a closely-held corporation.

[Again, read the memos from the partner carefully. The firm may have an established format regarding letters including the use of headings. Headings are appropriate in letters as well.]

[Include your analysis here.]

Thank you again for contacting me regarding your new business venture. Please feel free to contact me should you have further questions.

Sincerely,

[Do NOT put your name. Put your exam number, instead.]

BRIEF FORMAT

[Sometimes called Memorandum in Support of Motion . . .
or Suggestions in Support of Motion . . . .
Do not confuse with a predictive memorandum.
It is still a persuasive brief document.]

BRIEF IN SUPPORT OF MOTION TO SUPPRESS

Statement of Facts

Include only if instructions from supervising attorney require.

Argument

I. The Text Messages Between Plaintiff, Her Attorney, and the Investigator are Protected by Attorney-Client Privilege Because . . . . and Must be Suppressed. [Check memo from supervising attorney for format.]

[Argument for first issue.]

II. Plaintiff's Facebook Posts are Irrelevant to the Issues . . . and Must be Suppressed.

[Argument for second issue.]

Conclusion

Respectfully submitted,

[Do NOT put your name. Put your exam number, instead.]

Letters and memos usually start with at least one sentence that lays out the issues and is appropriate for that document. This should be brief. No need for a letter to start with a ton of trivial banter such as "Great to meet you," and "Thanks for meeting with us.

The second and more important part of format is the tone of the document. Memoranda are planning documents. Thus, the analysis must be objective and include the strengths and weaknesses of the client's situation. Letters can be objective or persuasive. For example, an initial settlement offer is a persuasive document to the opposing counsel as to why settlement serves both sides' best interests. A client letter, however, needs to be objective and state the strengths and weaknesses of the client's situation. A brief is always a persuasive document, but your audience is the judge. Use an advocacy tone. No need to inflate or embellish the argument, but use a strong voice.

Prepare for the MPT by reviewing formats for different documents in addition to doing practice questions. Your commercial bar preparation provider will usually provide you with several MPTs. You can also purchase additional MPTs directly from the NCBE. Use these to practice and to review format. For the MPTs you do not write out, spend time reading the MPT, bullet-outlining the law, and reviewing the format of the document.

IV. BOTTOM LINE IS ANALYSIS

An outline of your analysis is well worth the time invested. Consider drafting a thesis at the beginning of your analysis that briefly sets out the points you want to make. If you run short on time, the examiners will at least know what you planned to do. Then, in your analysis, bullet-outline the remaining points you want to make. You will receive some credit for those, although they are not fully developed.

The organization of your analysis should be a form of CRAC, whether your writing is objective or predictive. Always put the rule before the application. Make sure you have separate CRACs for each issue or sub-issue.

Most of the authority provided to you will be binding authority. Occasionally, the examiners will include authority from another jurisdiction—persuasive authority. If they do, consider that in your analysis and be careful not to treat it as binding authority. Likewise, if secondary authority is included, do not treat it the same as primary authority. Some of the authority may be irrelevant. Your job is to analyze and decide which authority to use. Remember that your analysis is to be based only on these authorities and no others.

As you do practice MPT questions, autopsy your answer the same way you do the practice essays. Identify each rule, application, and conclusion. Note the organization of the issues and sub-issues. Be brutally honest with yourself in your critique of your answer.

Most of the points are based on the analysis. Your ultimate conclusion often does not matter. Good grammar and punctuation count. Use headings so that organization is evident. Understand the format to quickly get it out of the way so that the majority of your time and written work is on the analysis.

V. PRACTICE MPT QUESTION

Wells v. Wells[3]

FILE

Broyles and Lemansky

Attorneys at Law

2398 S. 25th Street

Franklin City, Franklin 33173-3209

MEMORANDUM

To: Applicant
From: Pamela Broyles, Senior Partner
Re: *Wells v. Wells*
Date: July 29, 2004

We have just finished the evidentiary hearing in a family court proceeding in which our client, Joan Wells, petitioned the court for permission to remove her minor son, Sammy, from the State of Franklin to the State of Columbia. We ordered an expedited hearing transcript, and it is in the file.

Joan's petition is based on the assertion that she intends to relocate to Columbia to accept a new job. Sammy's father, Fred Wells, opposes the petition.

The judge has given us two days to submit concurrent briefs. This is where I need your help.

Please draft our brief in support of Joan's petition following the instructions in the Firm's memorandum on persuasive briefs. You should use all the relevant evidence as appropriate to support the arguments in the brief. Since we will not have the opportunity to present a rebuttal brief, be sure to anticipate and refute Fred's arguments.

Broyles and Lemansky
Attorneys at Law
2398 S. 25th Street
Franklin City, Franklin 33173-3209

MEMORANDUM   September 8, 1999

To: All Lawyers
From: Litigation Supervisor
Subject: Persuasive Briefs

_____

All persuasive briefs shall conform to the following guidelines:

All briefs shall include a Statement of Facts. The aim of the Statement of Facts is to persuade the tribunal that the facts support our client's position. The facts must be stated accurately, although emphasis is not improper. Select carefully the facts that are pertinent to the legal arguments. However, in a brief to a trial court, when the evidentiary hearing has just been completed, the Statement of Facts section of the brief may be abbreviated because it can be assumed that the court has the facts in mind.

The firm follows the practice of breaking the argument into its major components and writing carefully crafted subject headings that illustrate the arguments they cover. Avoid writing briefs that contain only a single broad argument heading. The argument heading should succinctly summarize the reasons the tribunal should take the position you are advocating. A heading should be a specific application of a rule of law to the facts of the case and not a bare legal or factual conclusion or a statement of an abstract principle. For example, improper: IT IS NOT IN THE CHILD'S BEST INTERESTS TO BE PLACED IN THE MOTHER'S CUSTODY. Proper: EVIDENCE THAT THE MOTHER HAS BEEN CONVICTED OF CHILD ABUSE IS SUFFICIENT TO ESTABLISH THAT IT IS NOT IN THE CHILD'S BEST INTERESTS TO BE PLACED IN THE MOTHER'S CUSTODY.

The body of each argument should analyze applicable legal authority and persuasively argue how the facts and law support our client's position. Authority supportive of our client's position should be emphasized, but contrary authority also should generally be cited, addressed in the argument, and explained or distinguished. Do not reserve arguments for reply or supplemental briefing.

The lawyer need not prepare a table of contents, a table of cases, a summary of argument, or an index. These will be prepared, when required, after the draft is approved.

TRANSCRIPT OF HEARING
July 28, 2004

THE COURT: This matter is here on the petition of Joan Wells for permission to remove the minor child, Sammy, from the state, specifically to Columbia. In 2002, when Joan and Fred Wells were divorced, this court awarded joint custody to the parents and designated Joan Wells primary physical custodian. Because Joan Wells indicated her intention to remove Sammy from Franklin and Fred Wells has opposed that move, this court must now decide if the custody arrangement ordered in 2002 should be modified. Present are Joan Wells, her attorney, Ms. Broyles, and Fred Wells, and his counsel, Mr. Simpson. We are ready to proceed with evidence. Ms. Broyles, call your first witness.

THE PETITIONER, Joan Wells, WAS SWORN AND IDENTIFIED.

PAMELA BROYLES: What are you asking the court to do, Ms. Wells?

JOAN WELLS: I am asking the court to permit me to take my six-year-old son, Sammy, to Columbia City so that I can take a position as an associate professor of Irish Literature and Studies in the Irish Studies Department at Columbia State University in Columbia City, Columbia, and can better care for Sammy.

Q: Why do you wish to relocate?

A: I have just completed my doctoral degree in Irish literature. Now I can obtain a position in my field at a higher salary. This will better my life and my ability to provide for Sammy.

Q: How will Sammy be cared for if you relocate?

A: Sammy will live with me. I have found a home near campus that is a bit larger than our present home. Sammy will attend elementary school at the McAuliff Elementary School, near campus. It is a wonderful school, being staffed with so many graduates of CSU. It has an after-school program for days when I must teach late. The quality of life for children in Columbia City is great—the parks, recreational programs, youth center, great cultural opportunities in music and the other arts—Sammy will have a great life.

Q: Can you tell us anything else about the educational opportunities for Sammy?

A: CSU offers a tuition discount to children of its professors so Sammy will be able to attend college at half the cost of tuition. That will save me and Fred a lot of money.

Q: What do you propose regarding Sammy's relationship with his father?

A: I want to be sure Sammy stays in touch with his father. I would never come between him and his father. Ever since we separated, I made sure that Sammy has a photo of himself and his father by his bed. Fred can send new photos from time to time. I also have a digital camera and can send Fred photos of Sammy via e-mail. Sammy still likes to be read to. Fred can tape books and Sammy can listen to the tapes before he goes to bed. I will have Sammy send Fred a packet of school papers and art projects every week so Fred can see how Sammy is doing. I know Fred is very interested in Sammy's music and other activities so we can even record events like Sammy's school plays, concerts, and sports activities, and send a videotape to Fred.

Q: Anything else regarding Sammy and his father?

A: Fred can call him whenever he wants, and when Sammy is older, he can e-mail his father as well. Whenever Sammy wants to call Fred, I will let him, of course. If Fred wants to purchase a computer camera for himself and Sammy, I will see that it gets hooked up at home and Sammy and Fred can see and talk with each other every day.

Q: What about visits with his father?

A: While Sammy is so young, he can fly with me to Franklin, for a week at Thanksgiving, a week in December, and a week during spring break. I would like Sammy to see my

continued on next page

family then too, but he can spend most of the time with Fred. Of course, I will see that Sammy gets to Fred's for several weeks in the summer, preferably two weeks with Fred in June and another two weeks in July. And if Fred wants to go on vacation with Sammy for a week or two, he can do that. When Sammy is older, he can fly to see Fred. Fred is also welcome to come visit in Columbia.

Q: Tell the court what brought about this relocation.

A: Well, teaching at the university level in Irish studies has always been my dream. When Fred and I had just started dating, I told him that my goal was to get a doctoral degree in Irish literature and teach at the best university possible.

Q: Fred has suggested that you are moving to get away from him and his new wife and that you refuse to talk to Kathleen, his new wife. Can you address that?

A: I never said that I refused to talk to her. What I said was this: Kathleen and I have a past history. When Fred married her, I suggested that it would be best if Fred and I limit our discussions about Sammy to just ourselves.

Q: Are you concerned that Sammy will have trouble adjusting if you move?

A: I am concerned that we make the move as easy on Sammy as possible. That is why I want to be settled before the school year starts. But Sammy is a very resilient child. He has just finished kindergarten, so this is an ideal time for the move—before he gets really settled into school.

BROYLES: I have nothing further for this witness.

THE COURT: Cross-examination, Mr. Simpson?

THOMAS SIMPSON: Thank you, Your Honor.

Q: Right now, Fred is with Sammy almost 40 percent of the time.

A: Yes, it comes to about that.

Q: If Sammy goes with you to Columbia, Fred will have less time with Sammy, isn't that right?

A: That depends on how frequently Fred comes to Columbia.

Q: Isn't it true that Sammy has been very active in the Franklin City Children's Choir here in Franklin City, Franklin?

A: Yes.

Q: Isn't it true that Fred has been an assistant director for the choir and has been able to encourage Sammy to develop his musical talent?

A: Yes. But let's not forget Sammy is only six years old.

Q: Isn't it true that there is no comparable children's choir in Columbia City?

A: So far, I have not found one, but I will encourage Sammy's musical talents.

Q: Fred cares more about Sammy's musical talent than you do, doesn't he?

A: I think it's important to develop all of Sammy's talents.

Q: Isn't it true that Fred has been a loving father who has cared for Sammy and been very involved in his life?

A: Yes. I have never said that Fred is anything but a caring parent.

Q: Fred also goes to teacher's conferences and to doctor's visits, and generally is very involved in all aspects of Sammy's life. Is that right?

A: All true.

Q: And isn't it true that Fred has participated in every important decision about Sammy's life?

A: Yes.

Q: Haven't there been times when the two of you have disagreed about Sammy's upbringing?

A: Occasionally.

Q: On those occasions, haven't the two of you been able to resolve your differences?

A: Sure. We've talked about the issues. I respect his opinion. In fact, because he teaches children, I usually go along with him on issues involving Sammy's schooling.

SIMPSON: No further questions, Your Honor.

continued on next page

COURT: Call the next witness.

THE WITNESS, Michael McBryan, WAS SWORN AND IDENTIFIED.

BROYLES: How do you know Joan Wells?

McBRYAN: I am the department chair for English and Irish Literature at Franklin State University and was the committee chair for Joan's doctoral dissertation. Joan was an excellent student and shows much promise in scholarship and teaching Irish literature.

Q: Is it possible that Franklin State University will offer her a position on the faculty?

A: No. We have a policy against hiring our own graduates. Even if we did not, the position she has been offered at CSU is a very prestigious one. We cannot meet the salary. Further, they have a whole department devoted to Irish studies so she will have colleagues who will encourage her in ways that we could not. Plus, she will be eligible for raises that will make her more financially secure.

BROYLES: I have no more questions for this witness Your Honor.

THE COURT: Mr. Simpson, any cross?

SIMPSON: Yes, Your Honor. Thank you.

SIMPSON: Isn't it true that Joan Wells has tenure at the community college?

A: True.

Q: Having tenure—in essence, doesn't that mean she is ensured employment at the community college for the rest of her life?

A: In general, yes, that is what it means.

SIMPSON: That is all I have for this witness, Your Honor.

THE COURT: Ms. Broyles, any other witnesses?

BROYLES: We call the court's attention to the stipulations previously presented to the court. Sammy's physician reports that Sammy, age six, is healthy and developing normally. His teacher indicates that he did well in school during his kindergarten year and is well prepared to move into first grade. He is progressing well in school and seems emotionally and socially well adjusted. Finally, the parties have stipulated that there are four nonstop flights a day between Franklin City, Franklin, and Columbia City, Columbia, and that the airlines offer unaccompanied minor service for children flying without an adult. Petitioner rests.

THE COURT: Very well. Mr. Simpson, call your first witness.

RESPONDENT, Fred Wells, WAS SWORN AND IDENTIFIED.

SIMPSON: Tell the court about your relationship with your son, Sammy.

FRED WELLS: Ever since Joan and I separated, I have made sure that Sammy is number one in my life. I talk to him on the phone several times a week. As the court ordered in the decree, Sammy is with me every weekend and one week in the summer, and on half the major holidays. In addition to what the court ordered, at least once during the week, year round, we have dinner together, and he and I go to movies and children's plays at least once a month. He has not yet shown much interest in sports but if he does, I will be at his games. We play T-ball in the yard when he is with me.

Q: What else do you and Sammy do when he is with you?

A: He and I play card games and board games and play trucks together. Normal father-son stuff. I put him to bed and work with him on his school projects, and help him get dressed in the morning, and prepare meals for him. When Joan and I were married, I was very involved in his day-to-day care. When he is with me on weekends, I read him several stories every night before he goes to bed.

Q: How is Sammy involved in the Franklin City Children's Choir?

A: Sammy is very musically talented. I am a music teacher and I could tell early on that he was talented. So we enrolled him in the Franklin City Children's Choir. The director loves Sammy's voice and has already given him several solos. At his age, they have practices three times a week for six weeks each fall and spring and put on two major

continued on next page

concerts a year. In a few years, he will tour with the choir. The choir goes all over the United States and to Europe every other year. If he stays in the choir until he is 18, he will have outstanding experiences and be well prepared for a college audition, if that is what he wants. There is no children's choir like this in Columbia City.

Q: Do you think Sammy has the talent to have a career in music?

A: It is very, very possible. Talent like his is rare and needs to be cultivated if he is to have a chance at a career. Joan will not develop it like I would. Taking him to choir is just too much hassle for her. Plus, I help him with singing practice and can really be his singing mentor.

Q: Where are Sammy's grandparents, cousins, and other family located?

A: My parents live about 80 miles south of Franklin City. Joan's parents are 40 miles away in the other direction. On Joan's side of the family, Sammy has two cousins his age and on my side there are also two cousins his age, all in Franklin City. They are his most frequent playmates. Plus, he has three older cousins and one younger one, all in the area.

Q: What concerns do you have if Joan moves away with Sammy?

A: Sammy had a lot of trouble adjusting after the divorce. He was almost four at the time. He regressed to baby talk for a while and went through a period of not wanting to play with other kids or go to anyone's home. In fact, Joan and I arranged for the daycare counselor to work with him. He has gotten over all that and seems fine now. I am afraid he will regress again if he moves. I am concerned that he will lose me as a father. A child needs a mother and a father. I would never take Sammy from his mother, but it seems she wants to take him from me. As far as I know, Joan knows no one in Columbia City. Sammy knows no one there—no school pals, no cousins, no playmates. He will be lonely. He could be here with me.

Q: You have remarried. How does Sammy relate to Kathleen, your new wife?

A: Sammy gets along with my new wife. I was very careful to introduce Kathleen to Sammy early in our relationship to be sure he could get along with her. The only problem since I remarried has been Joan. Joan used to work with Kathleen at the community college, and they did not get along. Joan will not even talk to her. If Kathleen answers the phone when Joan calls for Sammy at my house, Joan immediately asks for me and will not even say hello to Kathleen. I am afraid that Joan is moving in order to avoid dealing with Kathleen. Or else she is jealous that I have moved on with my life and she has to make a bigger splash by getting a new job and moving to a new city.

Q: If Joan did move away with Sammy, how would you be able to spend time with him?

A: There is no way I could see Sammy on a regular basis if he moves to Columbia. I cannot afford to fly out there and the drive is too much for a weekend. It's more than 10 hours one way. Even if I could get there, where would I stay with Sammy? I would have no way to be with him in a home environment. He is too young to fly to Franklin by himself. Joan's proposal means that I will see Sammy about eight weeks a year—eight out of 52! Now, if you add up all the time, he currently spends about 20 weeks a year with me. I am afraid he will forget me. I won't be there for school plays and concerts and his Little League games and whatever else he does. I cannot be a father to him and children need a father.

Q: Fred, how will you be able to make decisions about Sammy's education, health, and the like if Joan moves?

A: I won't be able to. Because I will be hundreds of miles away, I won't go to school conferences, doctor appointments, etc.

Q: Then, how would you have input into these decisions?

A: I would have to rely on Joan to fill me in. I would never feel that I had firsthand information or that I was involved in the decisions.

continued on next page

SIMPSON: Thank you, Mr. Wells. Your Honor, I have no more questions for this witness.

THE COURT: Ms. Broyles, do you wish to cross-examine?

BROYLES: Yes. Thank you, Your Honor.

BROYLES: Isn't it true that Joan has been a good mother?

A: Yes.

Q: Isn't it true that the choir was your idea, not Sammy's?

A: I believe it was a joint decision—mine, Joan's and Sammy's.

Q: Isn't it true that Joan has never gotten in the way of your time with Sammy?

A: True.

Q: In fact, she has voluntarily agreed that you can spend significantly more time with Sammy than even what the court ordered in the divorce decree, isn't that right?

A: Yes. I guess so.

Q: You can always telephone or e-mail doctors and teachers to get information about Sammy, can't you?

A: Yes.

Q: Except for this proposed move, you and Joan have resolved disagreements about Sammy's welfare, haven't you?

A: Yes.

BROYLES: That is all I have for this witness, Your Honor.

THE COURT: Mr. Simpson, call the next witness.

THE WITNESS, Maria Niro, WAS SWORN AND IDENTIFIED.

SIMPSON: How do you know Sammy Wells?

A: I am a counselor at the day care center Sammy attended. At the time of the divorce, his parents asked me to help Sammy through the adjustment period. I am trained to work with children going through losses, like death or divorce. I do play therapy to help them express their feelings. So I worked with Sammy for about eight weeks.

Q: Was Sammy having adjustment problems?

A: Yes, the normal ones. Like any child whose parents are divorcing, Sammy directly and indirectly expressed fears about where his bed and his clothes and toys would be, who would feed him and put him to bed and take him to day care.

SIMPSON: Thank you, Ms. Niro. I have no more questions, Your Honor.

THE COURT: Ms. Broyles?

Q: You are not a licensed social worker or counselor, are you?

A: No, no, but I have been trained to work with kids experiencing divorce and death. Had I thought Sammy needed professional counseling, I would have told the Wells family to take him to a professional. But all he needed was some help through some difficult months.

Q: So, Sammy didn't exhibit an unusual level of stress as a result of his parents' divorce?

A: No. It was a relatively mild case, as these matters go.

Q: And while you were working with him, Sammy got over these fears?

A: Yes. Like most children, he adapted to the new routine.

Q: So, he has adjusted well to living separately with his mother and father?

A: Yes.

Q: And you haven't worked with Sammy in the last year?

A: That's right.

BROYLES: No further questions, Your Honor.

SIMPSON: The respondent rests, Your Honor.

THE COURT: All right. We have concluded the evidence. It's clear that, constitutionally, the court does not have the authority to prohibit Ms. Wells from moving. The sole issue, therefore, before the court is whether Joan can take Sammy with her. I want to make a decision very soon. I want both counsel to submit a post-trial brief within 48 hours. There will be no rebuttal briefs, so address all the issues in this post-trial brief. We are adjourned.

LIBRARY

Franklin Dissolution Of Marriage Act

Section 30. Definitions.

For purposes of this article, the following words shall have the following meanings:

(1) JOINT CUSTODY. Joint legal custody and joint physical custody.

(2) JOINT LEGAL CUSTODY. Both parents have equal rights and responsibilities for major decisions concerning the child, including the child's education, health care, and religious training. The court may designate one parent to have sole power to make certain decisions while both parents retain equal rights and responsibilities for other decisions.

(3) JOINT PHYSICAL CUSTODY. Physical custody is shared by the parents in a way that assures the child frequent and substantial contact with each parent. Joint physical custody does not necessarily mean physical custody of equal durations of time. The court may designate one parent as the primary physical custodian.

(4) SOLE LEGAL CUSTODY. One parent has sole right and responsibility to make major decisions concerning the child, including the child's education, health care, and religious training.

(5) SOLE PHYSICAL CUSTODY. One parent has sole physical custody and the other parent has rights of visitation except as otherwise provided by the court.

Section 109. Removal of child.

The court may grant leave, before or after judgment, to any party having sole legal custody or sole or primary physical custody of any minor child or children to remove such child or children from Franklin whenever such approval is in the best interests of such child or children.

Section 402. Best interests of child.

The court shall determine custody in accordance with the best interests of the child. The court shall consider all relevant factors including:

(1) the mental and physical health of all individuals involved;

(2) the child's adjustment to the child's home, school, and community;

(3) the interaction and interrelationship of the child with the child's parent or parents, the child's siblings, and any other person who may significantly affect the child's best interests;

(4) the wishes of the child's parent or parents as to the child's custody.

Marshall v. Marshall
Franklin Supreme Court (2001)

Sue Ellen Marshall petitioned the court for leave to remove the parties' son, Michael, from the state of Franklin to the state of Columbia. As a result of their divorce in 1998, Sue Ellen and Forest were awarded joint custody of Michael, then three years old. The court designated Sue Ellen the primary physical custodian.

The record in this case reveals on Sue Ellen's side that Sue Ellen has been offered a job in her field of nursing administration in Phillips, Columbia, at a salary significantly higher than she is currently earning and with greater career potential; and Michael has an asthma condition that will be controlled more effectively in Columbia, although it is being adequately controlled in Franklin City.

The evidence on Forest's side shows that he has been a loving and involved parent; since the divorce, he has taken full advantage of all the time he has physical custody to be with Michael; he telephones Michael twice a week, although Sue Ellen requires advance notice of the calls and limits them to five minutes each; Forest coaches Michael to develop his swimming skills and, although Sue Ellen has lodged objections with Michael's school, Forest has chaperoned school-related field trips; both sets of grandparents, whom Michael visits frequently and who are an important part of Michael's life, live within 20 miles of Franklin City; Sue Ellen has steadfastly refused to allow Forest any flexibility in the physical custody arrangements or the telephone communications. Forest has been actively involved in decisions about Michael's medical care, education, and religious upbringing through direct contact with the pediatrician, teachers, coaches, and ministers.

The only evidence presented by Sue Ellen concerning her plans for visits between Forest and Michael after the move was that Michael would spend three weeks in the summer and one week during winter break with Forest, with flights to be at Forest's expense. She also agreed to permit the twice-weekly telephone calls of five minutes' duration, also at Forest's expense.

The trial court denied the petition because it was not in Michael's best interests to be separated from his father. The appellate court reversed, holding that the trial court had failed to properly apply the judicially created presumption that a parent with sole legal custody or sole or primary physical custody may move the child from Franklin. The appellate court noted that Sue Ellen had provided a valid reason for the move. The appellate court did not address Sue Ellen's motivation or the effects of the move on Michael.

On this appeal, Forest asserts that the appellate court's interpretation of Section 109 of the Franklin Dissolution of Marriage Act failed to account for the objecting parent's relationship with the child by not requiring findings concerning the effect of Michael's separation from his father in determining the best interests of the child.

In interpreting Section 109 in the context of joint custodial situations, the court must balance the benefits derived from the parent's move, the need for finality in custody decrees, the rights of both custodial parents to make decisions for the child, the interest of the child in having a loving relationship with both parents, and the rights of both parents.

We interpret Section 109 to require the parent with primary physical custody who wishes to move with the child from this state to present a legitimate reason for the

continued on next page

move. Once a legitimate reason has been established, a presumption is created in favor of the parent petitioning to move. The other parent can rebut the presumption by showing that the move is not in good faith or it is not in the best interests of the child. The parent seeking to rebut the presumption has the burden of persuading the court that the move is in bad faith or is not in the best interests of the child. This standard, although fact-based, recognizes the realities of a mobile society, while also seeking to prevent the primary custodial parent from undermining a child's relationship with the other parent.

Improved employment, educational opportunities, or health of the custodial parent, the new spouse, or the child are examples of legitimate reasons for a move. A move designed primarily to interfere with the relationship between the other parent and the child does not constitute a legitimate reason. Sue Ellen has established a legitimate reason for the move—better employment for herself and improved health for Michael. There is a question, however, as to whether Forest carried his burden of persuading the court that the move is not in the best interests of Michael. Unquestionably, the move will affect the time Forest spends with Michael. The amount of time alone is not sufficient to harm the parent-child relationship, where there is a strong relationship and where the parents take other steps to encourage the relationship.

More troubling was the evidence that in the past Sue Ellen may have sought to interfere with Forest's relationship with Michael through limiting telephone calls and other measures. Based on the record, this court cannot determine whether Forest demonstrated that the move is not in the best interests of Michael. Because we cannot determine whether the trial court understood the proper test or whether the court properly considered the factors concerning best interests, we must remand to the trial court to determine whether Forest has rebutted the presumption and carried his burden of persuasion.

Feldman v. Feldman
Franklin Court of Appeal (2002)

Howard and Ruth Feldman were granted joint custody of their daughters at the time of their divorce in 1998. Ruth, who is the primary physical custodian, now petitions for removal of the daughters from Franklin to Columbia.

The daughters lived with Howard between August of 2000 and December of 2001, while Ruth completed a master's degree in speech therapy, and thereafter, lived primarily with Ruth.

Ruth's new husband has recently been promoted and transferred by his company to Columbia. The daughters, who are now 13 and 15, are in good health, do well in school, and are active in tennis. Ruth has testified that the school district in Columbia has an active tennis team as well as a solid academic program.

Howard opposes the move because of its effect on his relationship with the girls. At a minimum, Howard sees the girls every weekend and has dinner with them once during the week. He regularly attends parent-teacher conferences and the girls' sports competitions, even when their mother does not. Because of the distance, if the girls move, the girls will not see their father on a regular basis. Further, Howard cannot afford to fly to Columbia to participate in their activities.

Howard concedes that, until now, he and Ruth have been able to jointly reach decisions about the girls and resolve disagreements about their care. However, he believes that Ruth is moving so far away so that the girls will develop a closer relationship with their new father that will drive a wedge between him and the girls.

Ruth proposes that the girls can fly, at her cost, to Franklin for one three-day weekend each month, September through February. She will bring the girls to Franklin for Thanksgiving, the winter break, and an extended summer break so they can spend time with their father, his family, and Ruth's family who remain in Franklin. Further, the girls have cell phones so that they can call their father regularly. She also suggests that Howard and the girls can e-mail every day to maintain contact. Finally, Ruth will arrange with the schools to send duplicate report cards to Howard.

In *Marshall v. Marshall*, our Supreme Court created a presumption that the primary custodial parent may remove the children from the state provided the parent seeking to relocate shows a legitimate reason for the move. Ruth has shown a legitimate reason for the move—improved employment of a parent or the spouse. Howard attempts to establish bad faith by presenting evidence that the move is designed to ruin his relationship with his daughters.

Howard relies on the case of *Davis v. Davis*, in which this court prohibited Mr. Davis from removing the children because he himself conceded that his reason for removing the children was to stop the mother's "bad influence." The court determined, however, that the mother was a loving parent whose influence was one of a concerned parent. Additionally, Ms. Davis presented evidence that Mr. Davis had a long history of trying to alienate the children from their mother. No such evidence was presented here, where Ruth has supported a close relationship between the girls and their father. Howard failed in his effort to show bad faith.

Howard's second contention is that the move is not in the best interests of the children. In determining "best interests," the court is guided by the factors listed in Section 402

continued on next page

of the Franklin Dissolution of Marriage Act. Section 402 directs the court to consider the child's health, adjustment to home, school, and community, and the interaction of the child with parents and siblings.

Howard cites the case of *Lewis v. Lewis*, in which this court denied a petition for removal because of the negative effect the move would have on the health and adjustment of the child. The child was developmentally disabled and deaf. Expert testimony established that she needed very specialized care that was available in Franklin but not in Columbia, and that any change in routine, especially a relocation, would set back her progress by a year or more.

Unlike the *Lewis* case, the Feldman girls are healthy, well adjusted in their present home, and capable of adjusting to a new environment. They have visited the school they will attend if the move is permitted. Whether they remain in Franklin or move to Columbia, they will have promising careers, educationally and socially.

The children have a strong and healthy relationship with each parent. Both parents have been closely involved in the upbringing of the girls. Certainly, if the move is permitted, it will affect the time the girls spend with their father. The issue, however, is whether the move is in their best interests. It is, of course, in their best interests to have a good relationship with their father, as well as with their mother. While their relationship with Howard will be changed, we do not believe it will be destroyed. Ruth's plans for continuing contact provide Howard meaningful involvement in the children's lives.

Ruth has proposed reasonable means by which the girls can communicate with Howard on a regular, indeed daily, basis. Further, they will see Howard face to face at least once every month, during all but spring tennis season.

The trial court's order permitting the removal is affirmed.

VI. POINT SHEET

I. Wells v. Wells
Drafters' Point Sheet[4]

In this performance test item, applicants are asked by the senior partner who represents Joan Wells to prepare a brief in support of Joan Wells' petition to remove her child from the state in order to take new employment in a neighboring state. Under the Franklin Dissolution of Marriage Act Section 109, Joan is required to submit the petition to the court because she has joint custody of the child with Fred Wells.

When Joan and Fred Wells were divorced in 2002, they were granted joint custody of their son, Sammy. Joint custody is defined as joint legal custody and joint physical custody. In Franklin, joint physical custody does not mean equal durations of time with each parent. Now Joan has the opportunity for a new position in her field, requiring her to relocate from Franklin to Columbia.

Joan wishes to move in order to accept a position as associate professor of Irish Literature and Studies at Columbia State University in Columbia City, Columbia. She wishes to take the couple's son, Sammy, with her. In anticipation of the move, Joan has arranged for Sammy's care and upbringing and for various means of maintaining a relationship with his father, Fred. Fred opposes the petition to remove the child from the state on several grounds. He argues that Sammy's development in general and especially in music will be adversely affected. Fred also claims that it will be hard for him to carry out his responsibilities as a legal custodian if Sammy is separated from him. He believes that the move is motivated by a desire to separate him from his son or by Joan's jealousy toward his new wife.

Both parties presented testimony to the court during a hearing and the senior partner ordered an expedited transcript of the testimony. At the conclusion of the testimony, the court ordered the parties to file concurrent briefs, with no rebuttal. The task for applicants is to prepare the persuasive brief that Joan will file.

The File contains the instructing memorandum from the senior partner, an office memorandum regarding persuasive briefs, and the transcript of the hearing, which includes the stipulations entered by the parties. The Library contains excerpts from the Franklin Dissolution of Marriage Act, a Franklin Supreme Court opinion, and a Franklin Court of Appeals opinion. The File does not contain evidence concerning the effect of separation of a six-year-old from his father. Nor does the Library contain any law that makes the child's wishes a factor to be considered. Applicants who discuss those issues are acting outside the materials given.

The following discussion covers all of the points the drafters intended to raise in the problem. Applicants need not cover them all to receive passing or even excellent grades. Grading is entirely within the discretion of the graders in the user jurisdictions.

---

4. The Multistate Bar Examination ("MBE®") questions, the Multistate Essay Examination ("MEE®") questions, and excerpts from the Multistate Performance Tests ("MPT®") have been reprinted by permission from the NCBE®. Copyright© by the National Conference of Bar Examiners. All rights reserved.

I. Overview: The office memorandum regarding persuasive briefs gives applicants the template for writing their answers in the form of a brief. Thus, it is expected that the work product will resemble a brief such as a lawyer would file with a court. Graders will have to decide how to weight the subjective components of "persuasiveness."

- There should be a statement of facts that explains the nature and essential features of the case, although, as the office memo explains, it should be abbreviated.
- The argument section should be broken down into carefully crafted headings that summarize the ensuing arguments. The arguments themselves should weave the law and the facts together into persuasive (as opposed to objective) statements of the case for the client.

Applicants are told that both sides are to file the briefs within 48 hours and that there will be no rebuttal briefs; therefore, applicants should anticipate the arguments of the opposite side and address them here.

II. Statement of Facts: This should include a brief recitation of the operative facts. Inasmuch as the trial judge already knows the facts, applicants should include only the key facts in the Statement of Facts and expand on them when they incorporate them into the legal argument part of the brief, but the Statement of Facts should at least describe the essence of the dispute.

- Essentially, applicants should explain that:
  - Joan and Fred Wells were divorced in 2002, and they were awarded joint custody of Sammy, now 6. Joan has primary physical custody of Sammy.
  - Joan Wells has completed her doctoral studies and has been offered a position as an associate professor in Irish Literature and Studies, her chosen field, at Columbia State University in Columbia City, Columbia.
  - She wishes to move to Columbia and take Sammy to live with her in Columbia.
  - Fred Wells, Sammy's father, opposes the move.

III. Argument: The argument section should reflect the steps in the legal analysis. Applicants should argue that the Franklin Supreme Court has interpreted Section 109 of the Franklin Dissolution of Marriage Act to require that the parent who has sole or primary physical custody and who seeks to remove the child from the state establish a legitimate reason for the move. *Marshall v. Marshall.* Once that parent has done so, there is a presumption that the parent may remove the child. The presumption may be rebutted by evidence from the objecting parent that the move is not being made in good faith or that it is not in the best interests of the child. *Marshall v. Marshall.*

The following headings are suggestions only and should not be taken by the graders to be the only acceptable ones.

- <u>Moving to Take a Position as Associate Professor Which Will Improve Her Employment Opportunities and Her Financial Security Constitutes a Legitimate Reason for the Move and Entitles Joan Wells to a Presumption That the Petition Should Be Granted.</u>

The first issue is whether Joan Wells has met her burden of offering a legitimate reason for the move. Franklin Dissolution of Marriage Act Section 109; *Marshall v. Marshall*. Legitimate reasons include improvements in the education, employment, or health of the parent or child. *Marshall v. Marshall*. Joan Wells has presented evidence of a legitimate reason for the move:

* The predicate for Joan's entitlement to the judicially created presumption is that she is a parent with "primary physical custody." She meets that requirement. *See* the court's introductory statement in the transcript.
* She has been offered a position as an associate professor in Irish Literature and Studies at Columbia State University, Columbia City, Columbia.
* The position is in her field of study and offers a better career path for her than her present position at the community college, and at Columbia State University, she will have colleagues to encourage her work.
* She is not likely to be hired by the Franklin State University, which has a policy against hiring its own graduates.
* The new position offers a higher salary, the promise of raises, and the potential for reduced tuition for Sammy, the child.

Thus, Joan has met her burden. She is entitled to a presumption in favor of granting her petition. *Marshall v. Marshall*.

Because the court instructed the parties that there will be no rebuttal briefs, applicants must anticipate the arguments that Fred Wells is likely to make and must address them as well.

* Sammy's Ability to Maintain a Father-Son Relationship with Fred Wells and Sammy's Health and Normal Development Rebut Any Speculation About Sammy's Possible Regression, the Lack of Opportunity to Join a Children's Choir, or the Possible Harm to the Father-Son Relationship.

A parent who objects to the petition to remove a child from the state may try to show that it is not in the best interests of the child. *Marshall v. Marshall*. To determine the best interests of the child, the court must consider the factors specified in Section 402 of the Franklin Dissolution of Marriage Act. *Feldman v. Feldman*. These factors include:

* The mental and physical health of all involved;
* The child's adjustment to the child's home, school, and community;
* The interaction and interrelationship of the child with the child's parents, siblings, and any other person who significantly affects the child's best interests; and
* The wishes of the child's parents as to custody.

The applicants should distinguish the *Lewis* case in which the court denied the petition to move where the *Lewis* child was deaf and developmentally disabled and in need of a routine. There, expert testimony supported the belief that the move would cause the *Lewis* child to regress by at least a year. Unlike the *Lewis* child, Sammy is developing normally and has demonstrated his ability to adjust to past changes. There is no expert testimony in this case predicting his likely regression, simply some speculation by a day care center counselor who also allowed that he is as likely to adjust well.

Fred may claim that the move is not in the best interests of Sammy. To prove that the move is not in the best interests of Sammy, Fred may assert:

* At the time of the divorce, Sammy regressed and needed assistance in dealing with the divorce;
* Sammy has no friends or family in Columbia;
* Sammy will not have the unique opportunities for developing his talent that he has with the Franklin City Children's Choir because Columbia does not have a comparable children's choir;
* Joan will not develop the talent as would Fred, who is a music teacher;
* Sammy will see his father only eight weeks a year instead of weekly as at present;
* Unlike the children in *Feldman*, Sammy is young;
* Fred will not be able to participate in Sammy's activities.

Applicants should argue, however, that Joan has effectively rebutted this evidence by showing:

* Sammy did adjust after the divorce with some limited assistance, and the counselor who worked with him at that time, a witness called by Fred, cannot predict that he will regress. The counselor had not worked with Sammy for over a year;
* Sammy is resilient as evidenced by his past ability to adapt, and the move is being made in advance of the start of the school year in order to give him a chance to adjust;
* Sammy is developing normally and is well adjusted and ready to advance in school;
* It is too early to realistically assess Sammy's musical talents but Joan will encourage the development of those talents along with others;
* As described above, Joan has a history of supporting Sammy's relationship with Fred.

Applicants should argue that the evidence taken as a whole fails to show that the move is not in the best interests of the child. In fact, the evidence shows that this move is much like that in the *Feldman* case where the court approved the petition to remove the children.

* <u>Fred Will Be Able to Carry Out His Responsibilities after the Move as a Joint Parent Through Telephone and E-mail Contact with Schools, Doctors, and Others.</u>

Fred may argue that he will be unable to carry out his responsibilities as a parent with joint legal custody (i.e., his decision-making responsibilities and his ability to maintain a loving relationship), if the move is permitted. He may suggest that the move is a ruse to set aside the court's original custody order because it will completely deprive him of joint *physical* custody. A parent, such as Fred, with joint legal custody has equal rights and responsibilities for major decisions concerning the child, including but not limited to the education of the child, health care, and religious training. *See* Section 30 of the Franklin Dissolution of Marriage Act. Fred may claim that he cannot effectively participate in decisions about Sammy because:

* He cannot effectively obtain firsthand information about Sammy and will have to rely on Joan for information about Sammy;

- He will not be able to be present for teacher-parent conferences or for doctor visits.

However, Joan has countered this evidence by testimony that:

- Fred can obtain this information through telephone or e-mail contact with the teachers and doctors;
- Joan will arrange for Sammy to regularly send packets of his schoolwork to Fred.
- Joan and Fred have a history of discussing issues that arise concerning Sammy and have been able to work out their differences in the past.

Based on this evidence, applicants should persuade the court that Fred will be able to continue to be a joint legal custodian for Sammy, even though his physical custody will be diminished.

- Evidence That Teaching Irish Literature Is a Lifelong Dream and That Joan Will Support the Father-Son Relationship through Telephone, E-mail, and Computer Conferencing as Well as In-Person Visits Rebuts Any Suggestion of Bad Faith.

A parent objecting to the removal of the child from the state may rebut the presumption by showing that the move is in bad faith. A move is in bad faith if it is designed to interfere with the parent-child relationship. *Marshall v. Marshall; Davis v. Davis.* Applicants should distinguish *Davis*, in which the father admitted that the reason for the move was to eliminate the "bad influence" of the mother. The court determined that the mother was a loving parent and denied the father's petition.

The facts in this case are much closer to those in *Feldman* where the court permitted the move. In *Feldman*, the mother had encouraged the close relationship between the children and their father and had proposed reasonable means of sustaining it, such as regular in-person visits, regular telephone contact, and daily e-mail communications.

Fred Wells may claim that the move interferes with the parent-child relationship:

- Fred's time with Sammy will be reduced from regular weekly contacts, totaling about 20 weeks a year, to eight weeks per year;
- Sammy will not see relatives on a regular basis;
- Fred will no longer engage in activities on a weekly basis with Sammy.

But time is not the only factor courts use in assessing bad faith. The courts have permitted moves where they affect the time a parent has with the child but where the relationship can be sustained through other means. *Feldman v. Feldman.* Courts are more suspicious of the moving parent's motive where there has been a history of interference with the relationship between the objecting parent and the child. *Marshall v. Marshall; Davis v. Davis.* Unlike the situations in those cases, Joan has been supportive of the father-son relationship and has proposed means of supporting the relationship despite the distance between Fred and Sammy. Applicants should detail what Joan has done and has offered to do in support of the father-son relationship:

- Joan has kept a photo of Sammy and his father in Sammy's room ever since the separation and has not interfered in the time Sammy spends with his father.

- If the move is permitted, Joan has offered that Fred may make tapes of books for Sammy to listen to, Fred may call Sammy whenever he wants, Fred and Sammy can communicate daily by computer conferencing and later, when Sammy is older, by e-mail.
- Joan will have Sammy send his father packets of his schoolwork every week.
- She will also record Sammy's activities and send them to his father.
- She will take Sammy to visit his father in person eight weeks a year and when Sammy is older, he can fly on his own for these visits.

Fred may also claim that the move is in bad faith because it is motivated by Joan's jealousy over Fred's remarriage to someone she dislikes:

- Joan will not talk with Fred's new wife, Kathleen.
- Joan is jealous of Kathleen or of Fred's remarriage or both.

Joan will rebut this evidence by showing that her desire to move to take the position in Irish Studies is part of a lifelong dream expressed long before Fred remarried.

Applicants should argue to the court that the sort of evidence Fred introduced is insufficient to show bad faith and is rebutted by Joan's history of pursuing her career goal.

IV. Conclusion: Applicants should persuade the court that Joan has met her burden by offering a legitimate reason for the move and that therefore she is entitled to a presumption in favor of the petition. While Fred has attempted to rebut that presumption by offering evidence of bad faith and evidence that the move is not in the best interests of Sammy, Joan has effectively rebutted such evidence. In light of the case law in Franklin, Joan is entitled to remove Sammy.

VII. SCORE SHEET

Stated	Implied	
_____	_____	**FORMAT:** Should resemble a brief that would be filed with a court. A persuasive document that includes a Statement of Facts, an Argument Section with Point Headings, and a Conclusion.
_____ _____ _____ _____ _____	_____ _____ _____ _____ _____	**STATEMENT OF FACTS** Joan and Fred Wells were divorced in 2002, and they were awarded joint custody of Sammy, now 6. Joan has primary physical custody. Joan Wells has completed her doctoral studies and has been offered a position as an associate professor in Irish Literature and Studies, her chosen field, at Columbia State University in Columbia City, Columbia. She wishes to move to Columbia and take Sammy to live with her. Fred Wells, Sammy's father, opposed the move.
_____ _____ _____ _____ _____ _____ _____ _____ _____ _____	_____ _____ _____ _____ _____ _____ _____ _____ _____ _____	**ARGUMENT** Heading I: *Moving to Take a Position as an Associate Professor, which will Improve her Employment Opportunities and her Financial Security, Constitutes a Legitimate Reason for the Move and Entitles Joan Wells to a Presumption That the Petition Should Be Granted.* **Rule:** Section 109 provides that parent with primary physical custody may remove the child from Franklin whenever such approval is in the best interests of the child. Legitimate reasons include improvements in the education, employment, or health of the parent or child. *Marshall.* Predicate is met—she has primary physical custody. Offered a position as an associate professor in Irish Literature and Studies at Columbia State University in Columbia City, Columbia. Position is in her field of study and offers a better career path for her than her present position at a community college, including colleagues who will encourage her work. Not likely to be hired by Franklin State University due to policy against hiring own graduates. The new position offers a higher salary, the promise of raises, and the potential for reduced tuition for Sammy. **Conclusion:** Joan has met her burden with a legitimate reason and is entitled to a presumption to grant her petition. Heading II: *Sammy's Ability to Maintain a Father-Son Relationship with Fred Wells and Sammy's Health and Normal Development Rebut Any Speculation About Sammy's Possible Regression, the Lack of Opportunity to Join a Children's Choir, or the Possible Harm to the Father-Son Relationship.* **Rule:** Parent who objects to the petition to remove a child from the state may try to show that it is not in the best interests of the child. *Marshall.*

continued on next page

Stated	Implied	
_____	_____	Section 402 outlines factors: mental and physical health of all involved; the child's adjustment to the child's home, school, and community; the interaction and interrelationship of the child with the child's parents, siblings, and any other person who significantly affects the child's best interests, wishes of the child's parents as to custody.
_____	_____	**Application:** Fred may assert: At the time of the divorce, Sammy regressed and needed assistance in dealing with the divorce.
_____	_____	Sammy has no friends or family in Columbia.
_____	_____	Sammy will not have the unique opportunities for developing his talent that he has with the Franklin City Children's Choir because Columbia does not have a comparable children's choir.
_____	_____	Joan will not develop the talent as would Fred, who is a music teacher.
_____	_____	Sammy will see his father only eight weeks a year instead of weekly as at present.
_____	_____	Unlike the children in *Feldman*, Sammy is young.
_____	_____	Fred will not be able to participate in Sammy's activities.
_____	_____	Unlike the deaf child in *Lewis*, Sammy is developing normally and has demonstrated his ability to adjust to past changes. No expert testimony, just a day care worker who predicted his regression.
_____	_____	Joan will effectively rebut: Sammy did adjust after the divorce. Counselor has not worked with him in a year.
_____	_____	Sammy is resilient as evidenced by past ability to adapt and move being made well in advance of start of school year to give him time to adjust.
_____	_____	Sammy is developing normally and is well-adjusted.
_____	_____	Too early to realistically assess Sammy's musical talent, but Joan will encourage the development of those talents.
_____	_____	Joan has a history of supporting Sammy's relationship with Fred.
_____	_____	**Conclusion:** Evidence taken as a whole fails to show that the move is not in Sammy's best interests.
_____	_____	Like the *Feldman* case, where permission to relocate was granted.
_____	_____	Heading III: *Fred Will Be Able to Carry Out his Responsibilities after the Move as a Joint Parent Through Telephone and E-mail Contact with Schools, Doctors, and Others.*
_____	_____	Fred may argue that he is unable to carry out his responsibilities as a parent with joint legal custody including making decisions and maintaining a loving relationship.
_____	_____	**Rule:** Section 30 of statute provides equal rights and responsibilities for major decisions including the education of the child, health care, and religious training.
_____	_____	**Application:** Fred cannot effectively obtain firsthand information about Sammy and will have to rely on Joan for information.
_____	_____	Will not be present for teacher-parent conferences or doctor visits.
_____	_____	Joan will counter that he can obtain information through telephone and email contact with teachers/doctors
_____	_____	Joan will arrange for Sammy to regularly send packets of schoolwork to Fred.
_____	_____	Joan and Fred have a history of discussing issues that arise concerning Sammy and have been able to work out their differences in the past.

continued on next page

Stated	Implied	
_____	_____	**Conclusion:** Fred will be able to continue to be a joint legal custodian for Sammy.
_____	_____	Heading IV: *Evidence That Teaching Irish Literature Is a Lifelong Dream and That Joan Will Support the Father-Son Relationship through Telephone, E-mail, and Computer Conferencing as Well as In-Person Visits Rebuts Any Suggestions of Bad Faith.*
_____	_____	**Rule:** A parent objecting to the removal of the child from the state may rebut the presumption by showing that the move is in bad faith.
_____	_____	A move is in bad faith if it is designed to interfere with the parent-child relationship. *Marshall; Davis.*
_____	_____	Time with child not only factor. Courts more suspicious of motive of moving parent where there has been interference already. *Marshall; Davis*
_____	_____	**Application:** Unlike *Davis* where the move was to eliminate the mother's "bad influence and court determined mother was a loving parent"; there is no bad faith here.
_____	_____	More like *Feldman* where move allowed and relationship with parent staying was encouraged
_____	_____	Fred's time with Sammy will be reduced from regular weekly contacts, totaling about 20 weeks a year, to eight weeks per year.
_____	_____	Sammy will not see relatives on a regular basis.
_____	_____	Fred will no longer engage in activities on a weekly basis with Sammy.
_____	_____	Joan has been supportive of relationship and has proposed means of supporting the relationship long distance.
_____	_____	Photo of Sammy and his dad in Sammy's room since the separation and has never interfered in the time Sammy spends with his father.
_____	_____	Fred may make tapes of books for Sammy to listen to; Fred may call whenever he wishes; Fred and Sammy can communicate daily by computer conferencing and by email when Sammy is older.
_____	_____	Packets of schoolwork and recording of activities will be sent.
_____	_____	Joan will take Sammy to visit his father in person eight weeks a year. When Sammy is old enough, he can fly alone.
_____	_____	Joan's desire to move is based on her lifelong dream and not because she doesn't care for Fred's new wife.
_____	_____	**Conclusion:** Fred's evidence is insufficient to show move is in bad faith.
_____	_____	**Overall Conclusion:** Joan has met her burden by offering a legitimate reason for the move and therefore she is entitled to a presumption in favor of the petition.

CHAPTER 6

Building Multistate Bar Examination Skills

While watching Sesame Street or in preschool, you actually took your first multiple choice assessment when you were asked, "Which of these things is different from the others?" You circled or pointed to the one out of four pictures on the page or screen that was different. A question was asked and you picked the one correct response out of several potential answers. Your elementary teachers, secondary teachers, and some undergraduate professors then continued to use multiple choice assessments throughout your education. Most of the Law School Admissions Test is set up in a multiple choice format.

The Multistate Bar Examination (MBE) is much more difficult than any other multiple choice assessment you have had for a number of reasons. First, the subject matter is more complex and more voluminous, spanning seven topics. Some law schools take two semesters just to cover one of the seven topics. In order to answer correctly, you must have detailed knowledge of each topic. A superficial understanding of the law will not suffice. You must be able to identify the issue, pull the detailed rule from your memory, and apply it correctly to the facts. Even then, more than one response can appear correct. The differences between answer responses can be subtle.

An applicant will often fall back on old test-taking strategies that worked in the past, but they will not work well on the MBE. An applicant may believe that the best way to prepare is by doing as many practice questions as possible, relying on remembering all of the answers. Unfortunately, this strategy frequently fails on the MBE. There are just too many topics. Doing hundreds of questions without autopsying the answers is a huge waste of time. Remember, in order to recall information, it must be encoded into your memory. A better preparation technique is similar to your preparation for the essay questions—focus on memorizing rules.

I. PREPARATION

The NCBE sets the number of questions for each topic. There is no deviation from these numbers. While taking the exam, there is absolutely no need to keep track of each topic. The count breaks out as:

- Constitutional Law—27 questions
- Contracts and Sales—28 questions
- Criminal Law and Procedure—27 questions

- Evidence—27 questions
- Federal Civil Procedure—27 questions
- Real Property—27 questions
- Torts—27 questions

Your preparation to do well on MBE questions is virtually identical to your preparation for essay questions. Just like essay questions, you must have the rules memorized for all Big Seven topics. Thus, you need a library of the materials to memorize in the format that you best memorize from. Fortunately, you may use the same library for the MBE questions that you are preparing for the essay questions. No need exists for separate libraries. Why? Your memorization of the rules works for both question styles. You should do practice questions in both formats, but the memorization is the same.

Just like your practice essay questions in Phase One, take as much time as you need on the MBE questions in Phase One. Look up the rule and delve into the particular subtopic. Really try to understand it.

During Phase Two, move to doing your practice MBE questions within time limits and closed-book. Now that does not mean practice 100 questions in a three-hour block of time every day. Indeed, you should only practice in that manner—half-day practice exams—two or three times throughout your preparation.

Instead, do 17 questions in a 30-minute block of time. Why? On the bar exam, you will do 100 questions in 180 minutes—the equivalent of 1.8 minutes per question. Keeping track of the time per multiple choice question is unworkable and unrealistic. Instead, keep track in half hour or hour time periods: 17 questions in one half hour and 34 questions in one hour. For your practice, keep to 17 questions in 30 minutes.

At the end of the 30 minutes, autopsy your answers. Just like essay questions, this is critical. Practice MBE questions provide a detailed critique of the question. Read all of it. Add any misunderstood rules and lucky guesses to your library or highlight them if they are already there. One month before the exam, push your question practice to 34 questions in an hour and then 50 questions in 90 minutes. Always take the time to put the misunderstood rules and the lucky guesses in your library.

Initially, you will study a topic and then do practice questions in just that topic area. Once you have covered all seven topics, do a mixed-topic set of questions at least once a week.

Your commercial bar preparation provider will probably have applications for practice questions that are used on your computer and other electronic devices. While doing questions on your smartphone is not a bad idea while waiting for your table at a restaurant, doing all of your questions in this manner is not a good idea. On the exam, it is paper and pencil. You need to time yourself doing them with paper and pencil.

A greater concern over doing questions only on an electronic device is that you will be tempted to skip the autopsy of your answers. You may fall back on the old habit of thinking that you will remember all your mistakes, failing to keep in mind that you will do hundreds of practice questions in seven different topics. Your memory will not hold rules over this length of time, in this depth, and over as many topics without conscious encoding of the material.

The last week before the exam, drop your MBE practice from 50 questions a day back to 34 questions a day. Your time is better spent working on memorizing the rules that week.

EXAM TIP

If you are someone that needs all the time allotted and more, use a regular #2 pencil rather than a mechanical pencil. The lead is thicker and you can fill in the circle in less time.

EXAM TIP

Are you a slow starter on MBE questions? Pick out 10 to 15 questions to do the morning of the MBE before you head to the exam. Then, you'll already be in the groove.

You will hear prior takers exclaim that one of the commercial provider's practice MBE questions are "more like" real MBE questions than another provider's questions. Do not believe it. No provider has any special relationship with the NCBE such that it has the inside scoop. The best test of "real" MBE questions is to take one of the NCBE online MBE exams. The NCBE provides several hundred question exams for a fee. These are actual bar questions used in prior exams. These are the best models. No matter which commercial provider you utilize, the heart and soul of doing well on MBE questions is knowing the rules so that you can apply the rules to the facts.

II. GO BACKWARDS

On the exam and in your practice, your analysis of an MBE question should be backwards. All MBE questions are set up with a hypothetical fact scenario, a call of the question, and four responses. Read the call of the question and the four responses first. You will immediately be able to pick which one of the seven topics is being tested. Reading the responses tells you the particular sub-issue that is being tested. After reading the responses, pull to mind the rule for that sub-issue. Write it down if you need to do that. Now, read the facts. Underline the facts that address that issue. Read the call and the responses again.

Do not try to pick the correct response. Instead, begin by eliminating responses you know are incorrect. Look at each response in isolation. To possibly be correct, every aspect of the response must be accurate from its characterization of the facts, its statement of the rule, its reasoning, and its focus on the central issue. This is not easy. Indeed, some calls of the question include qualifiers such as "most likely to prevail" or "what is the best argument." When you see this kind of qualifier, keep in mind that in reality only one of the responses is correct. Thus it's not just the *best* argument; it's the *only* argument that can prevail.

At times, it may seem that you are choosing between two correct responses. In reality, you need to choose the response with the most precision in its reasoning. Even if only a snippet of the legal rule is used, the rationale of that response may be the most accurate and precise.

Let's try an example to see how the rationale must be accurate and precise.

> **EXAM TIP**
> If two responses on an MBE question are the polar opposites of each other, chances are that one of them is the correct answer.

Driver ran into and injured Pedestrian. Pedestrian has sued Driver alleging that Driver, while drunk, struck Pedestrian, who was in a duly marked crosswalk. Pedestrian's counsel wishes to prove that after the accident Driver went to Pedestrian and offered $1,000 to settle Pedestrian's claim.

The trial judge should rule this evidence:

A. admissible as an admission of a party.
B. admissible as an admission to show Driver's liability, provided the court gives a cautionary instruction that the statement should not be considered as bearing on the issue of damages.
C. inadmissible since it is not relevant either to the question of liability or the question of damages.
D. inadmissible because even though it is relevant and an admission, the policy of the law is to encourage settlement negotiations.

First, what do the call of the question and the responses tell us? First, this is an Evidence question, and some of the responses deal with admissions of a party-opponent. Others deal with relevancy. Still others deal with both. What else can we tell from reading the responses? Response A gives no reasoning and does not address relevancy. Response C addresses relevancy, but not admissions. Responses B and D appear to address both admissions and relevancy. It is likely that one of those is the correct answer because they are more precise.

Now, read the facts. What is the central issue? Looks like the central issue deals with settlement offers. What is the rule for settlement offers? Federal Rules of Evidence (FRE) 408(a)(1) states that evidence of "furnishing, promising, or offering . . . a valuable consideration in compromising or attempting to compromise the claim" is inadmissible.[1] FRE 408(b) gives an exception if the settlement offer is offered for another purpose such as proving a witness's bias or prejudice.[2] You need to analyze both the general rule and the exception. Under the general rule, the settlement offer is inadmissible. Under the exception, is the offer being admitted for another purpose? In all likelihood, no. It is being offered to prove liability. As a result, you know response C is incorrect. Liability is certainly relevant, but relevancy is not the reason why settlement offers are inadmissible.

But, you are not finished. Now, you have to check admission by a party-opponent. Hearsay is a statement made by an out-of-court declarant that is being offered to prove the truth of the matter asserted.[3] Hearsay is inadmissible without an exception.[4] Is the offer hearsay? It was an out-of-court statement and is being offered to prove liability. Thus, it initially would be hearsay. However, certain out-of-court statements are not hearsay. Classified as non-hearsay, an admission is a statement "offered against an opposing party and was made by the party in an individual or representative capacity."[5] Is this a statement offered against an opposing party and made by that party? Yes.

Thus, you know this is an admission and that it is relevant, but inadmissible. Response A is correct, but does not address relevancy. Response B is incorrect. Evidence is either admissible or inadmissible. A cautionary instruction does not make the evidence admissible. Moreover, the settlement offer is being offered to prove liability, not just damages. Response C is incorrect because the settlement offer is relevant. You are left with response D. It is inadmissible, although relevant and an admission, because settlement offers are inadmissible. The reason why they are inadmissible is to encourage settlement negotiations. While response A is correct, it is not precise. Response D would be the correct answer.

Next, be sure to read the facts carefully. Don't skip over the details. Details matter. Ask yourself, why did the examiners include that he was an "experienced carpenter" instead of just "carpenter." Why does it matter that Tommy was four years old instead of seventeen years old? These details usually go to the core issue. In these examples, perhaps they are hinting at delegation of duty in a contract for

---

1. Fed. R. Evid. 408(a)(1).
2. Fed. R. Evid. 408(b).
3. Fed. R. Evid. 801 (c)(1)-(2).
4. Fed. R. Evid. 802.
5. Fed. R. Evid. 801(d)(2)(A).

the carpenter and witness competency for the child. Moreover, the examiners give you all the facts you need. Thus, read carefully and do not assume facts.

That's worth repeating. Try not to assume facts. For example, your impression is that the witness is a lying, cheating scumbag not to be trusted. But the response includes "if the jury believes him." Take that as fact—do not assume that it is impossible to believe him because he's a scumbag. The modifier, "if the jury believes him," takes care of that.

Let's try an example that requires careful reading of the facts.

> Painter, who has been in the painting and contracting business for ten years and has a fine reputation, contracts to paint Farmer's barn. Farmer's barn is a standard red barn with a loft. The contract has no provision regarding assignment. If Painter assigns the contract to Contractor, who has comparable experience and reputation, which of the following statements is correct?

> A. Painter is in breach of contract.
> B. Farmer may refuse to accept performance by Contractor.
> C. Farmer is required to accept performance by Contractor.
> D. There is a novation.

First, what do the call of the question and the responses tell us? First, this is a Contracts question and it deals with an assignment issue. What is the rule for assignments in contracts? One part of the rule is that an assignment cannot increase the risk that the promisee (Farmer) will not receive the promised performance. What else can we tell from reading the responses? Response A is very broad. Responses B and C are polar opposites. It is likely that one of those is the correct answer. Response D contains a term that you may not remember off the top of your head.

Now, read the facts. What is the central issue? Looks like the central issue is whether Farmer must accept the assignee's performance. What details are included in the description of the people involved? Painter has ten years' experience in the painting and contracting business and has a "fine reputation." That tells us that Painter is skilled and does good work. This is not someone that just decided to earn some money by painting. What about the assignee? Contractor has "comparable experience and reputation." Contractor's description tells us that he is also someone who is skilled and does good work.

Responses A and B state or allude to Painter having breached the contract. Responses C and D indicate that Painter has not breached the contract. Response A gives us no rationale and reasoning. It is the least precise answer and is unlikely to be correct unless all other responses are fundamentally incorrect. Response D requires that you know the term "novation." A novation requires the promisee's consent to the substitute performance. Did Farmer consent? No; thus, you can eliminate D. To determine which of the remaining three are correct, we must determine if Painter breached the contract by the assignment to Contractor.

Applying the assignment rule to the facts, did the assignment increase the risk that Farmer will not receive the promised performance—a barn painted by a skilled craftsman? As Contractor has comparable skill and experience, that answer is "no." Thus, Painter did not breach the contract and Farmer must accept the performance. Responses A and B are eliminated and response C is correct.

One fact made the difference: Contractor had comparable experience and reputation. Without that fact, a different response may have been correct. Just skimming the facts would not have highlighted that similarity.

EXAM TIP

If the response contains a Latin phrase or a rule that you have never heard, chances are that the response is incorrect. Don't assume that just because you don't recognize a concept that it must be correct.

III. AUTOPSY MBE QUESTIONS

To get the most out of your autopsy, keep track of your elimination process as you do practice questions. Indicate which response you eliminated first, second, and third. If you are guessing, include that as well.

Then, in your autopsy, review the answers you got correct, particularly lucky guesses, to see if your reasoning matches the examiners' reasoning. For incorrect answers, assess what stumped you. Was it an issue identification problem? Did you just not remember that rule? Did you skip over a detail in the reading? Did you apply the law to the facts incorrectly? Keeping track will show patterns in your answers so that you know what to focus upon in the rest of your preparation.

Keep track of when you go back and second-guess an answer and note whether your first choice was usually correct or your changed answer was correct. This may also indicate a trend that tells you quite a bit about your test-taking skills.

The chart on page 85 chart is designed for you to perform this autopsy in detail.[6] Those who regularly use the chart are better prepared for the MBE portion of the exam.

Let's attack this question from the autopsy point of view using the chart.

> In an automobile negligence action by Popkin against Dwyer, Juilliard testified for Popkin. Dwyer later called Watts, who testified that Julliard's reputation for truthfulness was bad.
>
> On cross-examination of Watts, Popkin's counsel asks, "Isn't it a fact that when you bought your new car last year, you made a false affidavit to escape paying the sales tax?"

This question is

A. proper, because it will indicate Watts's standard of judgment as to reputation for truthfulness.
B. proper, because it bears on Watts's credibility.
C. improper, because character cannot be proved by specific instances of conduct.
D. improper, because one cannot impeach an impeaching witness.

Analyze and answer this question before you continue reading.

If your answer was response A, this was probably a reading error. Although Watts's direct testimony was about Julliard's reputation, the cross examination had nothing to do with reputation and dealt with bad acts.

If your answer was response C, this was a result of not understanding the rule well enough. Under FRE 608(b), the general rule states that specific instances of conduct may not be proved through extrinsic evidence even for the purpose of attacking a witness's credibility.[7] An exception is that a judge may allow such evidence if it is brought out through cross examination of the witness whose credibility is being attacked and if the bad acts are probative of truthfulness.[8]

---

6. Idea originated with Denise Riebe & Michael Hunter Swartz, *Pass the Bar!* 138 (Carolina Acad. Press 2006).

7. Fed. R. Evid. 608(b).

8. Fed. R. Evid. 608(b)(1).

Here, Watts is being cross-examined with evidence of his own falsification of an affidavit. The act was probative of truthfulness and is being brought out on cross-examination and, thus, is proper. Therefore, response C is incorrect as it does not consider the exception to the rule.

If your answer was response D, this was a result of both an issue identification problem and not knowing the rule. There is no prohibition on impeaching an impeaching witness.

That leaves response B—the question was proper because it bore on Watts's credibility. You might have avoided this response because it seemed too straight-forward. Yet, it is correct and its rationale is correct. Moreover, there is a problem with each of the other responses.

As you autopsy each practice question, fill out the chart to see if there are any trends of common mistakes. This can tell you what you need to focus on as you do additional questions.

Without a doubt, focusing on memorizing rules and on autopsying your answers is the key to doing well on the MBE exam. Keep that in mind when you are tempted to just do practice questions in isolation.

MBE PRACTICE ANALYSIS				
Question	Order of elimination	Reason for correct answer	Reason my answer was incorrect	Type of Error [circle all that apply]
1	_____ _____ _____ _____			Issue identification Didn't know rule Reading error Application error
2	_____ _____ _____ _____			Issue identification Didn't know rule Reading error Application error
3	_____ _____ _____ _____			Issue identification Didn't know rule Reading error Application error
4	_____ _____ _____ _____			Issue identification Didn't know rule Reading error Application error
5	_____ _____ _____ _____			Issue identification Didn't know rule Reading error Application error
6	_____ _____ _____ _____			Issue identification Didn't know rule Reading error Application error

continued on next page

Question	Order of elimination	Reason for correct answer	Reason my answer was incorrect	Type of Error [circle all that apply]
7	_____ _____ _____ _____			Issue identification Didn't know rule Reading error Application error
8	_____ _____ _____ _____			Issue identification Didn't know rule Reading error Application error
9	_____ _____ _____ _____			Issue identification Didn't know rule Reading error Application error
10	_____ _____ _____ _____			Issue identification Didn't know rule Reading error Application error
11	_____ _____ _____ _____			Issue identification Didn't know rule Reading error Application error
12	_____ _____ _____ _____			Issue identification Didn't know rule Reading error Application error
13	_____ _____ _____ _____			Issue identification Didn't know rule Reading error Application error
14	_____ _____ _____ _____			Issue identification Didn't know rule Reading error Application error
15	_____ _____ _____ _____			Issue identification Didn't know rule Reading error Application error
16	_____ _____ _____ _____			Issue identification Didn't know rule Reading error Application error
17	_____ _____ _____ _____			Issue identification Didn't know rule Reading error Application error

CHAPTER 7

Building Confidence with Strategies

Throughout your third year of law school, if not all of law school, the bar exam has been the elephant in the room—always there, never moving. We don't have to deal with it or even look at it. We know that it is in the distant future. But now, we have to tackle it. But how do we do that? Just like the old riddle that asks, "How do you eat an elephant?" The answer is, "One bite at a time."

One day, one page, one topic at a time. Step-by-step you will study what you need to know and practice the skills you need to pass the exam. While you need to know what the elephant looks like, you conquer the task by focusing only on what you need to be doing that day, and then what needs to be done the next day, and the day after that, and the day after that.

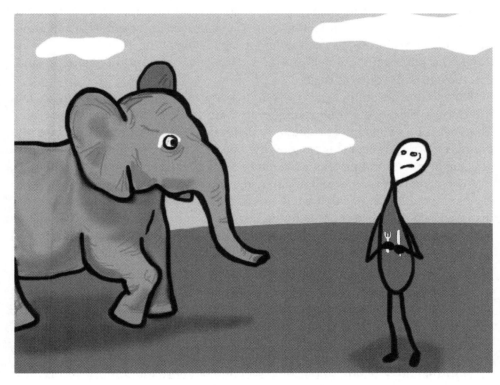

Tackling the Elephant

Bar preparation is similar to marathon training. A marathon is 26.2 miles. Yet, no marathon runner ever runs 26.2 miles in training. Instead, they follow a set schedule of shorter distances with a longer run every week. They run a certain number of miles on certain days and then they have rest days. They increase the number of miles they run as the marathon approaches.

Similarly, you will not take an entire bar exam during your bar preparation. You will tackle shorter tasks several days in a row and then accomplish a larger task on certain days. You will have rest days. You will have tasks that take a longer length of time to do, such as a one-day multiple choice practice exam and half-day essay and MPT exams. You will increase your preparation as the exam approaches.

The strategies included in this chapter help you to focus on the separate tasks ahead of you and to not be overwhelmed by the enormity of the overall task itself. The bar exam is the elephant. Here is your fork. One bite at a time.

I. LOW-HANGING FRUIT

The first strategy is straightforward. Focus on the basics of each question. You may identify a minor sub-issue or tangential issue that is fascinating to you. You believe that by analyzing that difficult-to-identify issue that you have nailed the "trick" of an essay question. Except, there is no trick. The points for a difficult-to-identify sub-issue or a tangential issue that is not essential to the analysis are only a small percentage of the points available for that question. No extra credit exists. Thus, if your answer focuses exclusively on that sub-issue, you will not pass that essay or MPT question—not because your analysis was deficient on what you analyzed, but because your answer failed to analyze the bulk of the points.

The bulk of the points lie in the low-hanging fruit—the basics and foundation of each issue's rule. When stating your rule, state all the elements, including those not at issue. Apply each element, again including those not at issue. Why? The bar examiners need to know that you know all the elements and can recognize the ones at issue.

Note that the examiners do *not* want to know everything about the topic. Do not start your essay question stating everything you remember about the topic. That just shows you could not identify the issue. They do want you to state the entire rule for the specific issue identified by the call of the question. But don't get caught rule dumping about the entire topic hoping something is right.

When you don't score well on an essay, you typically have gone over all the issues in your head, decided what was at issue, decided to focus only on the disputed issue, applied the rule to the facts in your head, reached your conclusion, and then only written down the conclusion on the disputed issue. In essence, you did a complete analysis in your head, but you did not communicate that analysis to the examiner. The examiner cannot give you points for what stays in your head. They can only give you points for what is written down.

Accordingly, put down every step of that analysis. This analysis going on in your head is the low-hanging fruit—the basics of each rule and the basics of applying each rule. While phrased differently in each jurisdiction, the essence of the standard to pass the bar examination and be admitted to practice law in that jurisdiction is that the applicant has demonstrated a minimum level of competence to practice law. Not the best potential, but a minimum level. That minimum is the low-hanging fruit, not the fruit at the top of the tree.

Low-Hanging Fruit

Focus on the Low-Hanging Fruit

If you sufficiently cover the low-hanging fruit on each and every topic, chances are good that you will pass the bar. There will be questions where you know more than just the low-hanging fruit and can address those mid- or high-level issues. In other questions, you don't quite get all the low-hanging fruit. The goal is an average essay score that equals 75%.

II. 75/15/10 STRATEGY

Your commercial bar prep materials have arrived—a large box or two. As you open the boxes, the enormity of the task will hit you. Book after book, page after page of material that you are expected to know to fulfill your dream of becoming a practicing lawyer are in front of you. How on earth can the bar examiners expect you to learn and memorize all that you are provided?

They don't. You do not have to memorize 100% of the material. You must have a substantial amount of the material learned and memorized, but that doesn't equate with having it all memorized. The question becomes, which parts do you have to have memorized? That's where the 75/15/10 strategy comes into play.

The low-hanging fruit accounts for approximately 75% of the material on each topic. Having a solid handle on 75% of the material will result in a passing score. That means 75% of *each topic*. You cannot have 75% of three-fourths or one-half of the topics and hope to pass. It must be 75% of each topic. Why can't it be 75% of all the material? The reason is that you may be faced with an exam where the 25% of the topics you do not concentrate on are indeed the essay questions! You just gave yourself absolutely no chance to pass the exam as your understanding of those topics would be minimal at best.

This begs the question—which 75% of each topic? The mind maps contained in Chapters 9 through 20 address that 75% and more. The mind maps are designed to help you sort through the material and decide where to concentrate your memorization efforts. During Phase One, you should build your library on all the material. During Phase Two, use the 75/15/10 strategy during your memorization process. Use this strategy to help you identify issues on the actual essay questions, both in practice and on the exam itself.

The next 15% is material that those having somewhat more exposure to the topic will know. If you took a class on that topic, you will have been exposed and possibly tested on this 15%. This 15% is a small cushion for that topic on the bar exam, but only for that topic. You cannot count on this cushion to pull up your 50% effort on all the other topics. First, your 15% of that topic may not be tested. Second, the math doesn't add up. If your jurisdiction scores on the 6 point scale recommended by the NCBE, you want to average 4 points to pass. That's a little less than 75% of the available points. Thus, if you count on the 5 you will receive on one question for the 15% extra knowledge, you will not pass if your other essays are all at 3. With 6 essays, your score is then 20 out of 36 or a 55.5%–a raw score that, when scaled, is still below most jurisdictions' pass point.

The last 10% is that material that delves into the far reaches of the topic. These issues are raised in the "Notes" sections after each case excerpt in your textbooks. These issues are the ones you may be able to identify if you have a special affinity for the topic. You took every course the law school offered in that area. You did extra reading on that topic. You wrote your law review article or wrote a seminar paper on that topic. The difficult-to-identify sub-issue and tangential issues are the ones that may peak your interest the most.

But this 10% of the topic is not the bulk of the points available for an essay. That issue may well be there. In fact most questions have sub-issues that deal with all three levels. The points are allocated between all the issues. The pass point does not require you to do well on every single point. You do not have to have 100% of the material memorized to pass the bar. You need a nice solid 75% of each topic.

In Chapter 2, mind maps were discussed as a tool to think about a topic in a way that helped you see the big picture of the topic and to see the relationships between ideas. The 75/15/10 strategy uses the mind map to focus on the core 75% of the material while allowing you to expand the map to include additional material. The mind map is your global positioning system (GPS) for that topic.

On any GPS, the first question it asks or determines for itself is where you are located. Similarly, as you read an essay question, the call of the question gives you your starting point. That tells you which topic's mind map to use and may tell you where on that mind map to begin. Next, you tell the GPS where you want to go. The GPS then gives you one or several routes to get where you need to go. With the call of the question as the starting point, you then use your mind map as your GPS to determine the route to take to answer the question.

That route is the 75% of the material. It includes the fundamental rules on the route you are taking. It goes step-by-step along the route. It gives signposts as to where you are going, similar to the name of the roads and whether to turn right or left on a GPS. No leap-frogging over issues or detours that are not explained. Go step-by-step and tell the reader how to navigate the analysis to reach the same conclusion. Note you are not discussing the entire map of the topic, but just the route for the issue.

The 15% are the additional comments provided regarding your route. It adds descriptors along the route such as restaurants and gas stations that occur at the points of turning. It doesn't just get you to the right destination. It gets you into the parking lot.

The 10% goes farther and takes you to the seat at the restaurant's table with menu in hand. The route is in full bloom with all descriptors and variants described in detail. No stone has been left unturned in order to flesh out all relevant issues and sub-issues.

Remember that focusing on that 10% is not what you need to pass. No one needs to strive to get an A on the bar exam by getting all the 10% points. It's just not needed. No one, truly no one, including an employer, cares how high you score on the bar exam as long as you have passed. The 10% issues can give you a cushion, but cannot make up for the failure to have the 75% of the material understood, memorized, and analyzed on every topic.

The 75/15/10 strategy is also helpful for issue identification on the questions themselves. When you have read the call of the question and the facts and you are still left with an unsettled feeling as to what the issue truly is, pull out your mind map to focus on the 75%. Visualize your map and peruse it going through each route. Pause at each stop along the route and ask yourself if you have any facts that would address that rule. As you go through each route, the issue will usually occur to you. This technique also works if you finish your answer and are left with doubt that you covered what you need to have covered. Run through your map to be sure you haven't missed an issue.

III. AVOID DUPING YOURSELF

It's so easy to dupe yourself. It's a psychological defense mechanism similar to denial. If we don't think about it, we don't have to acknowledge it as an issue. So, you tell yourself that you are working harder than you ever have, because you are. You have put in 500 hours of study. You have attended or watched the commercial bar preparation lectures—all of them. You have written essay answers and done the required number of MBE questions every day.

But you skip over the fact that you have not studied all the topics. You skip over the fact that you have spent almost all of your time on your two favorite topics and spent little to no time on your more troublesome topics. You skip over the fact that every essay you have done has been on your favorite topics. You skip over the fact that your MBE questions are only from three of the seven topics. You skip over the fact that you did not make your own library but used your buddy's, as his was better organized than yours would have been. You kid yourself when you look at a sample answer and think that even though your answer is deficient, you'll do better on the actual exam now that you have read the model answer because you will remember the issue and rule. You don't add the rule to your library of materials. Indeed, you may even just skim the model answer looking for a few buzz words. You dupe yourself that you will remember, because you do nothing to truly encode the information into your memory.

As human beings, we do not like to look at the hard truths about ourselves. We do not like to admit that we have not done "everything" asked because we did the easier stuff. But you must look at the hard truths. There is no replacement for the work you must do to pass the bar exam. You can choose not to do the work and take a chance. There are lots of folks willing to join you on that chance. You will see them all again at the next sitting of the exam, because your chances of passing the first time are negligible. This is an exam you only want to take once. There is no replacement for the work that must be done.

IV. GROWING YOUR MINDSET

How do you view your intellectual ability? Do you view yourself as someone with a fixed amount of intelligence? Or do you view yourself as someone that can cultivate your abilities through your efforts? Not anyone can be the next Bill Gates or Stephen Hawking, but the limit to your intelligence is unknown.

If you believe that you have a fixed amount of intelligence, called a fixed mindset, then your view of challenges becomes a running evaluation in your head. "Will I succeed or fail? Will I look smart or dumb? Will I be accepted or rejected? Will I feel like a winner or loser?"[1] Your goal becomes proving yourself. That you are smart enough. That you are a winner. What happens when some teacher, some coach, some test tells the fixed mindset that you did not succeed in getting the grade, making the team, etc.? Then, your commentary on your result becomes: "I'm a total failure. I'm an idiot. I'm a loser."[2] Then, you rationalize the result. "The test wasn't like the practice tests and that's not fair." "Something was wrong with the materials I was using." "My Property professor never explained future interests clearly, so how was I supposed to know it?" The fixed mindset gives little to no recognition of their efforts in reaching their goal.

If you believe your efforts make a difference in your intelligence, called a growth mindset, then the commentary in your head changes to, "I need to try hard" and "I need to put forth my best efforts." What is the growth mindset's commentary when your goal is not achieved? "I should study harder or study in a different way for the next time." "I'll look at what went wrong on my exam and resolve to do better." The growth mindset view of your self worth continues: "Failing this exam is not the end of my world. It is a stumbling block that I will work hard to overcome."

Both mindsets are naturally upset at not achieving their goal. But each mindset's view of why it happened and what to do next are different. Individuals with both mindsets pass the bar exam. But the fixed mindset limits achievement. Interfering thoughts disrupt your learning. It makes effort disagreeable because increased effort will probably not change the result after all, because you are probably just not smart enough any way. You study alone so others don't know how dumb you are. In contrast, the growth mindset seeks allies in learning. They focus, make an all-out effort, and pull from "a bottomless trunk of strategies."[3] That's why their abilities grow and they achieve.

Some words of wisdom from prior bar takers:

- "We have all achieved so much by the time we take the bar, but we seem to dwell on shortcomings, failure and disappointment and almost ignore

---

1. Carol Dweck, *Mindset: The New Psychology of Success* 6 (Random House 2012).
2. *Id.* at 8.
3. *Id.* at 67.

our own personal victories. I tried to remember how well I perform when I put in the effort."[4]

- "What goes with 'I'm probably going to fail' is the idea that 'why even try.' 'I'm going to do it' to me means 'I'm going to do it because I'm going to study hard and smart." To think otherwise is simply a self-defeating and, often, a self-fulfilling prophecy."[5]
- "I visualized my success and it didn't include failing the exam. I wrote a passing score on a piece of scratch paper during the exam to keep it positive."[6]
- Keep your perspective that there are bigger things in life than tests. "Find something else to focus on besides the test so you can step back and look at it with different perspective and it will eventually seem manageable."[7]
- "Even if you don't have faith in yourself, it's good to have faith in one's training."[8]

V. KEEPING COOL—MAINTAINING YOUR SANITY

Ever skipped breakfast to make it to class and then had your stomach grumble half way through the class? No doubt about it—you were hungry. At that point, your attention turned away from your Wills and Trusts class and focused on when you would get to eat and what you would have. Indeed, you may have spent several minutes focusing on lunch. Were you thinking about Wills and Trusts? No, your concentration was pulled away by hunger.

Abraham Maslow's Hierarchy of Needs theory is that we are motivated by certain needs and our motivation follows an order to achieve those needs. Our most basic needs must be met before we can seek the next level of needs. Our body's need for food, water, sleep, and warmth takes precedence. Only after those needs are met are we able to focus on the next level of needs.

One way to maintain your stress is to fulfill these needs first. You need a roof over your head, the ability to pay your utilities, and nourishing food to eat. You need sleep. Next, you need safety and security. To ensure that you have these throughout your preparation time, have your financial house in order so that you may spend the necessary time to prepare for the exam. If you are planning to fulfill these needs by working while you study, you must keep your hours at a minimum the first month of bar prep and do without working the last month of bar prep. Yes, it may be hard financially, but if you do not pass the bar the first time, you will have to go through the same financially difficult time again. Plan your finances in law school so that you are not relying on working during this time.

Avoid moving during bar preparation. Moving is more than just the physical acts of packing and unpacking possessions. Time is needed to locate a new residence. Time is needed to have utilities hooked up. Time is needed to arrange insurance, to have cars relicensed if moving to a different state, to set up new

---

4. Statement from D.M. (passed bar exam the first time).
5. Statement from T.S. (passed bar exam the first time).
6. Statement from J.C. (passed bar exam the first time).
7. Statement from L.P. (passed bar exam the first time).
8. Statement from D.W. (passed bar exam the first time).

bank accounts, etc. The list is endless. Thus, you cannot just write off the few days of packing and the actual relocation. Much more time will be involved. Either move before you begin bar preparation or arrange your move after the exam.

If you are a regular exerciser, keep it up! Exercise is a great stress reducer. If you run every day, keep running. If you go to the gym regularly, keep going. You may have to reduce the time you spend running and the time you spend at the gym, but there is no need to stop it completely. If you are not a regular exerciser, consider taking walks during breaks from studying. Moving around and getting your blood flowing to your extremities can only benefit you.

A word about sleep. Get some. As much as you can. Sleep is a physical need necessary for you to think clearly. All-nighters the week before the bar exam leave you exhausted and unable to concentrate. Cramming the days and nights before the exam will leave you unable to focus. If your fears and thoughts are keeping you up at night, here are a few tips:

- Avoid caffeine in the evenings.
- Try warm milk.
- Turn off the television as you try to go to sleep.
- Take a walk in the evening.
- Keep your room just a little cooler.
- Avoid drinking lots of liquids in the evening to avoid middle of the night trips to the bathroom.

If these tips don't work, an over-the-counter sleep aid used according to directions may help. If not, see your health care provider for sleep assistance.

After your physical needs are met, your need for love, friendship, and intimacy become your focus. The important people in your life also need your time. Be sure to have a regular date night with your significant other, even if it is just watching a movie together without you having your nose in a book. Spend time with your children every day. Take regular time away from study, either a half day on the weekends or, occasionally, a full day off. You need that time with your significant other as much as they need time with you. Spend time on those days off in recreation and relaxation. The idea is to have a true break from studying, so that when you hit it again you will be rejuvenated and more motivated to keep up the pace.

Likewise, if being part of a community group is important to you, there is no need to give it up. Just don't volunteer to chair the fundraising event in the middle of bar prep! If you regularly attend worship in your faith, keep attending! We need all the help we can get and you will be less stressed if your spiritual needs have been met.

Do not be surprised when you have an overwhelming feeling that this is an impossible task and one that you are deficient on in every category. All the stress and self-doubt have been building up and they come out all at once. You have a meltdown. Good! Good? How is that possibly good? It's good because continuing to study with that stress building up will not be good study. It will be distracted studying, at best. A meltdown means you probably need to take a break for the day and pick it back up the next day. You need some time away from this process. Most folks have at least two or three meltdowns during the bar preparation process. Expect them. Everyone gets them. Nothing is wrong with you when you have one. You just need to emotionally let it all hang out.

Lastly, remember that every single bar taker is in the same boat. You have the same test. The odd questions are odd to everyone. Everyone is stressed-out and nervous. Take a deep breath. You will have studied hard and your preparation will see you through the exam. Honest. You can do this!

All Together

CHAPTER 8

Not the First Time

All of the advice in this book is not just for first-time takers, but also applies to repeat takers. If this is not your first time taking a bar exam because you were unsuccessful, know that you are not alone. Even states with a high bar passage rate still have folks who do not pass. Usually, a combination of factors led to this result:

- Insufficient preparation
  - Lack of time spent
  - Lack of details in memorization materials
- Anxiety and mindset
- Personal issues

Let's address each cause and ways to remedy these issues.

I. INSUFFICIENT PREPARATION

A. Time Spent

There is no getting around it. Bar preparation takes a significant amount of time. If you worked during your preparation or had family issues that took substantial time away from your study, you likely were not able to cover all the materials and do sufficient practice questions. Take the time to sit down with your significant other, family members, and employer to discuss your need to spend more time on your bar preparation. Work with your employer to take more time off to study. At a minimum, you need the entire month of the exam. A better game plan would have you take two months off.

Plan on 400-500 hours to prepare. If you took a commercial bar prep course the first time, you most likely should not need to repeat the course your second time taking the exam. If it is your third or more time taking the exam, you should consider taking another commercial bar preparation course. The lapse of time makes it more difficult to remember details. If you did not take a commercial bar prep course the first time, you should take one the second time.

Generally, insufficient time preparing means you did not review all of the topics in detail. Remember, you cannot predict which essay topics will appear on the next exam. The examiners do repeat topics twice in a row, if not more than twice. You cannot game the exam by deciding which topics are less likely to appear. You must study all topics.

If you did not make your own flash cards, outlines, or flow charts the first time around, start making those for every topic before the eight weeks of bar preparation before the exam. Start with the "Big Seven"—the topics tested on the MBE: Constitutional Law, Contracts, Criminal Law and Procedure, Evidence, Federal Civil Procedure, Real Property, and Torts. Try to have four or more of those topics completely done prior to the start of the eight weeks. Do *not* start doing practice questions before the eight weeks. Your goal is to improve your memorization materials—to get ready to memorize. The eight weeks directly before the exam is plenty of time for practice questions.

B. Detail in Memorization Materials

If you relied on commercial bar prep materials for your memorization, your short-cut did not work. You need to make your own outlines or flash cards. That process encodes the information much better in your memory. Just reading someone else's organization and description of the material is insufficient. Autopsy each practice question and include the information in your materials. Take this time to make your materials focus on what you need to remember. It will be worth it.

If you did make your own outlines or flash cards and were not successful, two possible things happened. First, you may not have put enough detail in the rules you were memorizing. Or, you put too much detail into your rule such that you could not memorize much of it or it kept you from focusing on what was critical. Thus, you need to supplement or cull appropriately.

Use the mind maps contained in this book to guide you in your decision making about how to supplement or cull. Always, always autopsy your answers to practice questions and include the rules in your materials.

II. ANXIETY AND MINDSET

If you have experienced test anxiety prior to this exam, or if this is the first time, see a mental health professional to work on coping mechanisms. Some students with a high level of test anxiety find hypnosis beneficial.

If you have followed the advice in this book, you are more likely to pass the exam. Get to the place in your preparation where you feel that you have done your best—a positive mindset. You have done all that was asked and then some. Then, trust that preparation.

Anxiety can occur as a result of self-doubt and a mindset that you are likely to fail. Folks in the bottom of the class often feel this way. You may feel that because you did not perform in law school at the same level as the top 90% that you are more likely to fail. That mindset—"I'll probably fail"—will actually make it more likely that you will fail. In reality, folks at the bottom of the class can and do pass the exam on their first try all the time. The difference—their mindset. They maintain a growth mindset that their efforts make a difference. They then work very hard in their bar preparation. They put in their 500 hours of study. They know and feel that they have studied to the best of their abilities. Their mindset—"I can do this," "I have put forth my best effort"—carries them through the exam.

When you hear the voice in your head panic because you read a question that you don't know the answer to, immediately stop. Remember, you are not alone.

Everyone taking the exam is probably also flummoxed by this question. Everyone has their own topics they do not know as well as others and gets questions they do not immediately understand. Take a deep breath. More oxygen in the brain helps. Tell yourself—"I will do my best and this one question does not mean I will fail." Then, go through your mind map. Consider each branch and whether the facts give rise to any issue on that branch. That usually gives you something with which to begin your analysis.

If that doesn't do it, then guess. Now, it will be an educated guess and not willy-nilly. You have already gone through your mind map, but nothing jumped out at you. If you're not sure of the path, begin with the branch that is possibly related. Even if you are totally off, you will usually get a few points for the answer. Chapter 4 discusses in more detail how to guess in an intelligent manner.

Most importantly, change your mindset. Go into the exam knowing that you have done your best. Go into the exam knowing that your increased efforts will make a difference. Listen to those who had to make more than one attempt to pass successfully:

- "One word: Conquer. Owning the failure and being honest about my flaws. Embracing those flaws and conquering them on each subject. Also keeping my mind centered on the subject at hand not the overall big picture. The best thing . . . was the game plan and encouragement grounded in reality."[1]
- "After failing it once, it is really hard to convince yourself it isn't going to happen again. I know when I was studying the second time . . . and things clicked for me better . . . I would say to myself 'If I had only known that the first time I wouldn't have failed.' . . . When things made more sense the second time, it made it easier to think I was going to get it the second time."[2]
- "When I didn't pass the first time, I was very depressed. What kept me going were the words of encouragement from my professors. . . . Plus, I had to remind myself that I'd made it that far, with two very small children. If I could graduate, I could pass the stupid test."[3]

III. PERSONAL ISSUES

Life happens. It's unpredictable and unavoidable. Few things are under your control. Some of these were mentioned in Chapter 7: avoid working, avoid moving, etc. But most of life is not under your control. In February 2013, the test site of the Missouri bar exam was hit with a major snow storm. Being in the middle of the country, we can usually see our weather coming, and this would be a big one. Our applicants were told to travel the weekend before rather than the day before. All made it safely.

Then, during the exam, the power went out. Came on and went out again. The afternoon session was delayed. They started and it went out again. When they finally started, the exam software failed. All the typists had to handwrite.

---

1. Statement from S.P. (unsuccessful on first and second attempts, then passed).
2. Statement from L.H. (unsuccessful on first attempt, then passed).
3. Statement from P.R. (unsuccessful on first attempt, then passed).

The exam was not over until the early evening instead of the afternoon. They were hungry, anxious, and tired. All passed. They give credit to their preparation and that they were not as exhausted as other takers. They had listened to the advice in this book and were ready.

On the other hand, on another prior testing date, an applicant's hotel had a fire in the middle of the night. They were all displaced to another hotel. That applicant did not fare well. He needed to still study the night before. He had not taken the advice to heart.

Another applicant's wife asked for a divorce ten days before the bar. Talk about sabotage! She had graduated two years earlier and was an anxious test taker herself. She was working at the firm where he had accepted an offer. She insisted he look for a different job right then and move out of their residence ASAP. His whole life was turned around. It was a very tough time, emotionally. But, he persevered. He refused to move out and refused to renege on his employment with the firm. He had been running his game plan and was well-prepared prior to her announcement. The bar actually motivated him to show her. He passed.

Sometimes when life happens, it is a time to reevaluate your priorities. There will always be another test date. Spending time with a loved one who is terminally ill is more important than an exam. Most employers understand if you need to postpone. It is truly not the end of the world if you must postpone. Some states limit the number of times you can take the exam. Don't waste a try by letting a personal issue interfere; better to postpone.

As one applicant said, "[T]he bar exam is a test of how you handle real world situations, so relax and just do it one step at a time."[4]

---

4. Statement from J.C. (overheard from another applicant during the snowed-in exam in February 2013).

CHAPTER 9

Mapping MBE Topics—Constitutional Law

I. MIND MAP

Constitutional Law affects virtually every area of law. Federal law is "the supreme law of the land" and includes every federal statute, every federal regulation, and every federal treaty. A hierarchy of authority exists such that the Constitution[1] is at the top and all law below it on the hierarchy cannot conflict with the Constitution. In addition, the Constitution sets the parameters for our system of federalism—that is, the co-existence of the federal government with state governments. Specifically, the Constitution sets forth the federal government's powers. The Tenth Amendment provides that powers not delegated to the federal government nor prohibited by the Constitution to the States are reserved to the States.[2]

No need exists to memorize the Constitution word for word for the bar exam. What is needed is to understand the powers of the branches of the federal government, to understand the protections of due process and equal protection, and to achieve a sound understanding of the First Amendment. Use your mind map:

- Powers of Each Branch of Government
- Dormant Commerce Clause
- State Action
- Due Process
  - Procedural Due Process
  - Substantive Due Process
- Equal Protection
- First Amendment

---

1. All references to "Constitution" will be to the federal constitution unless otherwise stated.
2. U.S. Const. amend. X.

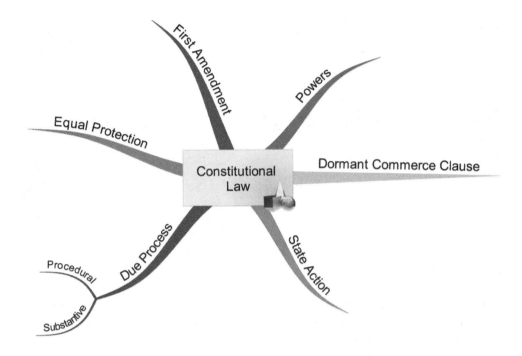

The drafters of the Constitution were concerned with creating a government with unfettered power. Thus, the Constitution limits the power of the federal government. The Constitution authorizes specific **powers** to each branch of government. Actions by each branch are valid only if authorized by the Constitution.

The judiciary's power emanates from Article III and from *Marbury v. Madison*,[3] which established judicial review. Under *Marbury*, the Court held that the Constitution is "law" and that the judiciary's province and duty was to declare what the law is.

The judiciary does not have to hear every case under its subject matter jurisdiction. Certain limitations are placed on the court's jurisdiction:

- Case or controversy
- Mootness
- Ripeness
- Abstention
- Standing
- Political questions

First, jurisdiction is limited to a "**case or controversy**"—a real and substantial dispute that touches the legal relations of parties with adverse interests and that can be resolved by a judicial decree of a conclusive character. The court does not give advisory opinions. Next, if the matter has already been resolved, the case will be dismissed as moot. Ripeness bars consideration of claims before they have fully developed. The court may abstain or refuse to hear a particular case when there are undecided issues of state law presented. Then, the state court resolves the issues of state law first, perhaps making a decision on the constitutional issue unnecessary. A person litigating a constitutional question

---

3. 5 U.S. (1 Cranch) 137 (1803).

must have standing. To prove standing, the litigant must show injury-in-fact, causation, and redressability.

The legislative branch, Congress, has a host of powers:

- Legislative
- Commerce
- Taxing
- Spending
- War and defense
- Investigatory
- Property
- Eminent domain
- Admiralty
- Bankruptcy
- Postal
- Copyright and patent
- Speech and debate
- Civil War amendments

Detailed knowledge of each power is not necessary to achieve the 75% competence you need to pass the bar exam. Focus your efforts on the legislative power, the commerce power, and the taxing power. Eminent domain is addressed under takings in Chapter 14.

Primarily, the legislature's power is to make laws. Incidental to that power is the right to conduct investigations and hearings, consider matters upon which legislation may be enacted, and do all other things "necessary and proper" to the enacting of legislation.[4] The Necessary and Proper Clause gives Congress the implied power "to make all Laws which shall be necessary and proper for carrying into Execution the foregoing Powers. . . ."[5]

The **Commerce Clause** and its later interpretations by the Supreme Court gives Congress the power to regulate:

- channels of interstate commerce, such as highways, waterways, and air traffic;
- instrumentalities of interstate commerce, such as cars, trucks, ships, and airplanes; and
- activities that have a "substantial economic effect" upon interstate commerce.

Under the substantially effects test, Congress must show that the regulated activity is economic in nature and that the regulated activity—when taken cumulatively throughout the nation—has a substantial effect on commerce.

Congress has the power to lay and **collect taxes**, duties, imposts, and excises.[6] A congressional act purporting to be a tax should be upheld as a valid exercise of the taxing power provided that it does, in fact, raise revenue—an objective standard—or that it was intended to raise revenue—a subjective standard. Congress can use its taxing power to achieve a regulatory effect as long as Congress has the power to regulate the activity taxed.

---

4. U.S. Const. art. I, § 1.
5. *Id.* § 8.
6. *Id.*

The **executive branch's powers** rest in the president as Chief Executive and Commander-in-Chief. The executive branch's power extends to international affairs. As Chief Executive, the president has appointment power to nominate and appoint ambassadors, justices of the Supreme Court, and all other officers of the United States.[7] The president also has **veto power** over Congress' legislation. The president has ten days in which to act upon legislation. If the president fails to act, the proposed legislation becomes law. The president can pocket veto a bill passed within ten days of the end of the congressional term by not signing it. Congress has the power to override a veto by a two-thirds vote of both houses of Congress. A line-item veto has been held unconstitutional. Only Congress has the power to amend legislation to delete provisions.

Congress can enact legislation that delegates **rulemaking power** to an executive or administrative agency in designated areas. This is an exception to the general rule that the executive branch does not "make law."

Additional powers vested in the executive branch include the **pardon power** and **executive privilege**. As Commander-in-Chief, the president also has the power to deploy military forces, but does not have the power to declare war. In international affairs, the president has the power to make treaties with foreign nations, which require the consent of two-thirds of the Senate before enactment.

Under the Commerce Clause, Congress has the power to regulate interstate commerce. States may regulate local transactions affecting interstate commerce as long as Congress has not enacted legislation. This state power is subject to certain limitations. These limitations are known as the **Dormant Commerce Clause**.

If a state law discriminates on its face between in-state and out-of-state economic actors, the state must show that the regulation serves a compelling state interest, and the regulation is narrowly tailed to serve that interest. If the state law merely incidentally burdens interstate commerce, the state must show that the regulation serves an important state interest and the burden on interstate commerce is not excessive in relation to the interest served.

State taxation of interstate commerce is permissible as long as the tax does not discriminate against or unduly burden interstate commerce. In reviewing a state tax of interstate commerce, courts generally require that:

- there must be a substantial nexus between the activity taxed and the taxing state;
- the tax must be fairly apportioned;
- the tax must not discriminate against interstate commerce; and
- the tax must be fairly related to the services provided by the taxing state.

Before analyzing any constitutional violation, you must show that there is government action and not action by a private citizen or entity. This **state action** requirement refers to actions by either the federal or state government. This requirement is based on the Fourteenth and Fifteenth Amendments. Therefore, analyzing whether a state action exists is the first step for both MBE and essay questions.

Private actors may be found to be state actors when the private entity is carrying on activities traditionally and exclusively performed by the government or where the government and private entity are so closely related that the action by the private party fairly can be treated as action by the government.

---

7. U.S. Const. art. II, § 2.

The **Supremacy Clause** provides that a federal law will supersede any state law with which it is in direct conflict. Thus, the federal law preempts the state law in an area in which the exercise of federal power is constitutional. For example, Congress passed legislation in the 1960s mandating warnings on cigarette packaging. As a result, states cannot demand different warnings as the federal legislation preempts state legislation.

Originally, the **Bill of Rights** applied only to the federal government. The Court has since interpreted the Fourteenth Amendment to apply the Bill of Rights to states by holding that fundamental rights are not privileges and immunities of national citizenship. For an essay question, always include how an amendment applies to the states through the Fourteenth Amendment.

The second portion of the Fourteenth Amendment is the **Due Process Clause**. The Due Process Clause (and the Equal Protection Clause) protects the rights of "persons," not just "citizens." Corporations and aliens are considered "persons." Corporations do not, however, have the privilege against self-incrimination.

The Fifth and Fourteenth Amendments protect against the deprivation of life, liberty, or property without due process of law. Thus, an individual is entitled to certain safeguards that include some form of notice and a meaningful hearing within a reasonable time. This is known as **procedural due process**. Protected liberty interests include freedom from bodily restraints, physical punishment, and commitment to a mental institution. Protected property interests include public education, welfare benefits, retention of driver's license, public employment, prejudgment garnishment, forfeiture of property, and business licensing. Without question, capital punishment is a deprivation of a life interest. As such, rigorous due process protections are employed. The Court has addressed other life interests such as abortion or right-to-die situations under other provisions of the Constitution.

For an economic regulation, **substantive due process** requires a more deferential standard than the standard for fundamental rights regulations. As such, an economic regulation will be upheld if it is rationally related to a legitimate government interest. When evaluating governmental regulations that affect fundamental rights of personhood, either **strict scrutiny** review or other forms of heightened scrutiny are used. These fundamental rights include the:

- right to travel,
- right to vote, and
- right to privacy.

Privacy rights may be remembered by the acronym CAMPERS:

- **C**ontraceptives
- **A**bortion
- **M**arriage
- **P**rocreation
- **P**rivate **E**ducation
- **F**amily **R**elations
- **S**exual relations (meaning private adult consensual activity[8])

---

8. *Lawrence v. Texas*, 539 U.S. 558 (2003) (Kennedy, J.) (holding that private adult consensual activity is a substantive due process liberty right, not a privacy right).

**Strict Scrutiny Applies in
Equal Protection Analysis
and in Other Contexts**

The guarantee of substantive due process assures that a law will be fair and reasonable, not arbitrary. Use substantive due process review when the law affects the rights of all persons with respect to the specific activity. Use equal protection when a law affects the rights of some persons with respect to a specific activity. A state statute must be involved for equal protection to be implicated.

Equal protection uses different standards of review depending upon the classification in the statute. Strict scrutiny puts the burden of persuasion on the government to prove that the measure being challenged is necessary to further a compelling governmental interest. In an equal protection analysis, strict scrutiny applies to suspect classifications—race, alienage, and national origin. In other contexts, strict scrutiny applies to the deprivation of fundamental rights, First Amendment rights, and access to courts.

Intermediate scrutiny also places the burden of persuasion on the government to prove that the measure being challenged is substantially related to the achievement of an important governmental interest. "Substantially related" means an exceedingly persuasive justification must be shown. Intermediate scrutiny applies to quasi-suspect classifications—gender and illegitimacy.

> **EXAM TIP**
> If a federal statute is used in a question, any response that implicates equal protection is automatically incorrect.

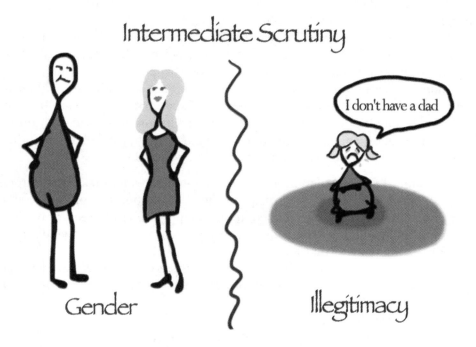

Intermediate Scrutiny

I don't have a dad

Gender   Illegitimacy

Rational basis scrutiny places the burden of persuasion on the plaintiff. The plaintiff must show that the measure being challenged serves no legitimate government interest or is not rationally related to any legitimate interest. Rational relationship means that the law cannot be arbitrary or unreasonable. Rational basis review applies to all classifications not falling under strict or intermediate scrutiny including classifications based on age, poverty, wealth, disability, and the need for necessities of life such as food, shelter, clothing, and medical care. As this is a more deferential standard, rarely does a regulation not meet rational basis scrutiny.

Focus your study of the **First Amendment** on freedom of religion, freedom of speech, freedom of the press, and freedom of association. **Freedom of religion** includes both the establishment of religion and the free exercise of religion. When analyzing an **establishment clause** issue, the first step is whether the law is a sect preference. All sect preference laws are subject to strict scrutiny analysis. Always include this rule in an essay answer. These are easy, low-hanging fruit points and they show the examiners that you know there is a difference between an explicit sect preference statute and one that is not.

If there is no explicit sect preference, then the Court analyzes the legislation or government program under the *Lemon* test:[9]

- The statute must have a secular legislative purpose;
- The principal or primary effect or purpose must neither advance nor inhibit religion; and
- The statute must not foster an excessive government entanglement with religion.

As a general rule, religious activities at public schools violate the Establishment Clause. Most government aid to religious schools is unconstitutional. If the program provides aid to all elementary and secondary school students including those attending parochial schools, however, then the program "passes" the *Lemon* test. Similarly, holiday displays on government property are generally permissible if they do not favor one religion over another.

Under the **Free Exercise Clause** of the First Amendment, religious beliefs are absolutely protected. The government may not punish an individual by denying benefits or imposing burdens based on religious belief.

Under the **Freedom of Speech Clause** of the First Amendment, "Congress shall make no law . . . abridging the freedom of speech. . . ."[10] The government may not censor all categories of speech or engage in content-based discrimination with some exceptions. Regulations are allowed if they pass strict scrutiny. Exceptions to the ban on government censorship include:

- Conduct-based regulation: If the regulation creates an incidental burden on speech, it is allowed if it furthers an important or substantial government interest unrelated to the suppression of free expression, and the incidental restriction on speech is no greater than is essential to the furtherance of that interest.
- Government as speaker: When the government is the speaker rather than a private actor, the government may discriminate based on the content of the speech.
- Unprotected speech:
  - Speech that advocates violence or unlawful action:
    - Speech "is directed to inciting or producing imminent lawless action and is likely to incite or produce such action."[11]
  - Fighting words:
    - Words likely to incite acts of immediate physical retaliation that are more than annoying or offensive. There must be a genuine likelihood of imminent violence.
  - Hostile audience speech:
    - Speech that elicits an immediate violent response against the speaker by an audience may be grounds for prosecution.
  - Obscene speech—three-part test:
    - An average person applying contemporary community standards would find that the work, taken as a whole, appeals to a prurient interest;

---

9. *Lemon v. Kurtzman*, 403 U.S. 602, 612-13 (1971).
10. U.S. Const. amend. I.
11. *Brandenburg v. Ohio*, 395 U.S. 444, 447 (1969).

- The work depicts or describes, in a patently offensive way, sexual conduct specifically defined by state law; and
- The work, taken as a whole, lacks serious literary, artistic, political, or scientific value.
- Defamatory speech:
  - Constitutional restrictions on what is considered defamatory speech apply where the plaintiff is either a public official or public figure or where the statement involves a matter of public concern.
  - Then, the plaintiff must prove actual malice; that is, knowledge of falsity or reckless disregard of the truth or falsity of the statement.[12]

Certain categories of speech receive lower levels of protection:

- Commercial speech:
  - Still highly protected, but not protected if false or deceptive or if related to unlawful activity. The government can regulate the speech only if the regulation:
    - Serves a substantial governmental interest;
    - Directly advances the substantial governmental interest; and
    - Is not more extensive than is necessary to serve that interest.
- Sexual speech: Regulation must serve a substantial government interest and leave open reasonable alternative channels of communication.

Regulations of time, place, and manner of speech are allowed. These restraints apply to public areas such as streets, sidewalks, and parks. A three-part test is used to determine the constitutionality of such restrictions:

1. Regulation must be content-neutral as to both subject matter and viewpoint,
2. Regulation must be narrowly tailored to serve a significant government interests, and
3. Regulation leaves alternative channels of communication open.

The freedom of speech and **association** bear a close nexus. State action that may curtail or have the effect of curtailing the freedom to associate is subject to the closest scrutiny.

Freedom of the press means that the press has no greater freedom to speak than any ordinary member of the general public. The press has no special right of access to government information. Both the public and the press have a right to attend criminal trials unless the judge finds an overriding interest that cannot be accommodated by less restrictive means. Gag orders on the press will almost never be held constitutional as the judge has other alternatives at her disposal.

Generally, radio and television broadcasting can be more closely regulated than the press, due to the limited number of airwaves available. Cable television receives First Amendment protection somewhere between broadcast television and newspapers.

---

12. *New York Times v. Sullivan*, 376 U.S. 254, 280 (1964).

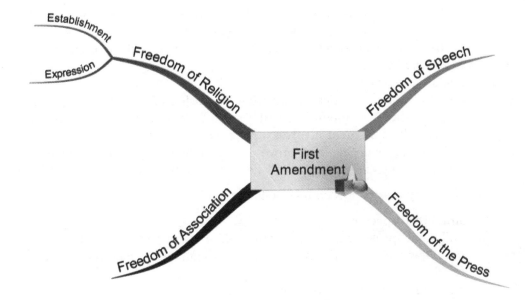

A Constitutional Law essay is ripe for low-hanging fruit points. Follow each step to set up the rule to be applied.

Constitutional Law Bill of Rights Analysis Steps

1. Identify the amendment.
2. State how amendment applies to states.
3. Identify the state action.
4. Give the language of the amendment itself.
5. Give the Court's interpretation of that language.

For example, in a takings question where a cable company seeks to lay cable on a private person's property, your rule statement should look like this:

The Fifth Amendment to the U.S. Constitution applies to the states through the Due Process Clause of the Fourteenth Amendment. Although a private company and not the government itself is doing the digging, the government is not shielded as state action is found because a government ordinance authorized the taking.

Under the Fifth Amendment, the government may take private property for public use so long as just compensation is paid to the owner. Any type of physical appropriation can constitute a taking. It does not have to be a physical appropriation of all of the property owner's rights to the property to constitute a taking.

The first paragraph identifies the amendment, showing how the amendment applies to the state and the source of state action. The second paragraph gives the language of the amendment itself and then the Court's interpretation of that language. Don't be tempted to just give the Court's interpretation of the language. Do all five steps of the analysis to show the examiners that you understand the Constitution's interplay with the Court's interpretation so you can rack up the points!

II. MBE STRATEGIES[13]

About half of the MBE questions will focus on state action, due process, equal protection, takings, and the First Amendment. The other half focuses on the powers of the different branches of government (including judicial review), and the relationship of a nation and its states in a federal system.

Unlike essay questions, answering MBE questions usually does not require you to set up the various provisions of the Constitution. Instead, they focus on the specific application of the provisions and whether each provision applies to the federal or state government or to individuals. Consider making a chart of the various clauses—whether the clause is a source of power or a prohibition on governmental action and whether the clause applies to the federal or state government or to individuals. Then, expand your chart to include what the provision does. This chart gives you a head start so that you can now fill in the rest of the provisions.

Constitutional Provisions			
Provision of Constitution	**Applies to:**	**Source, Prohibition, or Limitation**	**What does provision do?**
Commerce Clause	Federal Government	Source	Clause applies to: 1. Channels of interstate commerce; 2. Instrumentalities of interstate commerce; 3. Articles moving in interstate commerce; 4. Activities substantially affecting commerce. What else should be added?
Taxing & Spending Clauses	Federal Government	Source	Power to tax and spend for the general welfare. Only place where general welfare is addressed. What else should be added?
Contract Clause	States only	Prohibition	If a state is acting under a health and safety statute or regulation, the state's statute will trump the Contract Clause.
Privileges & Immunities Clause of the Fourteenth Amendment	States	Limitation	??
"Interstate" Privileges & Immunities Clause of Article IV	States	Limitation	??
Eleventh Amendment	Individuals	Limitation	??
Thirteenth Amendment	Federal & State Governments and Individuals	Limitation	??

---

13. Some of these strategies are from Steven L. Emanuel, *Strategies & Tactics for the MBE* 1-16 (5th ed. 2013).

Many MBE questions focus on the validity of a statute. The first step is to determine whether it is a federal or state statute. That, in and of itself, will eliminate answer responses. For a federal statute, look to see if the statute is rationally related to an enumerated power or if it is necessary and proper to effectuate an enumerated power:

- Remember the major enumerated powers: Civil Rights, Elections, Admiralty, Taxation, Eminent domain, Spending/taxing for general welfare, Defense, Interstate commerce, Citizenship, External (foreign) affairs (C-R-E-A-T-E-S D-I-C-E).
- On a Constitutional Law question, only the Constitution is tested. You must leave your understanding of other federal statutes and regulations at the door. Thus, your understanding of the requirements of the Americans with Disabilities Act is irrelevant to a question regarding whether a state can prohibit chair lifts on all stairs in public buildings. Avoid thinking "it's illegal to discriminate."

Use these strategies to analyze federal statutes questions:

- Congress can regulate an activity if the activity is commercial and the activity substantially affects (or is part of a class of activities that substantially affect) interstate commerce. If the activity is noncommercial, use a stricter test to find an "obvious connection" between the activity and interstate commerce.
- Federal regulation of an item that has finished traveling through the stream of commerce might not be permissible.
- If a regulated activity is noncommercial but part of a class of activities that are traditionally commercial and substantially affect interstate commerce, then federal regulation is permissible.
- If the question focuses on a federal statute, do not pick an equal protection answer choice. Instead, if it looks like equal protection, choose an answer choice involving the Fifth Amendment or Due Process.
- If the answer choice involves the general welfare, only the Taxing and Spending Clause applies.
- There is no federal police power.
- Taxpayers do not generally have standing except in cases alleging both the exercise of Congressional taxing/spending authority and a violation of the Establishment Clause of the First Amendment.

State statutes must meet a three-part test:

- The law must be enacted within the state's powers. Police powers are the most common source of state authority including public health, safety, welfare, or morals;
- It must not violate any person's constitutional rights (most common are due process and equal protection); and
- It must not unduly burden interstate commerce.

Use these strategies to analyze state questions:

- Only analyze a state statute under the Commerce Clause when there is no relevant federal regulation. If relevant federal legislation exists, analyze under the Supremacy Clause.

- Congress can expressly authorize state regulation. Under the Tenth Amendment, Congress cannot, however, *require* or "commandeer" the states to act.
- If Congress did not expressly authorize or prohibit state regulation, does a federal regulation preempt state law?
  - Yes, if there is a direct contradiction between the state and federal law.
  - If not, determine whether Congress intended federal law to occupy the field.
- Privileges and Immunities Clause of the Fourteenth Amendment: This "distractor" will almost never be the best answer choice on the MBE.
- "Interstate" Privileges and Immunities Clause of Article IV: could be a legitimate answer choice on the MBE.
- "Overbroad" if it prohibits not only unprotected speech but also some protected speech. "Vague" if so unclearly defined that a reasonable person would have to guess at its meaning.
- Special points regarding freedom of religion:
  - Government may only regulate religious practice with secular laws.
  - Protected beliefs must be sincerely held religious views, not mere philosophical or political views.
  - Watch for MBE questions on aid to private, religious schools; will parallel Supreme Court cases.
- A state court case must have addressed a federal question in order to reach the Supreme Court.
- The Supreme Court will not address a state court decision that rests on adequate and independent state law grounds.
- A purely economic regulation equals no due process or equal protection problem.

Constitutional law is myriad and complex. If you skip it, there is really little to no chance to pass the exam. Don't be intimidated thinking you need to have 100% understood and memorized. Your 75% is just right.

III. ESSAY PRACTICE QUESTION[14]

There are two nursing schools in State A: Public Nursing School (Public) and Private Nursing School (Private). Public is an agency of the state government, and all its faculty and staff are state employees. Private is owned by a private corporation and receives no direct funding from the state. The State A Board of Education regulates the curriculum of each nursing school and certifies all graduates of the two nursing schools as eligible to become licensed nurses in State A.

Both Public and Private have a long-standing policy of restricting admission to women. Neither school has ever admitted a male applicant. There has been general discrimination against women in State A in the health care field. Historically, however, 95 percent of State A nurses have been female.

A male resident of State A wants to be a nurse. The man first applied to Private and was denied admission. His rejection letter from Private stated that he was "not eligible to enroll because Private was established as an all-female institution and does not admit or enroll male students."

The man next applied to Public and was again denied admission. His letter from Public stated that "you are not eligible to enroll because Public does not enroll male students. Mindful of the historical discrimination that women have faced in State A, our state has established Public to remedy this discrimination and provide opportunities for women who want to work in the growing field of health care as nurses." The letter continued, "Because your grades and test scores would have been sufficient to admit you if you were female, we offer you admission to our new Male Nursing Opportunity Program instead."

The Male Nursing Opportunity Program allows male residents of State A to become nurses by studying at a nursing school in an adjacent state. Graduates of the program are certified by the State A Board of Education as eligible to become licensed nurses in State A. However, the Male Nursing Opportunity Program facilities are not as modem as those at Public, the faculty is not as experienced, and graduates of the Male Nursing Opportunity Program do not enjoy the same employment opportunities as graduates of either Public or Private.

1. Has Private violated the man's rights under the Equal Protection Clause of the Fourteenth Amendment? Explain.
2. Has Public violated the man's rights under the Equal Protection Clause of the Fourteenth Amendment? Explain.

---

14. The Multistate Bar Examination ("MBE®") questions, the Multistate Essay Examination ("MEE®") questions, and excerpts from the Multistate Performance Tests ("MPT®") have been reprinted by permission from the NCBE®. Copyright© by the National Conference of Bar Examiners. All rights reserved.

IV. SCORE SHEET

Stated	Implied	
		1. Has Private violated the man's rights under the Equal Protection Clause of the Fourteenth Amendment?
_____	_____	**Conclusion/Issue:** Private is not a state actor and its actions are not subject to the Equal Protection Clause.
_____	_____	**Rule:** Under the U.S. Constitution,
_____	_____	The Fourteenth Amendment provides that "No State shall . . . deny to any person within its jurisdiction the equal protection of the laws.""
_____	_____	While it applies to states, it generally does not apply to private parties.
_____	_____	But it does apply to private parties whose actions constitute state action.
_____	_____	Private parties may be found to be state actors where: (1) they have performed a traditional public function, (2) there is the enforcement of certain private contracts, (3) there is joint action or "entanglement" between a state and private actor, or (4) there is state encouragement of private discrimination.
_____	_____	If an unconstitutional action is attributable to the state, a violation of the Fourteenth Amendment has occurred.
_____	_____	**Application:** Here,
_____	_____	The allegedly unconstitutional action is the denial of admission based on gender.
_____	_____	But Private is a private entity and does not meet any of the factors that indicate a private party is a state actor.
_____	_____	Private is not performing a traditional public function and there is no enforcement of a private contract. In addition, state curriculum regulation and certification of graduates is not likely enough to constitute entanglement. Lastly, there is no indication that State A encouraged Private to discriminate.
_____	_____	**Conclusion:** Therefore,
_____	_____	Private, in running a private school, is not a state actor and is not subject to the Equal Protection Clause.
		2. Has Public violated the man's rights under the Equal Protection Clause of the Fourteenth Amendment?
_____	_____	**Conclusion/Issue for denying admission:** Public violated the Equal Protection Clause because a state college cannot deny admission on the basis of gender without justification that is exceedingly persuasive.
_____	_____	**Rule:** Classifications based on gender are usually subject to heightened scrutiny. Modernly, the intermediate scrutiny standard applies to gender classifications.
_____	_____	Laws that make classifications on the basis of gender are unconstitutional unless the state establishes an exceedingly persuasive justification for the classification.
_____	_____	The burden rests on the state to show the justification.
_____	_____	To be an exceedingly persuasive justification, it cannot rely on outdated/overbroad generalizations and stereotypes about the differences between men and women.
_____	_____	Must also serve an important government objective—must be a real state purpose.

continued on next page

Stated	Implied	
_____	_____	The discriminatory means employed (gender classifications) must be substantially related to achieving that objective.
_____	_____	A state can evoke a compensatory purpose to justify a classification only if the members of the gender benefitted by that classification actually suffer a disadvantage that is related to that classification.
_____	_____	**Application:** Here,
_____	_____	Public denied admission solely based on gender.
_____	_____	Public meets the criteria for being a state actor because it is a state nursing school—so the denial of admission by Public amounts to state action.
_____	_____	As such, the denial of admission is presumptively unconstitutional.
_____	_____	The state has an interest in remedying past discrimination against women, which is an important government objective.
_____	_____	But it is unclear from Public's letter if it actually sets forth the state's purpose—discrimination in the healthcare field does not equate to evidence of discrimination against women in the nursing field.
_____	_____	Instead, seems like State A is more likely reinforcing outdated stereotypes by restricting admission to women only at Public's school.
_____	_____	Moreover, it is unclear how the admissions policy advances the objective of ending discrimination against women in the healthcare field in general.
_____	_____	**Conclusion:** Therefore,
_____	_____	Public's denial of admission based on gender is unconstitutional.
_____	_____	**Conclusion for the male nursing program:** The Male Nursing Opportunity Program is inconsistent with the guarantees of equal protection.
_____	_____	**Rule:** A state may treat men and women differently consistent with the equal protection guarantee.
_____	_____	This includes providing separate facilities for gender.
_____	_____	The state has the burden.
_____	_____	State must (1) demonstrate the exceedingly persuasive justification for the separate treatment and (2) demonstrate that the separate facilities are substantially equivalent.
_____	_____	**Application:** Here,
_____	_____	The two programs are not substantially similar despite the fact that graduates from each program are eligible to become nurses.
_____	_____	Programs differ in overall quality. Also differ in employment opportunities offered to their graduates.
_____	_____	The faculty in the all-male program is not as experienced.
_____	_____	In terms of building and facilities, those available for the all-male program are not as modern as the all-female program.
_____	_____	**Conclusion:** Therefore,
_____	_____	The Male Nursing Opportunity Program is inferior to the all-female program at Public.
_____	_____	As a result, it is insufficient to satisfy as a substitute under Equal Protection Clause.

V. MBE PRACTICE QUESTIONS[15]

Question 1

A federal civil statute prohibited fishing in any body of water that was located within a national park and contained a particular endangered species of fish. The statute authorized federal district courts to enjoin knowing violators of the statute from the use of all national park facilities for up to two years. After a vacationer was found by a federal district court to have knowingly violated the statute, the court issued an injunction against his use of all national park facilities for two years. The vacationer appealed.

Before the appeals court heard the vacationer's case, Congress repealed the statute by a law that expressly made the repeal effective retroactive to a date one month before the vacationer's violation of the statute. The law also directly cited the vacationer's case and stated that it was intended to "repeal all the statutory prohibitions that formed the basis for decisions" such as that rendered against the vacationer.

On the basis of this law, the vacationer has asked the appeals court to vacate the injunction issued against him. Counsel for the United States has objected, contending that, as applied to the specific case pending in the appeals court, the law is unconstitutional.

How should the appeals court rule?

(A) For the United States, because Congress defied the constitutional prohibition against ex post facto laws by retroactively changing the consequences for violating the statute after the violation was proved in a trial court.
(B) For the United States, because the law's citation to the vacationer's case demonstrates that Congress intended to compel the appeals court to reach a particular result and, therefore, sought to exercise judicial powers vested exclusively in the courts by Article III.
(C) For the vacationer, because Congress has the power to determine the laws to be applied by the federal courts and to require retroactive application of those laws to any specifically identified case that it chooses.
(D) For the vacationer, because Congress is authorized to make substantive changes to federal civil statutes and to direct that those changes be applied by the courts to all actions in which a final judgment has not yet been rendered.

Question 2

The United States had long recognized the ruling faction in a foreign country as that country's government, despite an ongoing civil war. Throughout the civil war, the ruling faction controlled the majority of the country's territory, and the United States afforded diplomatic immunity to the ambassador representing the ruling faction.

A newly elected President of the United States decided to recognize a rebel group as the government of the foreign country and notified the ambassador from the ruling faction that she must leave the United States within 10 days.

---

15. *Id.*

The ambassador filed an action in federal district court for a declaration that the ruling faction was the true government of the foreign country and for an injunction against enforcement of the President's order that she leave the United States. The United States has moved to dismiss the action.

If the court dismisses the action, what will be the most likely reason?

(A) The action involves a nonjusticiable political question.
(B) The action is not ripe.
(C) The action is within the original jurisdiction of the U.S. Supreme Court.
(D) The ambassador does not have standing.

Question 3

An employer owed an employee $200 in unpaid wages. A law of the state in which the employer and the employee reside and in which the employee works provides that the courts of that state must decide claims for unpaid wages within 10 days of filing.

After the employee filed a claim in state court pursuant to this law, the employer filed a voluntary bankruptcy petition in federal bankruptcy court. In the bankruptcy proceeding, the employer sought to stay further proceedings in the unpaid wages claim on the basis of a federal statute which provides that a person who files a federal bankruptcy petition receives an automatic stay of all proceedings against him or her in all federal and state courts. No other federal laws apply.

In addition to the supremacy clause of Article VI, what is the most obvious constitutional basis for the imposition of a stay of the unpaid wages claim in the state court?

(A) Congress's power to provide for the general welfare.
(B) Congress's power to provide uniform rules of bankruptcy.
(C) Congress's power to regulate the jurisdiction and procedures of the courts.
(D) Congress's power to regulate commerce among the states.

Question 4

Congress enacted a statute directing U.S. ambassadors to send formal letters to the governments of their host countries, protesting any violations by those governments of international treaties on weapons sales. The President prefers to handle violations by certain countries in a less formal manner and has directed ambassadors not to comply with the statute.

Is the President's action constitutional?

(A) No, because Congress has the power to implement treaties, and therefore the statute is binding on the President.
(B) No, because Congress has the power to regulate commerce with foreign nations, and therefore the statute is binding on the President.
(C) Yes, because Congress has no jurisdiction over matters outside the U.S. borders.
(D) Yes, because the President and his subordinates are the exclusive official representatives of the United States in foreign affairs.

Question 5

Congress enacted a statute that authorized the construction of a monument commemorating the role of the United States in liberating a particular foreign nation during World War II. Another statute appropriated $3 million for the construction. When the United States became involved in a bitter trade dispute with the foreign nation, the President announced that he was canceling the monument's construction and that he would not spend the appropriated funds. Although the actual reason for the President's decision was the trade dispute, the announcement stated that the reason was an unexpected rise in the federal deficit.

Assume that no other statutes apply.

Is the President's decision constitutional?

(A) No, because the President failed to invoke his foreign affairs powers in his announcement.

(B) No, because the President is obligated to spend funds in accordance with congressional directions.

(C) Yes, because the President is vested with inherent executive power to control federal expenditures.

(D) Yes, because the President's decision is a valid exercise of his foreign affairs powers.

Question 6

A motorist who resided in State A was severely injured in a traffic accident that occurred in State B. The other vehicle involved in the accident was a truck owned by a furniture manufacturer and driven by one of its employees. The manufacturer's headquarters are in State B. Its products are sold by retailers in State A, but it has no office, plant, or agent for service of process there.

The motorist brought an action against the manufacturer in a state court in State A. The manufacturer appeared specially to contest that court's jurisdiction over it. The court ruled that it had jurisdiction over the manufacturer by virtue of State A's long-arm statute.

At trial, the court instructed the jury to apply State A law, under which a plaintiff's contributory negligence is a basis for reducing an award of damages but not for denying recovery altogether. Under State B law, contributory negligence is a complete defense. The jury found that the manufacturer was negligent and that its negligence was a cause of the motorist's injuries. It also found that the motorist was negligent, though to a lesser degree than the manufacturer, and that the motorist's negligence contributed to the accident. It returned a verdict in favor of the motorist and awarded her $1 million in damages.

The manufacturer appealed the judgment entered on this verdict, asserting error in the court's ruling on jurisdiction and in its application of State A law instead of State B law. The manufacturer raised all federal constitutional claims pertinent to these claims of error. The highest court in State A affirmed the trial court's judgment, and the U.S. Supreme Court denied the manufacturer's petition for a writ of certiorari.

The motorist has brought an action against the manufacturer in a state court in State B to collect on the judgment. The manufacturer has defended on all relevant federal constitutional grounds.

How should the State B court rule?

(A) For the manufacturer, because a judgment entered by a court that lacks jurisdiction over one of the parties is not entitled to full faith and credit, and the State A court could not constitutionally assert jurisdiction over the manufacturer because of the manufacturer's lack of a presence in that state.
(B) For the manufacturer, because the State A court was bound by the full faith and credit clause to apply State B law to an accident that occurred in State B and in which a State B company was involved.
(C) For the motorist, because the manufacturer litigated the issues of jurisdiction and choice of law in the State A court, and the final judgment of that court is entitled to full faith and credit in the State B court.
(D) For the motorist, because the Supreme Court's denial of certiorari to review the judgment of the highest court in State A conclusively establishes that the manufacturer's federal constitutional claims are invalid.

Question 7

Congress recently enacted a statute creating a program that made federal loans available to family farmers who had been unable to obtain loans from private lenders. Congress appropriated a fixed sum of money to fund loans made pursuant to the program and gave a designated federal agency discretion to decide which applicants were to receive the loans.

Two weeks after the program was established, a family farmer applied to the agency for a loan. Agency officials promptly reviewed her application and summarily denied it.

The farmer has sued the agency in federal district court, claiming only that the denial of her application without the opportunity for a hearing violated the due process clause of the Fifth Amendment. The farmer claims that she could have proved at such a hearing that without the federal loan it would be necessary for her to sell her farm.

Should the court uphold the agency's decision?

(A) No, because due process requires federal agencies to provide a hearing before making any factual determination that adversely affects an identified individual on the basis of his or her particular circumstances.
(B) No, because the denial of a loan may deprive the farmer of an established liberty interest to pursue her chosen occupation.
(C) Yes, because the applicable statute gives the farmer no legitimate claim of entitlement to receive a loan.
(D) Yes, because the spending clause of Article I, Section 8, gives Congress plenary power to control the distribution of appropriated funds in any manner it wishes.

Question 8

A state law provides that only U.S. citizens may serve as jurors in the state courts of that state. A woman who is a lawful resident alien and who has resided in the state for many years was summoned for jury duty in a state court. The woman's name was selected from a list of potential jurors that was compiled from a comprehensive list of local residents. She was disqualified from service solely because she is not a U.S. citizen.

The woman has filed an action for a declaratory judgment that the state law is unconstitutional. Who should prevail in this action?

(A) The state, because a state may limit to U.S. citizens functions that are an integral part of the process of self-government.
(B) The state, because jury service is a privilege, not a right, and therefore it is not a liberty interest protected by the due process clause of the Fourteenth Amendment.
(C) The woman, because the Constitution gives Congress plenary power to make classifications with respect to aliens.
(D) The woman, because the state has not articulated a legitimate reason for prohibiting resident aliens from serving as jurors in the state's courts.

Question 9

Congress enacted a statute that made it illegal for "any employee, without the consent of his or her employer, to post on the Internet any information concerning the employer." The purpose of the statute was to prevent employees from revealing their employers' trade secrets.

Is the statute constitutional?

(A) No, because it is not narrowly tailored to further a compelling government interest.
(B) No, because it targets a particular medium of communication for special regulation.
(C) Yes, because it leaves open ample alternative channels of communication.
(D) Yes, because it prevents employees from engaging in unethical conduct.

Question 10

A state law imposed substantial regulations on insurance companies operating within the state with respect to their rates, cash reserves, and financial practices.

A privately owned insurance company operating within the state advertised that it wanted to hire a new data processor. After reviewing applications for that position, the company hired a woman who appeared to be well qualified. The company refused to consider the application of a man who was better qualified than the woman, because he was known to have radical political views.

The man sued the company, alleging only a violation of his federal constitutional right to freedom of expression. Is the man likely to prevail?

(A) No, because hiring decisions are wholly discretionary and thus are not governed by the First Amendment.
(B) No, because the company is not subject to the provisions of the First and Fourteenth Amendments.
(C) Yes, because the company is affected with a public interest.
(D) Yes, because the company is substantially regulated by the state, and thus its employment decisions may fairly be attributed to the state.

Question 11

In order to foster an environment conducive to learning, a school board enacted a dress code that prohibited all public high school students from wearing in school shorts cut above the knee. Because female students at the school considered it unfashionable to wear shorts cut at or below the knee, they no longer wore shorts to school. On the other hand, male students at the school regularly wore shorts cut at or below the knee because they considered such shorts to be fashionable.

Female students sued to challenge the constitutionality of the dress code on the ground that it denied them the equal protection of the laws.

Should the court uphold the dress code?

(A) No, because the dress code is not necessary to further a compelling state interest.

(B) No, because the dress code is not substantially related to an important state interest.

(C) Yes, because the dress code is narrowly tailored to further an important state interest.

(D) Yes, because the dress code is rationally related to a legitimate state interest.

Question 12

A company owned a large tract of land that contained coal deposits that the company intended to mine. The company acquired mining equipment and began to plan its mining operations. Just as the company was about to begin mining, Congress enacted a statute that imposed a number of new environmental regulations and land-reclamation requirements on all mining operations within the United States. The statute made the company's planned mining operations economically infeasible. As a result, the company sold the tract of land to a farmer. While the sale price allowed the company to recover its original investment in the land, it did not cover the additional cost of the mining equipment the company had purchased or the profits it had expected to earn from its mining operations on the land.

In an action filed against the appropriate federal official, the company claims that the statute effected a taking of its property for which it is entitled to just compensation in an amount equal to the cost of the mining equipment it purchased and the profits it expected to earn from its mining operations on the land.

Which of the following is the most appropriate result in the action?

(A) The company should prevail on its claims for the cost of the mining equipment and for its lost profits.

(B) The company should prevail on its claim for the cost of the mining equipment, but not for its lost profits.

(C) The company should prevail on its claim for lost profits, but not for the cost of the mining equipment.

(D) The company should not prevail on its claim for the cost of the mining equipment or for its lost profits.

Question 13

A number of psychotherapists routinely send mailings to victims of car accidents informing the victims of the possibility of developing post-traumatic stress disorder (PTSD) as the result of the accidents, and offering psychotherapy services. Although PTSD is a possible result of a car accident, it is not common.

Many accident victims in a particular state who received the mailings complained that the mailings were disturbing and were an invasion of their privacy.

These victims also reported that as a result of the mailings, their regard for psychotherapists and for psychotherapy as a form of treatment had diminished. In response, the state enacted a law prohibiting any licensed psychotherapist from sending mailings that raised the concern of PTSD to any car accident victim in the state until 30 days after the accident. The state justified the law as an effort to address the victims' complaints as well as to protect the reputation of psychotherapy as a form of treatment.

Is this law constitutional?

(A) No, because the law singles out one type of message for prohibition while allowing others.

(B) No, because the mailings provide information to consumers.

(C) Yes, because mailings suggesting the possibility of developing PTSD as the result of an accident are misleading.

(D) Yes, because the law protects the privacy of accident victims and the public regard for psychotherapy without being substantially more restrictive than necessary.

Question 14

A clerical employee of a city water department was responsible for sending out water bills to customers. His work in this respect had always been satisfactory.

The employee's sister ran in a recent election against the incumbent mayor, but she lost. The employee had supported his sister in the election campaign. After the mayor found out about this, she fired the employee solely because his support for the sister indicated that he was "disloyal" to the mayor. The city's charter provides that "all employees of the city work at the pleasure of the mayor."

Is the mayor's action constitutional?

(A) No, because public employees have a property interest in their employment, which gives them a right to a hearing prior to discharge.

(B) No, because the mayor's action violates the employee's right to freedom of expression and association.

(C) Yes, because the employee has no property interest in his job since the city charter provides that he holds the job "at the pleasure of the mayor."

(D) Yes, because the mayor may require members of her administration to be politically loyal to her.

Question 15

An environmental organization's stated mission is to support environmental causes. The organization's membership is generally open to the public, but its bylaws permit its officers to refuse to admit anyone to membership who does not adhere to the organization's mission statement.

In a recent state administrative proceeding, the organization opposed plans to begin mining operations in the mountains surrounding a small town. Its opposition prevented the mine from being opened on schedule. In an effort to force the organization to withdraw its opposition, certain residents of the town attended a meeting of the organization and tried to become members, but the officers refused to admit them. The residents sued the organization, claiming that the refusal to admit them was discriminatory and violated a local ordinance that prohibits any organization from discriminating on the basis of an individual's political views. The organization responded that the ordinance is unconstitutional as applied to its membership decisions.

Are the residents likely to prevail in their claim?

(A) No, because the membership policies of a private organization are not state action.

(B) No, because the organization's right to freedom of association allows it to refuse to admit potential members who do not adhere to its mission statement.

(C) Yes, because the action of the officers in refusing to admit the residents as members violates equal protection of the laws.

(D) Yes, because the ordinance serves the compelling interest of protecting the residents' free speech rights.

Question 16

A fatal virus recently infected poultry in several nations. Some scientific evidence indicates that the virus can be transmitted from poultry to humans.

Poultry farming is a major industry in several U.S. states. In one such state, the legislature has enacted a law imposing a fee of two cents per bird on all poultry farming and processing operations in the state. The purpose of the fee is to pay for a state inspection system to ensure that no poultry raised or processed in the state is infected with the virus.

A company that has poultry processing plants both in the state and in other states has sued to challenge the fee. Is the fee constitutional?

(A) No, because although it attaches only to intrastate activity, in the aggregate, the fee substantially affects interstate commerce.

(B) No, because it places an undue burden on interstate commerce in violation of the negative implications of the commerce clause.

(C) Yes, because it applies only to activities that take place wholly within the state, and it does not unduly burden interstate commerce.

(D) Yes, because it was enacted pursuant to the state's police power, which takes precedence over the negative implications of the commerce clause.

VI. MBE PRACTICE ANALYSIS[16]

Question 1

A federal civil statute prohibited fishing in any body of water that was located within a national park and contained a particular endangered species of fish. The statute authorized federal district courts to enjoin knowing violators of the statute from the use of all national park facilities for up to two years. After a vacationer was found by a federal district court to have knowingly violated the statute, the court issued an injunction against his use of all national park facilities for two years. The vacationer appealed.

Before the appeals court heard the vacationer's case, Congress repealed the statute by a law that expressly made the repeal effective retroactive to a date one month before the vacationer's violation of the statute. The law also directly cited

---

16. *Id.*

the vacationer's case and stated that it was intended to "repeal all the statutory prohibitions that formed the basis for decisions" such as that rendered against the vacationer.

On the basis of this law, the vacationer has asked the appeals court to vacate the injunction issued against him. Counsel for the United States has objected, contending that, as applied to the specific case pending in the appeals court, the law is unconstitutional.

How should the appeals court rule?

(A) For the United States, because Congress defied the constitutional prohibition against ex post facto laws by retroactively changing the consequences for violating the statute after the violation was proved in a trial court.
Incorrect. The constitutional prohibition against ex post facto laws applies only to retroactive changes in statutes that result in the punishment of individuals for conduct that was legal before the changes. Congress's retroactive repeal of the statute in this case had the opposite effect. The appeals court should rule for the vacationer, because the vacationer's appeal of the district court's injunction was pending when Congress repealed the statute that authorized the injunction. Congress may change federal civil statutes and may direct federal courts to apply those changes in all actions in which a final judgment has not been rendered.

(B) For the United States, because the law's citation to the vacationer's case demonstrates that Congress intended to compel the appeals court to reach a particular result and, therefore, sought to exercise judicial powers vested exclusively in the courts by Article III.
Incorrect. Congress may not direct the outcome of a particular case under existing law, but Congress may effect a change in the law with retroactive application to pending actions. The appeals court should rule for the vacationer, because the vacationer's appeal of the district court's injunction was pending when Congress repealed the statute that authorized the injunction. Congress may change federal civil statutes and may direct federal courts to apply those changes in all actions in which a final judgment has not been rendered.

(C) For the vacationer, because Congress has the power to determine the laws to be applied by the federal courts and to require retroactive application of those laws to any specifically identified case that it chooses.
Incorrect. Although Congress may change the laws to be applied in federal courts, Congress may not direct federal courts to apply the new laws to reverse final judgments in already-decided actions. While it is correct that the appeals court should rule for the vacationer, it should do so because the vacationer's appeal of the district court's injunction was pending when Congress repealed the statute that authorized the injunction. Congress may change federal civil statutes and may direct federal courts to apply those changes to all actions in which a final judgment has not been rendered.

(D) For the vacationer, because Congress is authorized to make substantive changes to federal civil statutes and to direct that those changes be applied by the courts to all actions in which a final judgment has not yet been rendered.
Correct. The appeals court should rule for the vacationer, because the vacationer's appeal of the district court's injunction was pending when Congress repealed the statute that authorized the injunction. Congress may change federal civil statutes and may direct federal courts to apply those changes in all actions in which a final judgment has not been rendered.

Question 2

The United States had long recognized the ruling faction in a foreign country as that country's government, despite an ongoing civil war. Throughout the civil war, the ruling faction controlled the majority of the country's territory, and the United States afforded diplomatic immunity to the ambassador representing the ruling faction.

A newly elected President of the United States decided to recognize a rebel group as the government of the foreign country and notified the ambassador from the ruling faction that she must leave the United States within 10 days. The ambassador filed an action in federal district court for a declaration that the ruling faction was the true government of the foreign country and for an injunction against enforcement of the President's order that she leave the United States. The United States has moved to dismiss the action.

If the court dismisses the action, what will be the most likely reason?

(A) The action involves a nonjusticiable political question.

Correct. The action likely satisfies the political question doctrine and therefore should be dismissed as nonjusticiable. The President's Article II power to receive foreign ambassadors is likely a textually demonstrable commitment by the Constitution of exclusive authority to recognize foreign governments. Moreover, Article II provides no judicially manageable standards by which a court could review the constitutionality of a President's decision on whether to recognize a foreign government. Finally, because the action involves the President's administration of foreign affairs, the prudential elements of the political question doctrine also indicate that the court should dismiss the action as nonjusticiable.

(B) The action is not ripe.

Incorrect. The action is ripe for adjudication even though the ambassador may remain in the United States for 10 days. The ambassador has suffered immediate harm because she no longer represents the foreign country in the United States, she has lost her diplomatic immunity, and she is facing expulsion within a very short period of time. Also, the constitutional issues are fit for review without waiting for the ambassador's expulsion.

The reason the action should be dismissed is that it likely is nonjusticiable under the political question doctrine. The President's Article II power to receive foreign ambassadors is likely a textually demonstrable commitment by the Constitution of exclusive authority to recognize foreign governments. Moreover, Article II provides no judicially manageable standards by which a court could review the constitutionality of a President's decision on whether to recognize a foreign government. Finally, because the action involves the President's administration of foreign affairs, the prudential elements of the political question doctrine also indicate that the court should dismiss the action as nonjusticiable.

(C) The action is within the original jurisdiction of the U.S. Supreme Court.

Incorrect. Although Article III of the Constitution provides that the Supreme Court has original jurisdiction over actions involving ambassadors, federal district courts also may exercise original jurisdiction over actions within the Supreme Court's original jurisdiction.

The reason the action should be dismissed is that it likely is nonjusticiable under the political question doctrine. The President's Article II power to receive foreign ambassadors is likely a textually demonstrable commitment by the

Constitution of exclusive authority to recognize foreign governments. Moreover, Article II provides no judicially manageable standards by which a court could review the constitutionality of a President's decision on whether to recognize a foreign government. Finally, because the action involves the President's administration of foreign affairs, the prudential elements of the political question doctrine also indicate that the court should dismiss the action as nonjusticiable.

(D) The ambassador does not have standing.
Incorrect. The ambassador has standing, because she has been injured by the President's decision that her faction is no longer the government of her country, her injury is fairly traceable to this decision, and the injury is likely redressable by a court order invalidating the decision.

The reason the action should be dismissed is that it likely is nonjusticiable under the political question doctrine. The President's Article II power to receive foreign ambassadors is likely a textually demonstrable commitment by the Constitution of exclusive authority to recognize foreign governments. Moreover, Article II provides no judicially manageable standards by which a court could review the constitutionality of a President's decision on whether to recognize a foreign government. Finally, because the action involves the President's administration of foreign affairs, the prudential elements of the political question doctrine also indicate that the court should dismiss the action as nonjusticiable.

Question 3

An employer owed an employee $200 in unpaid wages. A law of the state in which the employer and the employee reside and in which the employee works provides that the courts of that state must decide claims for unpaid wages within 10 days of filing.

After the employee filed a claim in state court pursuant to this law, the employer filed a voluntary bankruptcy petition in federal bankruptcy court. In the bankruptcy proceeding, the employer sought to stay further proceedings in the unpaid wages claim on the basis of a federal statute which provides that a person who files a federal bankruptcy petition receives an automatic stay of all proceedings against him or her in all federal and state courts. No other federal laws apply.

In addition to the supremacy clause of Article VI, what is the most obvious constitutional basis for the imposition of a stay of the unpaid wages claim in the state court?

(A) Congress's power to provide for the general welfare.
Incorrect. Congress's power to provide for the general welfare authorizes only taxing and spending laws. Because the statute requiring the imposition of a stay of the unpaid wages claim concerns neither taxing nor spending, it is not authorized by the general welfare clause.

Congress's power to provide uniform rules of bankruptcy offers the most obvious constitutional basis for a federal statute requiring a stay of court proceedings against a person who has filed a federal bankruptcy petition.

(B) Congress's power to provide uniform rules of bankruptcy.

Correct. Congress's power to provide uniform rules of bankruptcy offers the most obvious constitutional basis for a federal statute requiring a stay of court proceedings against a person who has filed a federal bankruptcy petition.

(C) Congress's power to regulate the jurisdiction and procedures of the courts.
Incorrect. The constitutional provisions that give Congress the power to regulate the jurisdiction and procedures of federal courts do not authorize Congress to regulate state courts.

Congress's power to provide uniform rules of bankruptcy offers the most obvious constitutional basis for a federal statute requiring a stay of court proceedings against a person who has filed a federal bankruptcy petition.

(D) Congress's power to regulate commerce among the states.
Incorrect. A federal statute providing for a stay of court proceedings against a person who has filed a federal bankruptcy petition is not authorized by the commerce clause, because it is not a regulation of the channels or instrumentalities of interstate commerce, nor does it regulate an economic or commercial activity.

Congress's power to provide uniform rules of bankruptcy offers the most obvious constitutional basis for a federal statute requiring a stay of court proceedings against a person who has filed a federal bankruptcy petition.

Question 4

Congress enacted a statute directing U.S. ambassadors to send formal letters to the governments of their host countries, protesting any violations by those governments of international treaties on weapons sales. The President prefers to handle violations by certain countries in a less formal manner and has directed ambassadors not to comply with the statute.

Is the President's action constitutional?

(A) No, because Congress has the power to implement treaties, and therefore the statute is binding on the President.
Incorrect. Although Congress has the power, under the necessary and proper clause, to enact legislation in support of treaties, the President's action is constitutional, because the U.S. Supreme Court has ruled that the President alone has the authority to represent the United States in foreign affairs. Because the statute intrudes on that authority, it is unconstitutional and has no effect.

(B) No, because Congress has the power to regulate commerce with foreign nations, and therefore the statute is binding on the President.
Incorrect. Congress has the power to regulate commerce with foreign nations, but this statute does not concern commercial relationships between the United States and foreign nations. The President's action is constitutional, because the U.S. Supreme Court has ruled that the President alone has the authority to represent the United States in foreign affairs. Because the statute intrudes on that authority, it is unconstitutional and has no effect.

(C) Yes, because Congress has no jurisdiction over matters outside the U.S. borders.
Incorrect. Article I of the Constitution gives Congress several powers concerning matters outside the U.S. borders, including the power to declare war and the power to regulate commerce with foreign nations. However, because the U.S. Supreme Court has ruled that the President alone has the authority to represent the United States in

foreign affairs, the President's action is constitutional. Because the statute intrudes on the President's authority, it is unconstitutional and has no effect.

(D) Yes, because the President and his subordinates are the exclusive official representatives of the United States in foreign affairs.
Correct. The President's action is constitutional, because the U.S. Supreme Court has ruled that the President alone has the authority to represent the United States in foreign affairs. Because the statute intrudes on the President's authority, it is unconstitutional and has no effect.

Question 5

Congress enacted a statute that authorized the construction of a monument commemorating the role of the United States in liberating a particular foreign nation during World War II. Another statute appropriated $3 million for the construction. When the United States became involved in a bitter trade dispute with the foreign nation, the President announced that he was canceling the monument's construction and that he would not spend the appropriated funds. Although the actual reason for the President's decision was the trade dispute, the announcement stated that the reason was an unexpected rise in the federal deficit.

Assume that no other statutes apply.

Is the President's decision constitutional?

(A) No, because the President failed to invoke his foreign affairs powers in his announcement.
Incorrect. The constitutionality of the President's decision does not depend on whether he invoked a constitutional power to support the decision. While it is correct that the decision is unconstitutional, it is so because Article II of the Constitution obligates the President to take care that the laws are faithfully executed. Because the appropriations statute is a valid exercise of Congress's spending power, the President must abide by the requirements of the statute.

(B) No, because the President is obligated to spend funds in accordance with congressional directions.
Correct. The President's decision is unconstitutional, because Article II of the Constitution obligates the President to take care that the laws are faithfully executed. Because the appropriations statute is a valid exercise of Congress's spending power, the President must abide by the requirements of the statute.

(C) Yes, because the President is vested with inherent executive power to control federal expenditures.
Incorrect. The Constitution does not give the President power to control federal expenditures by refusing to authorize spending directed by Congress. The President's decision is unconstitutional, because Article II of the Constitution obligates the President to take care that the laws are faithfully executed. Because the appropriations statute is a valid exercise of Congress's spending power, the President must abide by the requirements of the statute.

(D) Yes, because the President's decision is a valid exercise of his foreign affairs powers.
Incorrect. The President's foreign affairs powers do not justify his refusal to authorize spending directed by Congress. The President's decision is unconstitutional, because

Article II of the Constitution obligates the President to take care that the laws are faithfully executed. Because the appropriations statute is a valid exercise of Congress's spending power, the President must abide by the requirements of the statute.

Question 6

A motorist who resided in State A was severely injured in a traffic accident that occurred in State B. The other vehicle involved in the accident was a truck owned by a furniture manufacturer and driven by one of its employees. The manufacturer's headquarters are in State B. Its products are sold by retailers in State A, but it has no office, plant, or agent for service of process there.

The motorist brought an action against the manufacturer in a state court in State A. The manufacturer appeared specially to contest that court's jurisdiction over it. The court ruled that it had jurisdiction over the manufacturer by virtue of State A's long-arm statute.

At trial, the court instructed the jury to apply State A law, under which a plaintiff's contributory negligence is a basis for reducing an award of damages but not for denying recovery altogether. Under State B law, contributory negligence is a complete defense. The jury found that the manufacturer was negligent and that its negligence was a cause of the motorist's injuries. It also found that the motorist was negligent, though to a lesser degree than the manufacturer, and that the motorist's negligence contributed to the accident. It returned a verdict in favor of the motorist and awarded her $1 million in damages.

The manufacturer appealed the judgment entered on this verdict, asserting error in the court's ruling on jurisdiction and in its application of State A law instead of State B law. The manufacturer raised all federal constitutional claims pertinent to these claims of error. The highest court in State A affirmed the trial court's judgment, and the U.S. Supreme Court denied the manufacturer's petition for a writ of certiorari.

The motorist has brought an action against the manufacturer in a state court in State B to collect on the judgment. The manufacturer has defended on all relevant federal constitutional grounds.

How should the State B court rule?

(A) For the manufacturer, because a judgment entered by a court that lacks jurisdiction over one of the parties is not entitled to full faith and credit, and the State A court could not constitutionally assert jurisdiction over the manufacturer because of the manufacturer's lack of a presence in that state.
Incorrect. The jurisdiction of the State A court was litigated in the State A court, and the ruling by that court in favor of jurisdiction is final and must be recognized by the State B court. The State B court should rule for the motorist, because the full faith and credit clause of the Constitution obligates the courts of each state to recognize the final judgments of the courts of every other state. Because the judgment of the State A court is final, it is entitled to full faith and credit in the State B court.

(B) For the manufacturer, because the State A court was bound by the full faith and credit clause to apply State B law to an accident that occurred in State B and in which a State B company was involved.
Incorrect. The full faith and credit clause of the Constitution obligates states to recognize laws enacted by other states, but it does not obligate a state court to apply the

laws of another state in cases before it. The State B court should rule for the motorist, because the full faith and credit clause of the Constitution obligates the courts of each state to recognize the final judgments of the courts of every other state. Because the judgment of the State A court is final, it is entitled to full faith and credit in the State B court.

(C) For the motorist, because the manufacturer litigated the issues of jurisdiction and choice of law in the State A court, and the final judgment of that court is entitled to full faith and credit in the State B court.

Correct. The State B court should rule for the motorist, because the full faith and credit clause of the Constitution obligates the courts of each state to recognize the final judgments of the courts of every other state. Because the judgment of the State A court is final, it is entitled to full faith and credit in the State B court.

(D) For the motorist, because the Supreme Court's denial of certiorari to review the judgment of the highest court in State A conclusively establishes that the manufacturer's federal constitutional claims are invalid.

Incorrect. The Supreme Court's denial of certiorari is not a ruling on the merits of the case; it is simply a decision not to review the case. The State B court should rule for the motorist, however, because the full faith and credit clause of the Constitution obligates the courts of each state to recognize the final judgments of the courts of every other state. Because the judgment of the State A court is final, it is entitled to full faith and credit in the State B court.

Question 7

Congress recently enacted a statute creating a program that made federal loans available to family farmers who had been unable to obtain loans from private lenders. Congress appropriated a fixed sum of money to fund loans made pursuant to the program and gave a designated federal agency discretion to decide which applicants were to receive the loans.

Two weeks after the program was established, a family farmer applied to the agency for a loan. Agency officials promptly reviewed her application and summarily denied it.

The farmer has sued the agency in federal district court, claiming only that the denial of her application without the opportunity for a hearing violated the due process clause of the Fifth Amendment. The farmer claims that she could have proved at such a hearing that without the federal loan it would be necessary for her to sell her farm.

Should the court uphold the agency's decision?

(A) No, because due process requires federal agencies to provide a hearing before making any factual determination that adversely affects an identified individual on the basis of his or her particular circumstances.

Incorrect. The due process clause obligates agencies to provide an individual with an opportunity for a hearing only when the agency makes an adjudicatory decision that deprives the individual of a property or liberty interest that is protected by the clause. The court should uphold the agency's decision, because the due process clause does not require the government to provide the farmer an opportunity for an administrative hearing on her loan application. The farmer had no legitimate claim of entitlement to a loan, because the statute gave the agency discretion to decide which applicants were to receive the loans. The agency's denial of the farmer's application therefore did not deprive her of a property or liberty interest protected by the due process clause.

(B) No, because the denial of a loan may deprive the farmer of an established liberty interest to pursue her chosen occupation.

Incorrect. The farmer's decision to pursue her chosen occupation does not qualify as a liberty interest protected by the due process clause. The court should uphold the agency's decision, because the due process clause does not require the government to provide the farmer an opportunity for an administrative hearing on her loan application. The farmer had no legitimate claim of entitlement to a loan, because the statute gave the agency discretion to decide which applicants were to receive the loans. The agency's denial of the farmer's loan application therefore did not deprive her of a property or liberty interest protected by the due process clause.

(C) Yes, because the applicable statute gives the farmer no legitimate claim of entitlement to receive a loan.

Correct. The court should uphold the agency's decision, because the due process clause does not require the government to provide the farmer an opportunity for an administrative hearing on her loan application. The farmer had no legitimate claim of entitlement to a loan, because the statute gave the agency discretion to decide which applicants were to receive the loans. The agency's denial of the farmer's application therefore did not deprive her of a property or liberty interest protected by the due process clause.

(D) Yes, because the spending clause of Article I, Section 8, gives Congress plenary power to control the distribution of appropriated funds in any manner it wishes.

Incorrect. Although Congress has broad authority to control the distribution of appropriated funds, that authority is subject to many constitutional limitations on the legislative power, including the due process clause of the Fifth Amendment. While the court should uphold the agency's decision, it should do so because the due process clause does not require the government to provide the farmer an opportunity for an administrative hearing on her loan application. The farmer had no legitimate claim of entitlement to a loan, because the statute gave the agency discretion to decide which applicants were to receive the loans. The agency's denial of the farmer's application therefore did not deprive her of a property or liberty interest protected by the due process clause.

Question 8

A state law provides that only U.S. citizens may serve as jurors in the state courts of that state. A woman who is a lawful resident alien and who has resided in the state for many years was summoned for jury duty in a state court. The woman's name was selected from a list of potential jurors that was compiled from a comprehensive list of local residents. She was disqualified from service solely because she is not a U.S. citizen.

The woman has filed an action for a declaratory judgment that the state law is unconstitutional. Who should prevail in this action?

(A) The state, because a state may limit to U.S. citizens functions that are an integral part of the process of self-government.

Correct. The state should prevail, because the law excluding aliens from jury service is rationally related to the state's legitimate interest in ensuring that only citizens perform functions that are central to self-government. Although strict scrutiny generally applies to state laws that discriminate against aliens, rational basis scrutiny is appropriate when alienage classifications restrict the right to participate in functions that are central to self-government, such as voting, running for office, or serving on a jury.

(B) The state, because jury service is a privilege, not a right, and therefore it is not a liberty interest protected by the due process clause of the Fourteenth Amendment.

Incorrect. Application of the due process clause no longer turns on whether the individual interest involved is a right or a privilege. In any event, the woman's constitutional challenge to the state law should be based on the equal protection clause rather than on the due process clause. While the state should prevail, it is because the law excluding aliens from jury service is rationally related to the state's legitimate interest in ensuring that only citizens perform functions that are central to self-government. Although strict scrutiny generally applies to state laws that discriminate against aliens, rational basis scrutiny is appropriate when alienage classifications restrict the right to participate in functions that are central to self-government, such as voting, running for office, or serving on a jury.

(C) The woman, because the Constitution gives Congress plenary power to make classifications with respect to aliens.

Incorrect. Although the Constitution gives Congress plenary power to control immigration, states may exercise their police powers to regulate the conduct of aliens within their borders unless the regulation is preempted by federal law or otherwise violates the Constitution. While strict scrutiny generally applies to state laws that discriminate against aliens, rational basis scrutiny is appropriate when alienage classifications restrict the right to participate in functions that are central to self-government, such as voting, running for office, or serving on a jury. The state should prevail here, because the law excluding aliens from jury service is rationally related to the state's legitimate interest in ensuring that only citizens perform functions that are central to self-government.

(D) The woman, because the state has not articulated a legitimate reason for prohibiting resident aliens from serving as jurors in the state's courts.

Incorrect. The state should prevail, because the law excluding aliens from jury service is rationally related to the state's legitimate interest in ensuring that only citizens perform functions that are central to self-government. Although strict scrutiny generally applies to state laws that discriminate against aliens, rational basis scrutiny is appropriate when alienage classifications restrict the right to participate in functions that are central to self-government, such as voting, running for office, or serving on a jury.

Question 9

Congress enacted a statute that made it illegal for "any employee, without the consent of his or her employer, to post on the Internet any information concerning the employer." The purpose of the statute was to prevent employees from revealing their employers' trade secrets.

Is the statute constitutional?

(A) No, because it is not narrowly tailored to further a compelling government interest.

Correct. The statute violates the freedom of speech protected by the First Amendment. The statute targets speech based on its content, because it prohibits employees from posting only "information concerning the employer" on the Internet. Because the statute is a content-based restriction on speech, it is subject to strict judicial scrutiny. Speech restrictions rarely survive strict scrutiny; the government must prove that the restriction is necessary to further a compelling government interest. Even if the government's interest in preventing employees from revealing trade secrets were deemed compelling, Congress could enact legislation utilizing less speech-restrictive means to protect trade secrets.

(B) No, because it targets a particular medium of communication for special regulation.

Incorrect. The statute does target one medium of communication—Internet postings—and this focus may cause a court to look more closely at the restriction when evaluating its constitutionality. However, a statute does not violate the First Amendment simply because it targets a particular medium. In this case, the statute violates the freedom of speech protected by the First Amendment because it targets speech based on its content; it prohibits employees from posting only "information concerning the employer" on the Internet. Because the statute is a content-based restriction on speech, it is subject to strict judicial scrutiny. Speech restrictions rarely survive strict scrutiny; the government must prove that the restriction is necessary to further a compelling government interest. Even if the government's interest in preventing employees from revealing trade secrets were deemed compelling, Congress could enact legislation utilizing less speech-restrictive means to protect trade secrets.

(C) Yes, because it leaves open ample alternative channels of communication.

Incorrect. The statute leaves open channels of communication other than the Internet, but this fact does not save the statute. The availability of ample alternative channels of communication is an element of the First Amendment test for evaluating speech restrictions that are content-neutral, but it is not as important with respect to content-based restrictions. In this case, the statute violates the freedom of speech protected by the First Amendment because it targets speech based on its content; it prohibits employees from posting only "information concerning the employer" on the Internet. Because the statute is a content-based restriction on speech, it is subject to strict judicial scrutiny. Speech restrictions rarely survive strict scrutiny; the government must prove that the restriction is necessary to further a compelling government interest. Even if the government's interest in preventing employees from revealing trade secrets were deemed compelling, Congress could enact legislation utilizing less speech-restrictive means to protect trade secrets.

(D) Yes, because it prevents employees from engaging in unethical conduct.

Incorrect. The statute may prevent employees from engaging in unethical conduct, but this fact does not save the statute. The statute violates the freedom of speech protected by the First Amendment because it targets speech based on its content; it prohibits employees from posting only "information concerning the employer" on the Internet. Because the statute is a content-based restriction on speech, it is subject to strict judicial scrutiny. Speech restrictions rarely survive strict scrutiny; the government must prove that the restriction is necessary to further a compelling government interest. Even if the government's interest in preventing employees from revealing trade secrets were deemed compelling, Congress could enact legislation utilizing less speech-restrictive means to protect trade secrets.

Question 10

A state law imposed substantial regulations on insurance companies operating within the state with respect to their rates, cash reserves, and financial practices.

A privately owned insurance company operating within the state advertised that it wanted to hire a new data processor. After reviewing applications for that position, the company hired a woman who appeared to be well qualified. The company refused to consider the application of a man who was better qualified than the woman, because he was known to have radical political views.

The man sued the company, alleging only a violation of his federal constitutional right to freedom of expression. Is the man likely to prevail?

(A) No, because hiring decisions are wholly discretionary and thus are not governed by the First Amendment.

Incorrect. The First Amendment applies to discretionary decisions of governments and government officials. The man is unlikely to prevail, but it is because the First and Fourteenth Amendments generally apply only to the actions of governments and government officials, not to the actions of privately owned companies such as the insurance company.

(B) No, because the company is not subject to the provisions of the First and Fourteenth Amendments.

Correct. The man is unlikely to prevail, because the First and Fourteenth Amendments generally apply only to the actions of governments and government officials, not to the actions of privately owned companies such as the insurance company.

(C) Yes, because the company is affected with a public interest.

Incorrect. The question whether the First and Fourteenth Amendments apply to the actions of a privately owned company does not turn on whether the company is affected with a public interest. The man is unlikely to prevail, because the First and Fourteenth Amendments generally apply only to the actions of governments and government officials, not to the actions of privately owned companies such as the insurance company.

(D) Yes, because the company is substantially regulated by the state, and thus its employment decisions may fairly be attributed to the state.

Incorrect. The fact that the company is substantially regulated by the state does not make the company's actions subject to the First and Fourteenth Amendments. The man is unlikely to prevail, because the First and Fourteenth Amendments generally apply only to the actions of governments and government officials, not to the actions of privately owned companies such as the insurance company.

Question 11

In order to foster an environment conducive to learning, a school board enacted a dress code that prohibited all public high school students from wearing in school shorts cut above the knee. Because female students at the school considered it unfashionable to wear shorts cut at or below the knee, they no longer wore shorts to school. On the other hand, male students at the school regularly wore shorts cut at or below the knee because they considered such shorts to be fashionable.

Female students sued to challenge the constitutionality of the dress code on the ground that it denied them the equal protection of the laws.

Should the court uphold the dress code?

(A) No, because the dress code is not necessary to further a compelling state interest.

Incorrect. The court should uphold the dress code, because the code is rationally related to the state's legitimate interest in fostering a proper educational environment. The dress code should not trigger heightened judicial scrutiny, because there are no facts to suggest that the purpose of the code is to discriminate against female students.

(B) No, because the dress code is not substantially related to an important state interest.

Incorrect. The court should uphold the dress code, because the code is rationally related to the state's legitimate interest in fostering a proper educational environment. The dress code should not trigger heightened judicial scrutiny, because there are no facts to suggest that the purpose of the code is to discriminate against female students.

(C) Yes, because the dress code is narrowly tailored to further an important state interest.

Incorrect. While the court should uphold the dress code, it should do so because the code is rationally related to the state's legitimate interest in fostering a proper educational environment. The dress code should not trigger heightened judicial scrutiny, because there are no facts to suggest that the purpose of the code is to discriminate against female students.

(D) Yes, because the dress code is rationally related to a legitimate state interest.

Correct. The court should uphold the dress code, because the code is rationally related to the state's legitimate interest in fostering a proper educational environment. The dress code should not trigger heightened judicial scrutiny, because there are no facts to suggest that the purpose of the code is to discriminate against female students.

Question 12

A company owned a large tract of land that contained coal deposits that the company intended to mine. The company acquired mining equipment and began to plan its mining operations. Just as the company was about to begin mining, Congress enacted a statute that imposed a number of new environmental regulations and land-reclamation requirements on all mining operations within the United States. The statute made the company's planned mining operations economically infeasible. As a result, the company sold the tract of land to a farmer. While the sale price allowed the company to recover its original investment in the land, it did not cover the additional cost of the mining equipment the company had purchased or the profits it had expected to earn from its mining operations on the land.

In an action filed against the appropriate federal official, the company claims that the statute effected a taking of its property for which it is entitled to just compensation in an amount equal to the cost of the mining equipment it purchased and the profits it expected to earn from its mining operations on the land.

Which of the following is the most appropriate result in the action?

(A) The company should prevail on its claims for the cost of the mining equipment and for its lost profits.

Incorrect. The company should not prevail on any aspect of its claim for just compensation. The statute did not effect a taking of the company's land or of the mining equipment, because the new regulations did not deny all economically viable use of the land. The company recovered its original investment in the land by selling it to the farmer, and the land is economically viable as farmland. The company may sell the mining equipment or use it for mining on other land. Finally, the profits the company expected to earn from its mining operations do not constitute a property interest subject to the takings clause.

(B) The company should prevail on its claim for the cost of the mining equipment, but not for its lost profits.

Incorrect. The company should not prevail on any aspect of its claim for just compensation. The statute did not affect a taking of the company's land or of the mining equipment, because the new regulations did not deny all economically viable use of the land. The company recovered its original investment in the land by selling it to the farmer, and the land is economically viable as farmland. The company may sell the mining equipment or use it for mining on other land. Finally, the profits the company expected to earn from its mining operations do not constitute a property interest subject to the takings clause.

(C) The company should prevail on its claim for lost profits, but not for the cost of the mining equipment.

Incorrect. The company should not prevail on any aspect of its claim for just compensation. The statute did not affect a taking of the company's land or of the mining equipment, because the new regulations did not deny all economically viable use of the land. The company recovered its original investment in the land by selling it to the farmer, and the land is economically viable as farmland. The company may sell the mining equipment or use it for mining on other land. Finally, the profits the company expected to earn from its mining operations do not constitute a property interest subject to the takings clause.

(D) The company should not prevail on its claim for the cost of the mining equipment or for its lost profits.

Correct. The company should not prevail on any aspect of its claim for just compensation. The statute did not affect a taking of the company's land or of the mining equipment, because the new regulations did not deny all economically viable use of the land. The company recovered its original investment in the land by selling it to the farmer, and the land is economically viable as farmland. The company may sell the mining equipment or use it for mining on other land. Finally, the profits the company expected to earn from its mining operations do not constitute a property interest subject to the takings clause.

Question 13

A number of psychotherapists routinely send mailings to victims of car accidents informing the victims of the possibility of developing post-traumatic stress disorder (PTSD) as the result of the accidents, and offering psychotherapy services. Although PTSD is a possible result of a car accident, it is not common.

Many accident victims in a particular state who received the mailings complained that the mailings were disturbing and were an invasion of their privacy. These victims also reported that as a result of the mailings, their regard for psychotherapists and for psychotherapy as a form of treatment had diminished.

In response, the state enacted a law prohibiting any licensed psychotherapist from sending mailings that raised the concern of PTSD to any car accident victim in the state until 30 days after the accident. The state justified the law as an effort to address the victims' complaints as well as to protect the reputation of psychotherapy as a form of treatment.

Is this law constitutional?

(A) No, because the law singles out one type of message for prohibition while allowing others.

Incorrect. It is true that the law singles out one type of message for prohibition while allowing other types. Such content-based restrictions on speech typically are subjected to strict judicial scrutiny and are invalidated. This law, however, is subject to a less exacting form of judicial scrutiny because it restricts commercial speech.

The law is constitutional, because it satisfies the First Amendment standards for government restrictions on commercial speech. The mailings qualify as commercial speech, because they advertise services provided by the psychotherapists. A restriction on commercial speech is subject to a form of intermediate judicial scrutiny, requiring the government to show that the restriction directly advances an important government interest and that the restriction is not substantially more extensive than necessary to protect that interest. The law here satisfies that standard; the 30-day waiting period for the psychotherapists' mailings narrowly serves the government's substantial interests in protecting both the privacy of accident victims and the public regard for psychotherapy.

(B) No, because the mailings provide information to consumers.

Incorrect. The fact that the mailings provide information to consumers entitles the mailings to First Amendment protection. However, because the mailings advertise the services of psychotherapists, they contain commercial speech and therefore are entitled to less constitutional protection than other forms of speech.

The law is constitutional, because it satisfies the First Amendment standards for government restrictions on commercial speech. A restriction on commercial speech is subject to a form of intermediate judicial scrutiny, requiring the government to show that the restriction directly advances an important government interest and that the restriction is not substantially more extensive than necessary to protect that interest. The law here satisfies that standard; the 30-day waiting period for the psychotherapists' mailings narrowly serves the government's substantial interests in protecting both the privacy of accident victims and the public regard for psychotherapy.

(C) Yes, because mailings suggesting the possibility of developing PTSD as the result of an accident are misleading.

Incorrect. Misleading commercial speech is not protected by the First Amendment, and governments therefore are free to restrict such speech. The mailings in this case are not misleading, however, because the facts state that "PTSD is a possible result" of car accidents.

The law is constitutional, because it satisfies the First Amendment standards for government restrictions on commercial speech. The mailings qualify as commercial speech because they advertise services provided by the psychotherapists. A restriction on commercial speech is subject to a form of intermediate judicial scrutiny, requiring the government to show that the restriction directly advances an important government interest and that the restriction is not substantially more extensive than necessary to protect that interest. The law here satisfies that standard; the 30-day waiting period for the psychotherapists' mailings narrowly serves the government's substantial interests in protecting both the privacy of accident victims and the public regard for psychotherapy.

(D) Yes, because the law protects the privacy of accident victims and the public regard for psychotherapy without being substantially more restrictive than necessary.

Correct. The law is constitutional, because it satisfies the First Amendment standards for government restrictions on commercial speech. The mailings contain commercial speech, because they advertise services provided by the psychotherapists. A restriction on commercial speech is subject to a form of intermediate judicial scrutiny, requiring the government to show that the restriction directly advances an important government interest and that the restriction is not substantially more extensive than necessary to protect that interest. The law here satisfies that standard; the 30-day waiting period for the psychotherapists' mailings narrowly serves the government's substantial interests in protecting both the privacy of accident victims and the public regard for psychotherapy.

Question 14

A clerical employee of a city water department was responsible for sending out water bills to customers. His work in this respect had always been satisfactory.

The employee's sister ran in a recent election against the incumbent mayor, but she lost. The employee had supported his sister in the election campaign. After the mayor found out about this, she fired the employee solely because his support for the sister indicated that he was "disloyal" to the mayor. The city's charter provides that "all employees of the city work at the pleasure of the mayor."

Is the mayor's action constitutional?

(A) No, because public employees have a property interest in their employment, which gives them a right to a hearing prior to discharge.

Incorrect. A public employee has a property interest in his or her employment if the employee can be fired only for cause. Because the city's charter provides that "all employees of the city work at the pleasure of the mayor," the clerical employee does not have a property interest in his employment.

Nevertheless, the mayor's action is unconstitutional, because it violates the employee's right to freedom of expression and association protected by the First Amendment. The U.S. Supreme Court has held that the government may not fire an employee because of the employee's political views or affiliations unless certain political views or affiliations are required for the effective performance of the employee's job. The political views or affiliations of a clerical employee of a city water department are not relevant to the employee's job, and thus the employee may not be fired because of them.

(B) No, because the mayor's action violates the employee's right to freedom of expression and association.

Correct. The mayor's action is unconstitutional, because it violates the employee's right to freedom of expression and association protected by the First Amendment. The U.S. Supreme Court has held that the government may not fire an employee because of the employee's political views or affiliations unless certain political views or affiliations are required for the effective performance of the employee's job. The political views or affiliations of a clerical employee of a city water department are not relevant to the employee's job, and thus the employee may not be fired because of them.

(C) Yes, because the employee has no property interest in his job since the city charter provides that he holds the job "at the pleasure of the mayor."

Incorrect. It is true that the employee has no property interest in his job, and therefore he is not entitled to the constitutional protections of procedural due process. Nevertheless, the mayor's action is unconstitutional, because it violates the employee's right to freedom of expression and association protected by the First Amendment. The U.S. Supreme Court has held that the government may not fire an employee because of the employee's political views or affiliations unless certain political views or affiliations are required for the effective performance of the employee's job. The political views or affiliations of a clerical employee of a city water department are not relevant to the employee's job, and thus the employee may not be fired because of them.

(D) Yes, because the mayor may require members of her administration to be politically loyal to her.

Incorrect. The mayor may require members of her administration to be politically loyal to her only if political loyalty is required for the effective performance of the job in question. The U.S. Supreme Court has held that the government may not fire an employee because of the employee's political views or affiliations unless certain political views or affiliations are required for the effective performance of the employee's job. The political views or affiliations of a clerical employee of a city water department are not relevant to the employee's job, and thus the employee may not be fired because of them. The mayor's action is unconstitutional, because it violates the employee's right to freedom of expression and association protected by the First Amendment.

Question 15

An environmental organization's stated mission is to support environmental causes. The organization's membership is generally open to the public, but its bylaws permit its officers to refuse to admit anyone to membership who does not adhere to the organization's mission statement.

In a recent state administrative proceeding, the organization opposed plans to begin mining operations in the mountains surrounding a small town. Its opposition prevented the mine from being opened on schedule. In an effort to force the organization to withdraw its opposition, certain residents of the town attended a meeting of the organization and tried to become members, but the officers refused to admit them. The residents sued the organization, claiming that the refusal to admit them was discriminatory and violated a local ordinance that prohibits any organization from discriminating on the basis of an individual's political views. The organization responded that the ordinance is unconstitutional as applied to its membership decisions.

Are the residents likely to prevail in their claim?

(A) No, because the membership policies of a private organization are not state action.

Incorrect. It is true that the membership policies of a private organization are not state action. The local ordinance on which the residents base their suit is state action, however, and it is subject to the requirements of the First Amendment.

The residents are not likely to prevail in their claim, because it would violate the environmental organization's First Amendment right to freedom of association if the state were to force the organization to accept the residents as members. The U.S. Supreme Court has held that the forced inclusion of an unwanted person in a group violates the group's freedom of association if including that person would significantly affect the group's ability to express its viewpoints. The freedom of association entitles the environmental organization to refuse membership to the residents, because admitting them would effect a change in the organization's viewpoint on the mining operations.

(B) No, because the organization's right to freedom of association allows it to refuse to admit potential members who do not adhere to its mission statement.
Correct. The residents are not likely to prevail in their claim, because it would violate the environmental organization's First Amendment right to freedom of association if the state were to force the organization to accept the residents as members. The U.S. Supreme Court has held that the forced inclusion of an unwanted person in a group violates the group's freedom of association if including that person would significantly affect the group's ability to express its viewpoints. The freedom of association entitles the environmental organization to refuse membership to the residents, because admitting them would effect a change in the organization's viewpoint on the mining operations.

(C) Yes, because the action of the officers in refusing to admit the residents as members violates equal protection of the laws.
Incorrect. The action of the officers in refusing to admit the residents as members is not subject to the equal protection clause, because the environmental organization is a private entity, and therefore the conduct of the organization's officers does not constitute state action.

The residents are not likely to prevail in their claim, because it would violate the environmental organization's First Amendment right to freedom of association if the state were to force the organization to accept the residents as members. The U.S. Supreme Court has held that the forced inclusion of an unwanted person in a group violates the group's freedom of association if including that person would significantly affect the group's ability to express its viewpoints. The freedom of association entitles the environmental organization to refuse membership to the residents, because admitting them would effect a change in the organization's viewpoint on the mining operations.

(D) Yes, because the ordinance serves the compelling interest of protecting the residents' free speech rights.
Incorrect. The U.S. Supreme Court has held that even statutes that support compelling interests do not justify the severe burden on an organization's freedom of association that would result from forcing an organization to accept members who would significantly affect the organization's ability to express its viewpoints. The residents are not likely to prevail in their claim, because it would violate the environmental organization's First Amendment right to freedom of association if the state were to force the organization to accept the residents as members. The U.S. Supreme Court has held that the forced inclusion of an unwanted person in a group violates the group's freedom of

association if including that person would significantly affect the group's ability to express its viewpoints. The freedom of association entitles the environmental organization to refuse membership to the residents, because admitting them would effect a change in the organization's viewpoint on the mining operations.

Question 16

A fatal virus recently infected poultry in several nations. Some scientific evidence indicates that the virus can be transmitted from poultry to humans.

Poultry farming is a major industry in several U.S. states. In one such state, the legislature has enacted a law imposing a fee of two cents per bird on all poultry farming and processing operations in the state. The purpose of the fee is to pay for a state inspection system to ensure that no poultry raised or processed in the state is infected with the virus.

A company that has poultry processing plants both in the state and in other states has sued to challenge the fee. Is the fee constitutional?

(A) No, because although it attaches only to intrastate activity, in the aggregate, the fee substantially affects interstate commerce.
Incorrect. Having a substantial effect on interstate commerce does not make the fee unconstitutional. The fee in this case is constitutional, because it does not violate the negative implications of the commerce clause: it does not discriminate against interstate commerce, and its burden on interstate commerce is not clearly excessive in relation to the legitimate public health benefit the inspection system will bring to the state.

(B) No, because it places an undue burden on interstate commerce in violation of the negative implications of the commerce clause.
Incorrect. The fee does not violate the negative implications of the commerce clause, because it does not discriminate against interstate commerce, and its burden on interstate commerce is not clearly excessive in relation to the legitimate public health benefit the inspection system will bring to the state. The fee is therefore constitutional.

(C) Yes, because it applies only to activities that take place wholly within the state, and it does not unduly burden interstate commerce.
Correct. The fee does not violate the negative implications of the commerce clause, because it does not discriminate against interstate commerce, and its burden on interstate commerce is not clearly excessive in relation to the legitimate public health benefit the inspection system will bring to the state.

(D) Yes, because it was enacted pursuant to the state's police power, which takes precedence over the negative implications of the commerce clause.
Incorrect. The fee was enacted pursuant to the state's police power, but the supremacy clause of the Constitution prohibits state laws that violate federal constitutional limits on state authority. The fee is constitutional, nonetheless, because it does not violate the negative implications of the commerce clause: it does not discriminate against interstate commerce, and its burden on interstate commerce is not clearly excessive in relation to the legitimate public health benefit the inspection system will bring to the state.

(C) Yes, because it applies only to activities that take place wholly within the state, and it does not unduly burden interstate commerce.
(D) Yes, because it was enacted pursuant to the state's police power, which takes precedence over the negative implications of the commerce clause.

CHAPTER 10

Mapping MBE Topics—Contracts

I. MIND MAP

Contracts is one of the few topics on the bar exam where you must make a decision about what law applies before you do any other analysis. Whether an MBE or essay question, your first decision must be whether the common law of contracts applies or whether the Uniform Commercial Code (UCC) Article 2 governing the sale of goods applies. Only then can you move forward with analyzing whether a contract exists, how the contract should be interpreted, whether each party performed its part of the bargain, whether the lack of performance constituted a breach of the contract, how third parties are impacted by the contract, and what remedies exist for the non-breaching party.

Your mind map then begins at contract formation, moving through interpretation and performance, before addressing remedies and third parties:

- UCC or common law?
  - Transaction in goods?
  - Mixed services and goods
  - Merchant?
- Contract formation
  - Offer/acceptance/consideration
  - Statute of Frauds
- Interpretation
  - Parol evidence
  - Warranties
- Performance
  - Conditions
- Remedies
- Third parties
  - Beneficiaries
  - Assignment
  - Delegation

Your analysis of whether the common law of contracts applies or whether the UCC applies is actually an analysis of whether this was a **transaction in goods**. The UCC only applies to a transaction in goods. Without a transaction in goods, the common law of contracts governs.

Real estate and services contracts are governed by common law. Thus, when the fact pattern involves services or real estate, just begin with a simple statement: "Because this is a services contract (or a real estate contract), the common law of contracts governs instead of the UCC." This sentence tells the examiners that you knew this was your first step and that you correctly determined the result.

If not a real estate and services contract, begin your answer with defining a transaction in goods, applying your facts, and concluding that the UCC applies. A transaction in goods is a sale of tangible, personal property. If the contract is a combination of services and the sale of goods, such as when one party sells the goods and agrees to install them, then your analysis determines which part is the most predominant and applies the law governing that aspect to the entire contract.

EXAM TIP

Common Law v. UCC? Always the first issue on every Contracts question!

If you decide that the UCC applies, then you have a second preliminary step: Are one or both parties a merchant? Several rules in Article 2 depend upon whether a party is a merchant. A merchant is "one who regularly deals in goods of the kind sold or who otherwise by his profession holds himself out as having special knowledge or skills as to the practices or goods involved."[1] Apply that definition to both parties.

Now that you know which law applies, you need to be sure a contract has been formed. If the fact pattern states that A and B entered into a valid contract, then you can skip this step. Do not analyze it, anyway. You would be wasting your time and the examiners would infer that you could not spot the actual issues.

Analyzing the **formation** of a contract focuses on the existence of mutual assent, consideration, and the absence of any defense to enforcement. Do not just state that a contract requires an offer, acceptance, and consideration. Always include that no defenses to enforcement must also exist.

EXAM TIP

An offer, acceptance, consideration, AND no defenses to enforcement are required for a contract. List all four requirements!

Understand that there are two types of contracts—bilateral and unilateral. A **bilateral contract** is formed by an exchange of promises. A **unilateral contract** is formed by a promise in exchange for performance.

Mutual assent is determined by whether there was an offer and an acceptance of that offer. An **offer** exists when there was intent to enter a contract through a promise or undertaking. The terms of the deal must be definite and certain, and the offer must be communicated to the offeree, giving her actual knowledge of the offer. An offer creates the power of acceptance in the person to whom the offer was made. However, an offer cannot be accepted if it has been terminated. Termination may be by the offeror or the offeree:

- By offeror—revocation
- By offeree
  - Rejection
  - Counteroffer

A **counteroffer** generally terminates the offer and creates a new offer. While mere bargaining is not a counteroffer, a conditional acceptance terminates the offer. The language will have an additional term, such as "provided," or "so long

---

1. U.C.C. § 2-104(1).

Bilateral v. Unilateral Contract

as," etc. If the acceptance does not contain the exact same terms as the offer, then the new terms are treated like a revocation of the original offer and a counteroffer under common law. This is known as the mirror-image rule.

Under the UCC, a change of terms is not a counteroffer and can constitute acceptance unless stated otherwise in one of the forms. This occurs when a buyer places an order and the seller's acceptance form contains different terms or the terms are not addressed in the order at all. Under the **battle of the forms**, this nonconforming acceptance is treated as a legally effective acceptance. Unless acceptance is expressly made conditional on assent to the additional or different terms, the nonconforming acceptance creates a valid and binding contract. If the buyer is a consumer, then the additional terms are treated as proposals. If both parties are merchants, additional terms become part of the contract unless the offer expressly limits acceptance to its terms, the offeror objects within a reasonable time, or the additional terms would materially alter the contract. If the terms are different, the knockout rule applies and omits the offeror's original provision and the offeree's differing provision from the resulting contract.

Under both the common law and the UCC, the offeror can control the method of **acceptance** by stating conditions. If the offer is silent as to the method of acceptance, the offeree may indicate its acceptance through starting performance. In a unilateral contract, the offeree must complete the performance for there to be a contract.

Acceptance by letter is valid upon dispatch—that is when the offeree places the letter in the mail. If the offeree changes its mind and sends a later acceptance, then whichever is received first controls.

A legally enforceable contract must also have **consideration**. In most situations, consideration is not an issue in real life. You do need to understand it as it will likely appear on MBE questions. Consideration is a bargained-for exchange.

The promise must induce the detriment and the detriment must induce the promise. An act of forbearance by the promisee is sufficient if it gives the promisor a benefit. The detriment and benefit must have legal value. Under the common law, a pre-existing contractual or statutory duty cannot act as consideration for a new promise. New consideration is required. Under the UCC, new consideration is not required to modify a sale of goods contract. Good faith is the test for changes to an existing sale of goods contract.

One substitute for consideration is **promissory estoppel** or detrimental reliance that requires:

1. Promise;
2. Reliance that is reasonable, detrimental, and foreseeable; and
3. Enforcement necessary to avoid injustice.

Defenses to the enforcement of a contract include lack of capacity; the statute of frauds; illegality; misrepresentation; nondisclosure; duress; unconscionability; and mistake of fact, whether mutual or unilateral. Individuals who lack capacity to contract include individuals under the age of 18; mental incompetents that lack the ability to understand the agreement; and intoxicated persons, if the other party has reason to know.

The **statute of frauds** is a heavily tested area on the bar exam. Spend considerable time understanding the doctrine. Five types of contracts fall within the statute of frauds:

- Promise to pay the debts of another (suretyship)
- Promise in consideration of marriage
- Service contract not capable of being performed within a year from the time of the contract
- Real estate contracts
- Sale of goods for $500 or more

These contracts must be evidenced by a writing signed by the parties sought to be bound. This does not mean the entire contract must be in writing, only that the party claiming a contract exists must show a writing signed by the defendant where the material terms of the contract are included. The UCC requirement does not look to the material terms, but instead that the writing states it is a contract for the sale of goods and contains the quantity of goods.

When both parties to a contract are mistaken about a material fact, then the contract is voidable by the adversely affected party. This mutual mistake of fact operates as a defense to contract enforcement. If, however, only one party is mistaken about the facts, the mistake does not prevent enforcement of the contract. But if the non-mistaken party knew or had reason to know about the mistake by the other party, the contract is voidable by the mistaken party.

Once the contract is formed, the next issues to address deal with the **interpretation** of the contract terms. Contracts are construed as a whole with a preference given to written or typed provisions using the ordinary meanings of words, and construed against the drafter if there is ambiguity. Two key areas should be considered in dealing with interpretation: gap filling provisions, such as warranties, and the parol evidence rule.

While parties generally reach explicit agreement on the essential parts of a contract, they often fail to be as explicit as to the details. Gaps result that are subject to more than one interpretation. Contract law supplies terms that govern areas where the contract is silent. The parties can override these terms by being explicit in their agreement. The UCC provides default rules for the sale of goods. One key area is warranties.

Applicants often confuse the different types of **warranties**: an express warranty, an implied warranty of merchantability, and an implied warranty of fitness for a particular purpose. Express warranties are created by the seller. These

Express Warranty

Implied Warranty of Merchantability

become part of the agreement if they are the basis of the bargain. The implied warranty of merchantability is included with every sale of goods. Goods must be fit for their ordinary purposes. Implied warranty of fitness for a particular purpose generally has unusual fact patterns. There must be a direct representation by the seller or the seller's representative that the product fits what the buyer wants. So look for the salesman who picks the product out for a buyer.

A seller can alter these implied warranties by explicitly excluding or modifying language mentioning merchantability. If in writing, it must be conspicuous. If the contract includes an expression such as "as is" or "with all faults" or similar language, that language is sufficient to call the buyer's attention to the exclusion of warranties. Course of dealing, course of performance, or usage of trade may also indicate that the warranty is excluded or modified.

Another gap filling issue is when the contract is missing terms completely. The UCC provides the missing terms. These missing terms include price, time, and place of delivery. The common law also provides missing terms including price and duration. Both sources of law include an obligation of good faith and fair dealing

Perhaps the most heavily tested contract interpretation topic is the **parol evidence rule**. The parol evidence rule governs whether the meaning of a document can be determined by the negotiations of the parties prior to the written contract. The admissibility of this evidence depends upon the answers to two questions. First, what is the purpose for which the evidence is being introduced? Second, does the evidence relate to a term or contract which is integrated?

Integration refers to whether the parties intended the written contract to be the final discussion as to specific terms. The court relies on whether a **merger clause** is included. The merger clause states words to the effect that the writing is the complete and entire agreement of the parties. The court may also look at how detailed the contract is.

Implied Warranty of Fitness for a Particular Purpose

If the purpose of the introduction of extrinsic evidence is to explain or interpret the terms of a written contract, parol evidence is admissible. Some jurisdictions first require a showing that the term is ambiguous. Unless the contract is completely integrated, parol evidence is admissible to supplement the terms of a written contract. The UCC will use usage of trade, course of dealing, and course of performance to supplement terms of the written contract. To contradict the terms of the agreement, parol evidence is admissible unless the contract is fully integrated. The UCC will again use course of dealing or course of performance to qualify the meaning of a term. The parol evidence rule does not bar evidence to prove the written agreement is invalid or unenforceable.

Other interpretation issues involve ambiguity, trade usage, and course of dealing.

A duty to perform is discharged by **performance**, by tender of performance, and by a completed condition subsequent. Performance is also discharged if performance is illegal, impossible, impractical, frustrated, or rescinded. Failure to fulfill a promise constitutes a breach of the contract.

Conditions in a contract can be express, implied, or constructive. Conditions can be precedent, concurrent, or subsequent. Constructive conditions are read into the contract by a court; or, if both performances can be performed simultaneously, then each is a constructive condition precedent to each other. If one party's performance will take longer, it is a constructive condition precedent to the other. Failure to fulfill a condition does not necessarily constitute breach of the contract, but may relieve the other party from performance.

Breach occurs when there is a failure to perform when under a duty to perform. If a minor breach, it does not relieve the non-breaching party from performance, but that party is entitled to damages. A material breach excuses the non-breaching party from performance and he is entitled to all available remedies.

Under the UCC, if the goods or their delivery fail to conform in any way with the contract, the buyer may reject them, accept them, or just accept certain ones. Buyer cannot reject after already accepting by inspecting and indicating the goods do conform or by failing to inspect. Acceptance may be revoked if the goods are so defective that their value is substantially impaired.

When considering modification issues, carefully consider the pre-existing duty rule under the common law. In essence, a promisor cannot provide consideration where that consideration is a duty the promisor is already obligated to perform. If the parties mutually agree to modify the contract terms, then the pre-existing duty rule is no longer at issue. Under the UCC, the pre-existing duty rule is abolished and an agreement modifying an existing contract needs no consideration. Instead, a good faith test is used.

Remedies issues require identifying whether monetary damages or an equitable remedy is available. Under the common law, **monetary damages** range from expectation damages, reliance damages, restitution, and liquidated damages. Under the UCC, the seller's remedies depend on whether the goods have been delivered. A buyer's remedies include damages or specific performance. One key factor is whether the buyer has covered its loss by purchasing replacement goods.

Equitable remedies include specific performance, restitution, unjust enrichment, and negative injunctive relief. **Specific performance** is an extraordinary remedy available only when a monetary award would be inadequate to grant relief to the aggrieved party. Specific performance is available for unique objects and real property. Specific performance is usually not available for personal services contracts or contracts requiring on-going cooperation between the parties. When considering an equitable remedy, the court will consider whether the aggrieved party has clean hands or whether the party has waited too long to seek recovery, a defense called "**laches.**"

Third parties come into play in three ways: as a beneficiary, through an assignment, or through delegation of the obligation. The issue with **third-party beneficiaries** is whether they have standing to sue the promisor. Incidental beneficiaries are those that benefit from a promisor's performance, but were not intended to benefit. An incidental beneficiary has no standing to enforce the contract.

Intended beneficiaries arise when the promisor's performance was intended to benefit that third party. Intended third-party beneficiaries may enforce the contract against a breaching promisor. They do not, however, have rights against the promisee in the event the performance is not forthcoming. There must be an independent obligation for the promisee to be liable.

An **assignment** is a transfer of a right to receive a performance under a contract. The owner of the right must manifest an intention to make a present transfer of the right. Partial assignments are valid. The assignee may then enforce the contract against the obligor. Certain rights are not assignable: those that substantially change the contract's risks/duties, those that are for future rights to arise under future contracts, and those that are illegal.

A **delegation** occurs when a third party agrees to satisfy a performance obligation owed by one of the parties to a contract. A delegation does not relieve the delegator from his obligations under the contract and the delegator remains liable for its performance unless there has been a **novation**. A novation occurs when the obligee agrees to release the delegator in return for the liability of the delagatee.

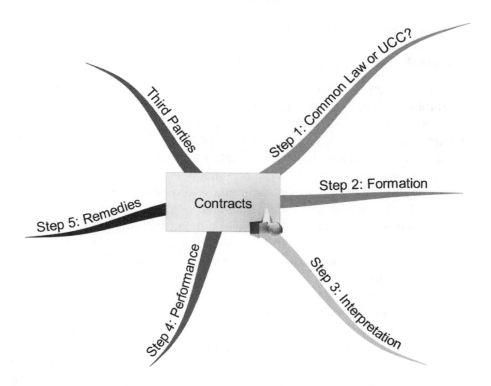

Certain duties are not delegable. These include personal performance con-tracts when the recipient relies on the quality of the party who is to render the performance. Duties cannot be delegated if the contract prohibits delegation.

Difficulties on contracts questions arise if the applicant does not understand when the UCC and the common law differ. It is useful to make a chart of the specific provisions that differ. When analyzing fact patterns, keep track of the parties' promises. Who promised what to whom? Watch for the details in the question. For example, if a promisor delegates to John with equivalent experience as a contractor or if a promisor delegates to John who is just starting his business—that small difference in facts probably makes the difference in whether the delegation is valid.

II. MBE STRATEGIES[2]

Common law questions and UCC questions cover most of the same topics. Approximately 50% of the questions will cover Formation and Performance. Interpretation, Remedies, and Third Party Rights constitute the remaining 50%. Approximately 25% of the total number of questions will be based on Articles 1 and 2 of the UCC.

Chart out the key differences between the UCC and the common law and have them solidly memorized. Particularly look at modification of agreements, irrevocability of offers, and delay in performance. MBE questions frequently focus on those distinctions with one response correctly laying out the UCC response and another response correctly laying out the common law response.

---

2. Some of these strategies are from Steven L. Emanuel, *Strategies & Tactics for the MBE* 69-80 (5th ed. 2013).

If you are not careful about which applies to the fact pattern, you will choose the wrong response.

Use these strategies to analyze contracts questions:

- Consideration is a bargained-for exchange, plus either detriment to the promisee or benefit to the promisor. Key is the bargain. Detriment to the promisee may be surrender of a legal claim.
- Find that a contract exists, wherever possible. Lack of an enforceable contract is a prerequisite to promissory estoppel or quasi contract.
- Determine what interpretation a reasonable person, knowing all that the parties know, would place on the terms. Avoid extraordinary or unusually strict interpretations of contract language.
- If the parties fully address a matter in the contract, the court will not go outside "the four corners" of the contract to use gap-filling provisions.
- When you encounter an oral contract on an MBE question, methodically check it against your memorized list of contracts covered by the Statute of Frauds. You must know when the need for a writing will be excused at common law and under the UCC.
- The parol evidence rule does not bar evidence of defects in contract formation, such as lack of consideration, fraud, and duress.
- Even if a court determines that an agreement is only partially integrated, the written agreement will be considered final as to the terms it does state.
- Only intended beneficiaries have enforceable rights.
- Beneficiary's rights are not enforceable until they vest—parties can modify or rescind before vesting.
- A third-party beneficiary's rights cannot vest until he knows about the contract.
- Meaningless details are relevant! They are there for a reason. If someone is retired, they are not a merchant. If someone is an experienced carpenter, then in all likelihood a duty to perform could be delegated to that person.
- Keep track of third-party beneficiaries and assignees. They are easy to keep track of as a beneficiary is created in the contract and an assignee gains rights later when a party transfers his contract rights to the assignee.

Because of the conflux of UCC and common law rules, contract MBE questions can be difficult. First determine if it is a transaction in goods. Keep track of the parties—offeror v. offeree, merchant v. non-merchant, third-party beneficiary v. assignee. Determine who promised what and then question if the promise was fulfilled. Follow your mind map to then consider at what stage in the contract's life the issue arises. Then you know what rule to apply to determine the correct response.

III. ESSAY PRACTICE QUESTION[3]

Baker is a renowned pastry chef. Café, a sole proprietorship, is a well-known restaurant in need of hiring a pastry chef. Baker and Café's Owner had extensive conversations regarding Baker coming to work at Café. On May 1, a week after those conversations occurred, Baker sent Café a signed letter dated May 1 stating: "I will work for Café as a head pastry chef for two years for an annual salary of $100,000."

On the morning of May 7, Café's Owner telephoned Baker and said: "The $100,000 is pretty stiff. Could you possibly consider working for less?" Baker replied: "I am a renowned pastry chef. I will not work for any less!"

Later that morning, Café's Owner sent Baker a signed letter by regular mail stating: "You obviously think you are too good for my restaurant. I am no longer interested in hiring you to work at Café."

Later that afternoon, Café's Owner had a change of heart and sent Baker a registered, express-mailed signed letter stating: "Okay, if you really won't work for less, I agree to pay you the $100,000 a year you demand to work as head pastry chef at Café for two years."

On May 10, the registered, express-mail letter was delivered to Baker's office. The regular-mail letter containing the rejection was still on its way. Baker accepted delivery of the registered, express-mail letter from the postal carrier and placed it on his desk without opening it.

On May 11, before Baker read the registered, express-mail letter on his desk, he accepted an offer to work for Restaurant. As a courtesy, Baker called Café's Owner and said, "Sorry, I just took a job at Restaurant. Too bad you couldn't afford me." Café's Owner responded, "You can't work for Restaurant, I already accepted your offer to work for Café for $100,000 a year."

Does Café have an enforceable contract with Baker? Explain.

---

3. The Multistate Bar Examination ("MBE®") questions, the Multistate Essay Examination ("MEE®") questions, and excerpts from the Multistate Performance Tests ("MPT®") have been reprinted by permission from the NCBE®. Copyright© by the National Conference of Bar Examiners. All rights reserved.

IV. SCORE SHEET

Stated	Implied	
		1. Formation
____	____	**Conclusion:** Café has an enforceable contract with Baker.
____	____	**Issue:** At issue is whether Café accepted an offer from Baker and, if so, whether the Statute of Frauds is available to Baker as a defense.
____	____	**Rule:** Under contract common law,
____	____	A contract requires mutual assent (offer and acceptance), consideration, and the absence of any formation defenses.
____	____	An offer is an expression of promise, undertaking, or commitment to enter into a contract. It contains terms that are definite and certain and is communicated to the offeree.
____	____	Once an offer is made, it may be accepted or rejected until and unless it is terminated.
____	____	At common law, which governs contracts for services (the U.C.C. governs contracts for the sale of goods), an offeree may accept an offer expressly or by other means not relevant here, or reject the offer.
____	____	An acceptance is a manifestation of assent to the terms of an offer in the manner prescribed or authorized by the offer.
____	____	Under the "mailbox rule," an acceptance is effective at the moment of dispatch.
____	____	Rejection of an offer may be made expressly or by making a counteroffer, i.e., an offer that contains the same subject matter as the original offer but that differs in its terms.
____	____	A counteroffer is both a rejection of the original offer, which terminates the offer, and a new offer.
____	____	A mere inquiry is not a counteroffer.
____	____	A rejection is effective upon receipt.
____	____	Note that the mailbox rule does not apply if an offeree sends a rejection and then sends an acceptance—in that case, whichever is received first is effective.
____	____	**Application:** Here,
____	____	The deal here is governed by common law because it involves a contract for services, i.e., an employment contract.
____	____	Baker's letter to Café on May 1, stating that he will work for Café as head pastry chef, was a valid offer because its terms were definite and certain (the letter included the job title, term of employment, and salary) and it was communicated to Café via mail. Thus, it was a valid offer.
____	____	Café's first response to Baker's offer on May 7, telling Baker that the salary amount contained in the offer was "pretty stiff," and asking Baker if he would "possibly consider working for less" was mere inquiry.
____	____	The response did not flatly reject the offer; it merely raised the question of whether Baker would consider working for less money. Thus, it was not a rejection and counteroffer and did not terminate Café's power to accept (or reject) Baker's offer.
____	____	Café's second communication regarding Baker's offer—made later that same morning— constituted a rejection.
____	____	In plain terms, Café rejected Baker's offer in a signed letter sent by regular mail.

continued on next page

Stated	Implied	
_____	_____	However, such a rejection would not be effective—i.e., would not terminate the offer and Café's power of acceptance—until it was received by Baker.
_____	_____	Café's third communication regarding Baker's offer was made later on the same day—he sent a letter accepting Baker's offer by registered, express mail.
_____	_____	Because Café had sent a rejection letter first, the mailbox rule did not apply to the acceptance and it was not effective upon dispatch.
_____	_____	Instead, whichever letter was received first was effective.
_____	_____	In this case, the acceptance letter was received first. Baker's act of accepting delivery of the letter from the postal carrier is all that matters; the fact that he did not open the letter or know its contents is irrelevant.
_____	_____	**Conclusion:** Therefore,
_____	_____	Because the facts do not reveal any formation defenses, such as lack of capacity, fraud, or duress, Baker's receipt of Café's acceptance before his receipt of Café's rejection was sufficient to form a contract.
		### 2. Statute of Frauds
_____	_____	**Conclusion on Statute of Frauds:** Moreover, the contract is enforceable, as no defense to enforcement is apparent on the facts. The only defense even remotely raised by the facts is the Statute of Frauds.
_____	_____	**Rule:** Under the Statute, contracts that cannot by their terms be performed within a year are unenforceable unless they are evidenced by a writing or writings signed by the party to be bound and containing the contract's essential terms, including the identity of the party to be charged and a description of the contract's subject matter.
_____	_____	**Application/Conclusion:** Here,
_____	_____	The subject matter of the contract is employment for two years. Thus, the contract must be evidenced by a writing signed by the party sought to be bound.
_____	_____	Here, Café Owner is seeking to hold Baker to the contract, so we must look for a sufficient writing signed by Baker.
_____	_____	In this case, Baker's letter constitutes a sufficient writing. It identifies himself as the person to be hired, describes the employment position at issue (head pastry chef), states the term of employment (two years), and includes the salary ($100,000/year).
_____	_____	**Conclusion:** Thus, the Statute of Frauds has been satisfied and the contract is enforceable against Baker.
_____	_____	However, as this is a contract for services, the court will not enforce it through an order for specific performance.
_____	_____	A court will not order specific performance of a contract for services, both because of difficulties in enforcing such an order and because it may constitute involuntary servitude.
_____	_____	Instead, the court would likely award damages against Baker or prohibit him from working for anyone else during the two-year term of the contract.

V. MBE PRACTICE QUESTIONS[4]

Question 1

A restaurant supplier sent a letter to a regular customer offering to sell the customer an industrial freezer for $10,000. Two days later, the customer responded with a letter that stated: "I accept your offer on the condition that you provide me with a warranty that the freezer is merchantable." In response to the customer's letter, the supplier called the customer and stated that the offer was no longer open. The supplier promptly sold the freezer to another buyer for $11,000.

If the customer sues the supplier for breach of contract, is the customer likely to prevail?

(A) No, because the customer's letter added a term, making it a counteroffer.
(B) No, because the subsequent sale to a bona fide purchaser for value cut off the claims of the customer.
(C) Yes, because the customer's letter was an acceptance of the supplier's offer, since the warranty of merchantability was already implied in the sale.
(D) Yes, because the supplier's letter was a firm offer that could not be revoked for a reasonable time.

Question 2

A seller sent an email to a potential buyer, offering to sell his house to her for $150,000. The buyer immediately responded via email, asking whether the offer included the house's front porch swing. The seller emailed back: "No, it doesn't." The buyer then ordered a front porch swing and emailed back to the seller: "I accept your offer." The seller refused to sell the house to the buyer, claiming that the offer was no longer open.

Is there a contract for the sale of the house?

(A) No, because the buyer's initial email was a counteroffer.
(B) No, because the offer lapsed before the buyer accepted.
(C) Yes, because the buyer relied on the offer by ordering the swing.
(D) Yes, because the buyer's initial email merely asked for information.

Question 3

In a telephone conversation, a jewelry maker offered to buy 100 ounces of gold from a precious metals company if delivery could be made within 10 days. The jewelry maker did not specify a price, but the market price for 100 ounces of gold at the time of the conversation was approximately $65,000. Without otherwise responding, the company delivered the gold six days later.

In the meantime, the project for which the jewelry maker planned to use the gold was canceled. The jewelry maker therefore refused to accept delivery of the gold or to pay the $65,000 demanded by the company.

---

4. *Id.*

Is there an enforceable contract between the jewelry maker and the company?

(A) No, because the parties did not agree on a price term.
(B) No, because the parties did not put their agreement in writing.
(C) Yes, because the absence of a price term does not defeat the formation of a valid contract for the sale of goods where the parties otherwise intended to form a contract.
(D) Yes, because the company relied on an implied promise to pay when it delivered the gold.

Question 4

A man sent an email to a friend that stated: "Because you have been a great friend to me, I am going to give you a rare book that I own." The friend replied by an email that said: "Thanks for the rare book. I am going to give you my butterfly collection." The rare book was worth $10,000; the butterfly collection was worth $100. The friend delivered the butterfly collection to the man, but the man refused to deliver the book.

If the friend sues the man to recover the value of the book, how should the court rule?

(A) For the man, because there was no bargained-for exchange to support his promise.
(B) For the man, because the consideration given for his promise was inadequate.
(C) For the friend, because she gave the butterfly collection to the man in reliance on receiving the book.
(D) For the friend, because she conferred a benefit on the man by delivering the butterfly collection.

Question 5

A farmer who wanted to sell her land received a letter from a developer that stated, "I will pay you $1,100 an acre for your land." The farmer's letter of reply stated, "I accept your offer." Unbeknownst to the farmer, the developer had intended to offer only $1,000 per acre but had mistakenly typed "$1,100." As both parties knew, comparable land in the vicinity had been selling at prices between $1,000 and $1,200 per acre.

Which of the following states the probable legal consequences of the correspondence between the parties?

(A) There is no contract, because the parties attached materially different meanings to the price term.
(B) There is no enforceable contract, because the developer is entitled to rescission due to a mutual mistake as to a basic assumption of the contract.
(C) There is a contract formed at a price of $1,000 per acre.
(D) There is a contract formed at a price of $1,100 per acre.

Question 6

A buyer and a seller entered into a written contract for the sale of a copy machine, using the same form contract that they had used a number of times in the past. The contract stated that payment was due 30 days after delivery and provided that the writing contained the complete and exclusive statement of the parties' agreement.

On several past occasions, the buyer had taken a 5% discount from the contract price when paying within 10 days of delivery, and the seller had not objected. On this occasion, when the buyer took a 5% discount for paying within 10 days, the seller objected because his profit margin on this particular machine was smaller than on his other machines.

If the seller sues the buyer for breach of contract, may the buyer introduce evidence that the 5% discount was a term of the agreement?

(A) No, because the seller timely objected to the buyer's proposal for different terms.
(B) No, because the writing contained the complete and exclusive agreement of the parties.
(C) Yes, because a modification made in good faith does not require consideration.
(D) Yes, because evidence of course of dealing is admissible even if the writing contains the complete and exclusive agreement of the parties.

Question 7

A buyer purchased a new car from a dealer under a written contract that provided that the price of the car was $20,000 and that the buyer would receive a "trade-in allowance of $7,000 for the buyer's old car." The old car had recently been damaged in an accident. The contract contained a merger clause stating: "This writing constitutes the entire agreement of the parties, and there are no other understandings or agreements not set forth herein." When the buyer took possession of the new car, she delivered the old car to the dealer. At that time, the dealer claimed that the trade-in allowance included an assignment of the buyer's claim against her insurance company for damage to the old car. The buyer refused to provide the assignment.

The dealer sued the buyer to recover the insurance payment. The dealer has offered evidence that the parties agreed during their negotiations for the new car that the dealer was entitled to the insurance payment.

Should the court admit this evidence?

(A) No, because the dealer's acceptance of the old car bars any additional claim by the dealer.
(B) No, because the merger clause bars any evidence of the parties' prior discussions concerning the trade-in allowance.
(C) Yes, because a merger clause does not bar evidence of fraud.
(D) Yes, because the merger clause does not bar evidence to explain what the parties meant by "trade-in allowance."

Question 8

A buyer agreed in writing to purchase a car from a seller for $15,000, with the price to be paid on a specified date at the seller's showroom. The contract provided, and both parties intended, that time was of the essence. Before the specified date, however, the seller sold the car to a third party for $20,000. On the specified date, the buyer arrived at the showroom but brought only $10,000.

When the seller did not appear at the showroom, the buyer called the seller and asked whether the seller would accept $10,000 for the car immediately and the remaining $5,000 in six weeks. The seller told the buyer that he had sold the car to the third party.

If the buyer sues the seller for breach of contract, will the buyer be likely to prevail?

(A) No, because the contractual obligations were discharged on the ground of impossibility.

(B) No, because the buyer was not prepared to tender her performance on the specified date.

(C) Yes, because the buyer's breach was not material.

(D) Yes, because the seller anticipatorily repudiated the contract when he sold the car to the third party.

Question 9

A mill and a bakery entered into a written contract that obligated the mill to deliver to the bakery 1,000 pounds of flour every Monday for 26 weeks at a specified price per pound. The mill delivered the proper quantity of flour in a timely manner for the first 15 weeks. However, the 16th delivery was tendered on a Tuesday, and amounted to only 800 pounds. The mill told the bakery that the 200-pound shortage would be made up on the delivery due the following Monday. The late delivery and the 200-pound shortage will not significantly disrupt the bakery's operations.

How may the bakery legally respond to the nonconforming tender?

(A) Accept the 800 pounds tendered, but notify the mill that the bakery will cancel the contract if the exact amount is not delivered on the following Monday.

(B) Accept the 800 pounds tendered, but notify the mill that the bakery will deduct from the price any damages for losses due to the nonconforming tender.

(C) Reject the 800 pounds tendered, but notify the mill that the bakery will accept delivery the following Monday if it is conforming.

(D) Reject the 800 pounds tendered, and notify the mill that the bakery is canceling the contract.

Question 10

A buyer agreed to purchase a seller's house for $250,000 "on condition that the buyer obtain mortgage financing within 30 days." Thirty days later, the buyer told the seller that the buyer would not purchase the house because the buyer had not obtained mortgage financing. The seller asked the buyer where the buyer had tried to obtain mortgage financing, and the buyer responded, "I was busy and didn't have time to seek mortgage financing."

If the seller sues the buyer for breach of contract, is the court likely to find the buyer in breach?

(A) No, because the buyer's performance was subject to a condition that did not occur.

(B) No, because the promise was illusory since the buyer was not obligated to do anything.

(C) Yes, because a promise was implied that the buyer had to make reasonable efforts to obtain mortgage financing.

(D) Yes, because a reasonable interpretation of the agreement is that the buyer had an obligation to purchase the house for $250,000 in 30 days.

Question 11

A producer contracted to pay an inexperienced performer a specified salary to act in a small role in a play the producer was taking on a six-week road tour. The contract was for the duration of the tour. On the third day of the tour, the performer was hospitalized with a stomach disorder. The producer replaced her in the cast with an experienced actor. One week later, the performer recovered, but the producer refused to allow her to resume her original role for the remainder of the tour.

In an action by the performer against the producer for breach of contract, which of the following, if proved, would be the producer's best defense?

(A) The actor, by general acclaim, was much better in the role than the performer had been.

(B) The actor was the only replacement the producer could find, and the actor would accept nothing less than a contract for the remainder of the six-week tour.

(C) The producer offered to employ the performer as the actor's understudy for the remainder of the six-week tour at the performer's original salary, but the performer declined.

(D) Both the producer and the performer knew that a year earlier the performer had been incapacitated for a short period of time by the same kind of stomach disorder.

Question 12

An art collector paid a gallery $1,000 to purchase a framed drawing from the gallery's collection. The price included shipping by the gallery to the collector's home. The gallery's owner used inadequate materials to wrap the drawing. The frame broke during shipment and scratched the drawing, reducing the drawing's value to $300. The collector complained to the gallery owner, who told the collector to take the drawing to a specific art restorer to have the drawing repaired. The collector paid the restorer $400 to repair the drawing, but not all of the scratches could be fixed. The drawing, after being repaired, was worth $700. The gallery owner subsequently refused to pay either for the repairs or for the damage to the drawing.

In an action by the collector against the gallery owner for damages, which of the following awards is most likely?

(A) Nothing.
(B) $300.
(C) $400.
(D) $700.

Question 13

A businesswoman sold her business to a company for $25 million in cash pursuant to a written contract that was signed by both parties. Under the contract, the company agreed to employ the businesswoman for two years as a vice president at a salary of $150,000 per year. After six months, the company, without cause, fired the businesswoman.

Which of the following statements best describes the businesswoman's rights after the discharge?

(A) She can recover the promised salary for the remainder of the two years if she remains ready to work.
(B) She can recover the promised salary for the remainder of the two years if no comparable job is reasonably available and she does not take another job.
(C) She can rescind the contract of sale and get back her business upon tender to the company of $25 million.
(D) She can get specific performance of her right to serve as a vice president of the company for two years.

Question 14

On June 15, a teacher accepted a contract for a one-year position teaching math at a public high school at a salary of $50,000, starting in September. On June 22, the school informed the teacher that, due to a change in its planned math curriculum, it no longer needed a full-time math teacher. The school offered instead to employ the teacher as a part-time academic counselor at a salary of $20,000, starting in September. The teacher refused the school's offer. On June 29, the teacher was offered a one-year position to teach math at a nearby private academy for $47,000, starting in September. The teacher, however, decided to spend the year completing work on a graduate degree in mathematics and declined the academy's offer.

If the teacher sues the school for breach of contract, what is her most likely recovery?

(A) $50,000, the full contract amount.
(B) $30,000, the full contract amount less the amount the teacher could have earned in the counselor position offered by the school.
(C) $3,000, the full contract amount less the amount the teacher could have earned in the teaching position at the academy.
(D) Nothing, because the school notified the teacher of its decision before the teacher had acted in substantial reliance on the contract.

Question 15

A produce distributor contracted to provide a grocer with eight crates of lettuce at the distributor's listed price. The distributor's shipping clerk mistakenly shipped only seven crates to the grocer. The grocer accepted delivery of the seven crates but immediately notified the distributor that the delivery did not conform to the contract. The distributor's listed price for seven crates of lettuce was 7/8 of its listed price for eight crates. The distributor shipped no more lettuce to the grocer, and the grocer has not yet paid for any of the lettuce.

How much, if anything, is the distributor entitled to collect from the grocer?

(A) Nothing, because the tender of all eight crates was a condition precedent to the grocer's duty to pay.

(B) The reasonable value of the seven crates of lettuce, minus the grocer's damages, if any, for the distributor's failure to deliver the full order.

(C) The listed price for the seven crates of lettuce, minus the grocer's damages, if any, for the distributor's failure to deliver the full order.

(D) The listed price for the seven crates of lettuce.

Question 16

A seller borrowed $5,000 from a bank. Soon thereafter the seller filed for bankruptcy, having paid nothing on his debt to the bank.

Five years after the debt had been discharged in bankruptcy, the seller contracted to sell certain goods to a buyer for $5,000. The contract provided that the buyer would pay the $5,000 to the bank "as payment of the $5,000 the seller owes the bank." The only debt that the seller ever owed the bank is the $5,000 debt that was discharged in bankruptcy. The seller delivered the goods to the buyer, who accepted them.

If the bank becomes aware of the contract between the seller and the buyer, and the buyer refuses to pay anything to the bank, is the bank likely to succeed in an action against the buyer for $5,000?

(A) No, because the buyer's promise to pay the bank was not supported by consideration.

(B) No, because the seller's debt was discharged in bankruptcy.

(C) Yes, because the bank was an intended beneficiary of the contract between the buyer and the seller.

(D) Yes, because no consideration is required to support a promise to pay a debt that has been discharged in bankruptcy.

Question 17

A builder borrowed $10,000 from a lender to finance a small construction job under a contract with a homeowner. The builder gave the lender a writing that stated, "Any money I receive from the homeowner will be paid immediately to the lender, regardless of any demands from other creditors." The builder died after completing the job but before the homeowner paid. The lender demanded that the homeowner pay the $10,000 due to the builder directly to the lender. The homeowner refused, saying that he would pay directly to the builder's estate everything that he owed the builder.

Is the lender likely to succeed in an action against the homeowner for $10,000?

(A) No, because the builder's death terminated the lender's right to receive payment directly from the homeowner.

(B) No, because the writing the builder gave to the lender did not transfer to the lender the right to receive payment from the homeowner.

(C) Yes, because the builder had manifested an intent that the homeowner pay the $10,000 directly to the lender.

(D) Yes, because the lender is an intended beneficiary of the builder-homeowner contract.

VI. MBE Practice Analysis[5]

Question 1

A restaurant supplier sent a letter to a regular customer offering to sell the customer an industrial freezer for $10,000. Two days later, the customer responded with a letter that stated: "I accept your offer on the condition that you provide me with a warranty that the freezer is merchantable." In response to the customer's letter, the supplier called the customer and stated that the offer was no longer open. The supplier promptly sold the freezer to another buyer for $11,000.

If the customer sues the supplier for breach of contract, is the customer likely to prevail?

(A) No, because the customer's letter added a term, making it a counteroffer.
Incorrect. It is true that a purported acceptance that is conditioned on an offeror's assent to a term additional to or different from the terms contained in an offer is a counteroffer. In this case, however, the customer's letter constituted an acceptance rather than a counteroffer. Under UCC §2-314, a warranty of merchantability is implied in every contract for the sale of a good by a seller who is a merchant with respect to goods of that kind. Therefore, the condition contained in the customer's letter merely stated a term that was already implied in the sale. A contract arose when the customer mailed its letter accepting the offer. Accordingly, the supplier's attempted revocation of its offer was ineffective, and its sale of the freezer to the third party breached its contract with the customer.

(B) No, because the subsequent sale to a bona fide purchaser for value cut off the claims of the customer.
Incorrect. Under some circumstances, the sale of goods to a bona fide purchaser may cut off the claims of other parties. In this case, however, the dispositive issue is whether the customer's letter in response to the supplier's offer constituted an acceptance or a counteroffer. Under UCC §2-314, a warranty of merchantability is implied in every contract for the sale of a good by a seller who is a merchant with respect to goods of that kind. Therefore, the condition contained in the customer's letter merely stated a term that was already implied in the sale. A contract arose when the customer mailed its letter accepting the offer. Accordingly, the supplier's attempted revocation of its offer was ineffective, and its sale of the freezer to the third party breached its contract with the customer.

(C) Yes, because the customer's letter was an acceptance of the supplier's offer, since the warranty of merchantability was already implied in the sale.
Correct. It is true that a purported acceptance that is conditioned on an offeror's assent to a term additional to or different from the terms contained in an offer is a counteroffer. In this case, however, the customer's letter constituted an acceptance rather than a counteroffer. Under UCC §2-314, a warranty of merchantability is implied in every contract for the sale of a good by a seller who is a merchant with respect to goods of that kind. Therefore, the condition contained in the customer's letter merely stated a term that was already implied in the sale. A contract arose when the customer mailed its letter accepting the offer. Accordingly, the supplier's attempted revocation of its offer was ineffective, and its sale of the freezer to the third party breached its contract with the customer.

---

5. *Id.*

(D) Yes, because the supplier's letter was a firm offer that could not be revoked for a reasonable time.

Incorrect. The supplier's letter did not create a firm offer because it failed to give assurance that the offer would be held open, a principal requirement of a firm offer under UCC §2-205. The dispositive issue here is whether the customer's response to the supplier's offer constituted an acceptance or a counteroffer. Under UCC §2-314, a warranty of merchantability is implied in every contract for the sale of a good by a seller who is a merchant with respect to goods of that kind. Therefore, the condition contained in the customer's letter merely stated a term that was already implied in the sale. A contract arose when the customer mailed its letter accepting the offer. Accordingly, the supplier's attempted revocation of its offer was ineffective, and its sale of the freezer to the third party breached its contract with the customer.

Question 2

A seller sent an email to a potential buyer, offering to sell his house to her for $150,000. The buyer immediately responded via email, asking whether the offer included the house's front porch swing. The seller emailed back: "No, it doesn't." The buyer then ordered a front porch swing and emailed back to the seller: "I accept your offer." The seller refused to sell the house to the buyer, claiming that the offer was no longer open.

Is there a contract for the sale of the house?

(A) No, because the buyer's initial email was a counteroffer.

Incorrect. A reply to an offer that merely requests information regarding the offer constitutes an inquiry rather than a counteroffer. The buyer's response asking whether the seller intended to include the front porch swing in his offer was an inquiry rather than a counteroffer. The buyer's subsequent email stating "I accept your offer" was an acceptance that created a contract between the parties. Therefore, the seller's attempted revocation of his offer was ineffective.

(B) No, because the offer lapsed before the buyer accepted.

Incorrect. An offeree's power of acceptance may terminate due to a lapse of time when the offeree fails to accept the offer within the time stated in the offer or within a reasonable time. In this case, the offer did not include an express time limitation. Therefore, the buyer could accept within a reasonable period of time. The email exchanges between the buyer and the seller demonstrate that the buyer accepted the seller's offer within a reasonable time period. The dispositive issue here is whether the buyer's reply to the seller's offer constituted an acceptance or a counteroffer.

A reply to an offer that merely requests information regarding the offer constitutes an inquiry rather than a counteroffer. The buyer's response asking whether the seller intended to include the front porch swing in his offer was an inquiry rather than a counteroffer. The buyer's subsequent email stating "I accept your offer" was an acceptance that created a contract between the parties. Therefore, the seller's attempted revocation of his offer was ineffective.

(C) Yes, because the buyer relied on the offer by ordering the swing.

Incorrect. An offeree's reliance on an offer can create a binding option contract that precludes an offeror from revoking its offer. In this case, however, there is no indication that the buyer's purchase of the swing was the type of act performed in substantial reliance on the offer that the seller reasonably could have expected at the time he communicated his offer. The dispositive issue here is whether the buyer's reply to the seller's offer constituted an acceptance or a counteroffer.

A reply to an offer that merely requests information regarding the offer constitutes an inquiry rather than a counteroffer. The buyer's response asking whether the seller intended to include the front porch swing in his offer was an inquiry rather than a counteroffer. The buyer's subsequent email stating "I accept your offer" was an acceptance that created a contract between the parties. Therefore, the seller's attempted revocation of his offer was ineffective.

(D) Yes, because the buyer's initial email merely asked for information.
Correct. A reply to an offer that merely requests information regarding the offer constitutes an inquiry rather than a counteroffer. The buyer's response asking whether the seller intended to include the front porch swing in his offer was an inquiry rather than a counteroffer. The buyer's subsequent email stating "I accept your offer" was an acceptance that created a contract between the parties. Therefore, the seller's attempted revocation of his offer was ineffective.

Question 3

In a telephone conversation, a jewelry maker offered to buy 100 ounces of gold from a precious metals company if delivery could be made within 10 days. The jewelry maker did not specify a price, but the market price for 100 ounces of gold at the time of the conversation was approximately $65,000. Without otherwise responding, the company delivered the gold six days later.

In the meantime, the project for which the jewelry maker planned to use the gold was canceled. The jewelry maker therefore refused to accept delivery of the gold or to pay the $65,000 demanded by the company.

Is there an enforceable contract between the jewelry maker and the company?

(A) No, because the parties did not agree on a price term.
Incorrect. Under UCC §2-305, a contract may be enforceable in the absence of a price term so long as the parties otherwise intended to enter into a contract. In this case, the dispositive issue is whether the parties' oral agreement is enforceable. Under UCC §2-201(1), a contract for the sale of goods for a price of $500 or more is not enforceable unless there is a writing indicating the contract that is signed by the party against whom enforcement is sought. In this case, the absence of such a writing signed by the jewelry maker renders the parties' oral agreement unenforceable. An exception to the writing requirement arises when a seller delivers goods that are accepted by the buyer, but in this case, the jewelry maker did not accept the gold.

(B) No, because the parties did not put their agreement in writing.
Correct. The parties failed to comply with the writing requirement of UCC §2-201(1). Under that section, a contract for the sale of goods for a price of $500 or more is not enforceable unless there is a writing indicating a contract of sale that is signed by the party against whom enforcement is sought. In this case, the absence of such a writing signed by the jewelry maker renders the parties' oral agreement unenforceable. An exception to the writing requirement arises when a seller delivers goods that are accepted by the buyer, but in this case, the jewelry maker did not accept the gold.

(C) Yes, because the absence of a price term does not defeat the formation of a valid contract for the sale of goods where the parties otherwise intended to form a contract.

Incorrect. Under UCC §2-305, a contract may be enforceable in the absence of a price term so long as the parties otherwise intended to enter into a contract. In this case, however, the dispositive issue is whether the parties' oral agreement is enforceable. Under UCC §2-201(1), a contract for the sale of goods for a price of $500 or more is not enforceable unless there is a writing indicating the contract that is signed by the party against whom enforcement is sought. The absence of such a writing signed by the jewelry maker renders the parties' oral agreement unenforceable. An exception to the writing requirement arises when a seller delivers goods that are accepted by the buyer. In this case, however, the jewelry maker did not accept the gold.

(D) Yes, because the company relied on an implied promise to pay when it delivered the gold.

Incorrect. The dispositive issue in this case is whether the parties' oral agreement is enforceable. Under UCC §2-201(1), a contract for the sale of goods for a price of $500 or more is not enforceable unless there is a writing indicating the contract that is signed by the party against whom enforcement is sought. The absence of such a writing signed by the jewelry maker renders the parties' oral agreement unenforceable. An exception to the writing requirement arises when a seller delivers goods that are accepted by the buyer. In this case, however, the jewelry maker did not accept the gold.

Question 4

A man sent an email to a friend that stated: "Because you have been a great friend to me, I am going to give you a rare book that I own." The friend replied by an email that said: "Thanks for the rare book. I am going to give you my butterfly collection." The rare book was worth $10,000; the butterfly collection was worth $100. The friend delivered the butterfly collection to the man, but the man refused to deliver the book.

If the friend sues the man to recover the value of the book, how should the court rule?

(A) For the man, because there was no bargained-for exchange to support his promise.

Correct. To constitute consideration, a return promise must be bargained for. A return promise is bargained for when it is sought by the promisor in exchange for his promise and is given by the promisee in exchange for that promise. Because the man's promise to give the rare book to the friend did not seek a return promise or performance, the friend's promise to give the man her butterfly collection did not constitute consideration for the man's promise. Accordingly, no contract arose between the parties, and the court should rule in favor of the man.

(B) For the man, because the consideration given for his promise was inadequate.

Incorrect. Instead of giving inadequate consideration, the friend gave no consideration at all. To constitute consideration, a return promise must be bargained for. A return promise is bargained for when it is sought by the promisor in exchange for his promise and is given by the promisee in exchange for that promise. Because the man's promise to give the rare book to the friend did not seek a return promise or performance, the friend's promise to give the man her butterfly collection did not constitute consideration for the man's promise. Accordingly, no contract arose between the parties, and the court should rule in favor of the man.

(C) For the friend, because she gave the butterfly collection to the man in reliance on receiving the book.

Incorrect. Although it is true that a promisee's reliance may provide the basis for the enforcement of a promise in the absence of consideration, that principle is inapplicable here. The man's promise failed to induce reliance by the friend of the type that the man reasonably might have expected when he promised to give her the rare book. In addition, this is not a case in which injustice could only be avoided by the enforcement of the man's promise. The dispositive issue here is whether the friend's promise to give her butterfly collection to the man constituted consideration for the man's promise. Because the man's promise to give the rare book to the friend did not seek a return promise or performance, the friend's promise did not constitute consideration for the man's promise. Accordingly, no contract arose between the parties, and the court should rule in favor of the man.

(D) For the friend, because she conferred a benefit on the man by delivering the butterfly collection.

Incorrect. The fact that a promisee confers a benefit on a promisor does not create an enforceable obligation on the part of the promisor. The dispositive issue here is whether the friend's promise to give her butterfly collection to the man constituted consideration for the man's promise. Because the man's promise to give the rare book to the friend did not seek a return promise or performance, the friend's promise did not constitute consideration for the man's promise. Accordingly, no contract arose between the parties, and the court should rule in favor of the man.

Question 5

A farmer who wanted to sell her land received a letter from a developer that stated, "I will pay you $1,100 an acre for your land." The farmer's letter of reply stated, "I accept your offer." Unbeknownst to the farmer, the developer had intended to offer only $1,000 per acre but had mistakenly typed "$1,100." As both parties knew, comparable land in the vicinity had been selling at prices between $1,000 and $1,200 per acre.

Which of the following states the probable legal consequences of the correspondence between the parties?

(A) There is no contract, because the parties attached materially different meanings to the price term.

Incorrect. There is a general rule that contract formation may be defeated, under some circumstances, where parties attach materially different meanings to a material term. That rule, however, is inapplicable here where the critical issue relates to the developer's intent, as manifested by his conduct, and the impact of the farmer's lack of knowledge of the developer's mistake. An enforceable contract requires mutual assent as determined by the parties' objective, rather than subjective, manifestations of that assent. Here, given the parties' knowledge of the price of comparable land, the developer's offer created a reasonable understanding that the developer would purchase the land for $1,100 per acre. Moreover, because the farmer neither knew nor had reason to know that the developer intended to purchase the land for only $1,000 per acre, the developer will be bound to purchase it for $1,100 per acre. Accordingly, the parties' conduct gave rise to a contract formed at $1,100 per acre when the farmer accepted the developer's offer.

(B) There is no enforceable contract, because the developer is entitled to rescission due to a mutual mistake as to a basic assumption of the contract.

Incorrect. While a mutual mistake may give rise to an action for rescission, there was no mutual mistake in this case. The critical issue here relates to the developer's intent as manifested by his conduct, and the impact of the farmer's lack of knowledge of the developer's mistake. An enforceable contract requires mutual assent as determined by the parties' objective, rather than subjective, manifestations of assent. Given the parties' knowledge of the price of comparable land, the developer's offer created a reasonable understanding that the developer would purchase the land for $1,100 per acre. Moreover, because the farmer neither knew nor had reason to know that the developer intended to purchase the land for only $1,000 per acre, the developer will be bound to purchase it for $1,100 per acre. Accordingly, the parties' conduct gave rise to a contract formed at $1,100 per acre when the farmer accepted the developer's offer.

(C) There is a contract formed at a price of $1,000 per acre.

Incorrect. An enforceable contract requires mutual assent as determined by the parties' objective, rather than subjective, manifestations of assent. Given the parties' knowledge of the price of comparable land, the developer's offer created a reasonable understanding that the developer would purchase the land for $1,100 per acre. Moreover, because the farmer neither knew nor had reason to know that the developer intended to purchase the land for only $1,000 per acre, the developer will be bound to purchase it for $1,100 per acre. Accordingly, the parties' conduct gave rise to a contract formed at $1,100 per acre when the farmer accepted the developer's offer.

(D) There is a contract formed at a price of $1,100 per acre.

Correct. An enforceable contract requires mutual assent as determined by the parties' objective, rather than subjective, manifestations of assent. Given the parties' knowledge of the price of comparable land, the developer's offer created a reasonable understanding that the developer would purchase the land for $1,100 per acre. Moreover, because the farmer neither knew nor had reason to know that the developer intended to purchase the land for only $1,000 per acre, the developer will be bound to purchase it for $1,100 per acre. Accordingly, the parties' conduct gave rise to a contract formed at $1,100 per acre when the farmer accepted the developer's offer.

Question 6

A buyer and a seller entered into a written contract for the sale of a copy machine, using the same form contract that they had used a number of times in the past. The contract stated that payment was due 30 days after delivery and provided that the writing contained the complete and exclusive statement of the parties' agreement.

On several past occasions, the buyer had taken a 5% discount from the contract price when paying within 10 days of delivery, and the seller had not objected. On this occasion, when the buyer took a 5% discount for paying within 10 days, the seller objected because his profit margin on this particular machine was smaller than on his other machines.

If the seller sues the buyer for breach of contract, may the buyer introduce evidence that the 5% discount was a term of the agreement?

(A) No, because the seller timely objected to the buyer's proposal for different terms.

Incorrect. Under UCC §1-303(b), course of dealing is defined as "a sequence of conduct concerning previous transactions between the parties to a particular transaction. . . ." In this case, on several past occasions the buyer had taken a 5% discount without objection from the seller, thus establishing a course of dealing. Given the course of dealing between the parties, the seller's objection to the 5% discount, after the buyer had acted in accordance with the course of dealing, was ineffective. Under the UCC's parol evidence rule, course-of-dealing evidence is admissible to explain or supplement a final written agreement.

(B) No, because the writing contained the complete and exclusive agreement of the parties.
Incorrect. Under UCC §1-303(b), course of dealing is defined as "a sequence of conduct concerning previous transactions between the parties to a particular transaction. . . ." In this case, on several past occasions the buyer had taken a 5% discount without objection from the seller, thus establishing a course of dealing. Under the UCC's parol evidence rule, course-of-dealing evidence is admissible to explain or supplement a final written agreement even if the parties intended the agreement to be complete and exclusive. Accordingly, the course-of-dealing evidence is admissible.

(C) Yes, because a modification made in good faith does not require consideration.
Incorrect. UCC Article 2 contains a general rule that a good-faith modification does not require consideration to be enforceable. However, the enforceability of a modification is not at issue here. The issue here is whether the UCC's parol evidence rule will preclude the admissibility of evidence of course of dealing. The facts indicate that in the parties' previous contracts the buyer had taken a 5% discount without objection from the seller. This conduct amounted to a course of dealing that is defined under UCC §1-303(b) as "a sequence of conduct concerning previous transactions between the parties to a particular transaction. . . ." Because the UCC's parol evidence rule explicitly allows for the admission of course-of-dealing evidence to explain or supplement a final written agreement, the evidence is admissible.

(D) Yes, because evidence of course of dealing is admissible even if the writing contains the complete and exclusive agreement of the parties.
Correct. Under UCC §1-303(b), course of dealing is defined as "a sequence of conduct concerning previous transactions between the parties to a particular transaction. . . ." In this case, on several past occasions the buyer had taken a 5% discount without objection from the seller, thus establishing a course of dealing. Under the UCC's parol evidence rule, course-of-dealing evidence is admissible to explain or supplement a final written agreement even if the parties intended the agreement to be complete and exclusive. Accordingly, the course-of-dealing evidence is admissible.

Question 7

A buyer purchased a new car from a dealer under a written contract that provided that the price of the car was $20,000 and that the buyer would receive a "trade-in allowance of $7,000 for the buyer's old car." The old car had recently been damaged in an accident. The contract contained a merger clause stating: "This writing constitutes the entire agreement of the parties, and there are no other understandings or agreements not set forth herein." When the buyer took possession of the new car, she delivered the old car to the dealer. At that time, the dealer claimed that the trade-in allowance included an assignment of the buyer's claim against her insurance company for damage to the old car. The buyer refused to provide the assignment.

The dealer sued the buyer to recover the insurance payment. The dealer has offered evidence that the parties agreed during their negotiations for the new car that the dealer was entitled to the insurance payment.

Should the court admit this evidence?

(A) No, because the dealer's acceptance of the old car bars any additional claim by the dealer.

Incorrect. A buyer's mere acceptance of goods does not waive its potential claims against a seller. The dispositive issue here is whether the parol evidence rule will allow the proffered evidence. Under that rule, a merger clause does not conclusively determine that an agreement is completely integrated. Moreover, a finding that an agreement is completely integrated does not necessarily bar the admission of extrinsic evidence. Although extrinsic evidence is inadmissible to supplement or contradict the express terms of a completely integrated agreement, such evidence is admissible to explain the terms of an agreement. In this case, evidence of the parties' discussions during their negotiations is admissible to aid in explaining whether they intended "trade-in allowance" to include an assignment of the buyer's claim against her insurance company.

(B) No, because the merger clause bars any evidence of the parties' prior discussions concerning the trade-in allowance.

Incorrect. Under the UCC's parol evidence rule, a merger clause does not conclusively determine that an agreement is completely integrated. Moreover, a finding that an agreement is completely integrated does not necessarily bar the admission of extrinsic evidence. Although extrinsic evidence is inadmissible to supplement or contradict the express terms of a completely integrated agreement, such evidence is admissible to explain the terms of an agreement. In this case, evidence of the parties' discussions during their negotiations is admissible to aid in explaining whether they intended "trade-in allowance" to include an assignment of the buyer's claim against her insurance company.

(C) Yes, because a merger clause does not bar evidence of fraud.

Incorrect. The UCC's parol evidence rule allows the introduction of extrinsic evidence to establish fraud even if an agreement is completely integrated. Because there is no indication of fraud in this case, the fraud exception is irrelevant. The dispositive issue here is whether the parol evidence rule will allow the proffered evidence. Under that rule, a merger clause does not conclusively determine that an agreement is completely integrated. Moreover, a finding that an agreement is completely integrated does not necessarily bar the admission of extrinsic evidence. Although extrinsic evidence is inadmissible to supplement or contradict the express terms of a completely integrated agreement, such evidence is admissible to explain the terms of an agreement. In this case, evidence of the parties' discussions during their negotiations is admissible to aid in explaining whether they intended "trade-in allowance" to include an assignment of the buyer's claim against her insurance company.

(D) Yes, because the merger clause does not bar evidence to explain what the parties meant by "trade-in allowance."

Correct. Under the UCC's parol evidence rule, a merger clause does not conclusively establish that an agreement is completely integrated. Moreover, a finding that an agreement is completely integrated does not necessarily bar the admission of extrinsic evidence. Although extrinsic evidence is inadmissible to supplement or contradict the express terms of a completely integrated agreement, such evidence is admissible to explain the terms of an agreement. In this case, evidence of the parties' discussions during their negotiations is admissible to aid in explaining whether they intended "trade-in- allowance" to include an assignment of the buyer's claim against her insurance company.

Question 8

A buyer agreed in writing to purchase a car from a seller for $15,000, with the price to be paid on a specified date at the seller's showroom. The contract provided, and both parties intended, that time was of the essence. Before the specified date, however, the seller sold the car to a third party for $20,000. On the specified date, the buyer arrived at the showroom but brought only $10,000. When the seller did not appear at the showroom, the buyer called the seller and asked whether the seller would accept $10,000 for the car immediately and the remaining $5,000 in six weeks. The seller told the buyer that he had sold the car to the third party.

If the buyer sues the seller for breach of contract, will the buyer be likely to prevail?

(A) No, because the contractual obligations were discharged on the ground of impossibility.

Incorrect. While the seller's sale of the car to a third party rendered it impossible for the seller to sell the car to the buyer, such conduct does not meet the standard to establish impossibility as a legal defense for nonperformance. Similarly, the buyer's tender of less than the full payment does not, without more, establish a legal basis for impossibility. The dispositive issue here relates to the effect of neither party tendering performance on the date specified in the contract. Under UCC Article 2, a seller's tender of delivery of goods and a buyer's tender of payment are concurrent conditions of exchange. Therefore, the buyer and the seller were obligated to simultaneously tender their respective performances. Because neither party was prepared to tender performance at the time or in the manner stipulated in the contract, each party's performance obligation was discharged. Accordingly, neither the buyer nor the seller has a claim for breach of contract.

(B) No, because the buyer was not prepared to tender her performance on the specified date.

Correct. Even though the facts demonstrate that the seller repudiated the contract by selling the car to a third party, the seller did not end up breaching the contract. Under UCC Article 2, a seller's tender of delivery of goods and a buyer's tender of payment are concurrent conditions of exchange. Therefore, the buyer and the seller were obligated to simultaneously tender their respective performances. Because neither party was prepared to tender performance at the time or in the manner stipulated in the contract, each party's performance obligation was discharged. Accordingly, neither the buyer nor the seller has a claim for breach of contract.

(C) Yes, because the buyer's breach was not material.

Incorrect. UCC Article 2 adopts the perfect tender rule, rather than the material breach rule, as the generally applicable standard. The dispositive issue here relates to the effect of neither party tendering performance on the date specified in the contract. Under Article 2, a seller's tender of delivery of goods and a buyer's tender of payment are concurrent conditions of exchange. Therefore, the buyer and the seller were obligated to simultaneously tender their respective performances. Because neither party was prepared to tender performance at the time or in the manner stipulated in the contract, each party's performance obligation was discharged. Accordingly, neither the buyer nor the seller has a claim for breach of contract.

(D) Yes, because the seller anticipatorily repudiated the contract when he sold the car to the third party.

Incorrect. While the seller's sale of the car to a third party would seem to constitute an anticipatory repudiation, as it turned out, neither party was prepared to tender performance at the time or in the manner specified in the contract. UCC Article 2 provides that a seller's tender of delivery of goods and a buyer's tender of payment are concurrent conditions of exchange. Therefore, the buyer and the seller were obligated to simultaneously tender their respective performances. Because neither party was prepared to tender performance at the time or in the manner stipulated in the contract, each party's performance obligation was discharged. Accordingly, neither the buyer nor the seller has a claim for breach of contract.

Question 9

A mill and a bakery entered into a written contract that obligated the mill to deliver to the bakery 1,000 pounds of flour every Monday for 26 weeks at a specified price per pound. The mill delivered the proper quantity of flour in a timely manner for the first 15 weeks. However, the 16th delivery was tendered on a Tuesday, and amounted to only 800 pounds. The mill told the bakery that the 200-pound shortage would be made up on the delivery due the following Monday. The late delivery and the 200-pound shortage will not significantly disrupt the bakery's operations.

How may the bakery legally respond to the nonconforming tender?

(A) Accept the 800 pounds tendered, but notify the mill that the bakery will cancel the contract if the exact amount is not delivered on the following Monday. **Incorrect.** Because the contract authorizes the delivery of flour in separate lots to be separately accepted, the parties entered into an installment contract. UCC §2-612 adopts a "substantial impairment" standard for determining whether a buyer can reject a particular installment or cancel the entire contract. A buyer can reject an installment if a nonconformity substantially impairs that installment and the nonconformity cannot be cured. A buyer can cancel the contract only when the nonconformity with respect to one or more installments substantially impairs the value of the whole contract. Here, the mill's tender of less than the contracted-for quantity did not amount to a nonconformity that substantially impaired the value of either the 16th installment or the whole contract. The mill's proposed cure, the delivery of the remaining 200 pounds on the following Monday, is sufficient given that the late delivery and the shortage will not significantly disrupt the bakery's business. Accordingly, not only must the bakery accept the delivery of the tendered 800 pounds of flour, it also must accept the remaining 200 pounds that the mill proposes to deliver on the following Monday.

(B) Accept the 800 pounds tendered, but notify the mill that the bakery will deduct from the price any damages for losses due to the nonconforming tender. **Correct.** Because the contract authorizes the delivery of flour in separate lots to be separately accepted, the parties entered into an installment contract. UCC §2-612 adopts a "substantial impairment" standard for determining whether a buyer can reject a particular installment or cancel the entire contract. A buyer can reject an installment if a nonconformity substantially impairs that installment and the nonconformity cannot be cured. Here the mill's tender of less than the contracted-for quantity did not amount to a nonconformity that substantially impaired either the value of the 16th installment or the whole contract. The mill's proposed cure, the delivery of the remaining 200 pounds on the following Monday, is sufficient given that the late delivery and the shortage will not significantly disrupt the bakery's business. Accordingly, the bakery must accept the delivery of the tendered 800 pounds of flour but may deduct from the price any damages for losses resulting from the late delivery.

(C) Reject the 800 pounds tendered, but notify the mill that the bakery will accept delivery the following Monday if it is conforming.

Incorrect. Because the contract authorizes the delivery of flour in separate lots to be separately accepted, the parties entered into an installment contract. UCC §2-612 adopts a "substantial impairment" standard for determining whether a buyer can reject a particular installment or cancel the entire contract. A buyer can reject an installment if a nonconformity substantially impairs that installment and the nonconformity cannot be cured. Here the mill's tender of less than the contracted-for quantity did not amount to a nonconformity that substantially impaired either the value of the 16th installment or the whole contract. The mill's proposed cure, the delivery of the remaining 200 pounds on the following Monday, is sufficient given that the late delivery and the shortage will not significantly disrupt the bakery's business. Accordingly, not only must the bakery accept the delivery of the tendered 800 pounds of flour, it also must accept the remaining 200 pounds that the mill proposes to deliver on the following Monday.

(D) Reject the 800 pounds tendered, and notify the mill that the bakery is canceling the contract.

Incorrect. Because the contract authorizes the delivery of flour in separate lots to be separately accepted, the parties entered into an installment contract. UCC §2-612 adopts a "substantial impairment" standard for determining whether a buyer can reject a particular installment or cancel the entire contract. A buyer can reject an installment if a nonconformity substantially impairs that installment and the nonconformity cannot be cured. Additionally, a buyer can cancel the contract only when the nonconformity with respect to one or more installments substantially impairs the value of the whole contract. Here, the mill's tender of less than the contracted-for quantity did not amount to a nonconformity that substantially impaired the value of the 16th installment or the whole contract. The mill's proposed cure, the delivery of the remaining 200 pounds on the following Monday, is sufficient given that the late delivery and the shortage will not significantly disrupt the bakery's business. Accordingly, the buyer has no right to reject the tender or to cancel the contract.

Question 10

A buyer agreed to purchase a seller's house for $250,000 "on condition that the buyer obtain mortgage financing within 30 days." Thirty days later, the buyer told the seller that the buyer would not purchase the house because the buyer had not obtained mortgage financing. The seller asked the buyer where the buyer had tried to obtain mortgage financing, and the buyer responded, "I was busy and didn't have time to seek mortgage financing."

If the seller sues the buyer for breach of contract, is the court likely to find the buyer in breach?

(A) No, because the buyer's performance was subject to a condition that did not occur.

Incorrect. A performance that is subject to an express condition cannot become due unless the condition occurs or its non-occurrence is excused. However, the duty of good faith, which is implied in every contract, imposed an obligation on the buyer to make reasonable efforts to secure mortgage financing. Because the buyer made no such efforts, the non-occurrence of the condition to the buyer's obligation to purchase the house—the buyer's securing financing—was excused. Accordingly, the court is likely to find that the buyer is in breach.

(B) No, because the promise was illusory since the buyer was not obligated to do anything.

Incorrect. The duty of good faith, which is implied in every contract, imposed an obligation on the buyer to make reasonable efforts to secure mortgage financing. Accordingly, the buyer's promise to secure financing was not illusory. A performance that is subject to an express condition cannot become due unless the condition occurs or its non-occurrence is excused. In this case, the non-occurrence of the condition to the buyer's obligation to perform was excused, because the buyer failed to make reasonable efforts to secure mortgage financing. Therefore, the court is likely to find that the buyer is in breach.

(C) Yes, because a promise was implied that the buyer had to make reasonable efforts to obtain mortgage financing.

Correct. A performance that is subject to an express condition cannot become due unless the condition occurs or its non-occurrence is excused. However, the duty of good faith, which is implied in every contract, imposed an obligation on the buyer to make reasonable efforts to secure mortgage financing. Because the buyer made no such efforts, the non-occurrence of the condition to the buyer's obligation to purchase the house—the buyer's securing financing—was excused. Accordingly, the court is likely to find that the buyer is in breach.

(D) Yes, because a reasonable interpretation of the agreement is that the buyer had an obligation to purchase the house for $250,000 in 30 days.

Incorrect. The contract explicitly stated that the buyer's obligation to perform was expressly conditioned on the buyer obtaining mortgage financing. A performance that is subject to an express condition cannot become due unless the condition occurs or its non-occurrence is excused. However, the duty of good faith, which is implied in every contract, imposed an obligation on the buyer to make reasonable efforts to secure mortgage financing. Because the buyer made no such efforts, the non-occurrence of the condition to the buyer's obligation to purchase the house—the buyer's securing financing—was excused. Accordingly, the court is likely to find that the buyer is in breach.

Question 11

A producer contracted to pay an inexperienced performer a specified salary to act in a small role in a play the producer was taking on a six-week road tour. The contract was for the duration of the tour. On the third day of the tour, the performer was hospitalized with a stomach disorder. The producer replaced her in the cast with an experienced actor. One week later, the performer recovered, but the producer refused to allow her to resume her original role for the remainder of the tour.

In an action by the performer against the producer for breach of contract, which of the following, if proved, would be the producer's best defense?

(A) The actor, by general acclaim, was much better in the role than the performer had been.

Incorrect. After the performer became ill, the temporary impracticability doctrine excused the performer's contractual obligation and also gave the producer the right to suspend his performance obligation during the period that the performer's illness prevented her from acting. The critical issue here is whether the producer also had the right to cancel the contract. Circumstances that would give the producer the right to cancel include the degree of uncertainty relating to the nature and duration of the performer's illness and the extent to which a delay in making substitute arrangements would have prevented the producer from continuing the tour. The relative quality of the actor's performance is not a circumstance that would give the producer the right to cancel the performer's contract.

(B) The actor was the only replacement the producer could find, and the actor would accept nothing less than a contract for the remainder of the six-week tour.
Correct. After the performer became ill, the temporary impracticability doctrine excused the performer's contractual obligation and also gave the producer the right to suspend his performance obligation during the period that the performer's illness prevented her from acting. The critical issue here is whether the producer also had the right to cancel the contract. Circumstances that would give the producer the right to cancel the contract include the degree of uncertainty relating to the nature and duration of the performer's illness and the extent to which a delay in making substitute arrangements would have prevented the producer from continuing the tour. The unwillingness of the actor, the only replacement available, to take a contract for less than the remainder of the six-week tour and the uncertainty surrounding when the performer might return to work would have discharged the producer's performance obligations and justified his cancellation of the contract with the performer.

(C) The producer offered to employ the performer as the actor's understudy for the remainder of the six-week tour at the performer's original salary, but the performer declined.
Incorrect. After the performer became ill, the temporary impracticability doctrine excused the performer's contractual obligation and also gave the producer the right to suspend his performance obligation during the period that the performer's illness prevented her from acting. The critical issue here is whether the producer also had the right to cancel the contract. Circumstances that would give the producer the right to cancel include the degree of uncertainty relating to the nature and duration of the performer's illness and the extent to which a delay in making substitute arrangements would have prevented the producer from continuing the tour. Because the producer had the right to cancel the contract, his action in offering the performer a job as understudy is irrelevant.

(D) Both the producer and the performer knew that a year earlier the performer had been incapacitated for a short period of time by the same kind of stomach disorder.
Incorrect. After the performer became ill, the temporary impracticability doctrine excused the performer's contractual obligation and also gave the producer the right to suspend his performance obligation during the period that the performer's illness prevented her from acting. The critical issue here is whether the producer also had the right to cancel the contract. Circumstances that would give the producer the right to cancel include the degree of uncertainty relating to the nature and duration of the performer's illness and the extent to which a delay in making substitute arrangements would have prevented the producer from continuing the tour. A history of having been ill for a short time would not justify the producer's cancellation of the contract. In fact, the short period of time that the performer had been incapacitated a year earlier from the same illness would weaken the producer's defense.

Question 12

An art collector paid a gallery $1,000 to purchase a framed drawing from the gallery's collection. The price included shipping by the gallery to the collector's home. The gallery's owner used inadequate materials to wrap the drawing. The frame broke during shipment and scratched the drawing, reducing the drawing's value to $300. The collector complained to the gallery owner, who told the collector to take the drawing to a specific art restorer to have the drawing repaired. The collector paid the restorer $400 to repair the drawing, but not all of the scratches could be fixed. The drawing, after being repaired, was worth $700. The gallery owner subsequently refused to pay either for the repairs or for the damage to the drawing.

In an action by the collector against the gallery owner for damages, which of the following awards is most likely?

(A) Nothing.
Incorrect. The gallery's use of inadequate materials to wrap the drawing constituted a breach of warranty. Therefore, the collector is entitled to be placed in the position he would have been in but for the gallery's breach. Awarding the collector nothing would violate the expectation damages principle. Under UCC §2-714(2), the generally applicable standard for measuring the collector's resulting damages would be the difference between the value of the drawing as accepted and the value of the drawing if it had been as warranted. Repair costs often are used to determine this difference in value, but when repairs fail to restore the goods to their value as warranted, an adjustment is required. The collector is entitled to recover the repair costs ($400) plus the difference between the value of the drawing if it had been as warranted and its value after the repairs ($1,000 - $700 = $300). Accordingly, the collector should recover $700.

(B) $300.
Incorrect. The gallery's use of inadequate materials to wrap the drawing constituted a breach of warranty. Therefore, the collector is entitled to be placed in the position he would have been in but for the gallery's breach. Awarding the collector $300 would violate the expectation damages principle. Under UCC §2-714(2), the generally applicable standard for measuring the collector's resulting damages would be the difference between the value of the drawing as accepted and the value of the drawing if it had been as warranted. Repair costs often are used to determine this difference in value, but when repairs fail to restore the goods to their value as warranted, an adjustment is required. The collector is entitled to recover the repair costs ($400) plus the difference between the value of the drawing if it had been as warranted and its value after the repairs ($1,000 - $700 = $300). Accordingly, the collector should recover $700.

(C) $400.
Incorrect. The gallery's use of inadequate materials to wrap the drawing constituted a breach of warranty. Therefore, the collector is entitled to be placed in the position he would have been in but for the gallery's breach. Awarding the collector $400 would violate the expectation damages principle. Under UCC §2-714(2), the generally applicable standard for measuring the collector's resulting damages would be the difference between the value of the drawing as accepted and the value of the drawing if it had been as warranted. Repair costs often are used to determine this difference in value, but when repairs fail to restore the goods to their value as warranted, an adjustment is required. The collector is entitled to recover the repair costs ($400) plus the difference between the value of the drawing if it had been as

warranted and its value after the repairs ($1,000 - $700 = $300). Accordingly, the collector should recover $700.

(D) $700.

Correct. The gallery's use of inadequate materials to wrap the drawing constituted a breach of warranty. Therefore, the collector is entitled to be placed in the position he would have been in but for the gallery's breach. Under UCC §2-714(2), the generally applicable standard for measuring the collector's resulting damages would be the difference between the value of the drawing as accepted and the value of the drawing if it had been as warranted. Repair costs often are used to determine this difference in value, but when repairs fail to restore the goods to their value as warranted, a further adjustment is required. Here the repairs failed to restore the drawing to its value as warranted. Therefore, the collector is entitled to recover the repair costs ($400) plus the difference between the value of the drawing if it had been as warranted and its value after the repairs ($1,000 - $700 = $300). Accordingly, the collector should recover $700.

Question 13

A businesswoman sold her business to a company for $25 million in cash pursuant to a written contract that was signed by both parties. Under the contract, the company agreed to employ the businesswoman for two years as a vice president at a salary of $150,000 per year. After six months, the company, without cause, fired the businesswoman.

Which of the following statements best describes the businesswoman's rights after the discharge?

(A) She can recover the promised salary for the remainder of the two years if she remains ready to work.

Incorrect. The company's unjustified termination of the businesswoman's employment constituted a breach of contract entitling the businesswoman to recover monetary damages. However, a wrongfully discharged employee is expected to mitigate damages by making reasonable efforts to seek comparable employment. In this case, to avoid a reduction in her damages, the businesswoman is required to do more than remain ready to work. Her recovery will be reduced by the compensation she earned or could have earned if she had made reasonable efforts to secure comparable employment.

(B) She can recover the promised salary for the remainder of the two years if no comparable job is reasonably available and she does not take another job.

Correct. The company's unjustified termination of the businesswoman's employment constituted a breach of contract entitling the businesswoman to recover monetary damages. A wrongfully discharged employee is expected to mitigate damages by making reasonable efforts to seek comparable employment. However, if no comparable employment is reasonably available and the businesswoman does not take another job, the businesswoman is entitled to recover the promised salary for the remainder of the two years.

(C) She can rescind the contract of sale and get back her business upon tender to the company of $25 million.

Incorrect. The company's unjustified termination of the businesswoman's employment constituted a material breach of contract. Nevertheless, a court would likely employ the concept of divisibility to preclude the businesswoman from rescinding the contract of sale. As stated in Restatement (Second) of Contracts §240, a contract is divisible where "the performances to be exchanged under an exchange of promises can be apportioned into corresponding pairs of part performances so that the parts of each pair are properly regarded as agreed equivalents." Here, the agreed equivalents would be the sale of the business and the corresponding $25 million purchase price, and the businesswoman's promise to work for the company and the corresponding yearly salary of $150,000. Applying this concept, the businesswoman would be able to recover damages for the company's breach of its promise to employ her, but she would not be permitted to rescind the contract of sale.

(D) She can get specific performance of her right to serve as a vice president of the company for two years.

Incorrect. The company's unjustified termination of the businesswoman's employment constituted a breach of contract entitling the businesswoman to recover monetary damages. The general rule is that employers cannot obtain specific performance requiring an employee who has breached a personal services contract to work for the employer. It is also true generally that courts refuse to grant specific performance of an employment contract against a breaching employer. Consequently, the businesswoman's recovery will consist of the unpaid salary under the contract, reduced by the compensation she earned or could have earned if she had made reasonable efforts to secure comparable employment.

Question 14

On June 15, a teacher accepted a contract for a one-year position teaching math at a public high school at a salary of $50,000, starting in September. On June 22, the school informed the teacher that, due to a change in its planned math curriculum, it no longer needed a full-time math teacher. The school offered instead to employ the teacher as a part-time academic counselor at a salary of $20,000, starting in September. The teacher refused the school's offer. On June 29, the teacher was offered a one-year position to teach math at a nearby private academy for $47,000, starting in September. The teacher, however, decided to spend the year completing work on a graduate degree in mathematics and declined the academy's offer.

If the teacher sues the school for breach of contract, what is her most likely recovery?

(A) $50,000, the full contract amount.

Incorrect. The teacher is entitled to recover damages that will place her in the position she would have been in but for the school's breach. However, an injured party is expected to make reasonable efforts to mitigate the loss resulting from the other party's breach. In the case of a wrongfully discharged employee, the employee is expected to accept an offer of comparable employment. If the employee fails or refuses to do so, the employee's recovery is reduced by the amount of the loss that the employee could have avoided by accepting comparable employment. Here, the teacher's damages of $50,000 should be reduced by the $47,000 she would have earned if she had accepted the comparable teaching position at the private academy. Therefore, the teacher is entitled to recover $3,000 from the school.

(B) $30,000, the full contract amount less the amount the teacher could have earned in the counselor position offered by the school.

Incorrect. The teacher is entitled to recover damages that will place her in the position she would have been in but for the school's breach. However, an injured party is expected to make reasonable efforts to mitigate the loss resulting from the other party's breach. In the case of a wrongfully discharged employee, the employee is expected to accept an offer of comparable employment. If the employee fails or refuses to do so, the employee's recovery is reduced by the amount of the loss that the employee could have avoided by accepting comparable employment. Because it is unlikely that a court would consider the counseling position to be comparable employment, the teacher's damages should not be reduced by the $20,000 she would have earned if she had accepted that position. On the other hand, her damages of $50,000 should be reduced by the $47,000 she would have earned if she had accepted the comparable teaching position at the private academy. Therefore, the teacher is entitled to recover $3,000 from the school.

(C) $3,000, the full contract amount less the amount the teacher could have earned in the teaching position at the academy.

Correct. The teacher is entitled to recover damages that will place her in the position she would have been in but for the school's breach. However, an injured party is expected to make reasonable efforts to mitigate the loss resulting from the other party's breach. In the case of a wrongfully discharged employee, the employee is expected to accept an offer of comparable employment. If the employee fails or refuses to do so, the employee's recovery is reduced by the amount of the loss that the employee could have avoided by accepting comparable employment. Here, the teacher's damages of $50,000 should be reduced by the $47,000 she would have earned if she had accepted the comparable teaching position at the private academy. Therefore, the teacher is entitled to recover $3,000 from the school.

(D) Nothing, because the school notified the teacher of its decision before the teacher had acted in substantial reliance on the contract.

Incorrect. The teacher and the school entered into an enforceable contract, and the school's unjustified nonperformance constituted a breach of contract. The teacher is therefore entitled to recover damages that will place her in the position she would have been in but for the breach and need not show reliance in order to recover. However, while she is entitled to damages from the breach, an injured party is expected to make reasonable efforts to mitigate the loss resulting from the other party's breach. In the case of a wrongfully discharged employee, the employee is expected to accept an offer of comparable employment. If the employee fails or refuses to do so, the employee's recovery is reduced by the amount of the loss that the employee could have avoided by accepting comparable employment. Here, the teacher's damages of $50,000 should be reduced by the $47,000 she would have earned if she had accepted the comparable teaching position at the private academy. Therefore, the teacher is entitled to recover $3,000 from the school.

Question 15

A produce distributor contracted to provide a grocer with eight crates of lettuce at the distributor's listed price. The distributor's shipping clerk mistakenly shipped only seven crates to the grocer. The grocer accepted delivery of the seven crates but immediately notified the distributor that the delivery did not conform to the contract. The distributor's listed price for seven crates of lettuce was 7/8 of its listed price for eight crates. The distributor shipped no more lettuce to the grocer, and the grocer has not yet paid for any of the lettuce.

How much, if anything, is the distributor entitled to collect from the grocer?

(A) Nothing, because the tender of all eight crates was a condition precedent to the grocer's duty to pay.

Incorrect. The distributor's nonconforming shipment constituted both an acceptance of the grocer's offer to purchase and a breach of the parties' contract. With respect to a nonconforming tender, UCC §2-601 allows a buyer to accept the whole, reject the whole, or partially accept or reject commercial units. A buyer who accepts a tender of goods, whether conforming or nonconforming, becomes obligated to pay the seller the contract price of the goods. Accordingly, the grocer's acceptance of the nonconforming shipment obligated it to pay the distributor's listed price for the seven crates, reduced by any damages for losses resulting from the nonconforming shipment.

(B) The reasonable value of the seven crates of lettuce, minus the grocer's damages, if any, for the distributor's failure to deliver the full order.

Incorrect. The distributor's nonconforming shipment constituted both an acceptance of the grocer's offer to purchase and a breach of the parties' contract. With respect to a nonconforming tender, UCC §2-601 allows a buyer to accept the whole, reject the whole, or partially accept or reject commercial units. A buyer who accepts a tender of goods, whether conforming or nonconforming, becomes obligated to pay the seller the contract price of the goods. Accordingly, the grocer's acceptance of the nonconforming shipment obligated it to pay the distributor's listed price for, rather than the reasonable value of, the seven crates of lettuce. The price paid by the grocer will be reduced by any damages for losses resulting from the nonconforming shipment.

(C) The listed price for the seven crates of lettuce, minus the grocer's damages, if any, for the distributor's failure to deliver the full order.

Correct. The distributor's nonconforming shipment constituted both an acceptance of the grocer's offer to purchase and a breach of the parties' contract. With respect to a nonconforming tender, UCC §2-601 allows a buyer to accept the whole, reject the whole, or partially accept or reject commercial units. A buyer who accepts a tender of goods, whether conforming or nonconforming, becomes obligated to pay the seller the contract price of the goods. Accordingly, the grocer's acceptance of the nonconforming shipment obligated it to pay the distributor's listed price for the seven crates, reduced by any damages for losses resulting from the nonconforming shipment.

(D) The listed price for the seven crates of lettuce.

Incorrect. The distributor's nonconforming shipment constituted both an acceptance of the grocer's offer to purchase and a breach of the parties' contract. With respect to a nonconforming tender, UCC §2-601 allows a buyer to accept the whole, reject the whole, or partially accept or reject commercial units. A buyer who accepts a tender of goods, whether conforming or nonconforming, becomes obligated to pay the seller the contract price of the goods. Accordingly, the grocer's acceptance of the nonconforming shipment obligated it to pay the distributor's listed price for the seven crates. However, that price should be reduced by any damages for losses resulting from the nonconforming shipment.

Question 16

A seller borrowed $5,000 from a bank. Soon thereafter the seller filed for bankruptcy, having paid nothing on his debt to the bank.

Five years after the debt had been discharged in bankruptcy, the seller contracted to sell certain goods to a buyer for $5,000. The contract provided that the buyer would pay the $5,000 to the bank "as payment of the $5,000 the seller owes the bank." The only debt that the seller ever owed the bank is the $5,000 debt that was discharged in bankruptcy. The seller delivered the goods to the buyer, who accepted them.

If the bank becomes aware of the contract between the seller and the buyer, and the buyer refuses to pay anything to the bank, is the bank likely to succeed in an action against the buyer for $5,000?

(A) No, because the buyer's promise to pay the bank was not supported by consideration.

Incorrect. The buyer and the seller entered into a bargained-for exchange for the sale and purchase of goods. Thus their agreement was supported by consideration. Moreover, a promisee (the seller) can intend that a third party be the beneficiary of the performance the promisee expects to receive from a promisor (the buyer). Because the parties' agreement provided that the buyer would pay to the bank the $5,000 that the buyer had promised to pay for the goods, the bank was an intended beneficiary of the enforceable agreement between the seller and the buyer, and the buyer is obligated to pay the bank.

(B) No, because the seller's debt was discharged in bankruptcy.

Incorrect. The bank was an intended beneficiary of the contract between the buyer and the seller, and the fact of discharge is irrelevant. The seller and the buyer entered into a bargained-for exchange for the sale and purchase of goods. Because their agreement provided that the buyer would pay to the bank the $5,000 that the buyer had promised to pay for the goods, the bank was an intended beneficiary of the enforceable agreement between the seller and the buyer, and the buyer is obligated to pay the bank.

(C) Yes, because the bank was an intended beneficiary of the contract between the buyer and the seller.

Correct. The buyer and the seller entered into a bargained-for exchange for the sale and purchase of goods. Because their agreement provided that the buyer would pay to the bank the $5,000 that the buyer had promised to pay for the goods, the bank was an intended beneficiary of the enforceable agreement between the seller and the buyer, and the buyer is obligated to pay the bank.

(D) Yes, because no consideration is required to support a promise to pay a debt that has been discharged in bankruptcy.

Incorrect. It is true that a promise by a debtor to pay a debt that has been discharged in bankruptcy requires no consideration to be enforceable. In this case, however, the discharge of the seller's debt is irrelevant. Here, the seller and the buyer entered into a bargained-for exchange for the sale and purchase of goods. Because their agreement provided that the buyer would pay to the bank the $5,000 that the buyer had promised to pay for the goods, the bank was an intended beneficiary of the enforceable agreement between the seller and the buyer, and the buyer is obligated to pay the bank.

Question 17

A builder borrowed $10,000 from a lender to finance a small construction job under a contract with a homeowner. The builder gave the lender a writing that stated, "Any money I receive from the homeowner will be paid immediately to the lender, regardless of any demands from other creditors." The builder died after completing the job but before the homeowner paid. The lender demanded that the homeowner pay the $10,000 due to the builder directly to the lender. The homeowner refused, saying that he would pay directly to the builder's estate everything that he owed the builder.

Is the lender likely to succeed in an action against the homeowner for $10,000?

(A) No, because the builder's death terminated the lender's right to receive payment directly from the homeowner.

Incorrect. The builder never gave the lender a valid assignment. An assignment arises when the holder of a right, an obligee, manifests the intent to make a present transfer of that right to another, the assignee. An assignment is to be distinguished from a promise to do something in the future, such as the payment of money. Here, the writing in which the builder promised to pay the lender the $10,000 he received from the homeowner did not transfer to the lender the right to receive payment directly from the homeowner, and thus it did not create an assignment.

(B) No, because the writing the builder gave to the lender did not transfer to the lender the right to receive payment from the homeowner.

Correct. An assignment arises when the holder of a right, an obligee, manifests the intent to make a present transfer of that right to another, the assignee. Upon an assignment, the assignor's rights are extinguished and transferred to the assignee. An assignment is to be distinguished from a promise to do something in the future, such as the payment of money. Here, the writing in which the builder promised to pay the lender the $10,000 he received from the homeowner did not transfer to the lender the right to receive payment directly from the homeowner, and thus it did not create an assignment.

(C) Yes, because the builder had manifested an intent that the homeowner pay the $10,000 directly to the lender.

Incorrect. It may have been the builder's subjective intent to have the homeowner pay the $10,000 directly to the lender if the builder died, but more was required in order for the lender to have the right to receive that direct payment. The dispositive issue here is whether the builder gave the lender a valid assignment. An assignment arises when the holder of a right, an obligee, manifests the intent to make a present transfer of that right to another, the assignee. An assignment is to be distinguished from a promise to do something in the future, such as the payment of money. Here, the writing in which the builder promised to pay to the lender the $10,000 he received from the homeowner did not transfer to the lender the right to receive payment directly from the homeowner, and thus it did not create an assignment.

(D) Yes, because the lender is an intended beneficiary of the builder-homeowner contract.

Incorrect. Because any rights that may have been granted to the lender were not created by the contract between the builder and the homeowner, the lender did not acquire third-party beneficiary status. The dispositive issue here is whether the builder gave the lender a valid assignment. An assignment arises when the holder of a right, an obligee, manifests the intent to make a present transfer of that right to another, the assignee. An assignment is to be distinguished from a promise to do something in the future, such as the payment of money. Here, the writing in which the builder promised to pay to the lender the $10,000 he received from the homeowner did not transfer to the lender the right to receive payment directly from the homeowner, and thus it did not create an assignment.

CHAPTER 11

Mapping MBE Topics—Criminal Law and Procedure

I. CRIMINAL LAW

Criminal law is based on three sources of law: common law, the Model Penal Code, and statutory law. If a statute is involved, the examiners will give you the statute. Thus, focus on common law and the Model Penal Code for memorization.

Your mind map focuses first on understanding the common law requirements of a crime before moving to the characteristics of particular crimes. Inchoate crimes are frequently tested, particularly attempt crimes. Understand the basics of each and understand that they can pop up with various offenses against persons or property:

- Elements of a crime
  - *Mens rea*
  - *Actus rea*
- Accomplice liability
- Inchoate crimes
- Offenses against persons
- Offenses against property
- Defenses

Mens rea refers to the level of intent required for specific crimes. The *mens rea* must occur simultaneously with the *actus rea*. Divide your memorization into the common law *mens rea* and the Model Penal Code *mens rea*. Under the common law, intent moves from no intent required to purposeful actions. The common law *mens rea* includes:

- Strict liability—no *mens rea* required (statutory rape, public health, and safety regulations).
- General intent—criminal negligence (rape, battery, kidnapping).
- Malice—gross negligence (murder, arson).
- Specific intent—purpose (first-degree murder, assault, inchoate crimes, property-related crimes).

The Model Penal Code *mens rea* includes:

- Negligently—gross deviation from norm in failing to perceive substantial and unjustifiable risk.

- Recklessly—gross deviation from norm in consciously disregarding substantial and unjustifiable risk.
- Knowingly—awareness.
- Purposely—conscious object.

A frequent test area is the intent required for attempt. The examiners want to know that you understand that specific intent is required. Another frequently tested area is **transferred intent**. In essence, the intent to harm a particular individual or object transfers if instead it causes similar harm to another person or object.

The component of *actus rea* includes a physical or external component and either a voluntary act or the omission to act that violates a legal duty. Just like torts, there is generally no legal duty to act or aid. A duty may arise from statute, contract, the relationship between the parties, the assumption of care, or the creation of the peril.

Accomplice liability refers to individuals that are accessories to a crime committed by someone else. Under the modern approach, one is liable for someone else's crime if they assisted by aiding, encouraging, or advising and they intended to assist in the commission of the crime.

Under the common law approach, there are four categories to parties to a crime:

- Principal in the first degree—present at scene and commits one element of the crime.
- Principal in the second degree—present at scene, assists but does not commit any element of the crime.
- Accessory before the fact—not at scene, provided assistance beforehand.
- Accessory after the fact—not at scene, provided assistance after crime completed.

The principals are liable for the crimes committed. An accessory before the fact is liable for every crime committed—both planned and all foreseeable crimes. An accessory after the fact is not liable for the crime committed, but is liable for the separate crime of being an accessory after the fact. If someone encourages the crime and then discourages the crime, they have withdrawn from liability. If an aider then neutralizes the aid, prevents the crime, or notifies the authorities, they have withdrawn from liability.

Spend considerable time understanding **inchoate crimes**. These include solicitation, conspiracy, and attempt. All are specific intent crimes. They cannot be committed through mere negligence or recklessness. **Solicitation** means asking or encouraging someone to commit a crime with the intent to commit that crime. Solicitation merges into the completed offense. That the crime was impossible to commit is not a defense.

Conspiracy requires an agreement to commit the unlawful act and the specific intent to achieve the object of the agreement. The majority approach, but not under the common law, is that an overt act in furtherance of the conspiracy is required. This can be a minor act. Conspirators are liable for the conspiracy, for the completed target crime, and for any foreseeable crimes by co-conspirators in furtherance of the conspiracy.

Under the common law, a conspirator can withdraw from the conspiracy by notifying co-conspirators in time for them to abandon their plans. They are still liable for the conspiracy and the crime itself, but are no longer liable for further crimes. Under the Model Penal Code, voluntarily withdrawing and thwarting the success of the conspiracy is a defense against the conspiracy itself. Impossibility is not a defense.

Under the common law, **attempt** requires an act with a dangerous propensity towards completion of the crime while the Model Penal Code requires a substantial step beyond mere preparation towards completion of the crime. Both require the specific intent to commit a crime. Attempt merges into the completed target offense. Factual impossibility is not a defense to attempt while legal impossibility is a defense.

Of all the **crimes against persons**, critical to your success on the bar exam is understanding and memorizing **homicide**. Common law murder requires an unlawful killing and "malice aforethought." There are four types of malice. Always analyze all of them. Some questions focus on differentiating these different types of malice. Don't stop when you find one that fits; quickly consider them all:

* Intent to kill.
* Intent to inflict serious bodily injury.
* Gross recklessness (depraved heart).
* Felony murder—killing during course of felony. Intent not required.

Under the common law, felony murder would stand if the killing was done by anyone. Under the modern approach, the killing must be done by the defendant or co-defendant.

Manslaughter can be voluntary or involuntary. Voluntary manslaughter is an intentional killing in the heat of passion. Heat of passion requires a sudden and intense reaction with adequate provocation and no cooling off period. Words

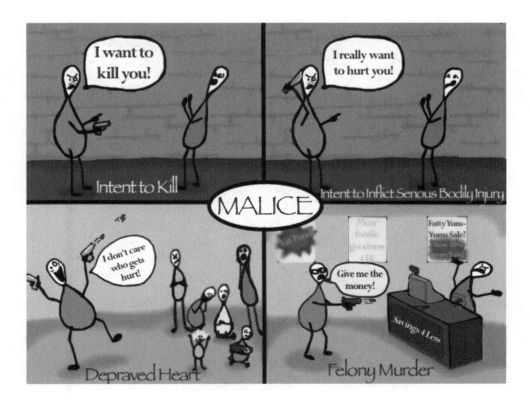

alone are insufficient. Involuntary manslaughter is either an unlawful killing with negligence or recklessness or a killing during the course of a misdemeanor or a felony not included in felony murder.

The modern approach to homicide includes classifying the murder by degrees. First-degree murder includes the only specific intent homicide—premeditated murder. First-degree felony murder occurs when the felony is enumerated by statute but typically includes rape, burglary, robbery, arson, and kidnapping. Second-degree murder is a catch-all for all other common law murders.

As for **crimes against property**, pay particular attention to the differences between larceny, embezzlement, and false pretenses:

- **Larceny**—taking away another's property by trespass with the intent to permanently deprive the person of their property.
- **Embezzlement**—conversion of property held in trust with the intent to defraud.
- **False pretenses**—taking title to property by misrepresentation with intent to defraud.

The key difference between larceny and embezzlement is that the owner was originally in possession with larceny. With embezzlement, the criminal originally had possession.

Robbery is larceny by force or threat of force. Thus, analyze the elements of larceny adding the element of "by force" or "threat of force."

Another key crime against property is **burglary**. Under the common law, burglary is the breaking and entering a dwelling of another at night with the intent to commit a felony within the dwelling. Thus, burglary is a specific intent crime. The modern approach expands dwelling to include any structure and is not limited to night time.

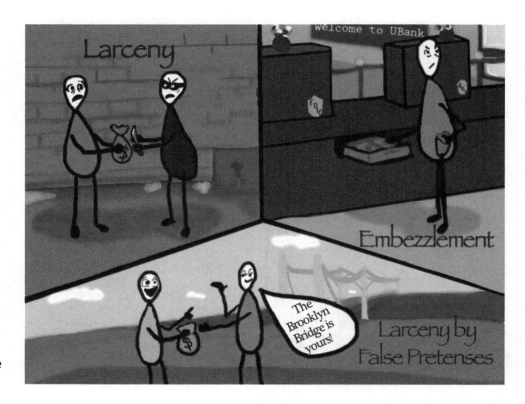

Larceny v. Embezzlement v. False Pretenses

Defenses to crimes include insanity, intoxication, infancy, mistake, self-defense, defense of others, defense of property, duress, necessity, and entrapment. For **insanity**, the common law rule is called the M'Naughten rule. Under that rule, mental illness precluded knowing right from wrong or understanding the nature and quality of act. Under the Model Penal Code, mental illness resulted in lack of substantial capacity to appreciate wrongfulness of conduct or to conform conduct to law.

Involuntary intoxication is a defense to all elements of a crime. Intoxication is caused by any substance including alcohol, drugs, and medicine. Involuntary intoxication results when the individual is taking the intoxicating substance without knowledge of its nature, under direct duress imposed by another, or pursuant to medical advice while unaware of the substance's intoxicating effect. Involuntary intoxication may be treated as a mental illness in some jurisdictions.

Voluntary intoxication is self-induced and results from intentional taking without duress a substance known to be intoxicating. The person need not have intended to become intoxicated. Voluntary intoxication may be a defense to crimes requiring intent or knowledge if the intoxication prevented the accused from formulating the requisite intent. Thus, voluntary intoxication may be a good defense to specific intent crimes, but not for general defense crimes including murder as malice aforethought includes recklessness.

A **mistake of fact** must negate the state of mind. For general intent crimes, the mistake must be reasonable. For specific intent crimes, reasonableness is not required as any mistake of fact is a defense. As strict liability offenses do not require a particular state of mind, mistake of fact is not a defense. **Mistake of law** is not a defense to a crime.

An individual may use non-deadly force in **self-defense** if she reasonably believed the force used was necessary to defend against imminent unlawful force. Deadly force is allowed only when the accused reasonably believes the force used is necessary to defend against imminent unlawful deadly force or serious bodily injury.

Criminal law is a topic that some applicants brush off thinking it is more manageable than others. Don't be mistaken. Keep your focus on the subtle

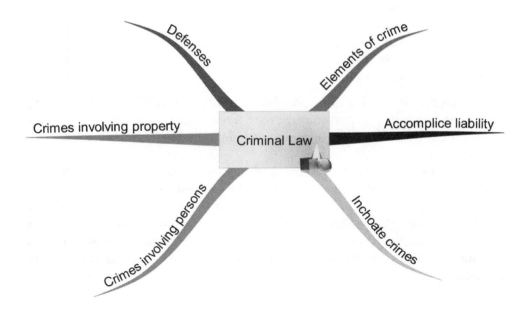

differences between similar crimes and the *mens rea* for each crime. On essays, generally give both the common law and Model Penal Code approach. For example, the *actus rea* required for attempt under the common law is an act with a dangerous propensity towards completion of the crime while under the Model Penal Code the act must be a substantial step in a course of conduct planned to culminate in the commission of the crime. In an attempt essay, analyze both. If a statute is given in either an essay or MBE question, hands down the central issue will focus on that statute. It's not just thrown in as a red herring. It's there for a purpose.

II. CRIMINAL PROCEDURE

Your mind map for criminal procedure follows the chronological progression of a suspect from evidence gathering and arrest until a guilty plea or conviction:

* Search and seizure
* Exclusionary rule
* Confession
* Guilty pleas
* Double jeopardy
* Privilege against self-incrimination

The Fourth Amendment of the U.S. Constitution provides that people should be free in their persons from unreasonable **searches and seizures**. "Search" is a government intrusion into an area where a person has a reasonable expectation of privacy. "Seizure" is the government exercising control over a person or thing. "Reasonableness" depends upon the circumstances—a valid warrant authorizing that the action is reasonable and an action that is reasonable without a warrant if the evidence is in plain view or another warrant exception makes the search reasonable.

Your analysis needs to follow each step:

* State action?
* Search or seizure?
* Warrant or warrant exception?
* Execution of warrant proper?
* Standing to protest?
* Evidence suppressed?

A **search** is a physical intrusion into a constitutionally protected area to obtain information. The person must have a reasonable expectation of privacy in that area, whether that is a home, an automobile, or a homeless person's sleeping space.

The **seizure** of a person is an **arrest**. Warrants are not required for arrests in public if supported by probable cause. While felonies only require probable cause, misdemeanors require both probable cause and that the misdemeanor was committed in the presence of an officer. Warrants are required for arrests in private, such as the person's home, unless an exception applies. If the person is in someone else's home, then a search warrant and an arrest warrant are necessary.

The seizure of a thing requires a meaningful interference with a possessory interest in the thing.

The only person who can challenge the constitutionality of a search or seizure is the person who was searched or seized. Thus, the accused has no **standing** to assert an unconstitutional search and seizure defense when the search occurred in a friend's home, where the accused has no reasonable expectation of privacy. This is an issue of standing and is a frequent test area.

To have a valid search or seizure, it must be authorized by a valid **warrant** or by a **warrant exception**. To have a valid warrant, there must be:

- Probable cause—fair probability, reasonable grounds, or reasonably trustworthy information sufficient for a prudent person to conclude that:
  - a crime has been or is being committed by the person to be seized, OR
  - there is evidence of criminality in place to be searched. (Note: hearsay and anonymous tips may support probable cause. Test is totality of circumstances.)
- Particularity—sufficiently definite for police to identify persons, places, or items to be searched or seized with reasonable certainty. Particularity must be on the face of the warrant or an incorporated affidavit.
- Oath or affirmation.
- Detached and neutral magistrate.

The warrant exceptions include:

- Plain view—police may seize an item they see in plain view or can "plain feel" if they have authority to be where they are and the item is connected with criminality.
- Consent—voluntary under totality of circumstances. May not search home over present objection of co-occupant.
- Exigent circumstances—police have reasonable belief to believe delay in obtaining warrant would result in evidence destruction, danger to public/police, or flight of suspect.
- Automobile search—probable cause that any area of car to be searched (including containers) harbors evidence of criminality.
- Search incident to lawful arrest:
  - Person: contemporaneous search of person, lunge area, and containers for weapons or evidence.
  - Car:
    - no search unless reasonable belief that arrested occupant or recent occupant may access car; OR
    - reasonable belief that car contains evidence of crime of arrest (not speeding).
  - Home: during the time it takes to complete arrest, may conduct a protective sweep for accomplices in adjoining rooms if reasonable suspicion of danger.
- Inventory—within scope of a reasonable and routine procedure to protect valuables, police, and public, police may inventory contents of possessions at time of booking and automobiles after impound.

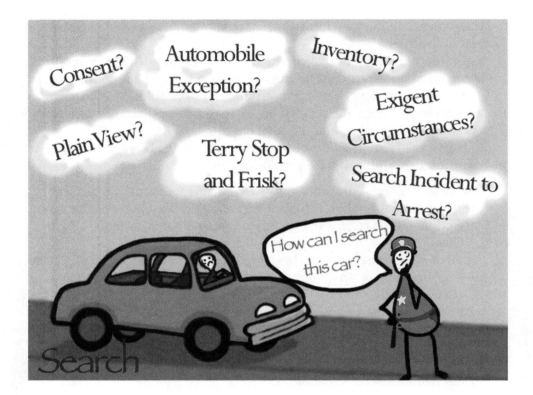

Automobile Searches

- *Terry:*
  - Stop: reasonable suspicion that suspect is engaged in criminal activity based on specific and articulate facts. Reasonable suspicion is less than probable cause, but more than a hunch.
  - Frisk: *Terry Stop* plus reasonable suspicion that suspect is armed and dangerous. May not frisk for evidence, only weapons.

The **execution of the warrant** must be reasonable. Before the search, police must knock and announce their presence and purpose before entering the premises unless they have reasonable grounds to believe it would be dangerous or futile. The requirement to knock and announce is also suspended if the police have reasonable grounds to believe evidence would be destroyed. During the search, police may take reasonable steps to secure premises including temporarily detaining individuals at the scene and ordering occupants out of a car.

The **exclusionary rule** is the main sanction against the state for violating an accused's constitutional rights. Any evidence gathered as a result of the state's unconstitutional conduct is inadmissible against the person whose rights were violated unless an exception applies. This rule is known as the "**fruit of the poisonous tree**." This includes all evidence downstream from the violation. In your analysis, once you have found a constitutional violation, state the exclusionary rule and that the evidence should be excluded. Only then do you address if an exception applies:

- Procedural exceptions:
  - Impeachment purposes
  - Grand jury proceedings

* Parole revocation hearing
* Civil proceedings such as immigration
* Doctrinal exceptions:
    * Knock and announce violation
    * Reasonable good faith reliance on facially valid warrant, although later found to be lacking probable cause
    * Clerical errors by court employees in maintaining records such as arrest warrants
    * Isolated negligence by police in maintaining records such as arrest warrants
* Found not to be fruit of the poisonous tree:
    * Independent source for obtaining evidence
    * Inevitable discovery
    * Attenuation

Confessions obtained by a state actor may be suppressed if obtained in violation of the Due Process Clause, the Sixth Amendment right to counsel, or the Fifth Amendment *Miranda* doctrine. The test for a due process violation is whether the confession was involuntary because the accused's will was overborne by state coercion.

The Sixth Amendment provides a **right to counsel** after the initiation of adversarial proceedings. The state cannot undermine this right by deliberate elicitation of a confession in the absence of counsel. If formal charges are brought such as an indictment and not a mere arrest, then the right to counsel arises. The test is violated by deliberate elicitation without counsel.

To protect the accused, the Supreme Court has construed the Fifth and Sixth Amendments to require a right to counsel and a **right to silence** when in a custodial interrogation. The state—the police—are required to inform the accused of their rights through *Miranda* **warnings**. When looking at confessions, go through each step of the analysis:

* Custody?
* Interrogation?
* Warnings given?
* Did accused invoke right to counsel? (unequivocally/expressly)
* Did accused waive rights? (voluntary, knowing, and intelligent)

The actual *Miranda* warnings are:

* Right to remain silent;
* Any statements can be used against you;
* Right to counsel before and during questions;
* If you cannot afford a lawyer, one will be appointed for you.

Once invoked, police must scrupulously honor both the right to silence and the right to counsel. If the suspect initiates conversation or a significant amount of time has elapsed, the police can resume interrogation after giving new warnings and receiving a valid waiver. Thus, if the first interrogation was invalid as without warnings and then a valid confession occurs, that confession will be admissible with proper warnings and proper waiver.

When an accused decides to make a **guilty plea**, the judge must follow the plea-taking colloquy on the record:

- Nature of charge;
- Maximum authorized sentence and any statutory minimum;
- Right to plead not guilty and to have a trial;
- Defendant waiving right to trial.

The accused cannot then withdraw her guilty plea unless:

- Defective plea-taking colloquy;
- Jurisdictional defect;
- Ineffective assistance of counsel, or;
- Prosecutor fails to fulfill his side of plea bargain. (Note: Judge is not bound by prosecutor's bargain.)

Double jeopardy prohibits a person being put twice in jeopardy of life or limb for the same offense by the same sovereign. Double jeopardy attaches when someone is put "in jeopardy"—when a jury is sworn in, when the first witness is sworn in during a bench trial, or when the judge accepts the plea unconditionally. Double jeopardy does not apply to civil proceedings. Double jeopardy is not implicated when the charges are not the same offense as when each offense has an element that the other does not.

Retrials are permitted if there is a hung jury, a mistrial due to manifest necessity, or a successful appeal.

The Fifth Amendment prohibits compelled testimony in a criminal case. Anyone may invoke the **privilege against self-incrimination** in a custodial interrogation and in any proceeding with testimony under oath. It does not apply to physical evidence or to prior uncompelled communication.

Most of your focus in your Criminal Procedure preparation should be on search and seizure, the exclusionary rule, and confessions. Without a doubt, that is where your 75% lies.

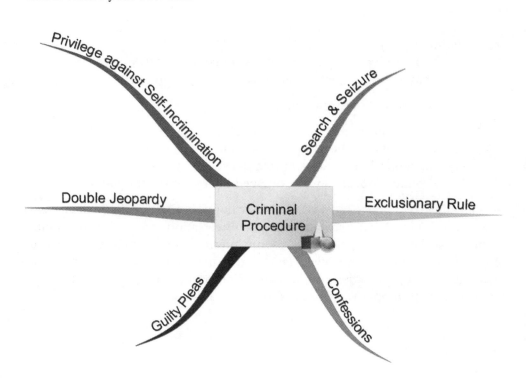

III. MBE STRATEGIES[1]

The split between Criminal Law questions and Criminal Procedure questions is almost exactly 50/50. The call of the question can range from whether the defendant should be found guilty to best argument questions. Always remember that best argument questions are really not the "best" argument. Only one of the responses is correct both in the result and the reasoning. Any mismatch and the response is incorrect.

A favorite topic is the differences between degrees and types of homicides. Remember, murder does not require intent. The *mens rea* can be satisfied by a "depraved heart"—a disregarding of an unreasonably high risk of harm to human life. In addition, look for any provocation. If the provocation is sufficient to anger this accused and it would provoke a reasonable person to kill, then the charge should be voluntary manslaughter if there was no cooling off and a reasonable person would not have cooled off under these circumstances.

Understand the differences between larceny, robbery, and burglary. These are frequent test topics. Make a chart of the differences to help you encode in your memory.

Memorize the list of warrantless searches allowed. If no warrant is in the fact pattern, go through this list to see if any apply. This type of question is frequently asked and the responses can trick you if they set out the reasoning for a different type of search not implicated by your facts.

Custodial interrogations and confessions are frequent topics. Look for whether the situation is custodial before you decide if the accused's rights were violated.

Use these strategies to analyze criminal law questions:

- Apply statutes verbatim. Criminal law questions frequently include a snippet of a statute. That snippet is loaded with potential issues, particularly concerning *mens rea*.
- Causation is always required for liability. Don't ignore if the defendant's conduct did not cause the victim's injury.
- Victim forgiveness (or settlement) does not negate the crime. Criminal violations are considered wrongs against the state, not against the individual.
- Once property is taken with the intent to steal, subsequent return of the property does not negate larceny.
- Categorize the *type* of search first; identifying the correct category will often allow elimination of one or more answer choices applying an inapplicable test.
- A person may object to a search only if she has a legitimate expectation of privacy as to the place being searched; this is a threshold issue.
- MBE questions dealing with witness testimony may state, before the call of the question, "If the jury believes him":
  - Always treat the testimony as fact.
  - Ignore any instinctual belief that the witness is lying.
  - Watch for hidden intent problems.

---

1. Some of these strategies are from Steven L. Emanuel, *Strategies & Tactics for the MBE* 127-35 (5th ed. 2013).

IV. ESSAY PRACTICE QUESTION[2]

John, age 18, and Crystal, age 14, walked into the Minit Mart, a convenience store. They wandered around the store for a few minutes and then walked up to the counter. John had his hand in a leather bag. He stared at the store clerk for about 10 seconds and started to sweat. At this point, Crystal began to cry. She said, "I don't want to do this," and ran out of the store. John remained for a few more seconds and then ran out of the store himself. The store clerk immediately called 911 and nervously said, "Two kids were about to rob me, but I guess they changed their minds."

Three days later, the police came to Crystal's home, where she lives with her parents. The police told Crystal's mother that Crystal was a suspect in an attempted robbery and that they wanted to search for evidence. Crystal's mother asked the police if they had a warrant. They said, "No, but we can get one." Crystal's mother let the police in.

When the police searched Crystal's room, they found John's zipped leather bag in Crystal's closet. Without first obtaining a search warrant, or asking Crystal's mother who owned the bag, the police opened the bag and found a gun and printouts of emails from John to a friend. The police read the emails, which described John's plans to rob the Minit Mart with the help of his girlfriend, Crystal.

Crystal later confessed that she and John had planned to rob the Minit Mart, but that she got scared and ran out of the store. She also said that John gave her the leather bag with the gun after they had left the Minit Mart and told her to "get rid of it."

John was charged with attempted armed robbery of the Minit Mart store. His lawyer filed a motion to suppress the leather bag and its contents on the grounds that the bag was seized and searched in violation of John's Fourth Amendment rights. The trial court denied the motion, and the issue was properly preserved for appeal.

At John's trial for attempted armed robbery, the Minit Mart clerk testified to the facts that he had told the police earlier. Crystal also testified for the prosecution, repeating what she had previously told the police. She also said that the leather bag belonged to John, that she and John had planned the robbery together, that she saw John load the gun and put it in his leather bag before they entered the Minit Mart, and that John's hand was in the leather bag with the gun for the entire time that they were in the Minit Mart. She testified that she "got scared" when she and John were standing at the counter, which is why she ran from the store. She said that when John got into the car after running out of the store, he said, "Well, that went bad," and then drove away from the store.

After Crystal's testimony, the prosecution introduced the leather bag, the emails, and the gun into evidence. The court admitted all of the evidence over the objection of John's lawyer.

John presented no evidence.

At the close of the case, the trial court denied both John's motion for judgment of acquittal and his request for a jury instruction on the defense of abandonment.

The jury convicted John of attempted armed robbery. Did the trial court err:

1. In denying John's motion to suppress the leather bag and its contents? Explain.
2. In denying John's motion for judgment of acquittal? Explain.
3. In failing to instruct the jury on the defense of abandonment? Explain.

---

2. The Multistate Bar Examination ("MBE®") questions, the Multistate Essay Examination ("MEE®") questions, and excerpts from the Multistate Performance Tests ("MPT®") have been reprinted by permission from the NCBE®. Copyright© by the National Conference of Bar Examiners. All rights reserved.

V. SCORE SHEET

Stated	Implied	
		1. John's motion to suppress the leather bag and its contents
_____	_____	**Conclusion/Issue:** Because John lacked a reasonable expectation of privacy in both his girlfriend's family home and the bag, the court likely did not err in denying his motion to suppress.
_____	_____	**Rule:** Under the rulings of the U.S. Supreme Court,
_____	_____	Only the actual victims of an alleged Fourth Amendment violation have standing to challenge it.
_____	_____	If a person is aggrieved by an illegal search and seizure only through the introduction of evidence secured by a search of a third person's premises or property, that person has not had any rights infringed.
_____	_____	Further, a person challenging the search and seizure must have a reasonable expectation of privacy in the object or place being searched and seized.
_____	_____	If a person turns over an object to another party, that person surrenders any reasonable expectation of privacy he might have had in that object.
_____	_____	**Application:** Here,
_____	_____	John lacks standing to challenge the search of his girlfriend's family home because it was not his own home and he lacks a reasonable expectation of privacy in it.
_____	_____	Crystal's mother consented to the warrantless search—but John cannot raise the issue of whether her consent was coerced or involuntary.
_____	_____	Even if John might have had a property interest in the bag found in Crystal's closet, he surrendered his reasonable expectation of privacy in that bag when he gave it to Crystal.
_____	_____	After passing it off to her, John could not control who had access to the bag or to the contents of the bag.
_____	_____	**Conclusion:** Therefore,
_____	_____	The court did not err in denying his motion to suppress the bag and its contents.
		2. John's motion for judgment of acquittal
_____	_____	**Conclusion/Issue:** Because the prosecution produced evidence sufficient to prove John intended to commit armed robbery and committed acts that exceeded mere preparation, the court did not err in denying his motion.
_____	_____	**Rule:** A court should grant a motion for judgment of acquittal only if the prosecution has failed to present sufficient evidence for a reasonable jury to find that the defendant committed each element of the offense beyond a reasonable doubt.
_____	_____	Under the Model Penal Code, the prosecution must prove two elements for attempted armed robbery: (1) the defendant intended to commit an armed robbery and (2) that his actions exceeded mere preparation and constituted an actual attempt of the crime itself.
_____	_____	To determine whether the defendant's conduct reaches the point of constituting an attempt to commit the crime, states employ a variety of tests.
_____	_____	Some require his conduct to be proximate to the crime and others require it to be dangerously proximate to the crime.
_____	_____	While the MPC only requires the defendant's actions be a substantial step toward committing the crime and corroborative of his criminal intent, some states require his behavior to unequivocally manifest his criminal intent.

continued on next page

Stated	Implied	
_____	_____	**Application:** Here,
_____	_____	The emails, testimony of the clerk, and Crystal's testimony evidence John's intent.
_____	_____	The evidence shows that John intended to commit essential elements of the crime of armed robbery because he planned to use force (the weapon) or the threat of force to make the clerk give him the money (stealing property of another).
_____	_____	Further, the evidence shows his actions to carry out his plan exceeded mere preparation—he loaded the gun, carried it to the store, and kept it within reach while in the store.
_____	_____	All of the above satisfy any proximity test and possibly the dangerously proximate test because he actually approached the clerk and likely would have completed the crime had his girlfriend remained in the store.
_____	_____	**Conclusion:** Therefore,
_____	_____	The court did not err in denying his motion for judgment of acquittal.
		3. Failure to instruct the jury on the defense of abandonment
_____	_____	**Conclusion/Issue:** Even though John left the premises without actually completing the robbery, the circumstances of his departure do not support this defense.
_____	_____	**Rule:** In the majority of states, if a defendant's conduct had exceeded mere preparation, then voluntary withdrawal or abandonment is not a defense.
_____	_____	The minority considers the abandonment of an attempt before the crime is committed to be an affirmative defense.
_____	_____	Abandonment cannot result merely from an extrinsic factor—it must be utterly voluntary in order to qualify as a defense under this approach.
_____	_____	**Application:** Here,
_____	_____	If the majority approach applies, John's conduct easily exceeded mere preparation and he would be guilty of attempt regardless of whether he ultimately renounced his plans voluntarily.
_____	_____	Under the minority approach, John's abandonment might qualify as a defense.
_____	_____	But he only abandoned the crime after his accomplice broke into tears and fled.
_____	_____	His decision to leave the store was likely based on his response to her flight and not an entirely voluntary decision on his part alone.
_____	_____	As such, it would ultimately fail to meet the requirements of the abandonment defense.
_____	_____	**Conclusion:** Therefore,
_____	_____	The court, under either approach, did not err by failing to instruct the jury of the defense of abandonment.

VI. MBE PRACTICE QUESTIONS[3]

Question 1

A state statute provides: "The sale of an alcoholic beverage to any person under the age of 21 is a misdemeanor."

A woman who was 20 years old, but who looked older and who had a very convincing fake driver's license indicating that she was 24, entered a convenience store, picked up a six-pack of beer, and placed the beer on the counter. The store clerk, after examining the driver's license, rang up the purchase.

Both the clerk and the store owner have been charged with violating the state statute.

If the court finds both the clerk and the store owner guilty, what standard of liability must the court have interpreted the statute to impose?

(A) Strict liability only.
(B) Vicarious liability only.
(C) Both strict and vicarious liability.
(D) Either strict or vicarious liability.

Question 2

A woman charged with murder has entered a plea of not guilty by reason of insanity. At her trial, in which the questions of guilt and sanity are being tried together, the evidence shows that the woman stalked the victim for several hours before following him to an isolated hiking trail where she shot and killed him. Expert witnesses for the defense have testified that the woman knew that killing was illegal and wrong, but that she suffered from a serious mental illness that left her in the grip of a powerful and irresistible compulsion to kill the victim.

If the jury believes the testimony of the defense experts, under what circumstances could the jury properly acquit the woman of murder?

(A) Only if the jurisdiction follows the M'Naghten test for insanity.
(B) Only if the jurisdiction follows the ALI Model Penal Code test for insanity.
(C) If the jurisdiction follows either the M'Naghten or the ALI Model Penal Code test for insanity.
(D) Even if the jurisdiction has abolished the insanity defense.

Question 3

A valid warrant was issued for a woman's arrest. The police learned that a person with the woman's name and physical description lived at a particular address. When police officers went to that address, the house appeared to be unoccupied: the windows and doors were boarded up with plywood, and the lawn had not been mowed for a long time. A neighbor confirmed that the house belonged to the woman but said that the woman had not been there for several months.

---

3. *Id.*

The officers knocked repeatedly on the front door and shouted, "Police! Open up!" Receiving no response, they tore the plywood off the door, smashed through the door with a sledgehammer, and entered the house. They found no one inside, but they did find an illegal sawed-off shotgun. Upon her return to the house a few weeks later, the woman was charged with unlawful possession of the shotgun.

The woman has moved to suppress the use of the shotgun as evidence at her trial. Should the court grant the motion?

(A) No, because the officers acted in good faith under the authority of a valid warrant.

(B) No, because the officers did not violate any legitimate expectation of privacy in the house since the woman had abandoned it.

(C) Yes, because the officers entered the house by means of excessive force.

(D) Yes, because the officers had no reason to believe that the woman was in the house.

Question 4

A woman was subpoenaed to appear before a grand jury. When she arrived, she was taken into the grand jury room to be questioned. She answered preliminary questions about her name and address. She was then asked where she had been at a certain time on a specified night when a murder had occurred. Before answering the question, the woman said that she wanted to consult her attorney, who was waiting outside the grand jury room, and she was allowed to do so. When she returned to the grand jury room, she stated that she refused to answer the question because the answer might incriminate her.

The prosecutor believes that the woman's nephew committed the murder. The nephew has said that he was with the woman at the time of the murder, and the prosecutor believes that this alibi is false. The prosecutor does not believe that the woman is guilty of the murder, either as a principal or as an accomplice, although he does believe that the woman may be guilty of other crimes. The prosecutor wants to compel the woman to answer the question by whatever means will result in the least harm to the prosecution's case.

Which of the following steps should the prosecutor take to get the woman to answer the question?

(A) Request the grand jury to order the woman to answer the question.

(B) Ask the woman's attorney to explain to the woman that the rules of evidence do not apply in grand jury proceedings, and to advise her that she cannot refuse to testify.

(C) Prepare the documents necessary to grant the woman immunity from any future use against her of her grand jury testimony or any evidence derived from it.

(D) Prepare the documents necessary to grant the woman immunity from any future prosecution for any crime she might disclose in the course of her testimony.

Question 5

A defendant was validly arrested for the murder of a store clerk and was taken to a police station where he was given Miranda warnings. When an interrogator asked the defendant, "Do you understand your Miranda rights, and are you willing to give up those rights and talk to us?" the defendant replied, "Yes." When asked, "Did you kill the clerk?" the defendant replied, "No." When asked, "Where were you on the day the clerk was killed?" the defendant replied, "Maybe I should talk to a lawyer." The interrogator asked, "Are you sure?" and the defendant replied, "I'm not sure." The interrogator then asked, "Why would you want to talk with a lawyer?" and the defendant replied, "Because I killed the clerk. It was an accident, and I think I need a lawyer to defend me." At that point all interrogation ceased. Later, the defendant was formally charged with murdering the clerk.

The defendant has moved to suppress evidence of his statement "I killed the clerk" on the ground that this statement was elicited in violation of his Miranda rights.

Should the defendant's motion be granted?

(A) No, because although the defendant effectively asserted the right to counsel, the question "Why would you want to talk with a lawyer?" did not constitute custodial interrogation.

(B) No, because the defendant did not effectively assert the right to counsel, and his conduct prior to making the statement constituted a valid waiver of his Miranda rights.

(C) Yes, because although the defendant did not effectively assert the right to counsel, his conduct prior to making the statement did not constitute a valid waiver of his Miranda rights.

(D) Yes, because the defendant effectively asserted the right to counsel, and the question "Why would you want to talk with a lawyer?" constituted custodial interrogation.

Question 6

Two defendants were being tried together in federal court for bank robbery. The prosecutor sought to introduce testimony from the first defendant's prison cellmate. The cellmate would testify that the first defendant had admitted to the cellmate that he and the second defendant had robbed the bank. The prosecutor asked the court to instruct the jury that the cellmate's testimony could be considered only against the first defendant.

Can the cellmate's testimony be admitted in a joint trial over the second defendant's objection?

(A) No, because the first defendant made the statement without Miranda warnings.

(B) No, because the limiting instruction cannot ensure that the jury will not consider the testimony in its deliberations regarding the second defendant.

(C) Yes, because the first defendant's statement was a declaration against penal interest.

(D) Yes, because the limiting instruction sufficiently protects the second defendant.

Question 7

A prosecutor presented to a federal grand jury the testimony of a witness in order to secure a defendant's indictment for theft of government property. The prosecutor did not disclose to the grand jury that the witness had been convicted four years earlier of perjury. The grand jury returned an indictment, and the defendant pleaded not guilty.

Shortly thereafter, the prosecutor took the case to trial, calling the witness to testify before the jury. The prosecutor did not disclose the witness's prior perjury conviction until the defense was preparing to rest. Defense counsel immediately moved for a mistrial, which the court denied. Instead, the court allowed the defense to recall the witness for the purpose of impeaching him with this conviction, but the witness could not be located. The court then allowed the defense to introduce documentary evidence of the witness's criminal record to the jury before resting its case. The jury convicted the defendant.

The defendant has moved for a new trial, arguing that the prosecutor's failure to disclose the witness's prior conviction in a timely manner violated the defendant's right to due process of law.

If the court grants the defendant's motion, what will be the most likely reason?

(A) The defendant was unable to cross-examine the witness about the conviction.
(B) The prosecutor failed to inform the grand jury of the witness's conviction.
(C) The court found it reasonably probable that the defendant would have been acquitted had the defense had timely access to the information about the witness's conviction.
(D) The court found that the prosecutor had deliberately delayed disclosing the witness's conviction to obtain a strategic advantage.

Question 8

A state statute divides murder into degrees and defines murder in the first degree as murder committed willfully with premeditation and deliberation. The statute defines murder in the second degree as all other murder at common law and defines voluntary manslaughter as at common law.

A man hated one of his coworkers. Upon learning that the coworker was at a neighbor's house, the man grabbed his gun and went to the neighbor's house hoping to provoke the coworker into attacking him so that he could then shoot the coworker. After arriving at the house, the man insulted the coworker and bragged that he had had sexual relations with the coworker's wife two weeks earlier. This statement was not true, but it enraged the coworker, who grabbed a knife from the kitchen table and ran toward the man. The man then shot and killed the coworker.

What is the most serious homicide offense of which the man could properly be convicted?

(A) Murder in the first degree.
(B) Murder in the second degree.
(C) Voluntary manslaughter, because he provoked the coworker.
(D) No form of criminal homicide, because he acted in self-defense.

Question 9

A wife decided to kill her husband because she was tired of his infidelity. She managed to obtain some cyanide, a deadly poison. One evening, she poured wine laced with the cyanide into a glass, handed it to her husband, and proposed a loving toast. The husband was so pleased with the toast that he set the glass of wine down on a table, grabbed his wife, and kissed her passionately. After the kiss, the wife changed her mind about killing the husband. She hid the glass of wine behind a lamp on the table, planning to leave it for the maid to clean up. The husband did not drink the wine.

The maid found the glass of wine while cleaning the next day. Rather than throw the wine away, the maid drank it. Shortly thereafter, she fell into a coma and died from cyanide poisoning.

In a common law jurisdiction, of what crime(s), if any, could the wife be found guilty?

(A) Attempted murder of the husband and murder or manslaughter of the maid.
(B) Only attempted murder of the husband.
(C) Only murder or manslaughter of the maid.
(D) No crime.

Question 10

In a crowded football stadium, a man saw a wallet fall out of a spectator's purse. The man picked up the wallet and found that it contained $100 in cash. Thinking that he could use the money and seeing no one watching, the man put the wallet in the pocket of his coat. Just then, the spectator approached the man and asked if he had seen a missing wallet. The man said no and went home with the wallet.

Of what crime, if any, is the man guilty?

(A) Embezzlement.
(B) False pretenses.
(C) Larceny.
(D) No crime.

Question 11

A woman went to an art gallery and falsely represented that she was an agent for a museum and wanted to purchase a painting that was hanging in the gallery. The woman and the gallery owner then agreed on a price for the painting to be paid 10 days later, and the woman took the painting. When the gallery failed to receive the payment when due, the owner called the museum and discovered that the woman did not work there. The owner then notified the police.

When interviewed by the police, the woman admitted making the false representation and acquiring the painting, but she said she believed that the painting had been stolen from her by someone who worked in the gallery.

Is the woman guilty of obtaining property by false pretenses?

(A) No, because she believed that the painting belonged to her.
(B) No, because the gallery owner would have sold the painting to anyone who agreed to pay the price.
(C) Yes, because even if her representation was not material, she never intended to pay for the painting.
(D) Yes, because she knowingly made a false representation on which the gallery owner relied.

Question 12

A woman broke off her engagement to a man but refused to return the engagement ring the man had given her. One night, the man entered the woman's house after midnight to retrieve the ring. Although the woman was not at home, a neighbor saw the man enter the house and called the police. The man unsuccessfully searched for the ring for 10 minutes. As he was walking out the front door, the police arrived and immediately arrested him.

The man has been charged with burglary in a jurisdiction that follows the common law. Which of the following, if proved, would serve as the man's best defense to the charge?

(A) The man knew that the woman kept a key under the doormat and he used the key to enter the house.
(B) The man incorrectly and unreasonably believed that he was legally entitled to the ring.
(C) The man knew that no one was at home when he entered the house.
(D) The man took nothing of value from the house.

Question 13

A woman wanted to kill a business competitor. She contacted a man who she believed was willing to commit murder for hire and offered him $50,000 to kill the competitor. The man agreed to do so and accepted $25,000 as a down payment. Unbeknownst to the woman, the man was an undercover police officer.

In a jurisdiction that has adopted the unilateral theory of conspiracy, is the woman guilty of conspiracy to murder the business competitor?

(A) No, because the man did not intend to kill the competitor.
(B) No, because it would have been impossible for the woman to kill the competitor by this method.
(C) Yes, because the woman believed that she had an agreement with the man that would bring about the competitor's death.
(D) Yes, because the woman took a substantial step toward bringing about the competitor's death by paying the man $25,000.

Question 14

A state statute provides as follows: "The maintenance of any ongoing enterprise in the nature of a betting parlor or bookmaking organization is a felony."

A prosecutor has evidence that a woman has been renting an office to a man, that the man has been using the office as a betting parlor within the meaning of the statute, and that the woman is aware of this use.

Which of the following additional pieces of evidence would be most useful to the prosecutor's effort to convict the woman as an accomplice to the man's violation of the statute?

(A) The woman was previously convicted of running a betting parlor herself on the same premises.
(B) The woman charges the man considerably more in rent than she charged the preceding tenant, who used the office for legitimate activities.
(C) The woman has personally placed bets with the man at the office location.

(D) The man has paid the woman the rent in bills that are traceable as the proceeds of gambling activity.

Question 15

After a defendant was indicted on federal bank fraud charges and released on bail, his attorney filed notice of the defendant's intent to offer an insanity defense. The prosecutor then enlisted the help of a forensic psychologist who was willing to participate in an "undercover" mental examination of the defendant. The psychologist contacted the defendant and pretended to represent an executive personnel agency. She told the defendant about an attractive employment opportunity and invited him to a "preliminary screening interview" to determine his qualifications for the job. As part of the purported screening process, the psychologist gave the defendant psychological tests that enabled her to form a reliable opinion about his mental state at the time of the alleged offense.

What is the strongest basis for a defense objection to the psychologist's testimony regarding the defendant's mental state?

(A) The Fourth Amendment prohibition against unreasonable searches and seizures.
(B) The Fifth Amendment privilege against compelled self-incrimination.
(C) The Sixth Amendment right to the assistance of counsel.
(D) The federal common law privilege for confidential communications between psychotherapist and patient.

Question 16

A defendant is charged with an offense under a statute that provides as follows: "Any person who, while intoxicated, appears in any public place and manifests a drunken condition by obstreperous or indecent conduct is guilty of a misdemeanor."

At trial, the evidence shows that the defendant was intoxicated when police officers burst into his house and arrested him pursuant to a valid warrant. It was a cold night, and the officers hustled the defendant out of his house without giving him time to get his coat. The defendant became angry and obstreperous when the officers refused to let him go back into the house to retrieve his coat. The officers left him handcuffed outside in the street, waiting for a special squad car to arrive. The arrest warrant was later vacated.

Can the defendant properly be convicted of violating the statute?

(A) No, because the defendant's claim of mistreatment is valid.
(B) No, because the statute requires proof of a voluntary appearance in a public place.
(C) Yes, because the defendant voluntarily became intoxicated.
(D) Yes, because the defendant voluntarily behaved in an obstreperous manner.

Question 17

A police officer had a hunch, not amounting to probable cause or reasonable suspicion, that a man was a drug dealer. One day while the officer was on highway patrol, her radar gun clocked the man's car at 68 mph in an area where the maximum posted speed limit was 65 mph. The officer's usual practice was not to stop a car unless it was going at least 5 mph over the posted limit, but contrary to her usual practice, she decided to stop the man's car in the hope that she might discover evidence of drug dealing. After she stopped the car and announced that she would be writing a speeding ticket, the officer ordered the man and his passenger to step out of the car. When the passenger stepped out, the officer saw that the passenger had been sitting on a clear bag of what the officer immediately recognized as marijuana. The officer arrested both the man and the passenger for possession of marijuana.

At their joint trial, the man and the passenger claim that their Fourth Amendment rights were violated because the officer improperly (1) stopped the car for speeding as a pretext for investigating a hunch rather than for the stated purpose of issuing a traffic ticket and (2) ordered the passenger to step out of the car even though there was no reason to believe that the passenger was a criminal or dangerous.

Are the man and the passenger correct?

(A) No, as to both the stop of the car and the officer's order that the passenger step out of the car.
(B) No as to the stop of the car, but yes as to the officer's order that the passenger step out of the car.
(C) Yes as to the stop of the car, but no as to the officer's order that the passenger step out of the car.
(D) Yes, as to both the stop of the car and the officer's order that the passenger step out of the car.

VII. MBE PRACTICE ANALYSIS[4]

Question 1

A state statute provides: "The sale of an alcoholic beverage to any person under the age of 21 is a misdemeanor."

A woman who was 20 years old, but who looked older and who had a very convincing fake driver's license indicating that she was 24, entered a convenience store, picked up a six-pack of beer, and placed the beer on the counter. The store clerk, after examining the driver's license, rang up the purchase.

Both the clerk and the store owner have been charged with violating the state statute.

If the court finds both the clerk and the store owner guilty, what standard of liability must the court have interpreted the statute to impose?

(A) Strict liability only.
Incorrect. The court must have applied strict liability to convict the clerk (who did not act knowingly, and arguably not even negligently), but must have applied vicarious liability to convict the store owner for the sale by the clerk.

(B) Vicarious liability only.
Incorrect. The court must have applied vicarious liability to convict the store owner for the sale by the clerk, but must have applied strict liability to convict the clerk (who did not act knowingly, and arguably not even negligently).

---

4. *Id.*

(C) Both strict and vicarious liability.
Correct. The court must have applied strict liability to convict the clerk (who did not act knowingly, and arguably not even negligently) and vicarious liability to convict the store owner for the sale by the clerk.

(D) Either strict or vicarious liability.
Incorrect. The court must have applied strict liability to convict the clerk (who did not act knowingly, and arguably not even negligently) and vicarious liability to convict the store owner for the sale by the clerk.

Question 2

A woman charged with murder has entered a plea of not guilty by reason of insanity. At her trial, in which the questions of guilt and sanity are being tried together, the evidence shows that the woman stalked the victim for several hours before following him to an isolated hiking trail where she shot and killed him. Expert witnesses for the defense have testified that the woman knew that killing was illegal and wrong, but that she suffered from a serious mental illness that left her in the grip of a powerful and irresistible compulsion to kill the victim.

If the jury believes the testimony of the defense experts, under what circumstances could the jury properly acquit the woman of murder?

(A) Only if the jurisdiction follows the M'Naghten test for insanity.
Incorrect. The jury could not find the woman to be legally insane under the M'Naghten test, which requires either that she did not know the nature and quality of the act she was committing or that she did not know the difference between right and wrong.

(B) Only if the jurisdiction follows the ALI Model Penal Code test for insanity.
Correct. The jury could find the woman to be legally insane under the ALI Model Penal Code test, because she could not conform her conduct to the requirements of the law.

(C) If the jurisdiction follows either the M'Naghten or the ALI Model Penal Code test for insanity.
Incorrect. The jury could not find the woman to be legally insane under the M'Naghten test, which requires either that she did not know the nature and quality of the act she was committing or that she did not know the difference between right and wrong. The jury could find the woman to be legally insane under the ALI Model Penal Code test, because she could not conform her conduct to the requirements of the law.

(D) Even if the jurisdiction has abolished the insanity defense.
Incorrect. The woman committed all the elements of murder and can be excused from responsibility only if she meets a recognized defense of insanity.

Question 3

A valid warrant was issued for a woman's arrest. The police learned that a person with the woman's name and physical description lived at a particular address. When police officers went to that address, the house appeared to be unoccupied: the windows and doors were boarded up with plywood, and the lawn had not been mowed for a long time. A neighbor confirmed that the house belonged to the woman but said that the woman had not been there for several months.

The officers knocked repeatedly on the front door and shouted, "Police! Open up!" Receiving no response, they tore the plywood off the door, smashed through the door with a sledgehammer, and entered the house. They found no one inside, but they did find an illegal sawed-off shotgun. Upon her return to the house a few weeks later, the woman was charged with unlawful possession of the shotgun.

The woman has moved to suppress the use of the shotgun as evidence at her trial. Should the court grant the motion?

(A) No, because the officers acted in good faith under the authority of a valid warrant.
Incorrect. Under the Fourth Amendment, the arrest warrant would have authorized forcible entry only if the officers had reason to believe that the woman was at home at the time of the entry. Here, the officers knew that the woman was not at home.

(B) No, because the officers did not violate any legitimate expectation of privacy in the house since the woman had abandoned it.
Incorrect. The facts here are legally insufficient to suggest that the woman had abandoned any reasonable expectation of privacy in the house.

(C) Yes, because the officers entered the house by means of excessive force.
Incorrect. Under the Fourth Amendment, the arrest warrant would have authorized forcible entry if the officers had reason to believe that the woman was at home at the time of the entry. Here, however, the officers knew that the woman was not at home.

(D) Yes, because the officers had no reason to believe that the woman was in the house.
Correct. Under the Fourth Amendment, the arrest warrant would have authorized forcible entry only if the officers had reason to believe that the woman was at home at the time of the entry. Here, the officers knew that the woman was not at home.

Question 4

A woman was subpoenaed to appear before a grand jury. When she arrived, she was taken into the grand jury room to be questioned. She answered preliminary questions about her name and address. She was then asked where she had been at a certain time on a specified night when a murder had occurred. Before answering the question, the woman said that she wanted to consult her attorney, who was waiting outside the grand jury room, and she was allowed to do so. When she returned to the grand jury room, she stated that she refused to answer the question because the answer might incriminate her.

The prosecutor believes that the woman's nephew committed the murder. The nephew has said that he was with the woman at the time of the murder, and the prosecutor believes that this alibi is false. The prosecutor does not believe that the woman is guilty of the murder, either as a principal or as an accomplice, although he does believe that the woman may be guilty of other crimes. The prosecutor wants to compel the woman to answer the question by whatever means will result in the least harm to the prosecution's case.

Which of the following steps should the prosecutor take to get the woman to answer the question?

(A) Request the grand jury to order the woman to answer the question.
Incorrect. The woman cannot be compelled to provide potentially incriminating testimony unless she is granted use and derivative-use immunity.

(B) Ask the woman's attorney to explain to the woman that the rules of evidence do not apply in grand jury proceedings, and to advise her that she cannot refuse to testify.

Incorrect. While the rules of evidence do not apply before grand juries, a witness cannot be compelled to provide potentially incriminating testimony unless the witness is granted use and derivative-use immunity.

(C) Prepare the documents necessary to grant the woman immunity from any future use against her of her grand jury testimony or any evidence derived from it.

Correct. A witness cannot be compelled to provide potentially incriminating testimony unless the witness is granted use and derivative-use immunity.

(D) Prepare the documents necessary to grant the woman immunity from any future prosecution for any crime she might disclose in the course of her testimony.

Incorrect. A witness cannot be compelled to provide potentially incriminating testimony unless the witness is granted use and derivative-use immunity, but the witness need not be granted transactional immunity.

Question 5

A defendant was validly arrested for the murder of a store clerk and was taken to a police station where he was given Miranda warnings. When an interrogator asked the defendant, "Do you understand your Miranda rights, and are you willing to give up those rights and talk to us?" the defendant replied, "Yes." When asked, "Did you kill the clerk?" the defendant replied, "No." When asked, "Where were you on the day the clerk was killed?" the defendant replied, "Maybe I should talk to a lawyer." The interrogator asked, "Are you sure?" and the defendant replied, "I'm not sure." The interrogator then asked, "Why would you want to talk with a lawyer?" and the defendant replied, "Because I killed the clerk. It was an accident, and I think I need a lawyer to defend me." At that point all interrogation ceased. Later, the defendant was formally charged with murdering the clerk.

The defendant has moved to suppress evidence of his statement "I killed the clerk" on the ground that this statement was elicited in violation of his Miranda rights.

Should the defendant's motion be granted?

(A) No, because although the defendant effectively asserted the right to counsel, the question "Why would you want to talk with a lawyer?" did not constitute custodial interrogation.

Incorrect. The defendant did not effectively assert his right to counsel, because such an assertion must be unambiguous. The defendant's statement "Maybe I should talk to a lawyer" is not an unambiguous request for counsel.

(B) No, because the defendant did not effectively assert the right to counsel, and his conduct prior to making the statement constituted a valid waiver of his Miranda rights.

Correct. The defendant did not effectively assert his right to counsel, because such an assertion must be unambiguous. The defendant's statement "Maybe I should talk to a lawyer" is not an unambiguous request for counsel. In addition, the defendant had unequivocally waived his Miranda rights prior to making this statement.

(C) Yes, because although the defendant did not effectively assert the right to counsel, his conduct prior to making the statement did not constitute a valid waiver of his Miranda rights.

Incorrect. The defendant unequivocally waived his Miranda rights, and his statement "Maybe I should talk to a lawyer" did not affect the validity of that waiver.

(D) Yes, because the defendant effectively asserted the right to counsel, and the question "Why would you want to talk with a lawyer?" constituted custodial interrogation.

Incorrect. The defendant did not effectively assert his right to counsel, because such an assertion must be unambiguous. The defendant's statement "Maybe I should talk to a lawyer" is not an unambiguous request for counsel.

Question 6

Two defendants were being tried together in federal court for bank robbery. The prosecutor sought to introduce testimony from the first defendant's prison cellmate. The cellmate would testify that the first defendant had admitted to the cellmate that he and the second defendant had robbed the bank. The prosecutor asked the court to instruct the jury that the cellmate's testimony could be considered only against the first defendant.

Can the cellmate's testimony be admitted in a joint trial over the second defendant's objection?

(A) No, because the first defendant made the statement without Miranda warnings.

Incorrect. Miranda warnings were not required, because the first defendant was not compelled by a known law enforcement agent to make the statement, and in any event the second defendant could not assert Miranda rights belonging to the first defendant.

(B) No, because the limiting instruction cannot ensure that the jury will not consider the testimony in its deliberations regarding the second defendant.

Correct. The limiting instruction is constitutionally insufficient to avoid the risk that the jury will consider the incriminating statement against the second defendant, who has no opportunity at trial to confront the first defendant.

(C) Yes, because the first defendant's statement was a declaration against penal interest.

Incorrect. The first defendant's statement incriminating the second defendant could not, under the Sixth Amendment confrontation clause, be considered against the second defendant on a theory that it constitutes a declaration against penal interest.

(D) Yes, because the limiting instruction sufficiently protects the second defendant.

Incorrect. The limiting instruction is constitutionally insufficient to avoid the risk that the jury will consider the incriminating statement against the second defendant, who has no opportunity at trial to confront the first defendant.

Question 7

A prosecutor presented to a federal grand jury the testimony of a witness in order to secure a defendant's indictment for theft of government property. The prosecutor did not disclose to the grand jury that the witness had been convicted four years earlier of perjury. The grand jury returned an indictment, and the defendant pleaded not guilty.

Shortly thereafter, the prosecutor took the case to trial, calling the witness to testify before the jury. The prosecutor did not disclose the witness's prior perjury conviction until the defense was preparing to rest. Defense counsel immediately moved for a mistrial, which the court denied. Instead, the court allowed the defense to recall the witness for the purpose of impeaching him with this conviction, but the witness could not be located. The court then allowed the defense to introduce documentary evidence of the witness's criminal record to the jury before resting its case. The jury convicted the defendant.

The defendant has moved for a new trial, arguing that the prosecutor's failure to disclose the witness's prior conviction in a timely manner violated the defendant's right to due process of law.

If the court grants the defendant's motion, what will be the most likely reason?

(A) The defendant was unable to cross-examine the witness about the conviction.
Incorrect. The court did not limit the defendant's right to cross-examine the witness. Rather, the constitutional violation, if any, was the prosecutor's untimely disclosure of impeachment information that would have created a reasonable probability of a different outcome had it been disclosed earlier.

(B) The prosecutor failed to inform the grand jury of the witness's conviction.
Incorrect. The prosecutor is not required to present a grand jury with evidence favorable to a defendant. Rather, the constitutional violation, if any, was the prosecutor's untimely disclosure of impeachment information that would have created a reasonable probability of a different outcome had it been disclosed earlier.

(C) The court found it reasonably probable that the defendant would have been acquitted had the defense had timely access to the information about the witness's conviction.
Correct. The untimely disclosure of evidence favorable to the defense (including impeachment information) violates the Constitution if the evidence would have created a reasonable probability of a different outcome had it been disclosed earlier.

(D) The court found that the prosecutor had deliberately delayed disclosing the witness's conviction to obtain a strategic advantage.
Incorrect. The prosecutor's motive is not an element of a constitutional claim involving untimely disclosure of evidence favorable to the defense (including impeachment information). Rather, such untimely disclosure would violate the Constitution only if the evidence would have created a reasonable probability of a different outcome had it been disclosed earlier.

Question 8

A state statute divides murder into degrees and defines murder in the first degree as murder committed willfully with premeditation and deliberation. The statute defines murder in the second degree as all other murder at common law and defines voluntary manslaughter as at common law.

A man hated one of his coworkers. Upon learning that the coworker was at a neighbor's house, the man grabbed his gun and went to the neighbor's house hoping to provoke the coworker into attacking him so that he could then shoot the coworker. After arriving at the house, the man insulted the coworker and bragged that he had had sexual relations with the coworker's wife two weeks earlier. This statement was not true, but it enraged the coworker, who grabbed a knife from the kitchen table and ran toward the man. The man then shot and killed the coworker.

What is the most serious homicide offense of which the man could properly be convicted?

(A) Murder in the first degree.
Correct. The killing was committed willfully with premeditation and deliberation. The killing cannot be justified as having been in self-defense, because the man was the clear aggressor who intentionally provoked the coworker so that he could shoot and kill him.

(B) Murder in the second degree.
Incorrect. Murder in the second degree is not the most serious homicide offense of which the man could properly be convicted. The man is guilty of first-degree murder, because he committed the killing willfully with premeditation and deliberation. The killing cannot be justified as having been in self-defense, because the man intentionally provoked the coworker so that he could shoot and kill him.

(C) Voluntary manslaughter, because he provoked the coworker.
Incorrect. Voluntary manslaughter is not the most serious homicide offense of which the man could properly be convicted, because he was not acting in the heat of passion when he killed the coworker. The man is guilty of first-degree murder, because he committed the killing willfully with premeditation and deliberation, and the killing cannot be justified as having been in self-defense.

(D) No form of criminal homicide, because he acted in self-defense.
Incorrect. The killing cannot be justified as having been in self-defense, because the man intentionally provoked the coworker so that he could shoot and kill him. The man is guilty of first-degree murder, because he committed the killing willfully with premeditation and deliberation.

Question 9

A wife decided to kill her husband because she was tired of his infidelity. She managed to obtain some cyanide, a deadly poison. One evening, she poured wine laced with the cyanide into a glass, handed it to her husband, and proposed a loving toast. The husband was so pleased with the toast that he set the glass of wine down on a table, grabbed his wife, and kissed her passionately. After the kiss, the wife changed her mind about killing the husband. She hid the glass of wine behind a lamp on the table, planning to leave it for the maid to clean up. The husband did not drink the wine.

The maid found the glass of wine while cleaning the next day. Rather than throw the wine away, the maid drank it. Shortly thereafter, she fell into a coma and died from cyanide poisoning.

In a common law jurisdiction, of what crime(s), if any, could the wife be found guilty?

(A) Attempted murder of the husband and murder or manslaughter of the maid.
Correct. As to the husband, the wife intended to murder him and took a substantial step to carry out that murder; the husband would have been killed had he drunk the wine. As to the maid, a trier of fact could view the wife's conduct as depraved-heart

recklessness (which would make her guilty of murder) or at the very least as criminal negligence (which would make her guilty of manslaughter).

(B) Only attempted murder of the husband.
Incorrect. The woman could be found guilty of attempted murder of the husband, because she intended to murder him and took a substantial step to carry out that murder; the husband would have been killed had he drunk the wine. However, the wife could also be found guilty of murder or manslaughter of the maid. As to the maid, a trier of fact could view the wife's conduct as depraved-heart recklessness (which would make her guilty of murder) or at the very least as criminal negligence (which would make her guilty of manslaughter).

(C) Only murder or manslaughter of the maid.
Incorrect. The wife could be found guilty of murder or manslaughter of the maid, because a trier of fact could view the wife's conduct as depraved-heart recklessness (which would make her guilty of murder) or at the very least as criminal negligence (which would make her guilty of manslaughter). However, the wife could also be found guilty of attempted murder of the husband. As to the husband, she intended to murder him and took a substantial step to carry out that murder; the husband would have been killed had he drunk the wine.

(D) No crime.
Incorrect. The wife could be found guilty of attempted murder of the husband and murder or manslaughter of the maid. As to the husband, the wife intended to murder him and took a substantial step to carry out that murder; the husband would have been killed had he drunk the wine. As to the maid, a trier of fact could view the wife's conduct as depraved-heart recklessness (which would make her guilty of murder) or at the very least as criminal negligence (which would make her guilty of manslaughter).

Question 10

In a crowded football stadium, a man saw a wallet fall out of a spectator's purse. The man picked up the wallet and found that it contained $100 in cash. Thinking that he could use the money and seeing no one watching, the man put the wallet in the pocket of his coat. Just then, the spectator approached the man and asked if he had seen a missing wallet. The man said no and went home with the wallet.

Of what crime, if any, is the man guilty?

(A) Embezzlement.
Incorrect. The initial taking of the wallet was a trespass, because the man knew that the wallet belonged to the spectator and he intended to convert the wallet to his own use in permanent deprivation of the spectator's right. Accordingly, and because the spectator never entrusted the man with the wallet, the man is guilty of larceny rather than embezzlement.

(B) False pretenses.
Incorrect. The initial taking of the wallet was a trespass, because the man knew that the wallet belonged to the spectator and he intended to convert the wallet to his own use in permanent deprivation of the spectator's right. Accordingly, and because the man never obtained title to the wallet, he is guilty of larceny rather than false pretenses.

(C) Larceny.

Correct. The initial taking of the wallet was a trespass, because the man knew that the wallet belonged to the spectator and he intended to convert the wallet to his own use in permanent deprivation of the spectator's right. Accordingly, the man is guilty of larceny.

(D) No crime.

Incorrect. The initial taking of the wallet was a trespass, because the man knew that the wallet belonged to the spectator and he intended to convert the wallet to his own use in permanent deprivation of the spectator's right. Accordingly, the man is guilty of larceny.

Question 11

A woman went to an art gallery and falsely represented that she was an agent for a museum and wanted to purchase a painting that was hanging in the gallery. The woman and the gallery owner then agreed on a price for the painting to be paid 10 days later, and the woman took the painting. When the gallery failed to receive the payment when due, the owner called the museum and discovered that the woman did not work there. The owner then notified the police.

When interviewed by the police, the woman admitted making the false representation and acquiring the painting, but she said she believed that the painting had been stolen from her by someone who worked in the gallery.

Is the woman guilty of obtaining property by false pretenses?

(A) No, because she believed that the painting belonged to her.

Correct. The crime of false pretenses, like other theft crimes, requires the intent to steal. The woman cannot properly be found guilty of obtaining property by false pretenses, because she made the false statements to obtain property that she subjectively believed belonged to her.

(B) No, because the gallery owner would have sold the painting to anyone who agreed to pay the price.

Incorrect. This fact does not excuse the woman for knowingly making false statements to obtain property that she would not otherwise have been able to obtain. The reason the woman cannot properly be found guilty of obtaining property by false pretenses is that she lacked the requisite intent to steal; she made the false statements to obtain property that she subjectively believed belonged to her.

(C) Yes, because even if her representation was not material, she never intended to pay for the painting.

Incorrect. In some jurisdictions, a false pretenses conviction can be based on a promise to make payment in the future if the promisor had no present intent to make the future payment. But the promisor must have the intent to steal the property. The woman cannot properly be found guilty of obtaining property by false pretenses, because she lacked the requisite intent to steal; she made the false statements to obtain property that she subjectively believed belonged to her.

(D) Yes, because she knowingly made a false representation on which the gallery owner relied.

Incorrect. Even assuming that the woman otherwise could be convicted of false pretenses, false pretenses requires the intent to steal required for other theft crimes. Accordingly, the woman cannot properly be found guilty of obtaining property by false pretenses, because she made the false statements to obtain property that she subjectively believed belonged to her.

Question 12

A woman broke off her engagement to a man but refused to return the engagement ring the man had given her. One night, the man entered the woman's house after midnight to retrieve the ring. Although the woman was not at home, a neighbor saw the man enter the house and called the police. The man unsuccessfully searched for the ring for 10 minutes. As he was walking out the front door, the police arrived and immediately arrested him.

The man has been charged with burglary in a jurisdiction that follows the common law. Which of the following, if proved, would serve as the man's best defense to the charge?

(A) The man knew that the woman kept a key under the doormat and he used the key to enter the house.
Incorrect. This fact does not provide a defense to burglary, because the man still broke into and entered the house without the woman's consent. Instead, the man's subjective belief that he was entitled to the ring (even if that belief was incorrect and unreasonable) negates the intent required for the underlying felony of larceny.

(B) The man incorrectly and unreasonably believed that he was legally entitled to the ring.
Correct. The crime of burglary requires that the breaking and entering of the dwelling have been done with the intent to commit an underlying felony (in most cases, larceny). The man's subjective belief that he was entitled to the ring (even if that belief was incorrect and unreasonable) negates the intent required for the underlying felony of larceny.

(C) The man knew that no one was at home when he entered the house.
Incorrect. This fact does not provide a defense, because the crime of burglary does not require that the dwelling be occupied at the time of the breaking and entering. Instead, the man's subjective belief that he was entitled to the ring (even if that belief was incorrect and unreasonable) negates the intent required for the underlying felony of larceny.

(D) The man took nothing of value from the house.
Incorrect. This fact does not provide a defense, because burglary requires that the person breaking and entering intend to commit a felony, not that the person be successful in committing the felony. Instead, the man's subjective belief that he was entitled to the ring (even if that belief was incorrect and unreasonable) negates the intent required for the underlying felony of larceny.

Question 13

A woman wanted to kill a business competitor. She contacted a man who she believed was willing to commit murder for hire and offered him $50,000 to kill the competitor. The man agreed to do so and accepted $25,000 as a down payment. Unbeknownst to the woman, the man was an undercover police officer.

In a jurisdiction that has adopted the unilateral theory of conspiracy, is the woman guilty of conspiracy to murder the business competitor?

(A) No, because the man did not intend to kill the competitor.

Incorrect. In jurisdictions that recognize unilateral conspiracies, it is enough that one person agree with another person to commit a crime (and in some jurisdictions, that an overt act in furtherance of that agreement be committed). It is no defense to unilateral conspiracy that the other person was feigning agreement or acting in an undercover capacity. Therefore, the man's lack of intent does not make the woman any less guilty.

(B) No, because it would have been impossible for the woman to kill the competitor by this method.

Incorrect. In jurisdictions that recognize unilateral conspiracies, it is enough that one person agree with another person to commit a crime (and in some jurisdictions, that an overt act in furtherance of that agreement be committed). It is no defense to unilateral conspiracy that the other person was feigning agreement or acting in an undercover capacity. Therefore, the woman cannot prevail on any impossibility defense.

(C) Yes, because the woman believed that she had an agreement with the man that would bring about the competitor's death.

Correct. In jurisdictions that recognize unilateral conspiracies, it is enough that one person agree with another person to commit a crime (and in some jurisdictions, that an overt act in furtherance of that agreement be committed). It is no defense to unilateral conspiracy that the other person was feigning agreement or acting in an undercover capacity. Here, the woman agreed to commit a crime and she committed an overt act in furtherance of that agreement when she paid the man $25,000. She therefore is guilty of conspiracy in a jurisdiction that recognizes unilateral conspiracies.

(D) Yes, because the woman took a substantial step toward bringing about the competitor's death by paying the man $25,000.

Incorrect. The woman is guilty, but not because she took a substantial step, which is a concept relevant under the Model Penal Code to attempt rather than conspiracy. The woman is guilty of conspiracy because in jurisdictions that recognize unilateral conspiracies, it is enough that one person agree with another person to commit a crime (and in some jurisdictions, that an overt act in furtherance of that agreement be committed). It is no defense to unilateral conspiracy that the other person was feigning agreement or acting in an undercover capacity.

Question 14

A state statute provides as follows: "The maintenance of any ongoing enterprise in the nature of a betting parlor or bookmaking organization is a felony."

A prosecutor has evidence that a woman has been renting an office to a man, that the man has been using the office as a betting parlor within the meaning of the statute, and that the woman is aware of this use.

Which of the following additional pieces of evidence would be most useful to the prosecutor's effort to convict the woman as an accomplice to the man's violation of the statute?

(A) The woman was previously convicted of running a betting parlor herself on the same premises.

Incorrect. The woman's prior conviction would not necessarily show that she has a personal stake in the continuing success of the man's criminal venture (and thus an intent to aid in that venture).

(B) The woman charges the man considerably more in rent than she charged the preceding tenant, who used the office for legitimate activities.
Correct. Showing that the woman benefits from the gambling would indicate her personal stake in the continuing success of the man's criminal venture (and thus her intent to aid in that venture).

(C) The woman has personally placed bets with the man at the office location.
Incorrect. Showing that the woman has placed bets would confirm that she knows that the premises are being used for gambling. However, it would not necessarily show that she has a personal stake in the continuing success of the man's criminal venture (and thus an intent to aid in that venture).

(D) The man has paid the woman the rent in bills that are traceable as the proceeds of gambling activity.
Incorrect. The source of the rent payments, assuming that the rent is not above the market price for the premises, would not necessarily show that the woman has a personal stake in the continuing success of the man's criminal venture (and thus an intent to aid in that venture).

Question 15

After a defendant was indicted on federal bank fraud charges and released on bail, his attorney filed notice of the defendant's intent to offer an insanity defense. The prosecutor then enlisted the help of a forensic psychologist who was willing to participate in an "undercover" mental examination of the defendant. The psychologist contacted the defendant and pretended to represent an executive personnel agency. She told the defendant about an attractive employment opportunity and invited him to a "preliminary screening interview" to determine his qualifications for the job. As part of the purported screening process, the psychologist gave the defendant psychological tests that enabled her to form a reliable opinion about his mental state at the time of the alleged offense.

What is the strongest basis for a defense objection to the psychologist's testimony regarding the defendant's mental state?

(A) The Fourth Amendment prohibition against unreasonable searches and seizures.
Incorrect. The Fourth Amendment does not prevent the government from using deception to obtain incriminating admissions.

(B) The Fifth Amendment privilege against compelled self-incrimination.
Incorrect. The Fifth Amendment privilege protects against compelled self-incrimination, not against the use of deception to obtain a suspect's voluntary admissions.

(C) The Sixth Amendment right to the assistance of counsel.
Correct. After a defendant is indicted, the right to counsel attaches, and authorities may not use deception to deliberately elicit statements related to the crime from the defendant without the representation of counsel.

(D) The federal common law privilege for confidential communications between psychotherapist and patient.
Incorrect. While there is such a federal common law privilege for communications intended to be kept confidential for the purpose of obtaining psychiatric services, the facts in this case do not support the privilege.

Question 16

A defendant is charged with an offense under a statute that provides as follows: "Any person who, while intoxicated, appears in any public place and manifests a drunken condition by obstreperous or indecent conduct is guilty of a misdemeanor."

At trial, the evidence shows that the defendant was intoxicated when police officers burst into his house and arrested him pursuant to a valid warrant. It was a cold night, and the officers hustled the defendant out of his house without giving him time to get his coat. The defendant became angry and obstreperous when the officers refused to let him go back into the house to retrieve his coat. The officers left him handcuffed outside in the street, waiting for a special squad car to arrive. The arrest warrant was later vacated.

Can the defendant properly be convicted of violating the statute?

(A) No, because the defendant's claim of mistreatment is valid.
Incorrect. The defendant cannot properly be convicted, regardless of whether his claim is valid, because of the general legal rule that a person is not guilty of a crime unless the act constituting the crime was committed voluntarily. This rule precludes the defendant's conviction, because he did not voluntarily appear in a public place.

(B) No, because the statute requires proof of a voluntary appearance in a public place.
Correct. The general legal rule is that a person is not guilty of a crime unless the act constituting the crime was committed voluntarily. This rule precludes the defendant's conviction, because he did not voluntarily appear in a public place.

(C) Yes, because the defendant voluntarily became intoxicated.
Incorrect. The general legal rule is that a person is not guilty of a crime unless the act constituting the crime was committed voluntarily. This rule precludes the defendant's conviction because, while the defendant voluntarily became intoxicated, he did not voluntarily appear in a public place.

(D) Yes, because the defendant voluntarily behaved in an obstreperous manner.
Incorrect. The general legal rule is that a person is not guilty of a crime unless the act constituting the crime was committed voluntarily. This rule precludes the defendant's conviction because, while the defendant voluntarily behaved obstreperously, he did not voluntarily appear in a public place.

Question 17

A police officer had a hunch, not amounting to probable cause or reasonable suspicion, that a man was a drug dealer. One day while the officer was on highway patrol, her radar gun clocked the man's car at 68 mph in an area where the maximum posted speed limit was 65 mph. The officer's usual practice was not to stop a car unless it was going at least 5 mph over the posted limit, but contrary to her usual practice, she decided to stop the man's car in the hope that she might discover evidence of drug dealing. After she stopped the car and announced that she would be writing a speeding ticket, the officer ordered the man and his passenger to step out of the car. When the passenger stepped out, the officer saw that the passenger had been sitting on a clear bag of what the officer immediately recognized as marijuana. The officer arrested both the man and the passenger for possession of marijuana.

At their joint trial, the man and the passenger claim that their Fourth Amendment rights were violated because the officer improperly (1) stopped the car for speeding as a pretext for investigating a hunch rather than for the stated purpose of issuing a traffic ticket and (2) ordered the passenger to step out of the car even though there was no reason to believe that the passenger was a criminal or dangerous.

Are the man and the passenger correct?

(A) No, as to both the stop of the car and the officer's order that the passenger step out of the car.

Correct. The stop of the car was constitutional, because it was objectively justifiable (regardless of the officer's subjective motivation), and both the driver and any passengers may be ordered to step out of a car during a lawful traffic stop.

(B) No as to the stop of the car, but yes as to the officer's order that the passenger step out of the car.

Incorrect. It is correct that the stop of the car was constitutional, because it was objectively justifiable (regardless of the officer's subjective motivation). However, it is also correct that both the driver and any passengers may be ordered to step out of a car during a lawful traffic stop.

(C) Yes as to the stop of the car, but no as to the officer's order that the passenger step out of the car.

Incorrect. It is correct that both the driver and any passengers may be ordered to step out of a car during a lawful traffic stop. However, it is also correct that the stop of the car here was constitutional, because it was objectively justifiable (regardless of the officer's subjective motivation).

(D) Yes, as to both the stop of the car and the officer's order that the passenger step out of the car.

Incorrect. The stop of the car was constitutional, because it was objectively justifiable (regardless of the officer's subjective motivation), and both the driver and any passengers may be ordered to step out of the car during a lawful traffic stop.

CHAPTER 12

Mapping MBE Topics—Evidence

I. MIND MAP

Among the topics tested on the bar exam, Evidence is unique. First, it deals only with the admission of proof in a trial of a lawsuit. It does not set out elements of a crime or a civil cause of action. Its focus is solely on whether a document, real evidence, or a witness's testimony should be admitted before a court to consider in deciding whether the elements of a cause of action or crime have been met.

Secondly, as a result of its sole mission, evidence has little interaction with other areas of the law. While most other topics have some overlap with another topic, evidence does not. Thus, your study focuses on only one source of law—the Federal Rules of Evidence (FRE).

Your mind map begins with the type of evidence. Is the evidence a document, a witness's testimony, or a piece of real evidence? Each type of evidence has its own mind map. Two considerations override the admission of every piece of evidence—relevancy and hearsay. These mind maps are then imbedded into each type of evidence:

- Relevancy
  - Definition
  - Legal relevance
  - Exceptions
  - Character
- Hearsay
  - Definition
  - Nonhearsay
  - Hearsay exceptions—declarant unavailable
  - Hearsay exceptions—declarant availability immaterial

Relevant evidence is evidence having any tendency to make the existence of any fact of consequence to the action more probable than it would be without the evidence.[1] Relevant evidence may still be excluded for public policy reasons including **legal relevance**. Under FRE 403, a court has the discretion to exclude relevant evidence if its probative value is substantially outweighed by the danger of unfair prejudice; confusion of the issues; misleading the jury; or by consideration of undue delay, waste of time, or needless presentation of cumulative

---

1. Fed. R. Evid. 401.

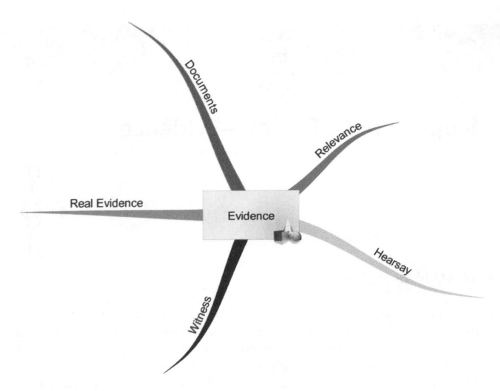

evidence.[2] Keep in mind that the requirement is unfair prejudice, not just prejudice. The evidence is always prejudicial to the party objecting to the evidence, but that does not mean it rises to the level of unfair prejudice.

Evidence may be admitted that does not relate to the particular event, but is a **prior similar event**. These **exceptions** to the relevancy rule include causation; similar accidents or injuries caused by the same event; and similar acts admissible to prove intent, habit, and industrial custom or routine.

Other exceptions are policy-based. **Liability insurance** may be admissible to prove ownership or control, although it is not admissible to show negligence or ability to pay.[3] Likewise, **subsequent remedial measures** are not admissible to prove negligence, but may be admissible to prove ownership or control, or to prove destruction of evidence.[4] **Settlement offers**[5] and **withdrawn guilty pleas**[6] are also inadmissible, although they may be admissible for other purposes.

Character evidence poses special problems and thus is a frequent test topic. Considerations include the purpose for the offer of character evidence and the means of proving character. Your mind map starts with asking whether this is a criminal or civil case. Then, ask whether this is testimony being offered on direct exam or on cross exam. Make a chart to insert the rules.

Hearsay is another overriding consideration. When dealing with hearsay, you can garner low-hanging fruit points by how you set out the rule. Even if you know from the get-go that the key issue revolves around a hearsay exception, do not jump to the exception. Still give the rule for the admissibility of hearsay evidence including the definition of hearsay. Continue by identifying whether the declarant is a party. Analyze both parts of the definition. Check for double hearsay and then begin your CRAC or IRAC on possible exceptions. For example:

---

2. Fed. R. Evid. 403.
3. Fed. R. Evid. 411.
4. Fed. R. Evid. 407.
5. Fed. R. Evid. 408(a).
6. Fed. R. Evid. 410(a).

CHARACTER EVIDENCE		
	Criminal	**Civil**
Direct Examination	Prosecution cannot initiate.	Generally not admissible. Only when character directly at issue: child custody, defamation, etc.
Cross Examination	Party: Defendant can introduce evidence of her good character to help prove innocence. Party/Witness: Impeachment.	Party or witness: Only for impeachment.

- State rule: "Hearsay is inadmissible without an exception."[7]
- Define hearsay: Hearsay is an out-of-court statement offered to prove the truth of the matter.[8]
- Party? Then, it is an admission of a party-opponent.[9]
- If not a party, analyze both parts of the rule: out-of-court statement and offered for the truth of the matter.
- Conclude if hearsay.
- Check for double hearsay. Do same analysis for each level of hearsay.
- Exception apply?
  - Declarant unavailability required?
  - Declarant unavailability immaterial?

One way to identify hearsay is to picture the witness on the stand and then identify who is making the actual statement.

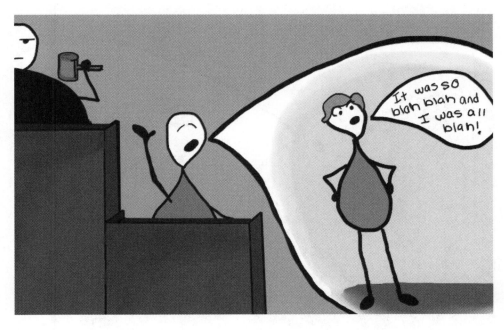

Hearsay with Person as Declarant

---

7. Fed. R. Evid. 802.
8. Fed. R. Evid. 801(c)(1)-(2).
9. Fed. R. Evid. 801(d)(2)(A).

Remember that a document can also be hearsay.

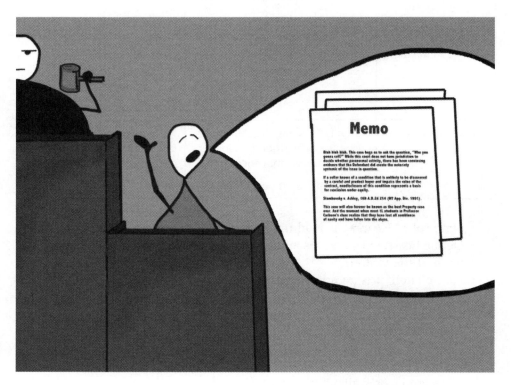

Hearsay with Document as Declarant

A regular issue on essay questions is **double or triple hearsay**. Each level of hearsay must be analyzed separately; again, look for documents and individuals.

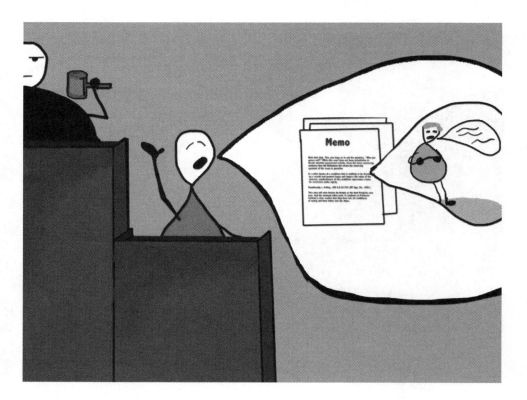

Double Hearsay with a Document

Double Hearsay with a Person

A twist that can throw some applicants off is **party-admissions**. To avoid that being you, see if the individual making the statement is wearing a party hat.

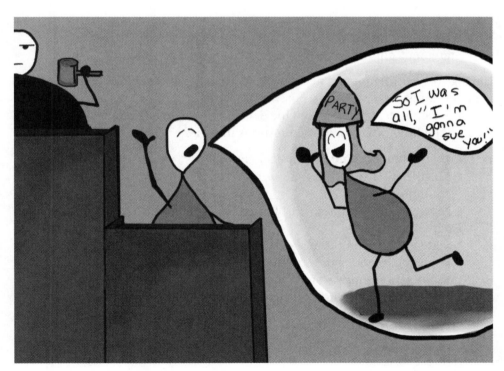

Party-Admission

Only after you have determined that it is hearsay and not a party-admission, then address whether a hearsay exception applies. Then, be careful that you also look for admissions in all double and triple hearsay questions.

Hearsay exceptions are divided into whether the declarant must be unavailable or not. Declarant unavailability results from:

* Privilege;
* Refusing to testify;
* Lack of memory;
* Death or physical/mental illness;
* Absent beyond the reach of the court's subpoena power and the proponent of the statement has been unable to procure attendance or testimony.[10]

Focus on the five exceptions that require the declarant to be unavailable:

* Former testimony:[11]
  * Given as a witness at a trial, hearing, or lawful deposition;
  * Offered against a party who had an opportunity and similar motive to develop it by direct, cross, or redirect examination;
* Statements against interest:[12]
  * Reasonable person in the declarant's position would have made only if the person believed it to be true;
  * Contrary to declarant's proprietary or pecuniary interest;
  * Supported by corroborating circumstances that clearly indicate its trustworthiness;
* Dying declarations:[13]
  * Statement made by declarant believing that declarant's death was imminent;
  * Statement about its cause or circumstances;
* Statement of personal or family history;[14]
* Statement offered against party procuring declarant's unavailability.[15]

Having this list memorized allows you to quickly eliminate declarant unavailability as an issue for all other possible exceptions.

The exceptions to the rule that the declarant need not be unavailable that are most frequently tested on essay questions include:

* Present state of mind or physical condition:[16]
  * Must be then-existing state of mind or emotional, sensory, or physical condition;
  * Not including a statement of memory or belief;
* Excited utterance:[17]
  * Statement relating to a startling event or condition;
  * Made while under the stress of excitement that it caused;
* Present sense impressions:[18]
  * Statement describing or explaining an event or condition;
  * Made while or immediately after the declarant perceived it;

---

10. Fed. R. Evid. 804(a).
11. Fed. R. Evid. 804(b)(3).
12. Fed. R. Evid. 804(b)(3).
13. Fed. R. Evid. 804(b)(2).
14. Fed. R. Evid. 804(b)(4).
15. Fed. R. Evid. 804(b)(6).
16. Fed. R. Evid. 803(3).
17. Fed. R. Evid. 803(2).
18. Fed. R. Evid. 803(1).

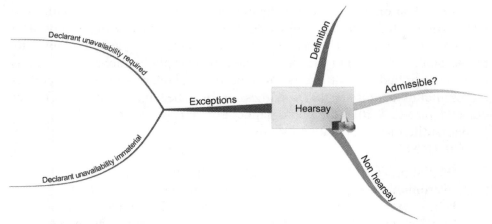

- Business records:[19]
  - Made at or near the time by someone with knowledge;
  - Kept in the course of a regularly conducted activity of a business or organization;
  - Making the record was a regular practice of that activity;
  - Shown by a custodian's testimony or by certification;
  - Neither the source of information nor the method of preparation indicate a lack of trustworthiness;
- Public records:[20]
  - Record sets out the office's activities;
  - Of a matter observed while under a legal duty to report;
  - Neither the source of information nor other circumstances indicate a lack of trustworthiness;
- Past recollection recorded:[21]
  - A record that:
    - is on a matter the witness once knew about but now cannot recall;
    - was made or adopted by the witness when the matter was fresh in the witness's memory; and
    - accurately reflects the witness's knowledge;
  - May be read into evidence;
  - May only be received as an exhibit if offered by an adverse party.

> **EXAM TIP**
> Sometimes, more than one exception potentially applies. Be sure to analyze all possibilities even if you decide that the requirements of one exception have been met—not all exceptions, just the possible ones. Don't eat all the candy—just the good ones!

Remember not to jump into analyzing a hearsay exception. Always, always analyze the general rule of hearsay. If hearsay and not an admission, state first that it's inadmissible without an exception. And then, analyze the potential exceptions. You will garner all the low-hanging fruit points.

These two overriding considerations—relevancy and hearsay—apply to both documents and witnesses. Relevancy also applies to real evidence.

The mind map for **documents** is fairly short:

- Relevant?
- Authentication
- Best evidence rule
- Hearsay?

---

19. Fed. R. Evid. 803(6).
20. Fed. R. Evid. 803(8).
21. Fed. R. Evid. 803(5).

Authentication means that the document is what the proponent claims it to be.[22] While a few writings are self-authenticating, most writings require a testimonial sponsor to prove that the writing was made, signed, or adopted by the particular relevant person. One frequent issue is photographs. Photographs must be identified by a witness as both a portrayal of relevant facts and a correct representation of those facts. The witness needs to be familiar with the scene or object depicted. Neither the photographer nor an expert is required.

Self-authenticating documents[23] include:

(OIL CANS)

* **O**fficial publications issued by public authority
* **I**nstruments—negotiable and commercial paper
* **L**abel, tag, or trademark affixed on item in regular course of business
* **C**ertified public documents (by clerk of agency or court that had custody)
* **A**cknowledged documents signed before notary, sworn to truth, content, and execution (except wills)
* **N**ewspapers and periodicals with reasonably wide circulation
* **S**ealed documents (government certified)

The **best evidence rule** only applies to documents. Any multiple choice question that has a response that indicates testimony unrelated to a document is inadmissible as it violates the best evidence rule is incorrect. The best evidence rule requires the "original writing, recording, or photograph, . . . to prove its content. . . ."[24] Thus, the rule applies only if the contents of the writing are at issue. Look for best evidence rule issues with operative or dispositive instruments such as contracts, deeds, and wills.

The mind map for **witnesses** or testimonial evidence is more detailed:

* Competency
* Relevance
* Opinion
  * Lay witness
  * Expert witness
* Character
* Impeachment
* Privileges
* Hearsay

Competency has four attributes. A witness must have the capacity to observe, to recollect, to communicate, and to appreciate the obligation to speak truthfully. The FRE requires that the witness have personal knowledge and must declare he will testify truthfully.[25]

Separate **opinion evidence** into lay opinions and expert opinions. **Lay opinion** testimony is generally inadmissible. Lay opinions may be allowed if no better evidence exists. In those situations, the lay opinion must be:

* based on the witness's perception,
* helpful for a clear understanding of a fact at issue, and
* not based on scientific, technical, or other specialized knowledge.[26]

---

22. Fed. R. Evid. 901(a).
23. Fed. R. Evid. 902.
24. Fed. R. Evid. 1002.
25. Fed. R. Evid. 602, 603.
26. Fed. R. Evid. 701.

Expert opinion testimony questions are usually not as difficult as actually presenting an expert at trial. The reason is that the examiners must give you sufficient facts to identify the issues, including qualification—an often heated area in trials. One area that is commonly tested is whether expert testimony is needed at all. Another area tested is whether the opinion is supported by a proper factual basis. Memorize all the requirements for expert testimony, but focus on whether the subject matter is appropriate for expert opinion and if the opinion is supported by a proper factual basis for detailed memorization:

- Subject matter appropriate for expert opinion:
  - Scientific knowledge
  - Technical knowledge
  - Other specialized knowledge
- Witness qualifies as expert
- Opinion backed with reasonable certainty
- Opinion supported by a proper factual basis[27]:
  - Personal knowledge
  - Facts made known at trial
  - Facts made known outside of court:
    - Facts need not be admissible in court
    - Of the kind that are reasonably relied upon by experts in the field

On direct examination in a criminal trial, **character** evidence is not allowed to prove conformity with the party's character. It is allowed for other purposes including motive, opportunity, intent, preparation, common scheme or plan, knowledge, identity, absence of mistake or accident. In a civil trial, character evidence is not allowed unless character is at issue, such as child custody. Character evidence issues also arise upon impeachment.

The purpose of **impeachment** is to cast an adverse reflection on a witness's truthfulness. Two methods of impeachment are cross examination and extrinsic evidence. Cross examination includes prior inconsistent statements, bias or interest, and criminal convictions.

A party need not show a **prior inconsistent statement** to a witness. The party must, on request, show it to an adverse party's attorney. Extrinsic evidence is admissible only if the witness has the opportunity to explain the statement and an adverse party has the opportunity to examine the witness about it or if justice requires. This rule does not apply to admissions by a party opponent under FRE 801(d)(2).

Divide crimes into two categories. First are **crimes involving dishonesty** such as fraud or perjury, whether a felony or misdemeanor. The court has no discretion to exclude these crimes and there is no time limitation on how old the crime is.

The second category is **felonies not involving dishonesty**. Here, the court does have discretion to exclude the conviction. The crime must not be too remote. Generally, if it has been over ten years since the date of conviction or release from confinement imposed for the conviction, the conviction is excluded. Additionally, the court employs a balancing test. For the accused, the government must show the probative value as impeachment is not outweighed by its prejudicial effect. This generally favors exclusion as the standard is just "outweighs" and not "substantially outweighs." For a witness other than an accused, the balancing test is FRE 403 and requires that the probative value is

---

27. Fed. R. Evid. 702.

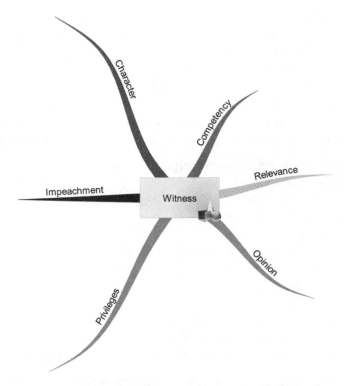

substantially outweighed by the danger of unfair prejudice. This favors admission. Extrinsic evidence of the crime is permitted.

Extrinsic evidence is most prevalent as an issue when dealing with **prior bad acts**. Most definitely, FRE 608 is a rule to spend significant time understanding. Generally, **interrogation** about prior bad acts is admissible within the court's discretion. The bad act must be probative of truthfulness. **Extrinsic evidence** of bad acts is not permitted. Thus, if the witness denies the act, the cross-examiner cannot refute the testimony by calling other witnesses or by producing other evidence.

Another area of extrinsic evidence is **reputation** evidence. A witness may be impeached by showing a poor reputation for truthfulness. This is done by calling another witness from the community where the impeached witness lives or from his business circle. The impeaching witness may also state her personal opinion based on acquaintance, subject to the court's discretion.

Impeachment is not allowed on a collateral matter, but impeachment is allowed of a hearsay declarant.

Like all other forms of evidence, **real evidence** must be relevant. In addition, the object must be authenticated—that it is what its proponent claims it to be. This is accomplished by recognition testimony or chain of custody. A witness may authenticate an object if it has significant features that make it identifiable upon inspection. Otherwise, the proponent must present evidence of the chain of custody of the object and that it has been held in a substantially unbroken chain of possession.

No specific provision of the FRE provides for federal **privileges**. FRE 501 states that privileges are governed by common law. The federal courts have recognized these privileges in states that provide for them and thus should be your focus:

- Attorney-client privilege:
  - Client may refuse to disclose and to prevent any other person from disclosing confidential communications made for the purpose of rendition of professional legal services to the client;

- Includes the attorney and its representatives;
- Only the client can waive the privilege.
- Physician, psychotherapist, or social worker patient privilege:
  - Confidential communications made for the purpose of diagnosis or treatment of the patient's physical, mental, or emotional condition.
- Spousal privilege:
  - Marital communication privilege: provides that either spouse has a privilege to refuse to disclose and to prevent her spouse from disclosing a confidential communication made between spouses while they were husband and wife.
  - Spousal testimony privilege: a spouse may not be called as a witness by the prosecution against his spouse in a criminal case and may not be compelled to testify against his spouse in any criminal proceeding including those where the spouse is not the defendant.

In sum, focus on the FRE. Always sort out the characters in the scenario. Who are the parties? Who is the witness? Is it a direct examination or a cross examination? If you aren't sure, is it your client's attorney who is questioning them or is it the opposing party's attorney? Once you have sorted out the players, then focus on the specific evidence. What is being offered into evidence? For what purpose is it being offered? Is this extrinsic evidence? That will get you through all Evidence MBE and essay questions.

II. MBE STRATEGIES[28]

On MBE questions, one-third of the questions are on hearsay, one-third are on presentation of evidence, and the last one-third covers relevance, privilege, and documents. These tend to be relatively short questions that are also easy to identify. When you read the call of the question and the responses, it will be immediately clear the question is about evidence because the responses will address admissibility. You should be able to tell which area of evidence and which rule should be applied. Keep in mind that not only do you need to know whether it is admissible, but you also need to know for what purpose it is being admitted.

Some answer choices are **always** wrong

- Latin terms that you have never studied or never seen are not correct. You may be fooled into thinking that the term is a correct answer that you just don't know. For example, *res gestae* is a relic from common law evidence. It is not in the Federal Rules of Evidence.
- Testimony on "ultimate issues" is an old rule from the common law. Ignore.
- "Testimony is inadmissible due to its self-serving nature" is always wrong because the self-serving nature goes to credibility, not admissibility.

Other answers require careful consideration:

- Have the exceptions that require unavailability of the declarant memorized. Then, any answer choice that states that the evidence is

---

28. Some of these strategies are from Steven L. Emanuel, *Strategies & Tactics for the MBE* 197-206 (5th ed. 2013).

inadmissible because the declarant is available to testify is easily identified as correct or incorrect.

- Beware of answer choices that state that the witness is not competent to give certain evidence. The answer is usually one of bias, not competence.

Some answer choices look wrong, but may actually be correct:

- Carefully analyze questions that include responses dealing with legal relevance (probative value substantially outweighed by undue prejudice). Legal relevance can be the best choice or can be wrong. Evidence excluded by FRE 403 must be shocking evidence, not merely prejudicial. If all other choices are incorrect, then FRE 403 may be correct.
- Another choice that looks wrong but that may be correct is "inadmissible because it is hearsay not within any exception." Avoid the instinct to try to find a way to make evidence admissible because your gut tells you it should be. Some evidence just isn't admissible.

Evidence is a technical area of the law. Understanding the FRE in detail is essential. Visualize the scene of the courtroom. Who is on the stand and who is doing the questioning? What is the evidence? Witness, document, or real evidence? Follow your mind maps and you will do well.

III. ESSAY PRACTICE QUESTION[29]

Plaintiff, an employee of Contractor, was injured while using a table saw manufactured by Defendant and owned by Contractor. Plaintiff sued Defendant in federal court to recover damages for his injuries.

At trial, Defendant called Witness, another employee of Contractor. Neither Witness nor Contractor is a party to Plaintiff's action against Defendant. On direct examination, Witness testified that he saw Plaintiff remove a safety guard from the table saw on the morning of the accident.

During cross-examination by Plaintiff's Counsel, Witness testified as follows:

Plaintiff's Counsel: At the time you applied for your job with Contractor, you had three years of previous construction experience, didn't you?

Witness: Yes.

Plaintiff's Counsel: Didn't you lie about how much construction experience you had when you applied for the job with Contractor?

Defense Counsel: Objection, inadmissible character evidence.

Plaintiff's Counsel: We are impeaching this witness with a specific instance of untruthful conduct under Rule 608(b), Your Honor.

Court: Overruled.

Plaintiff's Counsel: I'll repeat my question—didn't you lie about how much construction experience you had?

Witness: No, I did not.

Plaintiff's Counsel: Isn't Plaintiff's Exhibit 37 a genuine copy of your job application?

Witness: Yes, it is.

Plaintiff's Counsel: Didn't you lie on that application?

Witness: No.

Plaintiff's Counsel: We offer Plaintiff's Exhibit 37.

Defense Counsel: Objection, inadmissible character evidence.

Court: Approach the bench. (The following occurred outside the hearing of the jury.)

Plaintiff's Counsel: Judge, this is a copy of Witness's job application in which he represented that he had twelve years of construction experience when he actually had only three.

Court: Sustained.

Plaintiff's Counsel then asked Witness to review Plaintiff's Exhibit 37 to refresh his recollection about whether he had lied. Witness did so and then testified: "I didn't lie."

Plaintiff's Counsel thereafter re-offered Exhibit 37, claiming that it was admissible under Rule 612 to refresh Witness's recollection. Defense Counsel objected, and the Court sustained the objection.

Later, Plaintiff's Counsel called Contractor to testify. During direct examination, Plaintiff's Counsel asked Contractor, "Did Witness tell you that he had twelve years of construction experience during his job interview?" Defense

---

Counsel objected that this was inadmissible character evidence, and the Court sustained the objection.

Did the Court err in:

1. Overruling Defense Counsel's objection to cross-examination about an alleged lie by Witness? Explain.
2. Sustaining Defense Counsel's objection to the introduction of Exhibit 37 as inadmissible character evidence? Explain.
3. Sustaining Defense Counsel's objection to the introduction of Exhibit 37 to refresh the recollection of Witness? Explain.
4. Sustaining Defense Counsel's objection to Contractor's testimony? Explain.

IV. SCORE SHEET

Stated	Implied	
		1. Character Evidence—Asking Witness Directly
_____	_____	**Conclusion on Issue 1:** The trial court acted within its discretion in permitting cross-examination concerning the alleged lie on Witness's job application because lying about one's job experience is probative of untruthfulness.
_____	_____	**Rule:** The standard of review regarding an alleged error in an evidentiary ruling is abuse of discretion.
_____	_____	A trial court's ruling should be affirmed, even if the court of appeals would make a different ruling, if the challenged ruling lies within the zone of reasonable disagreement.
_____	_____	Character evidence is generally inadmissible to prove action in conformity with the character trait.
_____	_____	However, when a person testifies as a witness, that person's credibility becomes a material issue; a witness's credibility thus may be attacked by showing that the witness has an untruthful character.
_____	_____	Accordingly, a court may, in its discretion, admit evidence relating to a prior bad act if it is offered during cross-examination of the witness being impeached and is "probative of . . . untruthfulness."
_____	_____	Conduct that involves falsehood or deception is generally considered probative of untruthfulness.
_____	_____	**Application:** Here,
_____	_____	The trial court acted properly in allowing counsel to ask Witness if he had lied about his job experience on his application.
_____	_____	Witness's testimony was critical to establish that Plaintiff had removed a safety guard from the table saw. This testimony could be devastating to Plaintiff's claim.
_____	_____	**Conclusion on Issue 1:** Consequently, this line of inquiry was relevant and probative of Witness's truthfulness and the court was reasonable in its decision to permit counsel to cross-examine Witness about his job application.
		2. Character Evidence—Extrinsic Evidence
_____	_____	**Conclusion on Issue 2:** The trial court was within its discretion in excluding Exhibit 37 because Rule 608(b) forbids the use of extrinsic evidence to attack a witness's character for truthfulness.
_____	_____	**Rule:** The use of extrinsic evidence is prohibited to use to impeach a witness's character for truthfulness.
_____	_____	Although a witness may be cross-examined about a prior alleged lie, if he refuses to admit to lying, he may not be contradicted with extrinsic evidence.
_____	_____	Rule 608(b) does not define "extrinsic evidence," and there is disagreement among federal courts and evidence scholars about the term's meaning.
_____	_____	With respect to documents, one approach holds that a document is extrinsic evidence in all circumstances.

continued on next page

Stated	Implied	
_____	_____	The other, more lenient approach holds that a document is not extrinsic evidence if the witness being impeached can provide the foundation for admission of the document.
_____	_____	**Conclusion on Issue 2:** Thus, whether the Court should have admitted Exhibit 37 depends on which approach prevails in this jurisdiction.
		(Note: An applicant should receive full credit if the applicant recognizes the extrinsic evidence issue.)
		3. Exhibit to Refresh Recollection
_____	_____	**Conclusion on Issue 3:** Exhibit 37 was not admissible to refresh Witness's recollection because Rule 612 permits only counsel for the opposing party to offer such a document into evidence.
_____	_____	**Rule:** Since the Court permitted cross-examination concerning Exhibit 37, it was proper to allow the cross-examiner to try to get Witness to change his denial of lying on the job application.
_____	_____	The cross-examiner need not take the first answer a witness offers.
_____	_____	However, when an otherwise inadmissible document is shown to a witness to refresh his recollection, the witness must read it to himself.
_____	_____	It is improper to allow such a document to be read aloud to the jury.
_____	_____	It may be admitted as an exhibit only if offered by the lawyer who has not used the exhibit to refresh the recollection of the witness.
_____	_____	**Application/Conclusion on Issue 3:** The cross-examiner thus appropriately showed Exhibit 37 to Witness to refresh his recollection before asking him again whether he had lied.
		(Note: It may have been improper for the Court to permit Plaintiff's Counsel to attempt to "refresh" Witness's recollection, given that Witness did not testify to any lack of memory about what was said on the job application. However, Defense Counsel did not object to the attempt to refresh recollection, but only to the admission of the job application as an exhibit. Accordingly, only the admission of the exhibit is at issue.)
		4. Character Evidence—Extrinsic Evidence
_____	_____	**Conclusion on Issue 4:** The trial court properly excluded the testimony of Contractor because testimony by another witness represents extrinsic proof of the prior bad act and therefore is not admissible under Rule 608(b). (Note: same rule as issue 3.)
_____	_____	**Application/Conclusion on Issue 4:** The trial court correctly refused to permit testimony from Contractor that Witness had claimed 12 years of experience on his job application.
_____	_____	This testimony was relevant only to the witness's credibility and clearly constituted extrinsic evidence.

V. MBE PRACTICE QUESTIONS[30]

Question 1

A businessman was the target of a grand jury investigation into the alleged bribery of American and foreign officials in connection with an international construction project. The businessman had stated at a press conference that no bribes had been offered or taken and that no laws of any kind had been broken. The grand jury issued a subpoena requiring the businessman to testify before it. The businessman moved to quash the subpoena on the ground that his testimony could tend to incriminate him. The prosecutor responded with a grant of use immunity (under which the businessman's compelled statements before the grand jury could not be used against him in any state or federal prosecution). The businessman responded that the grant of use immunity was not sufficient to protect his Fifth Amendment rights.

Should the businessman be compelled to testify?

(A) No, because the businessman remains subject to the risk of foreign prosecution.
(B) No, because use immunity does not prevent the government from prosecuting the businessman on the bribery scheme.
(C) Yes, because the businessman has denied any criminal liability and therefore his Fifth Amendment rights are not at stake.
(D) Yes, because the grant of use immunity is coextensive with the businessman's Fifth Amendment rights.

Question 2

A defendant is on trial for knowing possession of a stolen television. The defendant claims that the television was a gift from a friend, who has disappeared. The defendant seeks to testify that he was present when the friend told her neighbor that the television had been given to the friend by her mother.

Is the defendant's testimony about the friend's statement to the neighbor admissible?

(A) No, because the friend's statement is hearsay not within any exception.
(B) No, because the defendant has not presented evidence of circumstances that clearly corroborate the statement.
(C) Yes, as nonhearsay evidence of the defendant's belief that the friend owned the television.
(D) Yes, under the hearsay exception for statements affecting an interest in property.

Question 3

A plaintiff has brought a civil suit against a defendant for injuries arising out of a fistfight between them. The day after the fight, a police officer talked to the plaintiff, the defendant, and an eyewitness, and made an official police report. At trial, the plaintiff seeks to introduce from the properly authenticated police report a statement attributed to the eyewitness, who is unavailable to testify at trial, that "[the defendant] started the fight."

Should the court admit the statement from the report?

(A) No, unless the entire report is introduced.
(B) No, because it is hearsay not within any exception.
(C) Yes, because it was based on the eyewitness's firsthand knowledge.
(D) Yes, because it is an excerpt from a public record offered in a civil case.

Question 4

A plaintiff has sued a defendant, alleging that she was run over by a speeding car driven by the defendant. The plaintiff was unconscious after her injury and, accompanied by her husband, was brought to the hospital in an ambulance.

At trial, the plaintiff calls an emergency room physician to testify that when the physician asked the plaintiff's husband if he knew what had happened, the husband, who was upset, replied, "I saw my wife get run over two hours ago by a driver who went right through the intersection without looking."

Is the physician's testimony about the husband's statement admissible?

(A) No, because it relates an opinion.
(B) No, because it is hearsay not within any exception.
(C) Yes, as a statement made for purposes of diagnosis or treatment.
(D) Yes, as an excited utterance.

Question 5

A plaintiff has sued a defendant for personal injuries the plaintiff suffered when she was bitten as she was trying to feed a rat that was part of the defendant's caged-rat experiment at a science fair. At trial, the plaintiff offers evidence that immediately after the incident the defendant said to her, "I'd like to give you this $100 bill, because I feel so bad about this."

Is the defendant's statement admissible?

(A) No, because it is not relevant to the issue of liability.
(B) No, because it was an offer of compromise.
(C) Yes, as a present sense impression.
(D) Yes, as the statement of a party-opponent.

Question 6

A defendant is charged with aggravated assault. The physical evidence at trial has shown that the victim was hit with a lead pipe in the back of the head and on the forearms and left in an alley. The medical examiner has testified that the injuries to the victim's forearms appear to have been defensive wounds. The victim has testified that he cannot remember who attacked him with the lead pipe. He would further testify that he remembers only that a passerby found him in the alley, and that he told the passerby that the defendant had hit him with the lead pipe; he then lost consciousness. The defendant objects to this proposed testimony, arguing that it is hearsay and that the victim had no personal knowledge of the identity of the perpetrator.

Is the victim's testimony concerning his previous statement to the passerby admissible?

(A) No, because the prosecutor has failed to show that it is more likely than not that the victim had personal knowledge of the perpetrator's identity.

(B) No, because the victim has no memory of the attack itself and therefore cannot be effectively cross-examined.

(C) Yes, because the victim is subject to cross-examination, and there is sufficient showing of personal knowledge.

(D) Yes, because it is the victim's own out-of-court statement.

Question 7

A man suffered a broken jaw in a fight with a neighbor that took place when they were both spectators at a soccer match.

If the man sues the neighbor for personal injury damages, which of the following actions must the trial court take if requested by the man?

(A) Prevent the neighbor's principal eyewitness from testifying, upon a showing that six years ago the witness was convicted of perjury and the conviction has not been the subject of a pardon or annulment.

(B) Refuse to let the neighbor cross-examine the man's medical expert on matters not covered on direct examination of the expert.

(C) Exclude nonparty eyewitnesses from the courtroom during the testimony of other witnesses.

(D) Require the production of a writing used before trial to refresh a witness's memory.

Question 8

A defendant is charged with robbing a bank. The prosecutor has supplied the court with information from accurate sources establishing that the bank is a federally insured institution and that this fact is not subject to reasonable dispute. The prosecutor asks the court to take judicial notice of this fact. The defendant objects.

How should the court proceed?

(A) The court must take judicial notice and instruct the jury that it is required to accept the judicially noticed fact as conclusive.

(B) The court must take judicial notice and instruct the jury that it may, but is not required to, accept the judicially noticed fact as conclusive.

(C) The court may refuse to take judicial notice, because judicial notice may not be taken of essential facts in a criminal case.

(D) The court must refuse to take judicial notice, because whether a bank is federally insured would not be generally known within the court's jurisdiction.

Question 9

The beneficiary of a decedent's life insurance policy has sued the life insurance company for the proceeds of the policy. At issue is the date when the decedent first experienced the heart problems that led to his death. The decedent's primary care physician has testified at trial that the decedent had a routine checkup on February 15. The physician then identifies a photocopy of a questionnaire completed by the decedent on that date in which the decedent wrote:

"Yesterday afternoon I broke into a big sweat and my chest hurt for a while." The beneficiary now offers the photocopy in evidence.

Should the court admit the photocopy?

(A) No, because the original questionnaire has not been shown to be unavailable.
(B) No, because the statement related to past rather than present symptoms.
(C) Yes, as a business record.
(D) Yes, as a statement for the purpose of obtaining medical treatment.

Question 10

A defendant is charged with mail fraud. At trial, the defendant has not taken the witness stand, but he has called a witness who has testified that the defendant has a reputation for honesty. On cross-examination, the prosecutor seeks to ask the witness, "Didn't you hear that two years ago the defendant was arrested for embezzlement?"

Should the court permit the question?

(A) No, because the defendant has not testified and therefore has not put his character at issue.
(B) No, because the incident was an arrest, not a conviction.
(C) Yes, because it seeks to impeach the credibility of the witness.
(D) Yes, because the earlier arrest for a crime of dishonesty makes the defendant's guilt of the mail fraud more likely.

Question 11

At a woman's trial for bank robbery, the prosecutor has called a private security guard for the bank who has testified, without objection, that while he was on a coffee break, the woman's brother rushed up to him and said, "Come quickly! My sister is robbing the bank!" The woman now seeks to call a witness to testify that the brother later told the witness, "I got my sister into trouble by telling a security guard that she was robbing the bank, but now I realize I was mistaken." The brother is unavailable to testify.

Is the witness's testimony admissible?

(A) No, because the brother will be afforded no opportunity to explain or deny the later statement.
(B) No, because the prosecutor will be afforded no opportunity to confront the brother.
(C) Yes, because it is substantive proof that the woman did not rob the bank.
(D) Yes, but only as an inconsistent statement to impeach the brother's credibility.

Question 12

A woman's car was set on fire by vandals. When she submitted a claim of loss for the car to her insurance company, the insurance company refused to pay, asserting that the woman's policy had lapsed due to the nonpayment of her premium. The woman sued the insurance company for breach of contract.

At trial, the woman testified that she had, in a timely manner, placed a stamped, properly addressed envelope containing the premium payment in the outgoing mail bin at her office. The woman's secretary then testified that every afternoon at closing time he takes all outgoing mail in the bin to the post office. The insurance company later called its mail clerk to testify that he opens all incoming mail and that he did not receive the woman's premium payment.

The woman and the insurance company have both moved for a directed verdict. For which party, if either, should the court direct a verdict?

(A) For the insurance company, because neither the woman nor her secretary has any personal knowledge that the envelope was mailed.

(B) For the insurance company, because the mail clerk's direct testimony negates the woman's circumstantial evidence.

(C) For the woman, because there is a presumption that an envelope properly addressed and stamped was received by the addressee.

(D) For neither the woman nor the insurance company, because under these circumstances the jury is responsible for determining whether the insurance company received the payment.

Question 13

At a defendant's trial for mail fraud, the defendant calls his wife to testify that she committed the fraud herself without the defendant's knowledge. On cross-examination, the prosecutor asks the wife, "Isn't it true that you have fled your home several times in fear of your husband?"

Is this question proper?

(A) No, because it is leading a witness not shown to be hostile.

(B) No, because its probative value is outweighed by the danger of unfair prejudice to the defendant.

(C) Yes, because by calling his wife, the defendant has waived his privilege to prevent her from testifying against him.

(D) Yes, because it explores the wife's possible motive for testifying falsely.

Question 14

A driver sued her insurance company on an accident insurance policy covering personal injuries to the driver. The insurance company defended on the ground that the driver's injuries were intentionally self-inflicted and therefore excluded from the policy's coverage.

The driver testified at trial that she had inflicted the injuries, as her negligence had caused the crash in which she was injured, but that she had not done so intentionally. She then called as a witness her treating psychiatrist to give his opinion that the driver had been mentally unbalanced, but not self-destructive, at the time of the crash.

Should the court admit the witness's opinion?

(A) No, because it is a statement about the driver's credibility.

(B) No, because it is an opinion about a mental state that constitutes an element of the defense.

(C) No, because the witness did not first state the basis for his opinion.

(D) Yes, because it is a helpful opinion by a qualified expert.

Question 15

A plaintiff has brought a products liability action against a defendant, the manufacturer of a sport-utility vehicle that the plaintiff's decedent was driving when she was fatally injured in a rollover accident. The plaintiff claims that a design defect in the vehicle caused it to roll over. The defendant claims that the cause of the accident was the decedent's driving at excessive speed during an ice storm. Eyewitnesses to the accident have given contradictory estimates about the vehicle's speed just before the rollover. It is also disputed whether the decedent was killed instantly.

Which of the following items of offered evidence is the court most likely to admit?

(A) A videotape offered by the defendant of a test conducted by the defendant showing that a sport-utility vehicle of the same model the decedent was driving did not roll over when driven by a professional driver on a dry test track at the top speed testified to by the eyewitnesses.

(B) A videotape offered by the plaintiff of a television news program about sport-utility vehicles that includes footage of accident scenes in which the vehicles had rolled over.

(C) Evidence offered by the defendant that the decedent had received two citations for speeding in the previous three years.

(D) Photographs taken at the accident scene and during the autopsy that would help the plaintiff's medical expert explain to the jury why she concluded that the decedent did not die instantly.

Question 16

At the start of the trial of a defendant and a codefendant for robbery, the codefendant and her attorney offered to give the prosecutor information about facts that would strengthen the prosecutor's case against the defendant in exchange for leniency toward the codefendant. The prosecutor refused the offer. Shortly thereafter, the codefendant committed suicide.

During the defendant's trial, the prosecutor called the codefendant's attorney and asked him to relate the information that the codefendant had revealed to the attorney.

Is the attorney's testimony admissible?

(A) No, because the codefendant's communications are protected by the attorney-client privilege.

(B) No, because the plea discussion was initiated by the codefendant rather than by the prosecutor.

(C) Yes, because the codefendant intended to disclose the information.

(D) Yes, because the information the codefendant gave to her attorney revealing her knowledge of the crime would be a statement against the codefendant's penal interest.

VI. MBE PRACTICE ANALYSIS[31]

Question 1

A businessman was the target of a grand jury investigation into the alleged bribery of American and foreign officials in connection with an international construction project. The businessman had stated at a press conference that no bribes had been offered or taken and that no laws of any kind had been broken. The grand jury issued a subpoena requiring the businessman to testify before it. The businessman moved to quash the subpoena on the ground that his testimony could tend to incriminate him. The prosecutor responded with a grant of use immunity (under which the businessman's compelled statements before the grand jury could not be used against him in any state or federal prosecution). The businessman responded that the grant of use immunity was not sufficient to protect his Fifth Amendment rights.

Should the businessman be compelled to testify?

(A) No, because the businessman remains subject to the risk of foreign prosecution.

Incorrect. While the businessman does face the possibility of foreign prosecution, the U.S. Supreme Court has squarely held that the Fifth Amendment does not protect against the risk of foreign prosecution. Because the businessman has been protected against the use of his statements in a domestic prosecution, his statements cannot tend to incriminate him in any sense protected by the Fifth Amendment. He should therefore be compelled to testify.

(B) No, because use immunity does not prevent the government from prosecuting the businessman on the bribery scheme.

Incorrect. It is true that the grant of use immunity does not protect the businessman from being prosecuted. Instead, it protects against the businessman's compelled statements—or any fruits of those statements—being used against him in any domestic prosecution. The U.S. Supreme Court has long held that the Fifth Amendment right is satisfied by a grant of use immunity. The Fifth Amendment does not require a grant of immunity from prosecution ("transactional immunity"). The businessman should therefore be compelled to testify.

(C) Yes, because the businessman has denied any criminal liability and therefore his Fifth Amendment rights are not at stake.

Incorrect. The fact that the businessman has denied liability does not mean that any statement he makes could never tend to incriminate him. Even an innocent person might say something that would tend to incriminate himself, and a tendency to incriminate is all that is required to trigger Fifth Amendment protection. However, because the grant of use immunity is coextensive with the businessman's Fifth Amendment rights, he should be compelled to testify.

(D) Yes, because the grant of use immunity is coextensive with the businessman's Fifth Amendment rights.

Correct. The U.S. Supreme Court has held that if a person is guaranteed, through a grant of use immunity, that neither his statements nor the fruits of those statements can be used against him in a domestic prosecution, then he loses his right to refuse to testify

---
31. *Id.*

because his statements cannot tend to incriminate him. Because the businessman has been protected against the use of his statements in a domestic prosecution, his statements cannot tend to incriminate him in any sense protected by the Fifth Amendment.

Question 2

A defendant is on trial for knowing possession of a stolen television. The defendant claims that the television was a gift from a friend, who has disappeared. The defendant seeks to testify that he was present when the friend told her neighbor that the television had been given to the friend by her mother.

Is the defendant's testimony about the friend's statement to the neighbor admissible?

(A) No, because the friend's statement is hearsay not within any exception.

Incorrect. The statement would be hearsay if it were offered to prove that the friend actually owned the television. But the defendant is offering the friend's statement as evidence that the defendant thought that the friend owned the television (i.e., that it had not been stolen). Because the defendant is charged with knowing possession of a stolen television, his state of mind is relevant. If the defendant had heard the friend say that the television was hers, that evidence would be relevant to the defendant's state of mind regardless of the truth of the statement. Therefore, the friend's out-of-court statement is not hearsay and is admissible.

(B) No, because the defendant has not presented evidence of circumstances that clearly corroborate the statement.

Incorrect. There is no requirement that a statement offered to prove its effect on the person who heard it must be corroborated. In this case, the defendant is offering the friend's statement as evidence that the defendant thought that the friend owned the television (i.e., that it had not been stolen). Because the defendant is charged with knowing possession of a stolen television, his state of mind is relevant. If the defendant had heard the friend say that the television was hers, that evidence would be relevant to the defendant's state of mind regardless of whether it was corroborated. Because the statement is not being offered for its truth, it is not hearsay and is admissible.

(C) Yes, as nonhearsay evidence of the defendant's belief that the friend owned the television.

Correct. The defendant is offering the friend's statement as evidence that the defendant thought that the friend owned the television (i.e., that it had not been stolen). Because the defendant is charged with knowing possession of a stolen television, his state of mind is relevant. If the defendant had heard the friend say that the television was hers, that evidence would be relevant to the defendant's state of mind regardless of the truth of the statement. Therefore, the friend's out-of-court statement is not hearsay.

(D) Yes, under the hearsay exception for statements affecting an interest in property.

Incorrect. The statement is offered for a nonhearsay purpose, so there is no need to find an applicable hearsay exception. The defendant is offering the friend's statement as evidence that the defendant thought that the friend owned the television (i.e., that it had not been stolen). Because the defendant is charged with knowing possession of a stolen television, his state of mind is relevant. If the defendant had heard the friend say that the television was hers, that evidence would be relevant to the defendant's state of mind regardless of the truth of the statement. Therefore, the friend's out-of-court statement is not hearsay.

Moreover, if an exception were required, the exception for statements affecting an interest in property would not be applicable, because that exception requires that the statement be contained in a document. Here the statement was oral.

Question 3

A plaintiff has brought a civil suit against a defendant for injuries arising out of a fistfight between them. The day after the fight, a police officer talked to the plaintiff, the defendant, and an eyewitness, and made an official police report. At trial, the plaintiff seeks to introduce from the properly authenticated police report a statement attributed to the eyewitness, who is unavailable to testify at trial, that "[the defendant] started the fight."

Should the court admit the statement from the report?

(A) No, unless the entire report is introduced.
Incorrect. The statement is inadmissible hearsay even if the entire report is introduced; the eyewitness's statement is hearsay within the hearsay report. The report itself could be admissible as a business or public record, but the hearsay within it is admissible only if it satisfies a separate hearsay exception or if it can be shown that the eyewitness had a business or public duty to report the information accurately. The eyewitness had no such duty, and no other hearsay exception applies.

(B) No, because it is hearsay not within any exception.
Correct. The eyewitness's statement is hearsay within the hearsay report. The report itself could be admissible as a business or public record, but the hearsay within it is admissible only if it satisfies a separate hearsay exception or if it can be shown that the eyewitness had a business or public duty to report the information accurately. The eyewitness had no such duty. The eyewitness's statement is also not a present sense impression, because it was made the day after the fight, and no other hearsay exception applies.

(C) Yes, because it was based on the eyewitness's firsthand knowledge.
Incorrect. The fact that the eyewitness purports to have personal knowledge does not solve the hearsay problem, which arises because the eyewitness might not have told the truth about the event he purportedly saw and is not subject to cross-examination about it. The eyewitness's statement is hearsay within the hearsay report. The report itself could be admissible as a business or public record, but the hearsay within it is admissible only if it satisfies a separate hearsay exception or if it can be shown that the eyewitness had a business or public duty to report the information accurately. The eyewitness had no such duty, and no other hearsay exception applies.

(D) Yes, because it is an excerpt from a public record offered in a civil case.
Incorrect. The eyewitness's statement is hearsay within the hearsay report. The report itself could be admissible as a business or public record, but the hearsay within it is admissible only if it satisfies a separate hearsay exception or if it can be shown that the eyewitness had a business or public duty to report the information accurately. The eyewitness had no such duty, and no other hearsay exception applies.

Question 4

A plaintiff has sued a defendant, alleging that she was run over by a speeding car driven by the defendant. The plaintiff was unconscious after her injury and, accompanied by her husband, was brought to the hospital in an ambulance.

At trial, the plaintiff calls an emergency room physician to testify that when the physician asked the plaintiff's husband if he knew what had happened, the husband, who was upset, replied, "I saw my wife get run over two hours ago by a driver who went right through the intersection without looking."

Is the physician's testimony about the husband's statement admissible?

(A) No, because it relates an opinion.

Incorrect. An out-of-court statement is not inadmissible simply because it contains an opinion. Statements of opinion by out-of-court declarants may be admitted if they qualify under a hearsay exception and otherwise satisfy the rules governing opinion testimony of in-court witnesses. This statement, however, is hearsay not within any exception and is inadmissible.

(B) No, because it is hearsay not within any exception.

Correct. The statement is offered to prove liability for the accident. As such, it is not a statement made for purposes of diagnosis or treatment. Moreover, the statement was made two hours after the accident, so it is very unlikely that the husband (who was not himself an accident victim) was under a continuous state of excitement between the time of the accident and the time he made the statement. Therefore, the statement is not admissible as an excited utterance, and no other hearsay exception applies.

(C) Yes, as a statement made for purposes of diagnosis or treatment.

Incorrect. The husband's statement is making an accusation of fault for the accident. Such a statement is not pertinent to the diagnosis or treatment of the plaintiff, as is required by the hearsay exception. No other hearsay exception applies, so the statement is inadmissible.

(D) Yes, as an excited utterance.

Incorrect. In order for this statement to be admissible as an excited utterance, the declarant must have been under a continuous state of excitement between the time of the event and the time of the statement. Here, the husband made the statement two hours after the accident, so it is very unlikely that the husband (who was not himself an accident victim) was under a continuous state of excitement between the time of the accident and the time he made the statement. Therefore, the statement is not admissible as an excited utterance, and no other hearsay exception applies, so the statement is inadmissible.

Question 5

A plaintiff has sued a defendant for personal injuries the plaintiff suffered when she was bitten as she was trying to feed a rat that was part of the defendant's caged-rat experiment at a science fair. At trial, the plaintiff offers evidence that immediately after the incident the defendant said to her, "I'd like to give you this $100 bill, because I feel so bad about this."

Is the defendant's statement admissible?

(A) No, because it is not relevant to the issue of liability.

Incorrect. The defendant's statement of contrition and offer of compensation clearly have a tendency to prove that he is liable, and a tendency is all that is required for the evidence to be relevant under Rule 401. The statement is admissible as the statement of a party-opponent.

(B) No, because it was an offer of compromise.

Incorrect. The statement would not be excluded under Rule 408, which excludes statements that are made to settle a claim, because that rule applies only when the statement is made as a compromise to a disputed claim. Here, at the time the defendant made the statement, he was not contesting that he was at fault. Therefore, there was no disputed claim, and the statement is admissible as the statement of a party-opponent.

(C) Yes, as a present sense impression.

Incorrect. The exception to the hearsay rule for present sense impressions covers a statement describing or explaining an event or condition made during or immediately after the event or condition. The defendant's statement is just an expression of contrition and not an attempt to explain any event or condition. However, the statement is admissible as the statement of a party-opponent.

(D) Yes, as the statement of a party-opponent.

Correct. An out-of-court statement by a party that is relevant to his or her liability is admissible under the exception to the hearsay rule for statements of a party-opponent. One might think that the statement would be excluded because of Rule 408, which excludes statements that are made to settle a claim. But that rule is inapplicable, because it applies only when the statement is made to compromise a disputed claim. Here, at the time the defendant made the statement, he was not contesting that he was at fault. Therefore, there was no disputed claim.

Question 6

A defendant is charged with aggravated assault. The physical evidence at trial has shown that the victim was hit with a lead pipe in the back of the head and on the forearms and left in an alley. The medical examiner has testified that the injuries to the victim's forearms appear to have been defensive wounds. The victim has testified that he cannot remember who attacked him with the lead pipe. He would further testify that he remembers only that a passerby found him in the alley, and that he told the passerby that the defendant had hit him with the lead pipe; he then lost consciousness. The defendant objects to this proposed testimony, arguing that it is hearsay and that the victim had no personal knowledge of the identity of the perpetrator.

Is the victim's testimony concerning his previous statement to the passerby admissible?

(A) No, because the prosecutor has failed to show that it is more likely than not that the victim had personal knowledge of the perpetrator's identity.

Incorrect. The standard for personal knowledge under Rule 602 is whether a reasonable juror could find that the witness is speaking on the basis of personal knowledge. This standard is referred to as "prima facie" proof and is significantly easier to satisfy than "more likely than not."

(B) No, because the victim has no memory of the attack itself and therefore cannot be effectively cross-examined.

Incorrect. The U.S. Supreme Court held in United States v. Owens that a declarant-witness is subject to cross-examination within the meaning of the hearsay exception for prior identifications even if the witness lacks all memory of the prior identification.

(C) Yes, because the victim is subject to cross-examination, and there is sufficient showing of personal knowledge.

Correct. The U.S. Supreme Court held in United States v. Owens that a declarant-witness is subject to cross-examination within the meaning of the hearsay exception for prior identifications even if the witness lacks all memory of the prior identification. As to personal knowledge, the evidence of defensive wounds is more than sufficient to persuade a reasonable juror that the victim saw his attacker.

(D) Yes, because it is the victim's own out-of-court statement.

Incorrect. The rule against hearsay applies to any out-of-court statement admitted for its truth, including earlier statements of trial witnesses. In this case, however, there is a hearsay exception for prior identifications when the declarant is testifying and subject to cross-examination.

Question 7

A man suffered a broken jaw in a fight with a neighbor that took place when they were both spectators at a soccer match.

If the man sues the neighbor for personal injury damages, which of the following actions must the trial court take if requested by the man?

(A) Prevent the neighbor's principal eyewitness from testifying, upon a showing that six years ago the witness was convicted of perjury and the conviction has not been the subject of a pardon or annulment.

Incorrect. A witness can never be excluded from testifying simply because there is impeachment evidence that could be used against that witness. Under Rule 601, all witnesses are presumed to be competent. The man can use this evidence to impeach the witness when the witness testifies.

(B) Refuse to let the neighbor cross-examine the man's medical expert on matters not covered on direct examination of the expert.

Incorrect. The trial court is not required to prohibit a cross-examiner from asking questions unrelated to the direct examination. Rule 611(b) states that the court "may allow inquiry into additional matters."

(C) Exclude nonparty eyewitnesses from the courtroom during the testimony of other witnesses.

Correct. Rule 615 provides that if a party moves to exclude prospective witnesses before they testify, "the court must order witnesses excluded so they cannot hear other witnesses' testimony."

(D) Require the production of a writing used before trial to refresh a witness's memory.

Incorrect. Under Rule 612, the trial court has discretion to order a party to produce for the adversary a writing used before trial to refresh the memory of a witness called by the party, but the court is not required to do so.

Question 8

A defendant is charged with robbing a bank. The prosecutor has supplied the court with information from accurate sources establishing that the bank is a federally insured institution and that this fact is not subject to reasonable dispute. The prosecutor asks the court to take judicial notice of this fact. The defendant objects.

How should the court proceed?

(A) The court must take judicial notice and instruct the jury that it is required to accept the judicially noticed fact as conclusive.

Incorrect. In criminal cases, the trial judge may not instruct the jury to accept a judicially noticed fact as conclusive. To do so would impermissibly limit the defendant's right to a jury trial. The court must take judicial notice of a fact if the court is supplied with the necessary information to indicate that the fact is not subject to reasonable dispute. However, Rule 201(f) provides that in a criminal case, "the court must instruct the jury that it may or may not accept the noticed fact as conclusive."

(B) The court must take judicial notice and instruct the jury that it may, but is not required to, accept the judicially noticed fact as conclusive.

Correct. The court must take judicial notice of a fact if the court is supplied with the necessary information to indicate that the fact is not subject to reasonable dispute. Rule 201(f) provides that in a criminal case, "the court must instruct the jury that it may or may not accept the noticed fact as conclusive."

(C) The court may refuse to take judicial notice, because judicial notice may not be taken of essential facts in a criminal case.

Incorrect. The court must take judicial notice of a fact if the court is supplied with the necessary information to indicate that the fact is not subject to reasonable dispute. Here the facts indicate that the court has been supplied with the necessary information. However, Rule 201(f) provides that in a criminal case, "the court must instruct the jury that it may or may not accept the noticed fact as conclusive."

(D) The court must refuse to take judicial notice, because whether a bank is federally insured would not be generally known within the court's jurisdiction.

Incorrect. Whether a bank is federally insured is a fact that would be generally known within the jurisdiction. Even if it were not, however, under Rule 201(b) judicial notice must be taken if the indisputability of a fact "can be accurately and readily determined from sources whose accuracy cannot be questioned." The facts here so provide. However, Rule 201(f) provides that in a criminal case, "the court must instruct the jury that it may or may not accept the noticed fact as conclusive."

Question 9

The beneficiary of a decedent's life insurance policy has sued the life insurance company for the proceeds of the policy. At issue is the date when the decedent first experienced the heart problems that led to his death. The decedent's primary care physician has testified at trial that the decedent had a routine checkup on February 15. The physician then identifies a photocopy of a questionnaire completed by the decedent on that date in which the decedent wrote: "Yesterday afternoon I broke into a big sweat and my chest hurt for a while." The beneficiary now offers the photocopy in evidence.

Should the court admit the photocopy?

(A) No, because the original questionnaire has not been shown to be unavailable.

Incorrect. This answer refers to the best evidence rule. Under the best evidence rule, a copy of a document is as admissible as the original unless a genuine question is raised about the authenticity of the original or the circumstances make it unfair to admit the copy. No such question or circumstances are present here. The photocopy should be admitted as a statement for the purpose of obtaining medical treatment.

(B) No, because the statement related to past rather than present symptoms.

Incorrect. Statements of medical history can be admitted under the hearsay exception in Rule 803(4) if they are pertinent to diagnosis or treatment, regardless of whether the statements relate to past or present symptoms. The decedent's statement clearly qualifies under this hearsay exception.

(C) Yes, as a business record.

Incorrect. For a recorded statement to be admissible as a business record under Rule 803(6), the business record must be kept in the course of a regularly conducted activity and it must be a regular practice of the business to make the record. Here, the record was made by the decedent, not by the physician, and there is no indication that the decedent regularly prepared such records. However, the photocopy should be admitted as a statement for the purpose of obtaining medical treatment.

(D) Yes, as a statement for the purpose of obtaining medical treatment.

Correct. The decedent's statement of his medical history was made for the purpose of diagnosis and treatment, and it is clearly pertinent to the physician's diagnosis and treatment. Therefore, it is admissible under Rule 803(4).

Question 10

A defendant is charged with mail fraud. At trial, the defendant has not taken the witness stand, but he has called a witness who has testified that the defendant has a reputation for honesty. On cross-examination, the prosecutor seeks to ask the witness, "Didn't you hear that two years ago the defendant was arrested for embezzlement?"

Should the court permit the question?

(A) No, because the defendant has not testified and therefore has not put his character at issue.

Incorrect. When a defendant calls a character witness, the prosecutor is permitted to test the character witness's knowledge of the defendant. The fact that the defendant has not put his character at issue is irrelevant.

(B) No, because the incident was an arrest, not a conviction.

Incorrect. For purposes of testing the witness's knowledge of the defendant's reputation for honesty, the bad act need not have resulted in a conviction. An arrest is sufficient to have an impact on the community's view of the defendant's honesty.

(C) Yes, because it seeks to impeach the credibility of the witness.

Correct. The witness has testified that she knows about the defendant's reputation. The prosecutor has the right to test the basis and adequacy of that knowledge, as well as the nature of the community itself. If the witness answers that she had not heard about the arrest, that admission could indicate that she is not very knowledgeable about the defendant's reputation in the community, because such an arrest would likely have a negative effect on that reputation. If the witness says that she had heard about the arrest, a negative inference could be raised about the community itself and its view of what it is to be an honest person.

(D) Yes, because the earlier arrest for a crime of dishonesty makes the defendant's guilt of the mail fraud more likely.

Incorrect. The prosecutor is not allowed to use a bad act to show that the defendant has a propensity to commit a similar bad act. Rule 404 limits the use of character evidence to prove conduct in accordance with a character trait.

Question 11

At a woman's trial for bank robbery, the prosecutor has called a private security guard for the bank who has testified, without objection, that while he was on a coffee break, the woman's brother rushed up to him and said, "Come quickly! My sister is robbing the bank!" The woman now seeks to call a witness to testify that the brother later told the witness, "I got my sister into trouble by telling a security guard that she was robbing the bank, but now I realize I was mistaken." The brother is unavailable to testify.

Is the witness's testimony admissible?

(A) No, because the brother will be afforded no opportunity to explain or deny the later statement.

Incorrect. What is being offered here is an inconsistent statement of a hearsay declarant. The goal is to impeach that declarant's credibility. The brother's original statement would have been admitted as an excited utterance under the Rule 803(2) hearsay exception. While it is ordinarily true that a witness impeached with a prior inconsistent statement must be given an opportunity to explain or deny the statement, that opportunity is not available when a hearsay declarant is not produced at trial. Rule 806 provides that the ordinary requirement of a "fair opportunity to explain or deny" is not applicable to hearsay declarants who are being impeached with prior inconsistent statements.

(B) No, because the prosecutor will be afforded no opportunity to confront the brother.

Incorrect. A prosecutor has no right to confrontation; only a criminal defendant has that right. In any case, here it is the prosecutor who offered the statement that the brother made at the time of the crime, so the prosecutor cannot argue a lack of opportunity to confront the brother.

(C) Yes, because it is substantive proof that the woman did not rob the bank.

Incorrect. The statement later made by the brother was an out-of-court statement, and if offered for its truth, it is hearsay. There is no applicable hearsay exception.

(D) Yes, but only as an inconsistent statement to impeach the brother's credibility.

Correct. It is ordinarily true that a witness impeached with a prior inconsistent statement must be given an opportunity to explain or deny the statement. That is not possible, however, when a hearsay declarant is not produced at trial. Therefore Rule 806 provides that the ordinary requirement of a "fair opportunity to explain or deny" is not applicable to hearsay declarants who are being impeached with prior inconsistent statements. The inconsistent statement is probative of the brother's credibility, and Rule 806 permits such impeachment.

Question 12

A woman's car was set on fire by vandals. When she submitted a claim of loss for the car to her insurance company, the insurance company refused to pay, asserting that the woman's policy had lapsed due to the nonpayment of her premium. The woman sued the insurance company for breach of contract.

At trial, the woman testified that she had, in a timely manner, placed a stamped, properly addressed envelope containing the premium payment in the outgoing mail bin at her office. The woman's secretary then testified that every afternoon at closing time he takes all outgoing mail in the bin to the post office. The insurance company later called its mail clerk to testify that he opens all incoming mail and that he did not receive the woman's premium payment.

The woman and the insurance company have both moved for a directed verdict. For which party, if either, should the court direct a verdict?

(A) For the insurance company, because neither the woman nor her secretary has any personal knowledge that the envelope was mailed.

Incorrect. Under Rule 301, the rule on presumptions, the woman has presented sufficient evidence that the envelope containing the premium payment was mailed. The rule does not require that the woman have personal knowledge that the envelope reached the post office. The insurance company then has the burden of producing evidence to rebut the presumption that the envelope was received. Because the insurance company has produced such evidence, the presumption is taken out of the case and it is up to the fact finder to determine whether the insurance company received the payment.

(B) For the insurance company, because the mail clerk's direct testimony negates the woman's circumstantial evidence.

Incorrect. Under Rule 301, once the woman provides evidence that the envelope containing the premium payment was mailed, the insurance company has the burden of producing evidence sufficient to rebut the presumption that the envelope was received. That does not mean, however, that if the insurance company does provide such evidence it is entitled to a directed verdict. Instead, the presumption is taken out of the case and it is up to the fact finder to determine whether the insurance company received the payment.

(C) For the woman, because there is a presumption that an envelope properly addressed and stamped was received by the addressee.

Incorrect. It is true that the woman's evidence has triggered the presumption that the envelope containing the premium payment was received. But under Rule 301, the insurance company then has the burden of producing enough evidence to rebut the presumption. Here the insurance company has done so. Consequently, the presumption is taken out of the case and it is up to the fact finder to determine whether the insurance company received the payment. Therefore, it would be error to grant a directed verdict for the woman.

(D) For neither the woman nor the insurance company, because under these circumstances the jury is responsible for determining whether the insurance company received the payment.

Correct. The woman has presented sufficient evidence to trigger the presumption that her payment was received. The insurance company has presented sufficient evidence to rebut that presumption. Consequently, the presumption is taken out of the case and it is up to the fact finder to determine whether the insurance company received the payment. Therefore, it would be error to grant a directed verdict for either the woman or the insurance company.

Question 13

At a defendant's trial for mail fraud, the defendant calls his wife to testify that she committed the fraud herself without the defendant's knowledge. On cross-examination, the prosecutor asks the wife, "Isn't it true that you have fled your home several times in fear of your husband?"

Is this question proper?

(A) No, because it is leading a witness not shown to be hostile.

Incorrect. Leading questions are generally permitted on cross-examination, and the question is proper because it explores the wife's possible motive for testifying falsely.

(B) No, because its probative value is outweighed by the danger of unfair prejudice to the defendant.

Incorrect. This answer applies the wrong balancing test. Under Rule 403, evidence that is probative is admissible unless its probative value is substantially outweighed by the risk of unfair prejudice. That test favors admitting probative evidence. It is not the case, therefore, that the probative value must outweigh the prejudicial effect for the evidence to be admissible. The question is proper because it explores the wife's possible motive for testifying falsely.

(C) Yes, because by calling his wife, the defendant has waived his privilege to prevent her from testifying against him.

Incorrect. The defendant does not have a privilege to prevent his wife from testifying against him. The privilege against adverse spousal testimony is held by the wife, as the witness, not by the defendant. The question is proper, however, because it explores the wife's possible motive for testifying falsely.

(D) Yes, because it explores the wife's possible motive for testifying falsely.

Correct. A cross-examiner is entitled to question in such a way as to raise inferences about the motive of a witness to testify falsely. Here, the question raises an inference that the wife is in fear of her husband and is therefore taking the blame for her husband's crime.

Question 14

A driver sued her insurance company on an accident insurance policy covering personal injuries to the driver. The insurance company defended on the ground that the driver's injuries were intentionally self-inflicted and therefore excluded from the policy's coverage.

The driver testified at trial that she had inflicted the injuries, as her negligence had caused the crash in which she was injured, but that she had not done so intentionally. She then called as a witness her treating psychiatrist to give his opinion that the driver had been mentally unbalanced, but not self-destructive, at the time of the crash.

Should the court admit the witness's opinion?

(A) No, because it is a statement about the driver's credibility.

Incorrect. The witness is not offering to testify that the driver is telling the truth. (If the witness were to do so, the testimony would be inadmissible, because credibility is a question for the jury to assess.) The witness is offering to testify only to the driver's pertinent mental state, which is permissible in a civil case such as this.

(B) No, because it is an opinion about a mental state that constitutes an element of the defense.

Incorrect. Rule 704(b), which prohibits an expert from testifying that a criminal defendant had or did not have the requisite mental state to commit the crime charged, is applicable to criminal cases only. There is no absolute bar to such testimony in a civil case such as this.

(C) No, because the witness did not first state the basis for his opinion.

Incorrect. Under Rule 705, an expert may state an opinion "without first testifying to the underlying facts or data."

(D) Yes, because it is a helpful opinion by a qualified expert.

Correct. The witness's opinion helps the jury understand a relevant mental state. The standard for qualification of an expert is not high; a psychiatrist is qualified to testify to a person's mental state.

Question 15

A plaintiff has brought a products liability action against a defendant, the manufacturer of a sport-utility vehicle that the plaintiff's decedent was driving when she was fatally injured in a rollover accident. The plaintiff claims that a design defect in the vehicle caused it to roll over. The defendant claims that the cause of the accident was the decedent's driving at excessive speed during an ice storm. Eyewitnesses to the accident have given contradictory estimates about the vehicle's speed just before the rollover. It is also disputed whether the decedent was killed instantly.

Which of the following items of offered evidence is the court most likely to admit?

(A) A videotape offered by the defendant of a test conducted by the defendant showing that a sport-utility vehicle of the same model the decedent was driving did not roll over when driven by a professional driver on a dry test track at the top speed testified to by the eyewitnesses.

Incorrect. In order for product demonstrations to be admissible under Rule 403 to prove how an accident happened, the conditions must be substantially similar to the conditions at the time in question. This test was conducted on a dry track with a professional driver. Even if the court admits this evidence in its discretion, the question calls for the evidence that the court is most likely to admit. This evidence is not it.

(B) A videotape offered by the plaintiff of a television news program about sport-utility vehicles that includes footage of accident scenes in which the vehicles had rolled over.

Incorrect. This evidence is not very probative, because it shows sport-utility vehicles in general, not necessarily the model used by the decedent, and there is no indication that the conditions in the accident scenes were in any way similar to the conditions in question. Under Rule 403, the probative value of this evidence is likely to be substantially outweighed by its prejudicial effect and risk of jury confusion. Even if the court admits this evidence in its discretion, the question calls for the evidence that the court is most likely to admit. This evidence is not it.

(C) Evidence offered by the defendant that the decedent had received two citations for speeding in the previous three years.

Incorrect. This evidence would not be admissible, because it is attempting to show that the decedent had a propensity to drive too fast, to create the inference that the decedent was driving too fast at the time in question. Under Rule 404, proof of character in order to show conduct consistent with that character is inadmissible in civil cases.

(D) Photographs taken at the accident scene and during the autopsy that would help the plaintiff's medical expert explain to the jury why she concluded that the decedent did not die instantly.

Correct. This evidence is most likely to be admitted. If these photographs are offered to illustrate the expert's testimony, the jury can be instructed to use the evidence only for that purpose. Moreover, this evidence is not as prejudicial or potentially confusing to the jury as the evidence in options (A) and (B), while the evidence in option (C) is inadmissible.

Question 16

At the start of the trial of a defendant and a codefendant for robbery, the codefendant and her attorney offered to give the prosecutor information about facts that would strengthen the prosecutor's case against the defendant in exchange for leniency toward the codefendant. The prosecutor refused the offer. Shortly thereafter, the codefendant committed suicide.

During the defendant's trial, the prosecutor called the codefendant's attorney and asked him to relate the information that the codefendant had revealed to the attorney.

Is the attorney's testimony admissible?

(A) No, because the codefendant's communications are protected by the attorney-client privilege.

Correct. The prosecutor is asking for confidential communications between the codefendant and her attorney, which is privileged information. If the codefendant had actually provided information to the prosecutor, the privilege would have been waived as to any communications previously made to her attorney. However, the codefendant did not disclose any confidential communications.

(B) No, because the plea discussion was initiated by the codefendant rather than by the prosecutor.

Incorrect. The prosecutor is asking for confidential communications between the codefendant and her attorney, which is privileged information, and it makes no difference who initiated the plea discussion. The question is whether the codefendant waived the privilege by offering information to the prosecutor, which she did not. Because the codefendant did not actually disclose any confidential communications to the prosecutor, there was no waiver.

(C) Yes, because the codefendant intended to disclose the information.

Incorrect. The prosecutor is asking for confidential communications between the codefendant and her attorney, which is privileged information. If the codefendant had actually provided information to the prosecutor, the privilege would have been waived as to any communications previously made to her attorney. However, the co-defendant did not disclose any confidential communications, and whether she intended to disclose the information is irrelevant.

(D) Yes, because the information the codefendant gave to her attorney revealing her knowledge of the crime would be a statement against the codefendant's penal interest.

Incorrect. A declaration against interest is one that tends to expose the declarant to criminal liability. Any statement to the attorney could not have subjected the codefendant to a risk of criminal liability, because the statement was privileged.

CHAPTER 13

Mapping MBE Topics—Federal Civil Procedure

I. MIND MAP

Federal Civil Procedure includes issues of jurisdiction and process. Statutes, rules, and case law serve as its foundation. Jurisdiction is laid out by statutes. The Federal Rules of Civil Procedure govern most issues regarding process. Case law further develops and interprets both.

The mind map moves chronologically through the decision-making process from bringing a lawsuit to its conclusion. Essentially, the same mind map can be used for federal civil procedure and state civil procedure:

- Jurisdiction and preliminary matters
  - Subject-matter jurisdiction
    - Original
    - Supplemental
    - Removal
  - Personal jurisdiction
  - Service of process
  - Venue v. transfer
- Pleadings
  - Joinder of claims
  - Joinder of parties
  - Amendments
- Discovery
- Jury trial
- Motions
- Preclusion
- Appealability and review

Jurisdiction, in this sense, is the power of the court. A court must have jurisdiction over the subject matter and jurisdiction over the person in order for any judgment it issues to be binding upon the parties. As to **subject-matter jurisdiction**, state courts have general jurisdiction while federal courts have limited jurisdiction. Always begin your rule statement for subject matter jurisdiction with "Federal courts are courts of limited jurisdiction." Each claim brought in federal court must have an independent basis for jurisdiction. Objections to subject-matter jurisdiction can never be waived.

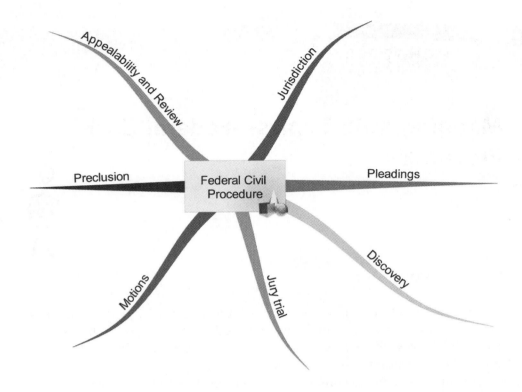

Subject-matter jurisdiction issues lend themselves well to practicing your organization as you always need to address both bases of jurisdiction. Always analyze both bases even if it is clear that one basis does or does not apply. You need to tell the examiner that you considered the other basis and your analysis is that it doesn't apply. First, the federal court has jurisdiction if the claim arises under federal law or is created by state law but depends on a substantial **federal question**, usually a constitutional question. Be clear that this basis of jurisdiction includes the constitution, laws, and treaties of the United States. This basis of jurisdiction is referred to as "federal question jurisdiction." A defense based on a federal question is insufficient to establish federal jurisdiction.

Secondly, the federal court also has jurisdiction based on **diversity jurisdiction**. This requires complete diversity of citizenship and over $75,000 in controversy. Complete diversity means that no single plaintiff may be a citizen of the same state as any single defendant. An individual's citizenship is determined by domicile. A corporation is a citizen of its state of incorporation and a citizen of a state where its principal place of business is located. The plaintiff's view governs the amount in controversy and only the alleged amount governs. A claimant may aggregate claims against a single defendant, but not against multiple defendants. Multiple claimants cannot aggregate claims to meet the $75,000 minimum.

Order of Analysis Federal Subject-Matter Jurisdiction

Overall **Rule:** Federal courts are courts of limited jurisdiction.

General **Rule:** Federal courts may only hear cases that involve a federal question or are based on diversity jurisdiction.

> **Rule 1:** Federal courts have jurisdiction over claims arising under the constitution, laws, and treaties of the United States.
>
> > **Apply** federal question jurisdiction to facts
> >
> > **Conclude** Issue 1: Federal question jurisdiction?
>
> **Rule 2:** Federal courts have jurisdiction over matters involving diverse citizens, where the amount in controversy is more than $75,000.
>
> > **Conclude:** Federal subject-matter jurisdiction exist?
> >
> > **Rule A:** Complete diversity is required, meaning no plaintiff and defendant can be citizens of the same state.
> >
> > (Note: May need further rule if a corporation is one of the parties.)
> >
> > > **Apply** complete diversity requirements to facts.
> > >
> > > **Conclude** Sub-issue A: Complete diversity exists?
> >
> > **Rule B:** A claimant may aggregate claims against a single defendant, but not against multiple defendants. Multiple claimants cannot aggregate claims to meet the $75,000 minimum.
> >
> > > **Apply** amount in controversy requirement to facts.
> > >
> > > **Conclude** Sub-issue B: Amount in controversy exists?
> > >
> > > **Conclude:** Diversity of jurisdiction?

Overall **conclusion:** Federal subject-matter jurisdiction exist?

When the plaintiff brings more than one claim, analyze subject-matter jurisdiction for each claim as there must be a jurisdictional basis for each claim. If you find that no subject-matter jurisdiction exists for one claim, then consider **supplemental jurisdiction**. A federal court has discretion to consider a pure state law claim if there is a common nucleus of operative facts between the state law claim and the federal claim. If the federal claim is based on diversity jurisdiction, then only claims involving diverse parties may be added provided they arise from a common nucleus of operative facts, although they do not need to have their own $75,000 in controversy. If one claim is based on a federal question, then a state law claim with non-diverse parties may be brought under supplemental jurisdiction, again provided they arise from a common nucleus of operative facts.

Defendants in state court may **remove** an action to the federal court that geographically embraces the state court if the federal court would have jurisdiction, all defendants consent, and a notice of removal is filed within 30 days of the service of the state court complaint. Notice must be served on all plaintiffs and on the state court. A defendant cannot remove the claim to federal court if the only federal component is a federal law-based defense.

If federal jurisdiction does not exist, the plaintiff can seek a **remand** back to the state court within 30 days of the filing of the notice of removal.

Personal jurisdiction exists if the court has *in personam* jurisdiction over the parties, *in rem* jurisdiction over property that is the subject of the claim, or *quasi in rem* jurisdiction over property that is attached to satisfy judgment in the action. The plaintiff must establish personal jurisdiction over each defendant. Be on the look-out for MBE questions where different defendants may have different bases of personal jurisdiction. Objections to personal jurisdiction must be brought in the first responsive pleading or they will be waived.

In personam jurisdiction exists if a person is located within the state by either domicile or service. Domicile exists if the person resides within the state and has expressed the intent to remain there indefinitely. If a defendant is served with process while in the forum state, *in personam* jurisdiction exists even if his presence is temporary and even if his presence is unrelated to the lawsuit. If the defendant's presence in the forum state is solely due to force, fraud, or participation in another judicial proceeding, service may not establish jurisdiction.

In personam jurisdiction also exists if the person consents to jurisdiction. Consent can be express, implied, or waived:

- Express consent.
- Implied consent: State has a substantial interest in regulating nonresidents in a particular in-state activity—for example, traffic laws. Driving within a state results in implied consent to personal jurisdiction in that state for traffic violations.
- Waived: Defendant fails to raise the defense of lack of personal jurisdiction in an answer or first responsive pleading. Defendant does not waive jurisdiction if he appears in court to contest jurisdiction.

In personam jurisdiction also exists over nonresidents through the operation of the state's long-arm jurisdiction even if they did not consent. Personal jurisdiction exists if the law of the forum grants personal jurisdiction and the law of the forum is constitutional. A long-arm statute provides specific jurisdiction over the defendant who does specific activities enumerated in the statute. Typical provisions include transacting business within the state, entering contracts within the state, and committing a tortious act within the state.

The assertion of personal jurisdiction must also meet constitutional requirements. The issue is whether the defendant engaged in minimum contacts such that it would not offend traditional notions of fair play and substantial justice. The issue then becomes whether the defendant purposely availed itself of the benefits of the forum state.

Personal jurisdiction through *in rem* jurisdiction is based on the parties' interest in a particular piece of property located within the state. Although rarely used, MBE questions may ask about *quasi in rem* jurisdiction. *Quasi in rem* jurisdiction exists in actions involving attachment of real or personal property as a part of the relief requested. A minimum contacts analysis is also required for *quasi in rem* jurisdiction.

Service of process is proper if the method of process follows the forum's rules and the method is constitutional. Service is not required for the action to be considered commenced, but must occur within 120 days of the filing of the complaint. Proper methods of service include:

- Abode service
- Waiver
- Agent service
- State methods
- Personal service

A summons is served with a copy of the complaint. If the service of process or the process itself is insufficient, the defendant must raise that defense in its first responsive pleading or those defenses will be waived.

Venue operates as a limit on a plaintiff's choice of where to file. Even if a court has subject-matter and personal jurisdiction, the plaintiff must also bring its claim in the proper venue.

Venue is proper:

* where any defendant resides, if all defendants reside in that state;
* in the federal district where a substantial part of the claim arose or where the property is located; or
* where the defendant can be found provided the court has personal jurisdiction, if there is no other district in which the action may otherwise be brought.

If the venue is improper, that is, if the claim does not meet any of these bases, then the remedy is to file a motion to dismiss based on **improper venue** in the first responsive pleading. If not raised then, that defense will be waived.

If a defendant would prefer a different venue, even though the current venue is proper, then the remedy is to file a **motion for transfer**. A motion to transfer is based on the doctrine of *forum non conveniens*. For the convenience of the parties and witnesses and in the interest of justice, a district court may transfer a civil action to any other district court where the action might have been brought. Note that substantial deference is given to the plaintiff's choice of forum.

The general requirements for a complaint, the initial **pleading**, are that it must contain sufficient facts to place the adversary on notice of plausible claims. A claim for relief must include a short and plain statement of the jurisdiction, a statement of a claim that would entitle the claimant to relief, and a demand of relief. Legal conclusions in a complaint are disregarded as are "formulaic recitation of elements."[1] A party may set out alternative claims and make inconsistent claims or defenses.

Once served with a complaint, the defendant must file a **responsive motion** or an **answer**. Either a motion or an answer, whichever is filed first, is considered the first responsive pleading. The defendant has 21 days from the date of service of the complaint to file its first responsive pleading. The 21 days includes weekends and holidays. If the twenty-first day falls on a weekend or holiday, the first responsive pleading or answer must be filed on the next business day.

Rule 12(b) defenses must be filed within the first responsive pleading. If not, these defenses are waived. Rule 12(b) defenses include:

* Motion to dismiss for lack of personal jurisdiction
* Motion to dismiss for insufficient service of process or insufficient process
* Motion to dismiss for improper venue
* Motion to dismiss for failure to state a claim
* Motion to dismiss for failure to join an indispensable party

Rule 12(b) also includes the defense of lack of subject-matter jurisdiction. This defense is never waived. It can be raised at any time and can be raised by the court itself.

If the defendant does not file a motion to dismiss or if its motion to dismiss is denied, it must file an **answer** that must fairly and precisely admit or deny every allegation in the complaint. In addition, the answer must include the previous

1. *Ashcroft v. Iqbal*, 129 S. Ct. 1937, 1949 (2008).

12(b) defenses and all **affirmative defenses** or they are waived. The affirmative defenses under Rule 8(c)(1) include:

- accord and satisfaction,
- arbitration and award,
- assumption of risk,
- contributory negligence,
- discharge in bankruptcy,
- duress,
- estoppel,
- failure of consideration,
- fraud,
- illegality,
- injury by fellow servant,
- laches,
- licenses,
- payment,
- release,
- *res judicata*,
- Statute of Frauds,
- statute of limitations, and
- waiver.

The plaintiff may **amend** its complaint once as of right within 21 days of service upon the defendant. After that, the plaintiff must file a leave to amend, which is granted freely by the court to do justice. The issues that arise with amending a complaint involve the relation back of amendments to conform to the statute of limitations. If the amendment is a new claim, then it relates back

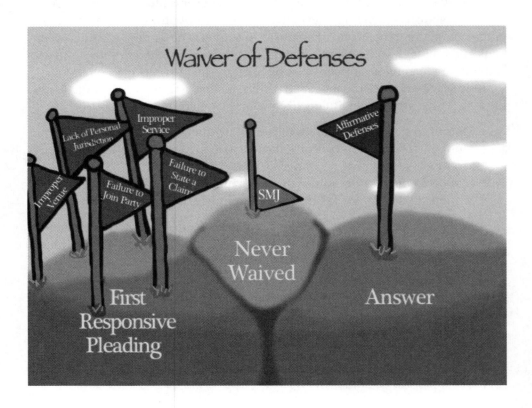

to the date of a timely-filed complaint if the new claim derives from the same transaction or occurrence as the earlier timely-filed complaint. If the amendment is a new party, relation back applies only if the amendment derives from the same transaction or occurrence, and the brand new party acquired knowledge within 120 days of the earlier timely-filed complaint that but for a mistake in name it would have been sued.

Joinder of parties and **joinder of claims** are frequently tested topics. The plaintiff may join parties to the same lawsuit if the claims involving those parties derive from the same transaction or occurrence or at least the same series of common transactions or occurrences. The plaintiff must join indispensable parties where there would be prejudice to any parties' right to a full and fair adjudication, including leaving an existing party subject to a substantial risk of incurring multiple inconsistent obligations.

The plaintiff may join as many claims as they have against a defendant regardless of whether there is any connection between those claims.

Third parties outside of the lawsuit may join a suit and bring claims. These actions are remembered by the three "I's":

- **Impleader**—Defendant may bring in a third party if that party may be liable to Defendant for all or part of Defendant's liability to Plaintiff.
- **Interpleader**—The holder of a common fund may file a lawsuit as a plaintiff and join as defendants all rival claimants to its common fund.
- **Intervention**—A non-party moves to enter into a lawsuit.
  - As of right: Non-party's interest will be adversely affected by the lawsuit, and that right is not protected by the parties.
  - Permissive: Court has discretion to permit if there is a commonality of issues between those in the ongoing lawsuit and those affecting the intervener.

A defendant may bring a **counterclaim** against the plaintiff. If it arises from the same transaction or occurrence, then it must be brought in that action and is called a mandatory or compulsory counterclaim. Failure to bring a mandatory counterclaim results in waiver of that claim. A defendant has a permissive counterclaim when it seeks to join claims that do not arise from the same transaction or occurrence. Failure to file a permissive counterclaim does not result in waiver. **Cross-claims** may be brought by any party against any co-party when the claim arises out of the same transaction or occurrence as the original claim or counterclaim. The court has subject-matter jurisdiction under supplemental jurisdiction for compulsory counterclaims and cross-claims if they arise out of the same transaction or occurrence in the absence of an independent basis for federal jurisdiction. If a claim is only a permissive counterclaim, then no supplemental jurisdiction exists because it did not arise out of the same transaction or occurrence and independent grounds for federal jurisdiction must exist.

Class actions are actions in which a named plaintiff represents a class of commonly-situated absent plaintiffs. The certification requirements for class actions can be remembered by the acrostic CANT:

- **Commonality**—there must be common issues of fact or law including common claims and common injuries.
- **Adequacy**—the named plaintiff and class counsel lawyers must fairly and adequately represent the class.

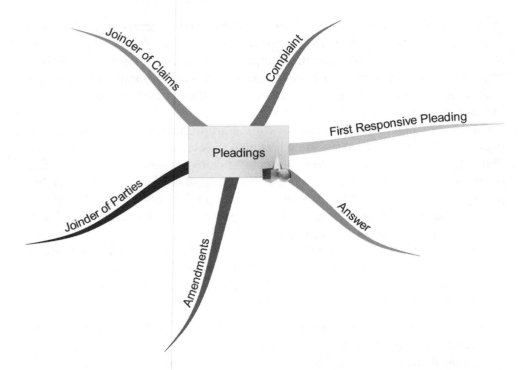

- **N**umbers—the class must be so numerous that joinder of them all would be impracticable (at least 40).
- **T**ypicality—the claims of the named plaintiff are typical of the class.

Additional requirements are predominance and superiority. Common questions must predominate over individual questions with class representation superior to other methods of adjudicating the controversy. Thus, a court is not likely to grant class certification where multiple state laws are involved and individual claims require separate investigation. Constitutional requirements include notice to the class and a chance to opt out if the claim involves money.

Discovery includes both mandatory disclosures and the more traditional means of discovery. Mandatory disclosures are required within two weeks of the initial discovery conference. A party has a duty to supplement the mandatory disclosures or be subject to the exclusion of that evidence at trial. The mandatory disclosures are:

- All supporting witnesses
- All supporting documents
- A damages computation
- Relevant insurance coverage

The traditional means of discovery are:

- Depositions: Direct questioning of a party or witness under oath.
- Interrogatories: Written questions that must be answered by another party in writing under oath within 30 days. Only served on parties, not witnesses.
- Request for admissions: Any request that is admitted is deemed established for all purposes in the litigation.

- Production of documents: A request to a party to produce documents or property for inspection and copying.
- Request for physical or mental examination: Only when a person's condition is in controversy. Advance court approval with a showing of "good cause" is required.

The scope of discovery is relevant information that is not privileged and it need not be admissible at trial. Parties can object to the requests for discovery or request a protective order.

One area of privilege that arises in discovery is the **work-product doctrine**, which covers any material that has been prepared for litigation and is not in the ordinary course of business. This includes the attorney's mental impressions, which are never discoverable, and all other forms of work product that are discoverable with a showing of substantial need and undue hardship. Sanctions for refusing to produce discovery can range from not being able to use the withheld information at trial to the striking of a claim or the dismissal of the case.

A party has a constitutional right to a **jury trial** if its claim primarily seeks monetary damages. The party must file a written demand within 14 days of service of the complaint. Each party is entitled to strike potential jurors for cause. Otherwise, each party receives three peremptory challenges that may be used to strike jurors without cause.

Motions are a major part of litigation and the practice of law. Focus on four critical motions:

- Summary judgment:
  - Filed within 30 days after close of discovery.
  - May be granted if there are no genuine issues of material fact and the movant is entitled to judgment as a matter of law.
  - Movant must produce evidence to support each element of the cause of action.
  - All inferences are drawn in favor of the non-movant.
- Judgment as matter of law: Formerly called a directed verdict, the motion is made at the close of the opponent's case. The grounds are that there is a legally insufficient evidentiary basis from which a reasonable jury could find for the non-moving party.
- Default judgment: Entered against a defendant who failed to respond to the complaint in a timely manner.
- Post-trial motions:
  - Renewed motion for judgment as a matter of law: Formerly called a judgment notwithstanding the verdict, the motion is made within 28 days of judgment. The basis of the motion is identical to that made at the close of the opponent's case.
  - Motion for new trial: Also made within 28 days, this motion will be granted in the court's discretion if either the errors at trial affected the parties' substantive trial rights or the verdict was against the manifest weight of the evidence.

Preclusion means that parties are barred from relitigating claims or issues that they have already fully and fairly litigated to a final judgment on the merits. These doctrines are intended to promote judicial economy and the finality of judgments. In essence, these doctrines mean that once a case has reached a final judgment, that case and its related claims and issues have been decided permanently and are not eligible for relitigation. ***Res judicata*** or claim preclusion means that a claim cannot be relitigated if the claim arises between the same parties or those in privity with them; it arises out of the same transaction or occurrence; and that the court determined the claim on the merits and had proper subject-matter and personal jurisdiction. *Res judicata* is an affirmative defense that is waived if not asserted in an answer.

Collateral estoppel or issue preclusion refers to an issue that cannot be relitigated. Collateral estoppel may not be used against someone who was not a party to the previous action. Issue preclusion may be used offensively by one who was not a party to the first action against one who was a party in the earlier suit. Courts are reluctant to permit offensive use of issue preclusion and will look to see if the plaintiff in the second suit could have joined the first action; whether there are procedural opportunities available to the defendant in the second suit that were unavailable in the earlier action; and whether the defendant had incentive to litigate the issue in the first action.

A judgment is **appealable** when it is a final order entered by a lower court. The party seeking to appeal must file its notice of appeal within 30 days from the entry of judgment. A **final judgment** is one that disposes of all issues as to all parties. If it is a partial final order that resolves only some of the claims, but not all of the claims, then an interlocutory appeal can be requested. Both the trial court and the appellate court must find that there is doubt as to a controlling legal issue and that appellate review would advance the litigation.

Within one year of a judgment, a party can file a **motion for relief from a judgment**. The requirements can be remembered by the acrostic MEND:

Post-Trial
Motion
Timing

- **M**erit
- **E**quity
- **N**ew facts
- **D**ue diligence

II. MBE STRATEGIES

Federal Civil Procedure is being added to the MBE portion of the exam effective with the February 2015 bar exam. As such, there are no questions to review for specific strategies at this time. In all likelihood, the 75% that is tested on the essays will be the same 75% tested by the MBE. Similar to essays, one area that is likely to be tested is the timing of motions and of pleadings. For example, did the defendant file its first responsive pleading or answer in time or was it late such that the defendant waived its Rule 12(b) defenses? Did the defendant fail to timely file a post-trial motion or a motion for relief of judgment? What are the consequences of failing to timely file? Was amending the complaint sufficient to trigger the doctrine of relation back?

Carefully lay out a timeline of what happened when. This is critical for the first responsive pleading, the answer, post-trial motions, and the notice of appeal, among others. Memorize the time requirements for each. Include those requirements in your mind maps. You could even make a chart of all the time requirements to help you memorize them.

Your mind maps will be more than adequate to help you through both styles of questions.

III. Essay Practice Question[2]

Ann and Bill, both citizens of State X, were walking by a construction site in State X when an overhead crane dropped a load of plate glass windows on the sidewalk near them. The windows shattered when they hit the pavement, and both Ann and Bill were struck by flying glass. Ann's injuries were severe; she incurred more than $450,000 in medical expenses. Bill suffered only minor injuries and had medical bills of $500.

At the time of the accident, the glass windows were being installed in a new skyscraper by GlassCo, Inc., a State Y corporation with its principal place of business in State Y. The crane operator was a GlassCo employee, and the crane was owned by GlassCo. A subsequent investigation by GlassCo's insurance company concluded that the accident was due to crane operator error and improper crane maintenance.

Ann and Bill have joined as plaintiffs and filed a suit against GlassCo in a state trial court in State X. Ann is seeking more than $1,000,000 in damages, and Bill is seeking $5,000. They have both refused GlassCo's request to enter into settlement negotiations.

You are an associate in the law firm that has been retained by GlassCo. The partner in charge of the case wants to remove the lawsuit from state to federal court. She has asked:

1. What must GlassCo do to remove the case from state to federal court? Explain.
2. If the case is removed to federal court, do the Federal Rules of Civil Procedure permit the separate claims of Ann and Bill to remain joined in a single lawsuit? Explain.
3. If Ann's and Bill's claims remain joined, will the federal court have jurisdiction over the case? Explain.

---

2. The Multistate Bar Examination ("MBE®") questions, the Multistate Essay Examination ("MEE®") questions, and excerpts from the Multistate Performance Tests ("MPT®") have been reprinted by permission from the NCBE®. Copyright© by the National Conference of Bar Examiners. All rights reserved.

IV. SCORE SHEET

Stated	Implied	
		1. What must GlassCo do to remove the case from state to federal court?
_____	_____	**Conclusion/Issue:** The process of removal consists of several steps.
_____	_____	**Rule:** Under federal statute,
_____	_____	The first step is for the defendant to file a notice of removal. It must be filed in the federal district court for the district and division within which the state action is pending.
_____	_____	In terms of timeframe, the notice must be filed within 30 days of the defendant's having received a copy of the initial pleading by service or otherwise, or within 30 days after the service or summons—whichever period is shorter.
_____	_____	Notice must be signed. It must also include a statement of the basis for federal jurisdiction. In addition, must also file a copy of the materials from the state court proceeding.
_____	_____	Then, defendant must serve the adverse party with notice of the filing.
_____	_____	Must also file a copy of the notice of removal with the state court.
_____	_____	Removal is then "automatic" and the state court cannot take any further action.
_____	_____	Note: If the defendant removes the action to federal court, and the plaintiff wishes to contest the removal, the plaintiff must file a motion to remand.
		2. If the case is removed to federal court, do the Federal Rules of Civil Procedure permit the separate claims of Ann and Bill to remain joined in a single lawsuit?
_____	_____	**Conclusion/Issue:** The claims may be joined in a single action because those claims arose out of the "same transaction [or] occurrence" and involve "common questions" of law and fact.
_____	_____	**Rule:** Under Federal Rules of Civil Procedure,
_____	_____	Claims may be joined in a single suit if they arise out of the same transaction, occurrence, or series of transactions or occurrences, and any question of law or fact common to all plaintiffs will arise in the action.
_____	_____	**Application:** Here,
_____	_____	Ann and Bill are each bringing claims that stem from the same accident involving the falling glass, which is one single occurrence.
_____	_____	Their claims will raise common questions of fact, such as whether the glass accident was caused by the negligence of GlassCo employees.
_____	_____	Their claims may also raise common questions of law, like the legal standard for measuring damages.
_____	_____	It is irrelevant that Ann and Bill are asserting separate claims and separate rights to relief—plaintiffs can still join when they assert their rights to relief severally.
_____	_____	**Conclusion:** Therefore,
_____	_____	The claims may be joined in one lawsuit, as both requirements are met.

continued on next page

Stated	Implied	
		3. If Ann's and Bill's claims remain joined, will the federal court have jurisdiction over the case?
_____	_____	**Conclusion/Issue:** The federal court will have subject-matter jurisdiction because Ann's claim is within original diversity jurisdiction and Bill's claim, while it does not meet the amount in controversy requirement, falls within the federal court's supplemental jurisdiction.
_____	_____	**Rule for original diversity jurisdiction:** Under the federal diversity statute, removal is proper only when the civil action that is removed is within the original jurisdiction of the federal court, meaning that citizenship must be completely diverse and the amount in controversy must exceed $75,000.
_____	_____	**Application:** Here,
_____	_____	Ann and GlassCo are citizens of different states. In addition, Ann's claim for $1,000,000 exceeds the amount in controversy requirement.
_____	_____	Even though Bill and GlassCo are diverse, Bill is seeking damages of only $5,000, which is substantially less than amount in controversy requirement. So Bill's claim does not fall within the original diversity jurisdiction of the court.
_____	_____	**Conclusion/Transition:** Therefore, only Anne's claim would fall under original diversity jurisdiction. However, the federal court will still have jurisdiction over Bill's claim.
_____	_____	**Rule for supplemental jurisdiction:** Under federal supplemental jurisdiction statute,
_____	_____	If federal court has original jurisdiction, the court also has supplemental jurisdiction over all other claims so related to the main claim that they form part of the same case or controversy.
_____	_____	**Application:** Here,
_____	_____	The claims of both Bill and Ann arose out of the same accident—which is a common nucleus of operative fact. Also, the claims are similar in the facts and law, so it is sensible to expect them to be tried in a single proceeding.
_____	_____	**Conclusion:** Therefore,
_____	_____	Bill's claim is sufficiently related to Ann's claim to be part of the same case or controversy and the court has supplemental jurisdiction over his claim.

CHAPTER 14

Mapping MBE Topics—Real Property

I. MIND MAP

While some mind maps have a predictable format because they can be organized along a chronological series of events, real property is not one of them. Instead, real property considers various interests in land including different ways to achieve ownership, different types of ownership interests, different types of future interests, and different types of temporary interests. Your mind map then focuses on these areas.

- Estates and future interests
- Adverse possession
- Conveyances
- Land use
- Landlord–tenant

Estates and Future Interests. Many students shy away from studying **estates and future interests** as the language seems awkward and a bit archaic. Don't give up before you start. Understand present possessory estates first. Then, memorize the future interests that can follow each possessory estate. Only certain future interests follow certain present possessory estates. After you have memorized these pairings, then work towards a deeper understanding.

Real Property Interests Analysis Steps

1. Nature and characteristics of the interests of real property.
2. How a particular interest can be created.
3. How to classify the interest.
4. The rights of possession and the rights of the user of the interest.
5. The legal and equitable remedies stemming from that interest.

Both the present possessory estate and the future estate attached to it can be determined by critical reading. Make a chart of the different types of present possessory estates and which future interests may be connected to each estate. Add additional detail to this chart from practice MBE and essay questions for your later memorization.

		PRESENT POSSESSORY ESTATES AND POSSIBLE FUTURE INTERESTS			
Words of Purchase	Words of Limitation	Present Possessory Estate	Possible Future Interests	Characteristics of Future Interest	RAP apply?
To A	None	Fee Simple Absolute	None	N/A	N/A
To A	and her heirs	Fee Simple Absolute	None	N/A	N/A
To A	and the heirs of his body	Fee Tail	Same as Life Estate	(Fill in)	(Fill in)
To A	for so long as; during; while; until	Fee Simple Determinable	Possibility of Reverter	Created in grantor	No
To A	provided; however; however if; but if; on condition that; or in the event that	Fee Simple Subject to a Condition Subsequent	Right of Entry or Power of Termination	Does not automatically terminate the estate; "O may reenter and terminate/retake A's estate"	(Fill in)
To A	Same as condition subsequent	Fee Simple subject to Executory Interest	Shifting/Springing executory interest (Power of Termination)	Automatically terminates the estate	Yes
To A	for life	Life Estate	Reversion/Remainder (Contingent or Vested)	(Fill in)	Reversion: No Remainder: Yes
To A	for life of B	Life Estate	Reversion/Remainder (Contingent or Vested)	(Fill in)	Reversion: No Remainder: Yes

Life estates have some special considerations because they can be made defeasible if the life estate holder breaches certain duties. Because the property is always going to pass to someone else upon the life estate holder's death, the life estate holder must maintain the property:

- Duty to not adversely affect the future interest (waste):
  - Duty to repair and maintain
  - Duty to pay mortgage interest
  - Duty to pay all ordinary taxes
  - Duty to pay the full cost of special assessments if the life of the public improvement is less than the duration of the life tenant's estate. Equitable apportionment is applied to improvements likely to last longer.

The **Rule Against Perpetuities (RAP)** has befuddled many a law student and many a bar applicant. Yet if you follow this analysis, you can work your way through any possible question:

- Identify whether or not the interest is subject to RAP:
  - Interests *not* subject to RAP:
    - Present possessory estates
    - Charitable trusts

- Resulting trusts
- Fully vested interests at creation, such as reversionary interests and completely vested remainders
  - Interests subject to RAP:
    - Options to purchase land
    - Powers of appointment
    - Rights of first refusal
    - Interests not fully vested at creation, such as:
      - Remainders subject to open
      - Contingent remainders
      - Executory interests
- Identify the life or lives in being, express or implied.
- Determine whether the interest will for certain either vest **or** fail to vest within 21 years of the life or lives in being.

Concurrent estates exist when two or more persons share an interest. Each is called a co-tenant. There are different types of joint estates:

- **Tenancy in Common:** Each co-tenant owns an undivided interest in the whole with no right of survivorship. Presumed form of co-ownership.
  - Possession: Unity of possession—each joint tenant has the right to possess the whole.
  - Transfer: Co-tenant may transfer his interest *inter vivos.*
  - Devisibility: Co-tenant may devise his interest and the interest can descend by intestacy.
- **Joint Tenancy:** Each co-tenant owns an undivided interest in the whole and has a right of survivorship.
  - Four unities required:
    - Unity of time—joint tenants must take at the same time.
    - Unity of title—joint tenants must take by the same instrument.
    - Unity of interest—joint tenants must take equal shares of the same type.
    - Unity of possession—each joint tenant has the right to possess the whole.
  - **Right of survivorship:** At the death of one joint tenant, the interest of the surviving joint tenant absorbs the interest of the deceased joint tenant. Only the last surviving joint tenant has an interest that is devisable.
  - Severed: Joint tenancy severed if one joint tenant conveys his interest voluntarily or involuntarily (creditor forces sale). Tenancy in common then results.
- **Tenancy by the Entirety:** Reserved for married couples. Presumed in some states if conveyance to a married couple. Gives each spouse an undivided interest in the whole and a right of survivorship.

A co-tenant has the right to seek partition of the property either voluntarily or involuntarily. A co-tenant who pays a mortgage or tax may seek contribution from the other co-tenant. A co-tenant does not have a right to seek a contribution or setoff for improvements made to the premises unless the improvements generate increased rents or profits. Then, those costs are recoverable only in a partition suit.

Keep in mind that **restraints on alienation** are usually unenforceable.

Adverse Possession. A favorite topic of bar examiners is **adverse possession**, particularly boundary disputes. Check for each requirement using the acrostic, OCEAN:

- **O**pen and notorious
- **C**ontinuous possession for the statutory period
- **E**xclusive
- **A**ctual
- **N**on-permissive (hostile)

An adverse possessor must possess the premises for the requisite time period. The specific timing requirements are set out by state statute. If the adverse possessor has not been in possession for the full statutory possession, he may still meet the time period by tacking his period of possession onto that period of possession of another possessor if the possessors are in privity of estate. Privity of estate exists when there has been a voluntary transfer of possession from the first adverse possessor to the second adverse possessor, such as by deed. The statutory period may also be tolled if the owner has a disability at the time the adverse possessor enters.

Conveyances. The topic of **conveyances** covers real estate contracts, including the statute of frauds, marketable title, duty to disclose defects, implied warranty of quality, and remedies for breach of a contract to sell real property; conveyance by deed; recording statutes; and mortgages.

Real property contracts fall within the **Statute of Frauds** and require a writing signed by the party to be charged. The writing must include:

- Description of the property
- Description of the parties
- Price
- Any conditions of price or payment agreed upon

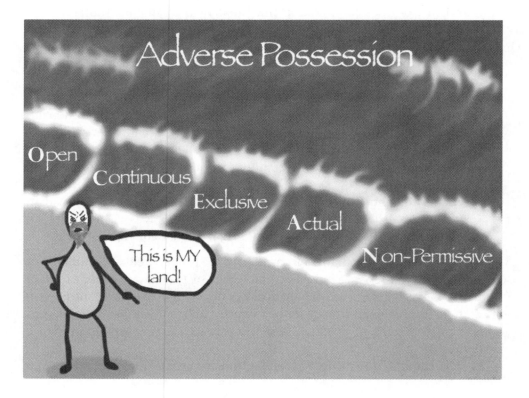

All contracts for the sale of real property include an implied promise to convey a **marketable title** to the purchaser at the time for performance (the closing). A marketable title is a title that is reasonably free from doubt in both fact and law. Title is not reasonably free from doubt if it contains any of the following defects:

* Defects in the chain of title, such as adverse possession, defective execution of a deed, or significant variation of the description of the land.
* Encumbrances such as mortgages, liens, easements, leases, and covenants.
    * Be careful: Seller may satisfy a mortgage or lien at closing with the proceeds.
* Encroachment of your improvements onto another's land, or encroachments of another onto your land.
* Zoning and other land use restrictions do not render title unmarketable unless a zoning violation exists.

Remedies for failure to convey a marketable title include rescission, money damages, or specific performance.

The seller has a **duty to disclose** all material latent defects known to the seller that are not readily observable or known to the buyer. Most jurisdictions recognize an implied warranty of quality. This warranty can be called of workmanlike quality, of habitability, of fitness, or of suitability. This runs from a seller/builder to subsequent purchasers.

A seller's **remedies** for a buyer's breach to purchase property include expectation damages, foreseeable consequential damages, reasonable reliance damages, retaining the down payment, or liquidated damages. If willful, punitive damages may be valid. In equity, the seller may seek rescission of the contract if property has increased in value or specific performance if property has decreased in value.

A buyer's remedies for a seller's breach include expectation damages, reliance damages, restitution of the down payment, and punitive damages. In equity, the buyer may seek rescission or specific performance.

Under the traditional rule, covenants in a real estate contract merge into the **deed** at closing. This typically means that a purchaser must sue under the deed's warranties rather than under the sales contract.

There are three types of deeds. In a **general warranty deed**, the grantor warrants that no title defects exist in the chain of title. In a **special warranty deed**, the grantor warrants that no title defects occurred during his ownership of the property, but does not warrant against title defects that occurred prior to his ownership. In a **quitclaim deed**, the grantor provides no warrants. The grantee takes whatever interest the grantor had.

A general or special warranty deed contains a series of covenants, divided into present and future covenants. Present covenants are broken, if at all, only at the time of conveyance, and a grantee has a limited time to make a claim. Present covenants do not generally run with the land to remote grantees. Future covenants may be broken after the time of conveyance and do run with the land to subsequent purchasers. Remember these points about covenants:

* Present covenants:
    * Covenant of seisin—grantor owns and possesses the estate granted. Existence of an encumbrance does not breach the covenant.

- Covenant of right to convey—grantor has the right to convey the property. This differs from the covenant of seisin as a trustee may be seised of the fee but barred from conveying the property by the trust document.
- Covenant against encumbrances—grantor promises that there are no encumbrances. No third person has a right that diminishes the value or limits the use of the land granted, including:
  - mortgage and judgment liens,
  - taxes,
  - leases,
  - water rights,
  - easements, and
  - restrictions on use.
- Future covenants:
  - Covenant of quiet enjoyment—grantor covenants that the grantee will not be disturbed by a superior claim.
  - Covenant of warranty—grantor covenants that he will assist in defending title against valid claims and will compensate the grantee for losses sustained by the assertion of superior title.
  - Covenant of further assurances—grantor promises to take whatever steps may be required to perfect title defects.

Conveyance of real property by deed requires donative intent, delivery, and acceptance. Grantor must intend to transfer the interest immediately. Will formalities must be observed if the deed is to take effect only upon the grantor's death. Delivery is usually accomplished by the physical act of handing the deed over to someone else. Mere words including a declaration of intent and relinquishment of control can accomplish delivery. A presumption of delivery arises if:

- the deed is later found in the grantee's possession;
- the deed is properly executed and recorded; or
- the deed contains an attestation clause that attests to delivery.

Handing the deed to an agent does not constitute delivery until the agent delivers the deed to the grantee or grantee's agent. That triggers the doctrine of relation back as long as the grantor relinquishes all control over the deed. When delivery is accomplished through the agent, delivery relates back to the date the grantor handed the deed to the agent.

When there are conflicting descriptions of the property contained in the deed, rules of construction determine which description prevails. The order of superiority relies first on natural deed descriptions:

- Natural monuments
- Artificial monuments
- Courses and angles
- Distances
- Name and quantity

Recording a deed is not required to validate the transfer of title. Recording becomes important when two or more parties claim that the owner has conveyed or mortgaged the property to them and their relative priority is at issue.

Title based on adverse possession is not recordable until title has been quieted. Because adverse possession is a nondocumented title, it is not recordable and is not made invalid by a *bona fide purchaser*. Other nondocumented interests include prescriptive easements, implied easements, and boundary adjustments by acquiescence or by oral agreement.

There are three types of recording statutes: race, notice, and race-notice. Under the **race statute**, the person who records first prevails. Under a **notice statute**, an unrecorded conveyance is invalid against a subsequent *bona fide* purchaser for value and without notice. To prevail under a notice statute, a claimant must prove:

- The claimant took subsequent in time to another person claiming ownership;
- The claimant was a *bona fide* purchaser for value; and
- The claimant took the property without actual, constructive, or inquiry notice.

Constructive notice exists if the other party's deed is recorded in the proper chain of title in the record books. Inquiry notice exists if the appearance of the property is such that the claimant should have asked more questions about the property's title. A quitclaim deed gives rise to inquiry notice.

Under a **race-notice statute**, an unrecorded conveyance is invalid against a subsequent *bona fide* purchaser for value who takes without notice and records first. To prevail under a race-notice statute, the claimant must prove:

- The claimant took subsequent in time to another person claiming ownership;
- The claimant was a *bona fide* purchaser for value;
- The claimant took the property without actual, constructive, or inquiry notice; and
- The claimant recorded first.

The **shelter rule** provides protection for a subsequent purchaser who does not satisfy the applicable recording statute. Under the shelter rule, a person who is a successor in interest to a person protected by the recording statute is also protected.

Two types of questions involve **mortgage** issues. The first concerns the sale of property encumbered by a mortgage. The second concerns multiple mortgages on the same property. Typically, unless the mortgagor is paying off the mortgage with the proceeds of a sale, a mortgagor must receive consent from a mortgagee before transferring property encumbered by a mortgage because of "due on sale" clauses. A key distinction to understand is the difference between assuming an existing mortgage on property and taking property "subject to" an existing mortgage.

Assuming an existing mortgage means the mortgage is transferred from the mortgagor/grantor to the grantee. The grantee assumes the mortgage via an agreement and must pay off the grantor's debt to the mortgagee. Absent a later modification agreement between the grantee and mortgagee that removes the mortgagor/grantor from the dispute, the mortgagor/grantor remains on the hook for a default. Thus, when a default occurs, the mortgagee may:

- Foreclose on the real property;
- Sue grantee on the debt as the grantee is primarily liable; or

Notice Recording Statute

**Race-Notice Recording
Statute**

- Sue mortgagor/grantor on the debt as secondarily liable.
  - Mortgagor/grantor could then seek reimbursement from the grantee personally.

Taking property "subject to" an existing mortgage also begins with a pre-existing mortgage on the property that is transferred from the mortgagor/

grantor to the grantee. The difference is that the grantee does not sign an assumption agreement and so does not assume the existing mortgage, but takes the property "subject to the mortgage." In this case, the mortgagor/grantor remains on the hook to the mortgagee, but the grantee is not on the hook to the mortgagee. Thus, when a default occurs, the mortgagee may:

- Foreclose on the real property now owned by the grantee; or
- Sue the mortgagor/grantor on the debt.
  - Could then foreclose on the property, but may not successfully pursue a personal action against the grantee.

The second topic that occurs regularly in relation to mortgages is multiple mortgages on the same property. Priority is determined by chronological order of recording. Every mortgagee may redeem "up" by paying off and acquiring any mortgages of higher priority. For example, mortgagee 2 could "redeem" from mortgagee 1, and mortgagor then owes both mortgages to mortgagee 2. In addition, a mortgagee can foreclose "down," thereby wiping out mortgages and other interests of lower priority. A foreclosure sale wipes out all later mortgages—those coming later in time than the mortgage being foreclosed—but does not wipe out prior mortgages.

Land Use. An **easement** is an interest to use the land of another. Easements may be either affirmative or negative and may be either appurtenant or in gross. Most easements are affirmative, which gives the holder the right to do something on the land of another. A negative easement gives the holder the right to prevent a landowner from doing something on the land. The common law recognizes negative easements regarding light, air, water, and lateral and subjacent support. A writing is always required for a negative easement. An easement appurtenant requires a dominant and servient tenement. An easement in gross is personal in nature, resulting in a servient but not a dominant estate.

Creation of an easement may be created through a writing, by implication, by prescription, or by estoppel. The Statute of Frauds applies to a writing. An affirmative easement may be created by implication either by prior use or by necessity. An affirmative easement may also be created by prescription, which is similar to adverse possession, requiring use of the property that is open and notorious, continuous, exclusive, actual, and non-permissive (hostile). These are the same requirements as adverse possession. Creation of an easement by estoppel requires proof of an act or representation by the owner of the burdened estate in respect to the easement, justifiable reliance on that act or representation by the owner, and damages suffered by the owner of the benefited estate.

Easements can be transferred. An easement may be terminated by any of the following methods:

- End of a time period, if easement created for a specific term;
- When the holder of the dominant estate releases his interest to the holder of the servient estate;
- When the dominant and servient estates come into common ownership;
- Abandonment;
- Estoppel;
- By prescription; or
- When a governmental body acquires the servient estate through an exercise of the eminent domain power.

Be sure to understand the difference between an easement and a license. A **license** is a privilege, usually to do something on someone else's property. A writing and consideration are not required. Licenses are not transferable unless the licensor intends it to be. Licenses expire upon the death of the licensor or the conveyance of the servient estate. Licenses are revocable at the will of the licensor unless the license is coupled with an interest in personal property that is on the land of another and has a privilege that is incidental to the personal property. Another exception to revocability is an executed license based on estoppel and involving a substantial expenditure of funds in reliance on the promisor's promise to allow the promisee to use the land. This becomes an easement by estoppel.

A **covenant** is a promise that attaches to land. The promise can be to do or to refrain from doing something on his land. A covenant that **runs with the land** is a promise that attaches to land. In contrast to easements, most running covenants are negative in nature. Running covenants include promises to pay rent, condominium common charges, and maintenance fees. These are said to touch and concern the land. Covenants run with the land when there is a writing, intent, horizontal and vertical privity, touch and concern, and notice. Horizontal privity refers to the relationship between the original covenantor and covenantee. This requirement is satisfied by a conveyance of land between the convenantee and covenantor, which occurs by the same deed that includes the covenant. Vertical privity refers to the relationship between an original party to a running covenant and the successor in interest to the original party. The successor steps into the shoes of the original party. A covenant touches and concerns the land when the covenant exercises direct influence on the occupation, use, or enjoyment of the premises.

A court may enforce a covenant as an **equitable servitude** if the plaintiff can establish all the elements for a covenant that runs with the land, but the plaintiff seeks equitable relief. An equitable servitude also exists when the plaintiff cannot establish at law all of the elements, but the plaintiff can demonstrate the relaxed requirements for an equitable servitude. For example, as an equity doctrine, if one of the covenant requirements is not met, a court may impose an equitable servitude such as when the covenant is not in writing. The plaintiff may prove the covenant through part performance or estoppel.

Zoning is another restriction on the use of land. The state possesses the power to regulate for the health, safety, and welfare of its citizens. A zoning ordinance may be challenged under the Due Process and Equal Protection Clauses. A zoning ordinance may also be subject to a First Amendment challenge if it regulates billboards or aesthetics.

A **taking** occurs when the government exercises its eminent domain power to take private property. The government may take the entirety of the land in fee simple or take an easement or an interest in the estate of the property. The Takings Clause of the Fifth Amendment, applicable to the states through the Fourteenth Amendment, provides that private property may not be taken for a public use without just compensation. A *per se* taking occurs when an act by the government results in a permanent occupation of private property. A governmental regulation may constitute a taking if it "goes too far." A court engages in a balancing test considering the economic impact on the property owner, the extent to which the regulation interferes with distinct investment-backed expectations, and the character of the governmental action.

A public **nuisance** is an unreasonable interference with a right common to the general public. To recover damages, an individual plaintiff must have suffered harm different from that suffered by other members of the public. A private nuisance is a substantial and unreasonable invasion of another's interest in his use and enjoyment of land.

Landlord-tenant. Under **landlord-tenant** law, a lease gives the tenant exclusive possession of the premises for a period of time. A lease can be created expressly or implied by conduct of the parties. An implied lease includes when a holdover tenant pays rent and the landlord accepts the rent. There are four types of leases:

* Term of years: definite beginning and end. No notice required to terminate.
* Periodic: set beginning and continues from period to period, such as month to month, without a set termination date until notice is given. Notice must be at the end of period. The required notice is measured by the rent payment clause (one full period), but no longer than six months.
* At will: no fixed duration. Terminates if either party dies; the tenant commits waste; the tenant attempts to assign his interest; the landlord transfers his interest; or the landlord transfers the premises to a third party for a term of years. Most states provide for 30 days' notice.
* Tenancy at Sufferance/Holdover Tenancy: tenant remains in possession of the leased premises after the end of the lease term. The landlord can recover possession and receive the reasonable rental value for the holdover period.

Both the landlord and tenant owe specific duties to each other:

* Duties of tenant:
  * Pay rent
  * Not commit waste
  * Repair
  * Other duties as contracted
* Duties of landlord:
  * Deliver legal right to possession of premises
  * Water and heat
  * Duties in lease document
  * Quiet enjoyment
  * Implied warranty of habitability

If the tenant fails to pay rent or commits another material breach of the lease, the landlord may seek to evict the tenant and/or to recover damages for the tenant's breach. Under the modern rule, rent acceleration clauses are permitted in leases. A tenant abandons the premises if he vacates the premises without intending to return and fails to pay rent. The landlord may then retake the premises, ignore the abandonment, and continue to hold the tenant liable for rent or reenter and relet the premises. The landlord has a duty to mitigate its damages. Retaliatory eviction in response to tenant's complaints about the landlord is prohibited in most states.

A tenant may seek money damages for the landlord's breach of the lease. A tenant may vacate the premises and terminate the lease if the tenant has been evicted by the landlord, actually or constructively. Statutes in some jurisdictions provide the tenant with additional remedies including withholding rent or repairing the premises and deducting the cost of repair from subsequent rent payments.

An assignment occurs when the tenant transfers to a third person all of his rights in the leased premises. The assignee then comes into privity of estate with the landlord. Thus, when the rent is not paid, the landlord may sue the assignee.

Assignment

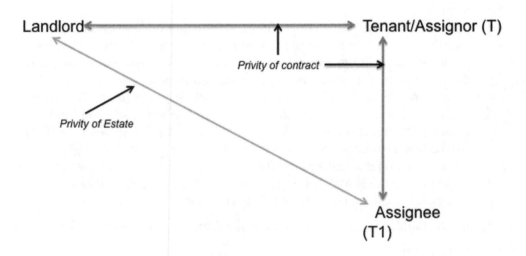

A sublease occurs when the tenant transfers less than all of his rights to a third person. A subtenant does not come into privity of estate with the landlord. Absent an express assumption of the duty to pay rent, the landlord may not sue the subtenant directly.

Sublease

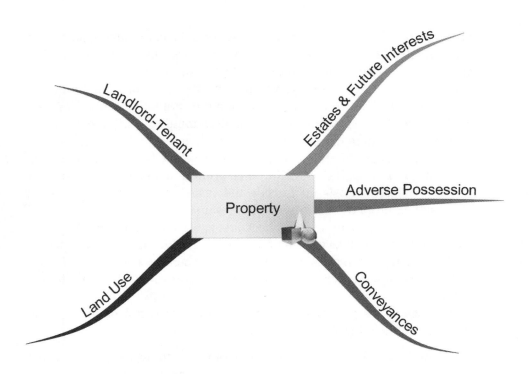

II. MBE STRATEGIES[1]

Property questions tend to have the longest fact patterns. They are complicated and require careful reading. As you work through the fact patterns, keep in mind a couple of things as you sort through the parties and each interest in the property.

Bona fide purchaser status does not matter between the original parties to a transaction and is only relevant if subsequent purchasers are involved. Most of these fact patterns involve recording statutes.

Marketable title is a frequent topic on the MBE. Remember that marketable title is implied in every real estate sales contract; but once the deed takes effect, the terms of the deed control.

Another popular topic is the difference between real covenants and equitable servitudes. Keep track of notice.

Know the differences between recording statutes. Pure race statutes do not come up very often on the MBE. The other two types of recording statutes are distinguishable by one point: whether the subsequent *bona fide* purchaser is protected before he records his own interest. Under a pure notice statute, the *bona fide* purchaser is protected from the moment of conveyance. Under a race-notice statute, he is not protected until he records his interest.

Use these strategies for analyzing property questions:

- Questions asking for the answer choice that is "most likely to succeed": Determine which answer choice most closely addresses the greatest

---

1. Some of these strategies are from Steven L. Emanuel, *Strategies & Tactics for the MBE* 267-276 (5th ed. 2013).

obstacle to success in the case; the answer choice containing a point that is extremely difficult to prove is likely the incorrect answer where another answer would also resolve the case but be easier to prove.

* Questions asking for the "most important point" or "which of the following is the best comment concerning the conflicting claims of A and B": Look for the answer choice that will determine who will prevail in the case, and determine the pivotal fact, if possible.

* Beware of constitutional answers: Answer choices voiding a zoning ordinance or covenant on constitutional grounds are likely to be incorrect unless the restriction is far outside the realm of standard restrictions; eliminate all property law answer choices first.

* In "class gift" problems, always check first to see if the gift is an *inter vivos* conveyance or a conveyance by a will. Why does it matter? There are no RAP problems with a class of grandchildren when the conveyance is by a will because the grantor/testator is deceased and cannot have additional children.

* In Rule Against Perpetuities problems, see if you can think of *any* scenario that won't satisfy the Rule.

Give future interests a chance before you punt the topic. Keep track of the language including the words of conveyance and any words of limitation. Identify the present possessory interest and remember which future interests can follow from that interest.

III. ESSAY PRACTICE QUESTION[2]

Owen owned vacant land (Whiteacre) in State B located 500 yards from a lake and bordered by vacant land owned by others. Owen, who lived 50 miles from Whiteacre, used Whiteacre for cutting firewood and for parking his car when he used the lake.

Twenty years ago, Owen delivered to Abe a deed that read in its entirety:

> Owen hereby conveys to the grantee by a general warranty deed that parcel of vacant land in State B known as Whiteacre.

Owen signed the deed immediately below the quoted language and his signature was notarized. The deed was never recorded.

For the next 11 years, Abe seasonally planted vegetables on Whiteacre, cut timber on it, parked vehicles there when he and his family used the nearby lake for recreation, and gave permission to friends to park their cars and recreational vehicles there. He also paid the real property taxes due on the land, although the tax bills were actually sent to Owen because title had not been registered in Abe's name on the assessor's books. Abe did not build any structure on Whiteacre, fence it, or post no-trespassing signs.

Nine years ago, Abe moved to State C. Since that time, he has neither used Whiteacre nor given others permission to used Whiteacre, and to all outward appearances the land has appeared unoccupied.

Last year, Owen died intestate, leaving his daughter Doris as his sole heir. After Owen's death, Doris conveyed Whiteacre by a valid deed to Buyer, who paid fair market value for Whiteacre. Neither Doris nor Buyer knew of the Owen-to-Abe deed. Both Doris and Buyer believed that Owen was the owner of Whiteacre at the time of his death. Buyer promptly and properly recorded the deed from Doris and immediately went into possession of Whiteacre.

Last month Abe returned to State B. When he discovered Buyer in possession of Whiteacre, he sued for possession.

State B has enacted the following statutes:

1. Actions to recover possession of real property shall be brought within 10 years after the cause of action accrues.
2. No conveyance or mortgage of real property shall be good against subsequent purchasers for value and without notice unless the same be recorded according to law.

Who is entitled to possession of Whiteacre? Explain.

2. *Id.*

IV. SCORE SHEET

Stated	Implied	
		1. Transfer by deed
_____	_____	**Conclusion:** Abe is entitled to possession of Whiteacre. The first issue is whether Abe acquired title to Whiteacre by deed from Owen.
_____	_____	**Rule:** To be valid, a deed must (i) be in writing, (ii) sufficiently describe the land, (iii) identify the grantor and grantee, (iv) evidence an intention to convey the land, and (v) be signed by the grantor.
_____	_____	The parties may be identified by name or by describing them in some other way (e.g., "to my eldest daughter," "to the trustee of my irrevocable trust").
_____	_____	If the deed is delivered with the identity of the grantee left blank, some courts presume that the person taking delivery has authority to fill in the name of the grantee, and if he does so, the deed is valid.
_____	_____	**Application:** Here,
_____	_____	The Owen-to-Abe deed is in writing, describes Whiteacre, identifies Owen as the grantor, shows a present intent to convey ("hereby conveys"), and is signed by Owen. However, it does not identify the grantee by name or otherwise.
_____	_____	Nothing in the facts indicates that Abe wrote in his name after accepting the deed from Owen.
_____	_____	**Conclusion:** Thus, the deed is invalid and Owen did not effectively convey title to Whiteacre to Abe.
		2. Adverse possession
_____	_____	**Issue:** The next issue is whether Abe acquired title to Whiteacre by adverse possession.
_____	_____	**Rule:** To establish title by adverse possession, the possession must be (i) actual and exclusive, (ii) open and notorious, (iii) adverse and under a claim of right (hostile), and (iv) continuous throughout the statutory period.
_____	_____	Exclusive possession generally means not sharing possession with the true owner or the general public.
_____	_____	Possession is open and notorious when it is such as the usual owner would make of the land and is sufficient to put the true owner on notice of the fact of possession.
_____	_____	Possession is hostile when it is without the owner's consent; it does not matter whether the possessor believes he is on his own land or knows he is trespassing on someone else's land.
_____	_____	Continuous possession is possession that the average owner would make of the property under the circumstances.
_____	_____	The statutory period is the limitations period for an ejectment action; in State B, the limitations period is ten years.
_____	_____	In most states, payment of property taxes is not required to establish title by adverse possession but is good evidence of a claim of right.
_____	_____	**Application:** Here,
_____	_____	Abe's possession of Whiteacre was clearly actual and exclusive, as he did not share possession with Owen or the general public (Abe's "friends" do not constitute the general public).
_____	_____	His possession was open and notorious, as he planted vegetables, cut timber, and parked vehicles there when using the nearby lake for recreation—similar uses to which Owen made of the property.

continued on next page

Stated	Implied	
_____	_____	Thus, it does not matter that Abe did not build structures on Whiteacre, fence it, or post no-trespassing signs.
_____	_____	Although Abe believed he was on his own land, his state of mind is irrelevant.
_____	_____	Because he did not enter Whiteacre with Owen's permission (the deed was void), Abe's possession was hostile.
_____	_____	He possessed the property for 11 years, one year beyond that required by the statute of limitations.
_____	_____	Finally, Abe paid the property taxes, although in most states this is not necessary to establish an adverse possession claim.
_____	_____	**Conclusion:** Thus, Abe has a strong claim that he acquired title to Whiteacre by adverse possession.
_____	_____	***3. Which title is superior?***
_____	_____	**Issue:** The final issue is whether Buyer's title to Whiteacre is superior to Abe's title. State B's recording act is a notice statute.
_____	_____	**Rule:** Under a notice statute, a subsequent bona fide purchaser ("BFP") prevails regardless of whether he records at all.
_____	_____	A BFP is a purchaser who takes for valuable consideration and without notice of a prior claim at the time of the conveyance.
_____	_____	There are three types of notice: actual, record, and inquiry.
_____	_____	Actual notice is what the purchaser actually knows.
_____	_____	Record notice is notice that the law imputes to the purchaser, which means that if there is a prior deed on record, the purchaser cannot be a BFP.
_____	_____	Inquiry notice is notice that the purchaser would have by inquiring into the property (e.g., by visiting it to determine who is occupying the land).
_____	_____	However, the recording acts do not protect a subsequent purchaser against interests that arise by **operation of law** (e.g., implied easements, title by adverse possession), because there is no instrument to record in order to perfect such interests.
_____	_____	**Application:** Here,
_____	_____	Buyer purchased Whiteacre for valuable consideration, namely fair market value. It is irrelevant that she obtained title from a donee (Doris).
_____	_____	Buyer seemingly took without notice of a prior claim. She had no actual knowledge that Abe had a potential claim to the property.
_____	_____	Because Abe moved to State C and has neither used Whiteacre nor permitted others to use Whiteacre, Buyer did not have inquiry notice, as inquiry would have revealed that Whiteacre was unoccupied.
_____	_____	Buyer did not have record notice of the void Owen-to-Abe deed because the deed was not recorded.
_____	_____	Instead, subsequent purchasers take subject to those interests.
_____	_____	**Conclusion:** Thus, Abe's title to Whiteacre, acquired by adverse possession, is superior to Buyer's title.

V. MBE PRACTICE QUESTIONS[3]

Question 1

A man obtained a bank loan secured by a mortgage on an office building that he owned. After several years, the man conveyed the office building to a woman, who took title subject to the mortgage. The deed to the woman was not recorded. The woman took immediate possession of the building and made the mortgage payments for several years.

Subsequently, the woman stopped making payments on the mortgage loan, and the bank eventually commenced foreclosure proceedings in which the man and the woman were both named parties. At the foreclosure sale, a third party purchased the building for less than the outstanding balance on the mortgage loan. The bank then sought to collect the deficiency from the woman.

Is the bank entitled to collect the deficiency from the woman?

(A) No, because the woman did not record the deed from the man.
(B) No, because the woman is not personally liable on the loan.
(C) Yes, because the woman took immediate possession of the building when she bought it from the man.
(D) Yes, because the woman was a party to the foreclosure proceeding.

Question 2

A credit card company obtained and properly filed a judgment against a man after he failed to pay a $10,000 debt. A statute in the jurisdiction provides as follows: "Any judgment properly filed shall, for 10 years from filing, be a lien on the real property then owned or subsequently acquired by any person against whom the judgment is rendered."

Two years later, the man purchased land for $200,000. He made a down payment of $20,000 and borrowed the remaining $180,000 from a bank. The bank loan was secured by a mortgage on the land. Immediately after the closing, the deed to the man was recorded first, and the bank's mortgage was recorded second.

Five months later, the man defaulted on the mortgage loan and the bank initiated judicial foreclosure proceedings. After receiving notice of the proceedings, the credit card company filed a motion to have its judgment lien declared to be the first lien on the land.

Is the credit card company's motion likely to be granted?

(A) No, because the bank's mortgage secured a loan used to purchase the land.
(B) No, because the man's down payment exceeded the amount of his debt to the credit card company.
(C) Yes, because the bank had constructive notice of the judgment lien.
(D) Yes, because the bank is a third-party lender and not the seller of the land.

---

3. The Multistate Bar Examination ("MBE®") questions, the Multistate Essay Examination ("MEE®") questions, and excerpts from the Multistate Performance Tests ("MPT®") have been reprinted by permission from the NCBE®. Copyright© by the National Conference of Bar Examiners. All rights reserved.

Question 3

A husband and wife acquired land as common law joint tenants with right of survivorship. One year later, without his wife's knowledge, the husband executed a will devising the land to his best friend. The husband subsequently died.

Is the wife now the sole owner of the land?

(A) No, because a joint tenant has the unilateral right to end a joint tenancy without the consent of the other joint tenant.
(B) No, because the wife's interest in the husband's undivided 50% ownership in the land adeemed.
(C) Yes, because of the doctrine of after-acquired title.
(D) Yes, because the devise to the friend did not sever the joint tenancy.

Question 4

A landlord leased a building to a tenant for a 10-year term. Two years after the term began, the tenant subleased the building to a sublessee for a 5-year term. Under the terms of the sublease, the sublessee agreed to make monthly rent payments to the tenant.

Although the sublessee made timely rent payments to the tenant, the tenant did not forward four of those payments to the landlord. The tenant has left the jurisdiction and cannot be found. The landlord has sued the sublessee for the unpaid rent.

There is no applicable statute.

If the court rules that the sublessee is not liable to the landlord for the unpaid rent, what will be the most likely reason?

(A) A sublessee is responsible to the landlord only as a surety for unpaid rent owed by the tenant.
(B) The sublease constitutes a novation of the original lease.
(C) The sublessee is not in privity of estate or contract with the landlord.
(D) The sublessee's rent payments to the tenant fully discharged the sublessee's obligation to pay rent to the landlord.

Question 5

A woman who owned a house executed a deed purporting to convey the house to her son and his wife. The language of the deed was sufficient to create a common law joint tenancy with right of survivorship, which is unmodified by statute in the jurisdiction. The woman mailed the deed to the son with a letter saying: "Because I intend you and your wife to have my house after my death, I am enclosing a deed to the house. However, I intend to live in the house for the rest of my life, so don't record the deed until I die. The deed will be effective at my death."

The son put the deed in his desk. The wife discovered the deed and recorded it without the son's knowledge. Subsequently, the son and the wife separated, and the wife, without telling anyone, conveyed her interest in the house to a friend who immediately reconveyed it to the wife.

The woman learned that the son and the wife had separated and also learned what had happened to the deed to the house. The woman then brought an appropriate action against the son and the wife to obtain a declaration that the woman was still the owner of the house and an order canceling of record the woman's deed and the subsequent deeds.

If the court determines that the woman owns the house in fee simple, what will be the likely explanation?

(A) The deed was not delivered.
(B) The wife's conduct entitles the woman to equitable relief.
(C) The woman expressly reserved a life estate.
(D) The woman received no consideration for her deed.

Question 6

A woman borrowed $100,000 from a bank and executed a promissory note to the bank in that amount. As security for repayment of the loan, the woman's brother gave the bank a mortgage on a tract of land solely owned by him. The brother did not sign the promissory note.

The woman subsequently defaulted on the loan, and after acceleration, the bank instituted foreclosure proceedings on the brother's land. The brother filed a timely objection to the foreclosure.

Will the bank succeed in foreclosing on the tract of land?

(A) No, because the bank has an equitable mortgage rather than a legal mortgage.
(B) No, because a mortgage from the brother is invalid without a mortgage debt owed by him.
(C) Yes, because the bank has a valid mortgage.
(D) Yes, because the bank is a surety for the brother's mortgage.

Question 7

A mother executed a will devising vacant land to her son. The mother showed the will to her son.

Thereafter, the son purported to convey the land to a friend by a warranty deed that contained no exceptions. The friend paid value for the land and promptly recorded the deed without having first conducted any title search. The friend never took possession of the land.

The mother later died, and the will devising the land to her son was duly admitted to probate.

Thereafter, the friend conducted a title search for the land and asked the son for a new deed. The son refused, because the value of the land had doubled, but he offered to refund the purchase price to the friend.

The friend has sued to quiet title to the land. Is the friend likely to prevail?

(A) No, because the friend failed to conduct a title search before purchasing the land.
(B) No, because the son had no interest in the land at the time of conveyance.
(C) Yes, because of the doctrine of estoppel by deed.
(D) Yes, because the deed was recorded.

Question 8

A woman inherited a house from a distant relative. The woman had never visited the house, which was located in another state, and did not want to own it. Upon learning this, a man who lived next door to the house called the woman and asked to buy the house. The woman agreed, provided that the house was sold "as is." The man agreed, and the woman conveyed the house to the man by a warranty deed.

The man had purchased the house for investment purposes, intending to rent it out while continuing to live next door. After the sale, the man started to renovate the house and discovered serious termite damage. The man sued the woman for breach of contract.

There are no applicable statutes. How should the court rule?

(A) For the woman, because the man planned to change the use of the house for investment purposes.

(B) For the woman, because she sold the house "as is."

(C) For the man, because of the doctrine of caveat emptor.

(D) For the man, because he received a warranty deed.

Question 9

A man owned a large tract of land. The eastern portion of the land was undeveloped and unused. A farmer owned a farm, the western border of which was along the eastern border of the man's land. The two tracts of land had never been in common ownership.

Five years ago, the farmer asked the man for permission to use a designated two acres of the eastern portion of the man's land to enlarge her farm's irrigation facilities. The man orally gave his permission for such use. Since then, the farmer has invested substantial amounts of money and effort each year to develop and maintain the irrigation facilities within the two-acre parcel. The man has been fully aware of the farmer's actions. Nothing regarding this matter was ever reduced to writing.

Last year, the man gave the entire tract of land as a gift to his nephew. The deed of gift made no reference to the farmer or the two-acre parcel. When the nephew had the land surveyed and discovered the facts, he notified the farmer in writing, "Your license to use the two-acre parcel has been terminated." The notice instructed the farmer to remove her facilities from the two-acre parcel immediately. The farmer refused the nephew's demand.

In an appropriate action between the nephew and the farmer to determine whether the farmer had a right to continue to use the two-acre parcel, the court ruled in favor of the farmer.

What is the most likely reason for the court's ruling?

(A) The investments and efforts by the farmer in reliance on the license estop the man, and now the nephew as the man's donee, from terminating the license.

(B) The nephew is merely a donee.

(C) The farmer has acquired an easement based on prior use.

(D) The farmer received a license coupled with an interest.

Question 10

Two friends planned to incorporate a business together and agreed that they would own all of the corporation's stock in equal proportion.

A businesswoman conveyed land by a warranty deed to "the corporation and its successors and assigns." The deed was recorded.

Thereafter, the friends had a disagreement. No papers were ever filed to incorporate the business. There is no applicable statute.

Who owns the land?

(A) The businesswoman, because the deed was a warranty deed.

(B) The businesswoman, because the deed was void.

(C) The two friends as tenants in common, because they intended to own the corporation's stock in equal proportion.

(D) The two friends as tenants in common, because they were the intended sole shareholders.

Question 11

A landlord leased a building to a tenant for a term of six years. The lease complied with the statute of frauds and was not recorded. During the lease term, the tenant sent an email to the landlord that stated: "I hereby offer to purchase for $250,000 the building that I am now occupying under a six-year lease with you." The tenant's name was placed below the word "signed" on the message.

In response, the landlord emailed the tenant: "That's fine. We'll close in 60 days." The landlord's name was placed below the word "signed" on the reply message.

Sixty days later, the landlord refused to tender the deed to the building when the tenant tendered the $250,000 purchase price. The tenant has sued for specific performance.

Who is likely to prevail?

(A) The landlord, because formation of an enforceable contract to convey the building could not occur until after the lease term expired.

(B) The landlord, because the landlord's email response did not contain a sufficient signature under the statute of frauds.

(C) The tenant, because the email messages constitute an insufficient attornment of the lease.

(D) The tenant, because the email messages constitute a sufficient memorandum under the statute of frauds.

Question 12

A tenant leased a commercial property from a landlord for a 12-year term. The property included a large store and a parking lot. At the start of the lease period, the tenant took possession and with the landlord's oral consent installed counters, display cases, shelving, and special lighting. Both parties complied with all lease terms.

The lease is set to expire next month. Two weeks ago, when the landlord contacted the tenant about a possible lease renewal, she learned that the tenant had decided not to renew the lease, and that the tenant planned to remove all of the above-listed items on or before the lease termination date. The landlord claimed that all the items had become part of the real estate and had to remain on the premises. The tenant asserted his right and intention to remove all the items.

Both the lease and the statutes of the jurisdiction are silent on the matter in dispute. At the time the landlord consented and the tenant installed the items, nothing was said about the tenant's right to retain or remove the items.

The landlord has sued the tenant to enjoin his removal of the items. How is the court likely to rule?

(A) For the landlord, because the items have become part of the landlord's real estate.
(B) For the landlord as to items bolted or otherwise attached to the premises, and for the tenant as to items not attached to the premises other than by weight.
(C) For the tenant, provided that the tenant reasonably restores the premises to the prior condition or pays for the cost of restoration.
(D) For the tenant, because all of the items may be removed as trade fixtures without any obligation to restore the premises.

Question 13

For 22 years, the land records have shown a man as the owner of an 80-acre farm. The man has never physically occupied the land.

Nineteen years ago, a woman entered the farm. The character and duration of the woman's possession of the farm caused her to become the owner of the farm under the adverse possession law of the jurisdiction.

Three years ago, when the woman was not present, a neighbor took over possession of the farm. The neighbor repaired fences, put up "no trespassing" signs, and did some plowing. When the woman returned, she found the neighbor in possession of the farm. The neighbor vigorously rejected the woman's claimed right to possession and threatened force. The woman withdrew.

The woman then went to the man and told him of the history of activity on the farm. The woman orally told the man that she had been wrong to try to take his farm. She expressly waived any claim she had to the land. The man thanked her.

Last month, unsure of the effect of her conversation with the man, the woman executed a deed purporting to convey the farm to her son. The son promptly recorded the deed.

The period of time to acquire title by adverse possession in the jurisdiction is 10 years. Who now owns the farm?

(A) The man, because the woman's later words and actions released title to the man.
(B) The neighbor, because the neighbor succeeded to the woman's adverse possession title by privity of possession.
(C) The son, because he succeeded to the woman's adverse possession title by privity of conveyance.
(D) The woman, because she must bring a quiet title action to establish her title to the farm before she can convey the farm to her son.

Question 14

In the most recent deed in the chain of title to a tract of land, a man conveyed the land as follows: "To my niece and her heirs and assigns in fee simple until my niece's daughter marries, and then to my niece's daughter and her heirs and assigns in fee simple."

There is no applicable statute, and the common law Rule Against Perpetuities has not been modified in the jurisdiction. Which of the following is the most accurate statement concerning the title to the land?

(A) The niece has a life estate and the daughter has a contingent remainder.
(B) The niece has a fee simple and the daughter has no interest, because after the grant of a fee simple there can be no gift over.
(C) The niece has a fee simple and the daughter has no interest, because she might not marry within 21 years after the date of the deed.
(D) The niece has a defeasible fee simple determinable and the daughter has an executory interest.

Question 15

A businessman executed a promissory note for $200,000 to a bank, secured by a mortgage on commercial real estate owned by the businessman. The promissory note stated that the businessman was not personally liable for the mortgage debt.

One week later, a finance company obtained a judgment against the businessman for $50,000 and filed the judgment in the county where the real estate was located. At the time the judgment was filed, the finance company had no actual notice of the bank's mortgage.

Two weeks after that filing, the bank recorded its mortgage on the businessman's real estate.

The recording act of the jurisdiction provides: "Unless the same be recorded according to law, no conveyance or mortgage of real property shall be good against subsequent purchasers for value and without notice or against judgment creditors without notice."

The finance company sued to enforce its judgment lien against the businessman's real estate. The bank intervened in the action, contending that the judgment lien was a second lien on the real estate and that its mortgage was a first lien.

Is the bank's contention correct?

(A) No, because the judgment lien was recorded before the mortgage, and the finance company had no actual notice of the mortgage.
(B) No, because the businessman was not personally liable for the mortgage debt, and the mortgage was therefore void.
(C) Yes, because a mortgage prior in time has priority over a subsequent judgment lien.
(D) Yes, because the recording of a mortgage relates back to the date of execution of the mortgage note.

Question 16

A seller conveyed residential land to a buyer by a warranty deed that contained no exceptions and recited that the full consideration had been paid. To finance the purchase, the buyer borrowed 80% of the necessary funds from a bank. The seller agreed to finance 15% of the purchase price, and the buyer agreed to provide cash for the remaining 5%.

At the closing, the buyer signed a promissory note to the seller for 15% of the purchase price but did not execute a mortgage. The bank knew of the loan made by the seller and of the promissory note executed by the buyer to the seller. The buyer also signed a note to the bank, secured by a mortgage, for the 80% advanced by the bank.

The buyer has now defaulted on both loans. There are no applicable statutes. Which loan has priority?

(A) The bank's loan, because the seller can finance a part of the purchase price only by use of an installment land contract.
(B) The bank's loan, because it was secured by a purchase-money mortgage.
(C) The seller's loan, because a promissory note to a seller has priority over a bank loan for residential property.
(D) The seller's loan, because the bank knew that the seller had an equitable vendor's lien.

Question 17

A seller and a buyer signed a contract for the sale of vacant land. The contract was silent concerning the quality of title, but the seller agreed in the contract to convey the land to the buyer by a warranty deed without any exceptions.

When the buyer conducted a title search for the land, she learned that the applicable zoning did not allow for her planned commercial use. She also discovered that there was a recorded restrictive covenant limiting the use of the land to residential use.

The buyer no longer wants to purchase the land. Must the buyer purchase the land?

(A) No, because the restrictive covenant renders the title unmarketable.
(B) No, because the zoning places a cloud on the title.
(C) Yes, because the buyer would receive a warranty deed without any exceptions.
(D) Yes, because the contract was silent regarding the quality of the title.

VI. MBE PRACTICE ANALYSIS[4]

Question 1

A man obtained a bank loan secured by a mortgage on an office building that he owned. After several years, the man conveyed the office building to a woman, who took title subject to the mortgage. The deed to the woman was not recorded. The woman took immediate possession of the building and made the mortgage payments for several years.

Subsequently, the woman stopped making payments on the mortgage loan, and the bank eventually commenced foreclosure proceedings in which the man and the woman were both named parties. At the foreclosure sale, a third party purchased the building for less than the outstanding balance on the mortgage loan. The bank then sought to collect the deficiency from the woman.

Is the bank entitled to collect the deficiency from the woman?

(A) No, because the woman did not record the deed from the man.

---

4. *Id.*

Incorrect. The woman took title to the office building subject to the mortgage debt, which means that the debt was to be satisfied out of the building. The building is the principal, and the man, as transferor, is the only party liable for any deficiency. This situation can be contrasted with one in which a buyer expressly assumes the mortgage debt. In that case, the buyer would be primarily liable for any deficiency and the seller, absent a release by the mortgagee, would be secondarily liable. Recording the deed would give the bank constructive notice of the transfer but would have no effect on the collection of the deficiency.

(B) No, because the woman is not personally liable on the loan.
Correct. The woman took title to the office building subject to the mortgage but did not assume the mortgage debt. The debt is to be satisfied out of the building. The building is the principal, and the man, as transferor, is the only party liable for any deficiency. This situation can be contrasted with one in which a buyer expressly assumes the mortgage debt. In that case, the buyer would be primarily liable for any deficiency and the seller, absent a release by the mortgagee, would be secondarily liable.

(C) Yes, because the woman took immediate possession of the building when she bought it from the man.
Incorrect. The woman took title to the building subject to the mortgage. Her title to the building allowed her to take possession of the building, but her possession has no effect on the payment of any deficiency judgment. Taking title to the building subject to the mortgage means that the debt is to be satisfied out of the building. The building is the principal, and the man, as transferor, is the only party liable for any deficiency. This situation can be contrasted with one in which a buyer expressly assumes the mortgage debt. In that case, the buyer would be primarily liable for any deficiency and the seller, absent a release by the mortgagee, would be secondarily liable.

(D) Yes, because the woman was a party to the foreclosure proceeding.
Incorrect. Because the woman took title to the building subject to the mortgage debt, she was a necessary party to the foreclosure proceeding. However, the fact that she took title to the building subject to the mortgage means that the debt is to be satisfied out of the building. The building is the principal, and the man, as transferor, is the only party liable for any deficiency. This situation can be contrasted with one in which a buyer expressly assumes the mortgage debt. In that case, the buyer would be primarily liable for any deficiency and the seller, absent a release by the mortgagee, would be secondarily liable.

Question 2

A credit card company obtained and properly filed a judgment against a man after he failed to pay a $10,000 debt. A statute in the jurisdiction provides as follows: "Any judgment properly filed shall, for 10 years from filing, be a lien on the real property then owned or subsequently acquired by any person against whom the judgment is rendered."

Two years later, the man purchased land for $200,000. He made a down payment of $20,000 and borrowed the remaining $180,000 from a bank. The bank loan was secured by a mortgage on the land. Immediately after the closing, the deed to the man was recorded first, and the bank's mortgage was recorded second.

Five months later, the man defaulted on the mortgage loan and the bank initiated judicial foreclosure proceedings. After receiving notice of the proceedings, the credit card company filed a motion to have its judgment lien declared to be the first lien on the land.

Is the credit card company's motion likely to be granted?

(A) No, because the bank's mortgage secured a loan used to purchase the land.
Correct. The bank's mortgage is a purchase-money mortgage, meaning that the funds the bank advanced were used to purchase the land. A purchase-money mortgage executed at the same time as the purchase of the real property encumbered takes precedence over any other claim or lien, including a previously filed judgment lien. Therefore, the bank's purchase-money mortgage takes precedence over the credit card company's judgment lien.

(B) No, because the man's down payment exceeded the amount of his debt to the credit card company.
Incorrect. The relative amounts of the down payment and the credit card debt are irrelevant. The bank's mortgage is a purchase-money mortgage, meaning that the funds the bank advanced were used to purchase the land. A purchase-money mortgage executed at the same time as the purchase of the real property encumbered takes precedence over any other claim or lien, including a previously filed judgment lien.

(C) Yes, because the bank had constructive notice of the judgment lien.
Incorrect. It is true that the judgment lien was properly filed and thus provided the bank with constructive notice of the lien. The bank's mortgage, however, is a purchase-money mortgage, meaning that the funds the bank advanced were used to purchase the land. A purchase-money mortgage executed at the same time as the purchase of the real property encumbered takes precedence over any other claim, including a previously filed judgment lien.

(D) Yes, because the bank is a third-party lender and not the seller of the land.
Incorrect. The bank's mortgage is a purchase-money mortgage, meaning that the funds the bank advanced were used to purchase the land. A purchase-money mortgage may be granted by a seller, by a third party, or both. A purchase-money mortgage executed at the same time as the purchase of the real property encumbered takes precedence over any other claim, including a previously filed judgment lien. Therefore, the bank's purchase-money mortgage takes precedence over the credit card company's judgment lien.

Question 3

A husband and wife acquired land as common law joint tenants with right of survivorship. One year later, without his wife's knowledge, the husband executed a will devising the land to his best friend. The husband subsequently died.

Is the wife now the sole owner of the land?

(A) No, because a joint tenant has the unilateral right to end a joint tenancy without the consent of the other joint tenant.
Incorrect. As a general rule, a joint tenant's interest is freely alienable during his or her lifetime without the consent of the other joint tenant. However, a joint tenant's interest cannot be devised in a will. In this case, on the death of the husband, the wife's interest in the joint tenancy immediately swelled and she became the sole owner of the land as the surviving joint tenant.

(B) No, because the wife's interest in the husband's undivided 50% ownership in the land adeemed.

Incorrect. The doctrine of ademption applies only when an individual dies testate and attempts to devise land that the testator no longer owns. Although as a general rule a joint tenant's interest is freely alienable during his or her lifetime without the consent of the other joint tenant, that interest cannot be devised in a will. In this case, on the death of the husband, the wife's interest in the joint tenancy immediately swelled and she became the sole owner of the land as the surviving joint tenant.

(C) Yes, because of the doctrine of after-acquired title.

Incorrect. The doctrine of after-acquired title applies when an individual attempts to convey title (usually by warranty deed) at a time when the individual does not have title to the land but later acquires title to the land. Although as a general rule a joint tenant's interest is freely alienable during his or her lifetime without the consent of the other joint tenant, that interest cannot be devised in a will. In this case, on the death of the husband, the wife's interest in the joint tenancy immediately swelled and she became the sole owner of the land as the surviving joint tenant.

(D) Yes, because the devise to the friend did not sever the joint tenancy.

Correct. Although as a general rule a joint tenant's interest is freely alienable during his or her lifetime without the consent of the other joint tenant, that interest cannot be devised in a will. In this case, on the death of the husband, the wife's interest in the joint tenancy immediately swelled and she became the sole owner of the land as the surviving joint tenant.

Question 4

A landlord leased a building to a tenant for a 10-year term. Two years after the term began, the tenant subleased the building to a sublessee for a 5-year term. Under the terms of the sublease, the sublessee agreed to make monthly rent payments to the tenant.

Although the sublessee made timely rent payments to the tenant, the tenant did not forward four of those payments to the landlord. The tenant has left the jurisdiction and cannot be found. The landlord has sued the sublessee for the unpaid rent.

There is no applicable statute.

If the court rules that the sublessee is not liable to the landlord for the unpaid rent, what will be the most likely reason?

(A) A sublessee is responsible to the landlord only as a surety for unpaid rent owed by the tenant.

Incorrect. In a sublease, the tenant transfers a right of possession for a time shorter than the balance of the leasehold. Therefore, the sublessee and the tenant are in privity of estate with each other, but only the tenant remains in privity of estate with the landlord. There also is no privity of contract between the sublessee and the landlord, because the sublessee made no promise, either to the landlord or to the tenant, to pay rent to the landlord. Lacking privity, the sublessee is not liable to the landlord for the rent and also is not a surety for the tenant.

(B) The sublease constitutes a novation of the original lease.

Incorrect. A novation occurs when a tenant seeks to avoid future liability for rent after an assignment and the landlord agrees to release the tenant from such liability. An assignment occurs when the tenant transfers the entire period of time remaining on the lease agreement. Here, the tenant only transferred a portion of the remaining time on the lease agreement, and the tenant did not seek a release or novation from the landlord.

(C) The sublessee is not in privity of estate or contract with the landlord.
Correct. In a sublease, the tenant transfers a right of possession for a time shorter than the balance of the leasehold. Therefore, the sublessee and the tenant are in privity of estate with each other, but only the tenant remains in privity of estate with the landlord. There also is no privity of contract between the sublessee and the landlord, because the sublessee made no promise, either to the landlord or to the tenant, to pay rent to the landlord. Lacking privity, the sublessee is not liable to the landlord for the rent. Although privity may not be required under an equitable servitude theory, a finding for the sublessee would mean that the court did not use such a theory.

(D) The sublessee's rent payments to the tenant fully discharged the sublessee's obligation to pay rent to the landlord.
Incorrect. The sublessee had no obligation to pay rent to the landlord. In a sublease, the tenant transfers a right of possession for a time shorter than the balance of the leasehold. Therefore, the sublessee and the tenant are in privity of estate with each other, but only the tenant remains in privity of estate with the landlord. There also is no privity of contract between the sublessee and the landlord, because the sublessee made no promise, either to the landlord or to the tenant, to pay rent to the landlord. Lacking privity, a sublessee is not liable to the landlord for the rent. Although privity may not be required under an equitable servitude theory, a finding for the sublessee would mean that the court did not use such a theory.

Question 5

A woman who owned a house executed a deed purporting to convey the house to her son and his wife. The language of the deed was sufficient to create a common law joint tenancy with right of survivorship, which is unmodified by statute in the jurisdiction. The woman mailed the deed to the son with a letter saying: "Because I intend you and your wife to have my house after my death, I am enclosing a deed to the house. However, I intend to live in the house for the rest of my life, so don't record the deed until I die. The deed will be effective at my death."

The son put the deed in his desk. The wife discovered the deed and recorded it without the son's knowledge. Subsequently, the son and the wife separated, and the wife, without telling anyone, conveyed her interest in the house to a friend who immediately reconveyed it to the wife.

The woman learned that the son and the wife had separated and also learned what had happened to the deed to the house. The woman then brought an appropriate action against the son and the wife to obtain a declaration that the woman was still the owner of the house and an order canceling of record the woman's deed and the subsequent deeds.

If the court determines that the woman owns the house in fee simple, what will be the likely explanation?

(A) The deed was not delivered.
Correct. To be valid, a deed must be properly executed and delivered. Delivery is a question of the grantor's intent. In this case, the woman did not intend the deed to be

effective until her death. An intent to have a transfer be effective at the grantor's death is valid in a will but not in a deed unless the deed expressly reserves a life estate, which this deed did not do. The woman remained in possession of the house and intended to retain title to the house until her death. The deed was not delivered, so she owns the house in fee simple.

(B) The wife's conduct entitles the woman to equitable relief.

Incorrect. The wife's conduct may have been inappropriate, but it is not relevant to whether the woman properly delivered the deed to the son and the wife. To be valid, a deed must be properly executed and delivered. Delivery is a question of the grantor's intent. In this case, the woman did not intend the deed to be effective until her death. An intent to have a transfer be effective at the grantor's death is valid in a will but not in a deed unless the deed expressly reserves a life estate, which this deed did not do. The woman remained in possession of the house and intended to retain title to the house until her death. The deed was not delivered, so she owns the house in fee simple.

(C) The woman expressly reserved a life estate.

Incorrect. The woman did not expressly reserve a life estate, and she remained in possession of the house. To be valid, a deed must be properly executed and delivered. Delivery is a question of the grantor's intent. In this case, the woman did not intend the deed to be effective until her death. An intent to have a transfer be effective at the grantor's death is valid in a will but not in a deed unless the deed expressly reserves a life estate, which this deed did not do. The woman remained in possession of the house and intended to retain title to the house until her death. The deed was not delivered, so she owns the house in fee simple.

(D) The woman received no consideration for her deed.

Incorrect. A grantor may convey property for no consideration. To be valid, however, a deed must be properly executed and delivered. Delivery is a question of the grantor's intent. In this case, the woman did not intend the deed to be effective until her death. An intent to have a transfer be effective at the grantor's death is valid in a will but not in a deed unless the deed expressly reserves a life estate, which this deed did not do. The woman remained in possession of the house, and the deed was not delivered, so she owns the house in fee simple.

Question 6

A woman borrowed $100,000 from a bank and executed a promissory note to the bank in that amount. As security for repayment of the loan, the woman's brother gave the bank a mortgage on a tract of land solely owned by him. The brother did not sign the promissory note.

The woman subsequently defaulted on the loan, and after acceleration, the bank instituted foreclosure proceedings on the brother's land. The brother filed a timely objection to the foreclosure.

Will the bank succeed in foreclosing on the tract of land?

(A) No, because the bank has an equitable mortgage rather than a legal mortgage.

Incorrect. A mortgage is security for the performance of an act. The performance may be by the mortgagor or by some other person. Therefore, the mortgage granted by the brother to secure the debt of the woman is valid, and the bank may foreclose on it.

(B) No, because a mortgage from the brother is invalid without a mortgage debt owed by him.

Incorrect. A mortgage is security for the performance of an act. The performance may be by the mortgagor or by some other person. Therefore, the mortgage granted by the brother to secure the debt of the woman is valid, and the bank may foreclose on it.

(C) Yes, because the bank has a valid mortgage.

Correct. A mortgage is security for the performance of an act. The performance may be by the mortgagor or by some other person. The mortgage granted by the brother to secure the debt of the woman is valid even though the woman also has personal liability on the debt.

(D) Yes, because the bank is a surety for the brother's mortgage.

Incorrect. The bank is the mortgagee under the mortgage and not a surety. The bank may foreclose on the mortgage, however, because the mortgage is valid and the debt is in default. A mortgage is security for the performance of an act. The performance may be by the mortgagor or by some other person.

Question 7

A mother executed a will devising vacant land to her son. The mother showed the will to her son.

Thereafter, the son purported to convey the land to a friend by a warranty deed that contained no exceptions. The friend paid value for the land and promptly recorded the deed without having first conducted any title search. The friend never took possession of the land.

The mother later died, and the will devising the land to her son was duly admitted to probate.

Thereafter, the friend conducted a title search for the land and asked the son for a new deed. The son refused, because the value of the land had doubled, but he offered to refund the purchase price to the friend.

The friend has sued to quiet title to the land. Is the friend likely to prevail?

(A) No, because the friend failed to conduct a title search before purchasing the land.

Incorrect. A buyer may want to search the title before purchasing land to determine if title is as called for in the contract, but such a search is not required. The doctrine of estoppel by deed (sometimes referred to as after-acquired title) provides that even if the grantor has no title to the land at the time the deed is delivered, title automatically passes to the grantee when title is so acquired, provided that the grantor asserts the quality of title conveyed in the deed. In this case, the son conveyed to the friend by a warranty deed with no exceptions.

(B) No, because the son had no interest in the land at the time of conveyance.

Incorrect. It is true that the son had no interest in the land at the time of conveyance. The doctrine of estoppel by deed (sometimes referred to as after-acquired title), however, provides that in such a case title automatically passes to the grantee when the title is so acquired, provided that the grantor asserts the quality of title conveyed in the deed. In this case, the son conveyed to the friend by a warranty deed with no exceptions.

(C) Yes, because of the doctrine of estoppel by deed.

Correct. The doctrine of estoppel by deed (sometimes referred to as after-acquired title) provides that even if the grantor has no title to the land at the time the deed is delivered, the title automatically passes to the grantee when title is so acquired, provided that the grantor asserts the quality of title conveyed in the deed. In this case, the son conveyed to the friend by a warranty deed with no exceptions.

(D) Yes, because the deed was recorded.
Incorrect. Recording has no effect on title in this case. The doctrine of estoppel by deed (sometimes referred to as after-acquired title) provides that even if the grantor has no title to the land at the time the deed is delivered, the title automatically passes to the grantee when title is so acquired, provided that the grantor asserts the quality of title conveyed in the deed. In this case, the son conveyed to the friend by a warranty deed with no exceptions. It is irrelevant to the doctrine of estoppel by deed whether the deed was recorded or not.

Question 8

A woman inherited a house from a distant relative. The woman had never visited the house, which was located in another state, and did not want to own it. Upon learning this, a man who lived next door to the house called the woman and asked to buy the house. The woman agreed, provided that the house was sold "as is." The man agreed, and the woman conveyed the house to the man by a warranty deed.

The man had purchased the house for investment purposes, intending to rent it out while continuing to live next door. After the sale, the man started to renovate the house and discovered serious termite damage. The man sued the woman for breach of contract.

There are no applicable statutes. How should the court rule?

(A) For the woman, because the man planned to change the use of the house for investment purposes.
Incorrect. The man's proposed change of use was not known to the woman, nor was it stated in the contract. His planned change to the use of the house is irrelevant to the outcome of the case. The woman should prevail, but it is because she sold the house "as is."

(B) For the woman, because she sold the house "as is."
Correct. A seller may disclaim any duty to disclose defects if the disclaimer is sufficiently clear and specific. In this case, the contract specifically noted that the house was being sold "as is." The woman made no misrepresentations regarding the condition of the house. There are no statutes that might require an owner-occupier to disclose known defects, and in any case the woman inherited the house and had never visited or lived in it. In addition, this is not the sale of a new house by a builder/seller, which may impose a warranty of habitability.

(C) For the man, because of the doctrine of caveat emptor.
Incorrect. The doctrine of caveat emptor states that the buyer accepts the property in its current condition. Therefore, the caveat emptor doctrine would not protect the man as the buyer. In fact, a seller may disclaim any duty to disclose defects if the disclaimer is sufficiently clear and specific. In this case, the contract specifically noted that the house was being sold "as is," and therefore the woman should prevail.

(D) For the man, because he received a warranty deed.

Incorrect. A warranty deed provides remedies for breaches of title matters. Termite damage affects the physical quality of the property, not title to the property. A seller may disclaim any duty to disclose physical defects if the disclaimer is sufficiently clear and specific. In this case, the contract specifically noted that the house was being sold "as is," and therefore the woman should prevail.

Question 9

A man owned a large tract of land. The eastern portion of the land was undeveloped and unused. A farmer owned a farm, the western border of which was along the eastern border of the man's land. The two tracts of land had never been in common ownership.

Five years ago, the farmer asked the man for permission to use a designated two acres of the eastern portion of the man's land to enlarge her farm's irrigation facilities. The man orally gave his permission for such use. Since then, the farmer has invested substantial amounts of money and effort each year to develop and maintain the irrigation facilities within the two-acre parcel. The man has been fully aware of the farmer's actions. Nothing regarding this matter was ever reduced to writing.

Last year, the man gave the entire tract of land as a gift to his nephew. The deed of gift made no reference to the farmer or the two-acre parcel. When the nephew had the land surveyed and discovered the facts, he notified the farmer in writing, "Your license to use the two-acre parcel has been terminated." The notice instructed the farmer to remove her facilities from the two-acre parcel immediately. The farmer refused the nephew's demand.

In an appropriate action between the nephew and the farmer to determine whether the farmer had a right to continue to use the two-acre parcel, the court ruled in favor of the farmer.

What is the most likely reason for the court's ruling?

(A) The investments and efforts by the farmer in reliance on the license estop the man, and now the nephew as the man's donee, from terminating the license.
Correct. In most jurisdictions, the farmer may acquire the unconditional right to use the land following the oral license, provided that the farmer expended money and labor in reliance on the license. The farmer has acquired what is known as an irrevocable license or an equitable easement.

(B) The nephew is merely a donee.
Incorrect. It does not matter if the nephew acquired title to the property as a donee or as a purchaser. The farmer, by her expenditure of labor and money in reliance on the oral license, has acquired an irrevocable license (also known as an equitable easement).

(C) The farmer has acquired an easement based on prior use.
Incorrect. The two parcels of land have never been in common ownership and therefore an easement based on prior use cannot be implied. The farmer, by her expenditure of labor and money in reliance on the oral license, has acquired an irrevocable license (also known as an equitable easement).

(D) The farmer received a license coupled with an interest.
Incorrect. The license granted to the farmer was not a license coupled with an interest. A license coupled with an interest permits a person who owns personal property on the land of another to enter the land to retrieve the personal property. The farmer, by her

expenditure of labor and money in reliance on the oral license, has acquired an irrevocable license (also known as an equitable easement).

Question 10

Two friends planned to incorporate a business together and agreed that they would own all of the corporation's stock in equal proportion.

A businesswoman conveyed land by a warranty deed to "the corporation and its successors and assigns." The deed was recorded.

Thereafter, the friends had a disagreement. No papers were ever filed to incorporate the business. There is no applicable statute.

Who owns the land?

(A) The businesswoman, because the deed was a warranty deed.

Incorrect. The businesswoman owns the land, but she does so because the deed was void. To be valid, a deed must be properly executed and delivered. A deed to a nonexistent grantee, such as a corporation that has not yet been legally formed, is void. It does not matter whether the deed is a warranty, quitclaim, or special warranty deed. At the time the businesswoman attempted to convey the land to the corporation, the corporation had not yet been legally formed, so the deed was void.

(B) The businesswoman, because the deed was void.

Correct. To be valid, a deed must be properly executed and delivered. A deed to a nonexistent grantee, such as a corporation that has not yet been legally formed, is void. At the time the businesswoman attempted to convey the land to the corporation, the corporation had not yet been legally formed, so the deed was void.

(C) The two friends as tenants in common, because they intended to own the corporation's stock in equal proportion.

Incorrect. To be valid, a deed must be properly executed and delivered. A deed to a nonexistent grantee, such as a corporation that has not yet been legally formed, is void and thus conveys no title. It is irrelevant that the two friends intended to own the corporation's stock in equal proportion.

(D) The two friends as tenants in common, because they were the intended sole shareholders.

Incorrect. To be valid, a deed must be properly executed and delivered. A deed to a nonexistent grantee, such as a corporation that has not yet been legally formed, is void and thus conveys no title. It is irrelevant that the two friends intended to be the sole shareholders. At the time the businesswoman attempted to convey the land to the corporation, the corporation had not yet been legally formed, so the deed was void.

Question 11

A landlord leased a building to a tenant for a term of six years. The lease complied with the statute of frauds and was not recorded. During the lease term, the tenant sent an email to the landlord that stated: "I hereby offer to purchase for $250,000 the building that I am now occupying under a six-year lease with you." The tenant's name was placed below the word "signed" on the message.

In response, the landlord emailed the tenant: "That's fine. We'll close in 60 days." The landlord's name was placed below the word "signed" on the reply message.

Sixty days later, the landlord refused to tender the deed to the building when the tenant tendered the $250,000 purchase price. The tenant has sued for specific performance.

Who is likely to prevail?

(A) The landlord, because formation of an enforceable contract to convey the building could not occur until after the lease term expired.

Incorrect. A contract to convey the building could be made during the lease term or thereafter. The email exchange satisfied the statute of frauds, the contract was valid, and the tenant is entitled to specific performance.

(B) The landlord, because the landlord's email response did not contain a sufficient signature under the statute of frauds.

Incorrect. The statute of frauds does require a signature by the party against whom enforcement is sought. However, courts are liberal regarding the nature of a signature; it need only reflect an intent to authenticate the writing. Both the tenant's and the landlord's names were placed below the word "signed," which adequately reflected their desire to be bound. The other requirements of the statute of frauds were also met: the writings identified the parties and the property, expressed an intent to buy and sell, and contained a price term.

(C) The tenant, because the email messages constitute an insufficient attornment of the lease.

Incorrect. Attornment is not an issue in this case, because it is the tenant who wants to purchase the property. The tenant is likely to prevail, but it is because there was a valid contract of sale. The exchange of emails satisfies the statute of frauds, because the writings identified the parties and the property, expressed an intent to buy and sell, and contained a price term and adequate signatures.

(D) The tenant, because the email messages constitute a sufficient memorandum under the statute of frauds.

Correct. The statute of frauds requires a contract for the sale of land to identify the parties, contain a description of the land, evidence an intent to buy and sell, recite (usually) a price term, and be signed by the party against whom enforcement is sought. The email messages here fulfill those requirements. Courts are liberal regarding the nature of a signature; it need only reflect an intent to authenticate the writing. Both the tenant's and the landlord's names were placed below the word "signed," which adequately reflected their desire to be bound.

Question 12

A tenant leased a commercial property from a landlord for a 12-year term. The property included a large store and a parking lot. At the start of the lease period, the tenant took possession and with the landlord's oral consent installed counters, display cases, shelving, and special lighting. Both parties complied with all lease terms.

The lease is set to expire next month. Two weeks ago, when the landlord contacted the tenant about a possible lease renewal, she learned that the tenant had decided not to renew the lease, and that the tenant planned to remove all of the above-listed items on or before the lease termination date. The landlord claimed that all the items had become part of the real estate and had to remain on the premises. The tenant asserted his right and intention to remove all the items.

Both the lease and the statutes of the jurisdiction are silent on the matter in dispute. At the time the landlord consented and the tenant installed the items, nothing was said about the tenant's right to retain or remove the items.

The landlord has sued the tenant to enjoin his removal of the items. How is the court likely to rule?

(A) For the landlord, because the items have become part of the landlord's real estate.

Incorrect. This is a commercial lease, and the tenant has been using the items in his business. Therefore, even if the items have become fixtures, they are trade fixtures, which may be removed by the tenant before the end of the lease term unless very substantial damage would be done by the removal. It is unlikely that the removal of these items will cause substantial damage; if so, however, the tenant must either restore the premises or pay the cost of restoration.

(B) For the landlord as to items bolted or otherwise attached to the premises, and for the tenant as to items not attached to the premises other than by weight.

Incorrect. This is a commercial lease, and the tenant has been using the items in his business. Therefore, even if the items have become fixtures, they are trade fixtures, which may be removed by the tenant before the end of the lease term unless very substantial damage would be done by the removal. It is unlikely that the removal of these items will cause substantial damage; if so, however, the tenant must either restore the premises or pay the cost of restoration. Whether an item is bolted or otherwise attached to the premises is only a factor in determining if it is a fixture.

(C) For the tenant, provided that the tenant reasonably restores the premises to the prior condition or pays for the cost of restoration.

Correct. This is a commercial lease, and the tenant has been using the items in his business. Therefore, the items are trade fixtures, and the tenant may remove them before the end of the lease term unless very substantial damage would be done by the removal. It is unlikely that the removal of these items will cause substantial damage; if so, however, the tenant must either restore the premises or pay the cost of restoration.

(D) For the tenant, because all of the items may be removed as trade fixtures without any obligation to restore the premises.

Incorrect. The tenant may be obligated to restore the premises. This is a commercial lease, and the tenant has been using the items in his business. Therefore, the items are trade fixtures, and the tenant may remove them before the end of the lease term unless very substantial damage would be done by the removal. It is unlikely that the removal of these items will cause substantial damage; if so, however, the tenant must either restore the premises or pay the cost of restoration.

Question 13

For 22 years, the land records have shown a man as the owner of an 80-acre farm. The man has never physically occupied the land.

Nineteen years ago, a woman entered the farm. The character and duration of the woman's possession of the farm caused her to become the owner of the farm under the adverse possession law of the jurisdiction.

Three years ago, when the woman was not present, a neighbor took over possession of the farm. The neighbor repaired fences, put up "no trespassing" signs, and did some plowing. When the woman returned, she found the neighbor in possession of the farm. The neighbor vigorously rejected the woman's claimed right to possession and threatened force. The woman withdrew.

The woman then went to the man and told him of the history of activity on the farm. The woman orally told the man that she had been wrong to try to take his farm. She expressly waived any claim she had to the land. The man thanked her.

Last month, unsure of the effect of her conversation with the man, the woman executed a deed purporting to convey the farm to her son. The son promptly recorded the deed.

The period of time to acquire title by adverse possession in the jurisdiction is 10 years. Who now owns the farm?

(A) The man, because the woman's later words and actions released title to the man.

Incorrect. The woman acquired her title to the farm by adverse possession. The woman's title was an original title and did not derive from the man's title. The statute of frauds requires that any conveyance of real property be in writing. Therefore, the woman's oral statement was insufficient to release the title to the man, and the woman validly conveyed the farm to her son.

(B) The neighbor, because the neighbor succeeded to the woman's adverse possession title by privity of possession.

Incorrect. The woman acquired title to the farm by adverse possession. The woman's title was an original title and did not derive from the man's title. The neighbor's actions may have started the statute of limitations running on his adverse possession of the farm, but he has been in possession of the farm for only three years. In addition, the neighbor was never in privity with the woman.

(C) The son, because he succeeded to the woman's adverse possession title by privity of conveyance.

Correct. The woman acquired title to the farm by adverse possession. The woman's title was an original title and did not derive from the man's title. The statute of frauds requires that the conveyance of the farm be in writing. Therefore, the woman's oral statement was insufficient to release the title to the man, and the woman validly conveyed the farm to her son.

(D) The woman, because she must bring a quiet title action to establish her title to the farm before she can convey the farm to her son.

Incorrect. The woman acquired title to the farm by adverse possession. The woman's title was an original title and did not derive from the man's title. The statute of frauds requires that any conveyance of real property be in writing. Therefore, the woman's oral statement was insufficient to release the title to the man. Having established title to the farm by adverse possession, there is no requirement that the woman sue to establish title. Therefore, she could convey the farm to her son.

Question 14

In the most recent deed in the chain of title to a tract of land, a man conveyed the land as follows: "To my niece and her heirs and assigns in fee simple until my niece's daughter marries, and then to my niece's daughter and her heirs and assigns in fee simple."

There is no applicable statute, and the common law Rule Against Perpetuities has not been modified in the jurisdiction. Which of the following is the most accurate statement concerning the title to the land?

(A) The niece has a life estate and the daughter has a contingent remainder.
Incorrect. The gift to the niece was to the niece "and her heirs and assigns," thereby creating a fee estate rather than a life estate. The fee simple estate was made defeasible by the addition of the words of limitation "until my niece's daughter marries." A remainder interest may follow a life estate; however, a remainder does not follow a fee simple estate. A future interest created in a grantee following a defeasible estate is an executory interest. The executory interest in this case does not violate the Rule Against Perpetuities, because it will be known within the lifetime of the validating lives—the niece and the niece's daughter—whether the condition of marriage has occurred.

(B) The niece has a fee simple and the daughter has no interest, because after the grant of a fee simple there can be no gift over.
Incorrect. The niece was given a defeasible fee simple. A limitation may be expressly attached to a fee simple estate. The express limitation attached to the grant was "until my niece's daughter marries." A future interest held by a grantee following a defeasible estate is an executory interest. The executory interest in this case does not violate the common law Rule Against Perpetuities, because it will be known within the lifetime of the validating lives—the niece and the niece's daughter—whether the condition of marriage has occurred.

(C) The niece has a fee simple and the daughter has no interest, because she might not marry within 21 years after the date of the deed.
Incorrect. The niece was granted a defeasible fee simple. The express limitation was the marriage of the niece's daughter. If the limitation occurs, the estate transfers automatically to the niece's daughter. The future interest held by a grantee following a defeasible estate is an executory interest. Executory interests are subject to the common law Rule Against Perpetuities; however, the niece and the niece's daughter are both validating lives and the condition of the marriage either will or will not occur during their lifetimes. The additional 21 years after the death of all validating lives is not needed, and the rule is not violated.

(D) The niece has a defeasible fee simple determinable and the daughter has an executory interest.
Correct. The niece has a defeasible fee simple because of the limitation placed on the estate by the words "until my niece's daughter marries." If the niece's daughter marries, the estate in the niece will end automatically and will pass to the holder of the future interest (the niece's daughter). The future interest given to the daughter, a grantee, is an executory interest. The executory interest in this case does not violate the common law Rule Against Perpetuities, because it will be known within the lifetime of the validating lives—the niece and the niece's daughter—whether the condition of marriage has occurred.

Question 15

A businessman executed a promissory note for $200,000 to a bank, secured by a mortgage on commercial real estate owned by the businessman. The promissory note stated that the businessman was not personally liable for the mortgage debt.

One week later, a finance company obtained a judgment against the businessman for $50,000 and filed the judgment in the county where the real estate was located. At the time the judgment was filed, the finance company had no actual notice of the bank's mortgage.

Two weeks after that filing, the bank recorded its mortgage on the businessman's real estate.

The recording act of the jurisdiction provides: "Unless the same be recorded according to law, no conveyance or mortgage of real property shall be good against subsequent purchasers for value and without notice or against judgment creditors without notice."

The finance company sued to enforce its judgment lien against the businessman's real estate. The bank intervened in the action, contending that the judgment lien was a second lien on the real estate and that its mortgage was a first lien.

Is the bank's contention correct?

(A) No, because the judgment lien was recorded before the mortgage, and the finance company had no actual notice of the mortgage.

Correct. The judgment lien was recorded first in a jurisdiction that expressly protects judgment creditors without notice. The finance company had no actual notice of the mortgage and had no constructive notice because the mortgage was not recorded until two weeks after the judgment was filed. The bank's mortgage was not a purchase-money mortgage, which would have given it priority.

(B) No, because the businessman was not personally liable for the mortgage debt, and the mortgage was therefore void.

Incorrect. The fact that the businessman was not personally liable for the mortgage debt is irrelevant and does not make the mortgage void. The judgment was recorded first in a jurisdiction that expressly protects judgment creditors without notice. The finance company had no actual notice of the mortgage and had no constructive notice because the mortgage was not recorded until two weeks after the judgment was filed. The bank's mortgage was not a purchase-money mortgage, which would have given it priority.

(C) Yes, because a mortgage prior in time has priority over a subsequent judgment lien.

Incorrect. The judgment was recorded first in a jurisdiction that expressly protects judgment creditors without notice. The finance company had no actual notice of the mortgage and had no constructive notice because the mortgage was not recorded until two weeks after the judgment was filed. The bank's mortgage was not a purchase-money mortgage, which would have given it priority. Priority is determined under these facts by the order of filing.

(D) Yes, because the recording of a mortgage relates back to the date of execution of the mortgage note.

Incorrect. The recording of a mortgage does not relate back to the date of execution of the mortgage note. The mortgage gives constructive notice as of the date of its recording. Therefore, at the time the judgment was recorded, the finance company had neither actual nor constructive notice of the mortgage and is protected under the jurisdiction's recording act. The bank's mortgage was not a purchase-money mortgage, which would have given it priority.

Question 16

A seller conveyed residential land to a buyer by a warranty deed that contained no exceptions and recited that the full consideration had been paid. To finance the purchase, the buyer borrowed 80% of the necessary funds from a bank. The seller agreed to finance 15% of the purchase price, and the buyer agreed to provide cash for the remaining 5%.

At the closing, the buyer signed a promissory note to the seller for 15% of the purchase price but did not execute a mortgage. The bank knew of the loan made by the seller and of the promissory note executed by the buyer to the seller. The buyer also signed a note to the bank, secured by a mortgage, for the 80% advanced by the bank.

The buyer has now defaulted on both loans. There are no applicable statutes. Which loan has priority?

(A) The bank's loan, because the seller can finance a part of the purchase price only by use of an installment land contract.
Incorrect. A seller may finance the purchase of property in a number of ways, including by an installment land contract, by securing the note with a purchase-money mortgage, or by an equitable vendor's lien. However, the seller did not secure the note with a mortgage, nor was an installment land contract used. The seller may have had an equitable vendor's lien for the unpaid purchase price, but the deed recites that the full consideration was paid. Therefore, the bank's purchase-money mortgage takes priority over the seller's unsecured loan and any implied equitable vendor's lien even if the bank knew of the vendor's lien.

(B) The bank's loan, because it was secured by a purchase-money mortgage.
Correct. The bank has a purchase-money mortgage, because the loan proceeds were used to help purchase the land. A purchase-money mortgage, executed at the same time as the deed to the land, takes precedence over any other lien that attaches to the property. The seller's loan could also have been secured by a purchase-money mortgage, but it was not; the buyer signed an unsecured note to the seller. The seller also may have had an equitable vendor's lien for the unpaid purchase price, but the deed recites that the full consideration was paid. Therefore, the bank's purchase-money mortgage takes priority over the seller's unsecured loan and any implied equitable vendor's lien even if the bank knew of the vendor's lien.

(C) The seller's loan, because a promissory note to a seller has priority over a bank loan for residential property.
Incorrect. The seller's promissory note could have been secured by a mortgage, but it was not. The seller may have had an equitable vendor's lien for the unpaid purchase price, but the deed recites that the full consideration was paid. Therefore, the bank's purchase-money mortgage takes priority over the seller's unsecured loan and any implied equitable vendor's lien even if the bank knew of the vendor's lien.

(D) The seller's loan, because the bank knew that the seller had an equitable vendor's lien.
Incorrect. The seller may have had an equitable vendor's lien for the unpaid purchase price, but the deed recites that the full consideration was paid. Therefore, the bank's purchase-money mortgage takes precedence over the seller's unsecured loan as well as any implied equitable vendor's lien, and it is irrelevant that the bank knew of the vendor's lien.

Question 17

A seller and a buyer signed a contract for the sale of vacant land. The contract was silent concerning the quality of title, but the seller agreed in the contract to convey the land to the buyer by a warranty deed without any exceptions.

When the buyer conducted a title search for the land, she learned that the applicable zoning did not allow for her planned commercial use. She also discovered that there was a recorded restrictive covenant limiting the use of the land to residential use.

The buyer no longer wants to purchase the land. Must the buyer purchase the land?

(A) No, because the restrictive covenant renders the title unmarketable.
Correct. Unless the contract provides to the contrary, the law will imply that the seller will provide the buyer with a marketable title on the date of closing. A marketable title is not a perfect title but is a title a court will force an unwilling buyer to purchase. A right held in the land by a third party, such as the right to enforce a restrictive covenant, renders the title unmarketable, and the buyer need not purchase the land.

(B) No, because the zoning places a cloud on the title.
Incorrect. Although in some cases an existing violation of a zoning code may render title unmarketable, the mere existence of a zoning code does not render the title unmarketable or place a cloud on the title. Unless the contract provides to the contrary, the law will imply that the seller will provide the buyer with a marketable title on the date of closing. A right held in the land by a third party, such as the right to enforce a restrictive covenant, renders the title unmarketable, and the buyer need not purchase the land.

(C) Yes, because the buyer would receive a warranty deed without any exceptions.
Incorrect. Unless the contract provides to the contrary, the law will imply that the seller will provide the buyer with a marketable title on the date of closing. However, after a buyer accepts the deed, the doctrine of merger prevents the buyer from raising the issue of marketability of title, and the buyer's remedy regarding title issues, if any, will be based on the deed.

(D) Yes, because the contract was silent regarding the quality of the title.
Incorrect. Unless the contract provides to the contrary, the law will imply that the seller will provide the buyer with a marketable title on the date of closing. This contract was silent on the quality of title and therefore a marketable title will be implied. A marketable title is not a perfect title but is a title a court will require an unwilling buyer to purchase. A right held in the land by a third party, such as the right to enforce a restrictive covenant, renders the title unmarketable, and the buyer need not purchase the land.

CHAPTER **15**

Mapping MBE Topics—Torts

I. MIND MAP

Torts questions are answered by the law of general applicability. Applicants are instructed to make several assumptions:

- No statutes apply unless specified.
- The jurisdiction has survival actions and claims for wrongful death are allowed.
- Pure comparative fault applies.
- Joint and several liability applies.

Torts can be divided into four major categories. The torts in each category share common characteristics and similar defenses. Map each category separately to visualize the common characteristics. The four categories are:

- Intentional torts
- Harm to economic/dignitary interests
- Strict liability
- Negligence

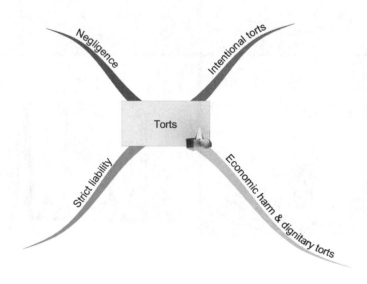

Liability for an **intentional tort** requires:

- a voluntary act,
- intent,
- the elements of a prima facie claim for that tort,
- causation,
- harm, and
- lack of a privilege or defense.

Intent is established if the defendant either desires that his act will cause the harmful result or knows with a substantial certainty that the result will follow. Children and mentally incompetents can be held liable for an intentional tort if the required intent is met. In certain situations, the defendant intends to commit one tort, but commits a different tort against that person or another person. The defendant's intent is transferred to the second tort. **Transferred intent** is limited to certain torts:

- Assault
- Battery
- False imprisonment
- Trespass to land
- Trespass to chattels

After mapping intent, then map the intentional torts by three sections: torts against persons, torts against property, and defenses.

Torts against persons include:

Intentional Torts Against Persons

- **Battery**: Harmful or offensive contact with the plaintiff or something closely connected with the plaintiff.
  - Reasonable person standard.
  - Includes anything connected to the person. Direct touching not required.
  - Liable if sets in motion a force that brings about the harmful or offensive contact (throwing a baseball).
  - Apprehension is not required.
  - Lack of consent.
- **Assault**: Plaintiff experiences a reasonable apprehension of an immediate harmful or offensive contact.
  - Apparent ability is all that is required. That defendant could not have committed the harmful or offensive contact does not defeat liability.
  - Harmful or offensive contact exists if a reasonable person would regard it as offensive.
    - Exaggerated fears are not actionable unless the defendant knew about that fear and used it to put plaintiff in apprehension.
    - Fear is not required, only harmful or offensive contact.
  - Words alone are insufficient. Some overt act is required.
  - Actual damages not required; can recover nominal damages.
- **False imprisonment**: Intentional act that causes a plaintiff to be confined or restrained to a bounded area against plaintiff's will and the plaintiff knows of the confinement or is injured.
  - Confinement includes:
    - confining by physical barriers,
    - failing to release the plaintiff where the defendant has a legal duty to do so, or
    - asserting invalid legal authority.
  - Very brief time is sufficient. No specific duration of time required.
  - No duty to resist if defendant makes a credible threat to use physical force.
  - Not confined if there is a reasonable means of escape that plaintiff is actually aware of.
  - Requires knowledge of confinement or actual harm.
  - Defense: Shopkeeper's privilege requires detention that is:
    - in a reasonable manner,
    - for a reasonable period of time, and
    - based on a reasonable belief as to theft.
- **Intentional infliction of emotional distress**: Intentional or reckless act amounting to extreme and outrageous conduct that causes the plaintiff severe mental distress.
  - Reckless conduct is sufficient if defendant acts in deliberate disregard of a high degree of probability that emotional distress will follow.

EXAM TIP
Be leery of concluding that intentional infliction of emotional distress exists. Raise the issue of a possible cause of action wherever the facts justify, but be careful of concluding that the elements are met. It must be outrageous conduct.

- Extreme and outrageous conduct is beyond the bounds of decency. Conduct a civilized society would not tolerate.
- Mental distress must be severe and substantial. More than a reasonable person could be expected to endure.

Torts against property include:

- **Trespass to land**: Tortfeasor's intentional act is a physical invasion of property.
  - Intentional entry is all that is required. No intent to cause harm required.
  - Mistake is not a defense. Need not know they are trespassing.
  - Plaintiff must be in actual possession or have the right to immediate possession of that land. Note: not ownership.
  - Satisfied if plaintiff causes a third person to enter onto plaintiff's land or remains upon the plaintiff's land when under a legal duty to leave.
  - Plaintiff's land includes the area both above and below the surface.
  - Liable for nominal damages and actual harm.
- **Trespass to chattels**: Intentional act that interferes with the plaintiff's chattel, causing harm.
  - Chattel means tangible personal property or intangible property that has a physical representation.
  - Mistake is not a defense.
  - Interference includes dispossession or intermeddling.
  - More serious interference may amount to conversion.
- **Conversion**: Intentional act that causes the destruction or serious interference with the plaintiff's chattel.

EXAM TIP

To differentiate trespass to chattel and conversion, remember that trespass to chattel involves an interference with the plaintiff's right of possession while conversion raises the interference to a serious enough level that warrants the defendant paying the full value of the chattel.

Intentional Torts Against Property

- Mistake is not a defense.
- Interference is more serious than trespass to chattel and includes
  - a greater use of the chattel and
  - a longer period of interference.
- Plaintiff entitled to fair market value at the time of conversion plus consequential damages, or replevin.
- Defendant's offer to return the chattel does not alleviate the conversion.

Defenses to intentional torts include self-defense, defense of others, defense of property, necessity, and consent. **Self-defense** means a defendant may use force reasonably necessary to protect against injury when he reasonably believes he is being or is about to be attacked. The defendant cannot be the initial aggressor and reasonable mistakes as to the danger are allowed. Look for when a duty to retreat may be imposed. The same considerations apply to the "**defense of others**" defense.

Defense of property requires the defendant to request the plaintiff to stop or leave unless it would be futile. Defendant may not use deadly force.

Necessity requires that injuring plaintiff's property was reasonably necessary to avoid a substantially greater harm to the public, to the defendant, or to save the defendant's more valuable property. A reasonable person standard is used.

Consent can be express or implied, and defendant will still be liable if he exceeds the scope of the consent.

When you have an intentional torts essay question that asks which claims can be brought or which claims will be successful, give the defenses that apply as well. Don't stop with one intentional tort if more than one may apply. Raise all the intentional torts that potentially apply, even if your conclusion is that the plaintiff will not be successful. Likewise, don't stop with one defense if more than one potentially applies.

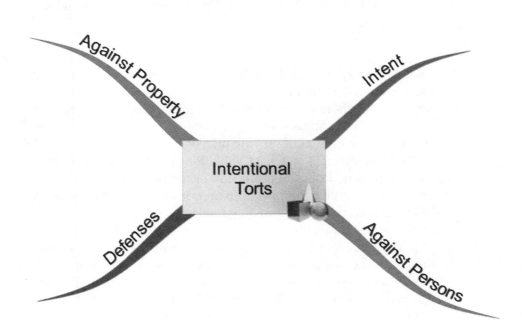

After you have read the call of the question and the fact pattern and decided that no intentional torts issues are raised, then consider **economic harm and dignitary torts**. These torts include defamation, fraud/misrepresentation, invasion of privacy, and nuisance.

Defamation is a defamatory message of or concerning the plaintiff that is communicated to a third person and damages the plaintiff's reputation:

- Elements:
  - Defamatory message: Message lowers a plaintiff in the community's esteem or discourages a third person from associating with him.
  - Of or concerning the plaintiff.
  - Publication: A third person received the defamatory message and understood it to be about the plaintiff.
  - Harm to reputation.
- Types:
  - Libel is a written form of defamation.
  - Slander is defamation not preserved in permanent form, including the spoken word.
  - Slander *per se*:
    - Commission of a crime.
    - Allegations of a loathsome disease.
    - Imputes improper conduct of business or profession.
    - Serious sexual misconduct.
- Damages:
  - General damages: No proof of actual damages required.
    - Slander *per se*
  - Pecuniary or special damages: Quantifiable monetary losses.
    - Slander
  - Punitive damages: Need additional showing of malice.
- Defenses:
  - Truth: Historical defense. Now, plaintiff must prove falsity of claim in *prima facie* case.
  - Privileges:
    - Absolute:
      - Defendant may not be held liable for an otherwise defamatory statement as a matter of law.
      - Applies to legislator, participant in judicial proceeding, policy-making officials, and spouses.
      - Defendant has burden of proving privilege.
    - Qualified: Defendant is not held liable for an otherwise defamatory message unless he loses the protection of the privilege.
      - Applies to communications of a matter of interest to the recipient.
      - Defendant has burden of proving privilege.
      - Privilege does not apply or is lost if:
        - the matter is outside the scope of the privilege (includes matters not relevant to the interests protected by the privilege), or
        - defendant acts out of malice (defendant's primary motive was something other than furthering the interest that justified the privilege).
  - Consent

- Constitutional considerations: The U.S. Supreme Court has modified the standards of common law defamation as applied to the nature of the plaintiff and the subject matter of the defamatory statement. *New York Times v. Sullivan*, 376 U.S. 254 (1964).
  - Malice is required: knowing falsity or recklessness as to truth or falsity.
    - Nature of the Plaintiff:
      - Public official.
      - Public figure: A person who has achieved pervasive fame or notoriety or as to specific limited issues.
    - Subject matter of the controversy:
      - Matter of public concern.
      - Actual malice required for presumed or punitive damages.

Order of Analysis Defamaion

1. **Rule:** Defamatory message of or concerning the plaintiff published to a third person that harms the plaintiff's reputation.
   Apply defamation definition to facts.
   Conclude: Defamation?
2. **Rule:** Malice required for public official, public figure, or matter of public concern (only if facts support).
   Define malice: Knowing falsity or reckless disregard for truth or falsity.
   Apply malice to facts.
   Conclude: Malice?
3. **Rule:** Damages
   Apply damages rules to facts.
   Conclude: Available damages?
4. **Rule:** Defenses—truth, privilege, consent.
   Apply defenses to facts.
   Analyze if outside scope of privilege or malice.
   Conclude: Defense exists?
   Conclude: Liable for defamation?

EXAM TIP
Defamation questions almost always include a qualified privilege defense. Look for it!

Misrepresentation or fraud is an intentional assertion of a material false fact that a plaintiff justifiably relied upon and that causes damages to the plaintiff:

- Misstatement of fact, not an opinion unless rendered by someone with superior skill:
  - False, affirmative statement
  - Active concealment
  - Omissions of fact/failure to disclose
- Scienter/malice; statement was made:
  - Knowing it was false, or
  - With reckless disregard as to its truth or falsity
- Intent to induce reliance
- Justifiable reliance; reasonable person standard
- Causation/damages

In a commercial setting, the scienter element can drop to negligence.

Invasion of Privacy is actually four separate torts:

- Appropriation of the plaintiff's name or picture: Unauthorized use of the the plaintiff's identity or likeness for the defendant's commercial advantage.

- Intrusion on the plaintiff's affairs/seclusion: Defendant unreasonably intrudes into the plaintiff's seclusion:
  - Physical or non-physical intrusion.
  - Must be highly objectionable to a reasonable person.
  - Refers to the plaintiff's physical solitude and the privacy of personal affairs or concerns. The plaintiff must have a reasonable expectation of privacy.
- Publication of facts placing plaintiff in a false light: Defendant publishes matters that portray a plaintiff in a false light.
  - Attributing to the plaintiff views he does not hold or actions he did not take.
  - Reasonable person would find offensive.
  - Must be communicated to a substantial number of people.
- Public disclosure of private facts about the plaintiff: Defendant unreasonably discloses private facts about a plaintiff to the public.
  - Needs to be highly offensive to a reasonable person and not of legitimate public concern.
  - Must be publication to the public.
  - Does not apply if publication is newsworthy.

Both consent and privilege defenses apply to all invasion of privacy torts; truth only applies to portrayal in a false light.

The last economic/dignitary tort is **nuisance**. Nuisance can be public or private. A public nuisance is an unreasonable interference with a right common to the general public. The court will consider:

- whether the conduct involves a significant interference with the public health, safety, peace, comfort, or convenience;
- whether the conduct is proscribed by a statute, ordinance, or regulation; and
- whether the conduct is of a continuing nature or has produced a permanent or long-lasting effect.

Types of Invasion of Privacy Torts

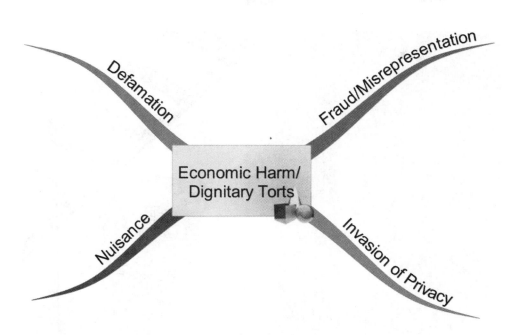

An individual cannot recover personally for public nuisance unless the individual suffers something the rest of the public did not.

Private nuisance is an activity or thing that substantially and unreasonably interferes with the plaintiff's use and enjoyment of the land. The interference must be substantial including offensive, inconvenient, or annoying to an average person in the community. The interference must be unreasonable.

The next area of torts to analyze is **strict liability**. Strict liability has three common law bases:

- Abnormally dangerous activity
- Wild animals
- Products liability

Strict liability can also be grounded in a statute. When that occurs, the bar examiners will give you the actual statute. Thus when you see a statute embedded in the facts of a torts question, think strict liability!

An **abnormally dangerous activity** must create a foreseeable risk of serious harm even with the exercise of reasonable care, and must be an activity that is not a matter of common usage. While driving a vehicle is dangerous, it is a matter of common usage. Moreover, if reasonable care is used, it is not abnormally dangerous.

Liability for **animals** depends upon the nature of the animal. Injury by a wild animal will almost always result in strict liability even if the defendant claims it is "domesticated." Likewise, the owner is strictly liable for damages when his animal trespasses, if it is reasonably foreseeable. Strict liability for domesticated animals typically arises by statute and is dependent on the owner's knowledge.

Products liability is not a separate theory of strict liability. Thus, you do not do an analysis of strict liability and an additional analysis of products liability. It is one analysis, but it requires consideration of proof unique to products:

- Defect:
  - Manufacturing defect: Product was dangerous beyond the expectation of the ordinary consumer because of a departure from its intended design.

**Strict Liability:
Abnormally Dangerous
Activity, Wild Animals,
and Products**

- Food products treated same way—consumer expectations standard.
- Design defect: Plaintiff must show a reasonable alternative design that is a less dangerous modification or alteration and was economically feasible:
  - Warning defect: While adequate warnings insulate a defendant, inadequate warnings result in liability.
  - Seller must anticipate reasonably foreseeable misuses of the product.
  - No requirement of contractual privity.

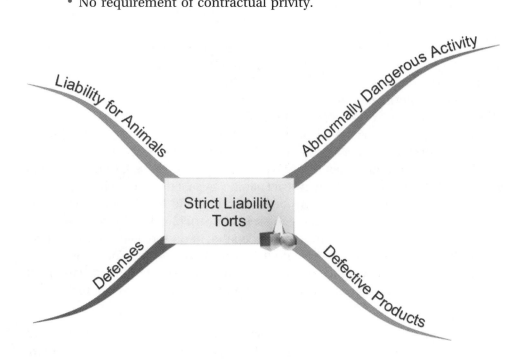

- Reasonable alternative design must exist at the time of the original design. Later improvements, so-called "state of the art," do not constitute a reasonable alternative design.
- Control: Defect must have existed at the time the product left that defendant's control.
- Changes: Product must reach the user without substantial change in the condition in which it was supplied.
- Business: Only commercial suppliers can be held liable. Casual sellers are not liable.
- Causation: Both actual cause and proximate cause required.
- Damages: Compensatory and punitive damages available. Most states deny recovery under strict liability when the sole claim is for economic loss.

Additional theories of recovery are also possible when a person is injured by a product. Intentional conduct, negligence, and breach of warranties claims can also be brought. Defenses to strict liability claims include comparative fault and assumption of risk.

Once you have decided that no intentional torts and economic or dignitary torts are evoked by your fact pattern and the fact pattern does not involve abnormally dangerous activity, wild animals, or a product, then the theory to analyze is **negligence**. Negligence accounts for over half of the Torts essay questions in whole or in part.

You probably have had the basic rule for negligence memorized since the first semester of law school: duty, breach, causation, and damages. For the bar exam, stating the rule in such a simple manner is insufficient. You must establish each element in more detail. Most of the time, each element will require its own CRAC. Occasionally, only one CRAC is appropriate.

The first part of your analysis is whether a **duty** exists. Include the appropriate additional rules when they are raised by the facts. Do not rule dump all of them. To analyze whether a duty exists, consider:

- Defendant must meet a certain standard of conduct for the protection of others against unreasonable risk.
- When action is taken, a duty of care is owed to all foreseeable plaintiffs.
- No affirmative duty to act exists.
  - Exceptions to no affirmative duty:
    - innkeepers
    - common carriers
    - special relationships
  - One can assume a duty to act. Besides standard of care, also liable if leaves plaintiff in worse condition.
    - Remember, assume no statute.
    - Fact pattern may give you a statute.
    - In an essay, include "if jurisdiction has a Good Samaritan statute, it would govern and relieve liability under certain conditions."
- No duty to control others.
  - Exception: special relationship.
  - Parents have duty to exercise reasonable care to control child if knows or has reason to know of the necessity and has ability to control child.
  - Masters have duty to control servants while acting within the scope of employment.

- Masters have a duty of care in hiring employees. Look for knowledge of a servant's prior bad acts.
- Negligent infliction of emotional distress.
  - Plaintiff must be in zone of danger.
    - Suffered a physical manifestation.
    - Exceptions to zone of danger and physical manifestation: Negligent death notice and mishandling of corpse.
  - Bystander.
    - Located near the scene of the accident.
    - Suffered severe emotional distress from the sensory and contemporaneous observation of scene.
    - Had a close personal relationship with victim.
- Possessors of Land.
  - Invitee: Duty to prevent injuries and duty to discover dangerous conditions.
  - Licensee: Duty to exercise reasonable care and to warn of dangerous conditions.
  - Trespasser:
    - Unknown trespassers: No duty of care.
    - Known trespassers: Jurisdictions take different approaches.
    - Children: Heightened standard of care as to artificial conditions.

The second part of your duty analysis is determining the **standard of care**. A defendant's conduct is measured against a reasonable, ordinary, prudent person. By utilizing a reasonable person, the standard is an objective one. A higher standard of care is imposed on professionals. The standard also varies depending upon the relationship between the parties such as bailor/bailee, owners/occupiers of land, and landlord/tenant. A child's conduct is held to the

Defendants with Affirmative Duty to Act: Innkeepers, Common Carriers, Professionals, Parents

standard of care of a reasonable child of the same age, education, intelligence, and experience. Some jurisdictions divide by age: For ages 6 and below it is conclusively presumed that they are incapable of negligence; for ages 7 through 13 there is a rebuttable presumption of no negligence; and for ages 14 and up there is a rebuttable presumption of capability for negligence.

Next, **breach** occurs when the defendant's conduct falls short of the standard of care. Two special situations should be considered. The first is **negligence *per se***. When a statute provides for a criminal penalty, that statute's specific duty replaces the common law duty. The plaintiff must prove that he was in the class intended to be protected by the statute, the harm suffered is the particular harm that the statute was designed to prevent, and the standards of conduct are clearly defined.

The second situation is ***res ispa loquitur***. *Res ispa* applies based on the particular injury. It is a circumstantial evidence doctrine. The accident that caused the injury would not normally occur unless someone was negligent, and the negligence is attributable to the defendant. When a jet crashes into a mountain on a clear day and there are no survivors to tell what happened, *res ispa* applies as, whether it was a mechanical error or pilot error, the airline is still responsible.

The third element of negligence is **causation**. Always address both actual cause and legal cause. **Actual cause** is also called cause-in-fact. But for the defendant's actions, the plaintiff's injury would not have occurred. Or, the defendant's actions were a significant factor in bringing about the injury. When two or more defendants have been negligent, but uncertainty exists about which one caused the injury, the burden of proof shifts to the

EXAM TIP
If you know what caused the injury, then *res ispa* does not apply. It only applies when the instrument of injury is in the defendant's sole control.

plaintiff to prove that harm has been caused by one of them. The burden then shifts back to the defendants to show their negligence was not the actual cause.

The plaintiff must also prove that the defendant's actions were the **proximate or legal cause** of her injury. The test is based on foreseeability and is actually a limitation on liability in that every actual cause case does not rise to legal cause. Defendants are liable for the normal incidents within the increased risk caused by their acts. As duty arises only to foreseeable plaintiffs who are within the zone of danger, proximate cause requires that the risk also be foreseeable. An exception to the foreseeable risk doctrine is the **eggshell plaintiff**. Defendants take the full consequence for a plaintiff's injuries, even if the injuries are more severe than they would have been with a normal person.

If there is an uninterrupted chain of events between a defendant's negligent act and the plaintiff's injury, then it is a **direct cause** case. Defendant is liable for all foreseeable harmful results. An **indirect cause** case is one where a force came into motion after the defendant's act and combined with the negligent act to cause the plaintiff's injury. The intervening force may break the chain of causation between the initial act and the ultimate injury.

Foreseeable intervening acts do not cut off a defendant's liability. These include subsequent medical malpractice, negligence of rescuers, and subsequent accidents. The key is again foreseeability. **Unforeseeable intervening acts** do cut off liability. Such superseding causes may include naturally occurring phenomena, criminal acts of third persons (unless foreseeable), intentional torts of third persons, or extraordinary forms of negligent conduct by the third person.

The element of **damages** means actual harm or injury. Unlike some intentional torts, a plaintiff cannot recover nominal damages. Plaintiff is compensated for all past, present, and prospective damages including economic damages, such as medical expenses and lost earnings, and noneconomic

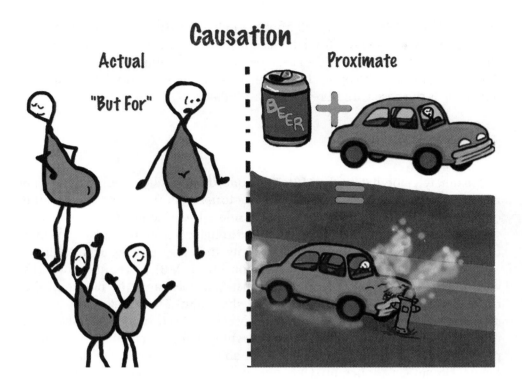

damages, such as pain and suffering. Punitive damages may be recoverable if defendant's actions were wanton and willful, reckless, or malicious.

Defenses include contributory fault, comparative fault, and assumption of risk. The examiners tell applicants to assume that pure comparative fault applies in the jurisdiction of the case. Thus, detail regarding contributory fault is generally not needed. Instead, spend your time on comparative fault and assumption of the risk. **Comparative fault** means that the plaintiff's conduct contributed to her injury and is compared to defendant's negligence. Damages are reduced accordingly. Comparative fault does not apply to intentional torts.

Assumption of risk requires that the plaintiff must have known of the risk and still voluntarily proceeded with the action. Essentially, assumption of risk means that the plaintiff consented to the defendant's actions. Assumption of the risk can be express or implied.

In addition to these elements, issues arise when two or more tortious acts combine to cause an indivisible injury. When this occurs, each defendant is liable for the entirety of plaintiff's damages—the doctrine of **joint and several**

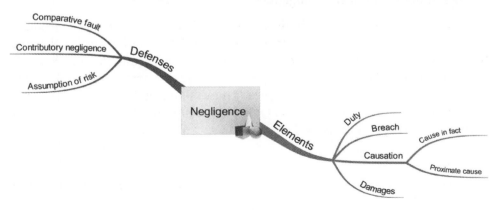

liability. If plaintiff recovers in full from one defendant, then there is satisfaction and she cannot also recover from the second defendant. The rule of contribution allows the tortfeasor that paid to seek recovery for the amount that was more than his share from the other defendant. This occurs when the fault is apportioned, as is the case with pure comparative fault.

II. MBE STRATEGIES[1]

Approximately one-half of the MBE Torts questions will be on negligence. The rest will consist of questions on all the other torts. Thus, first read the call of the question. The responses may concern only one cause of action. Other questions will consider different causes of action. Go through your mind map on the other torts to determine if any apply. If none apply, then it's a negligence question.

The most common call of the question on an MBE Torts question asks whether the plaintiff will prevail. You must first determine the nature of the claim. Then, determine the elements of the claim. Then, determine if any defenses to the claim arise. Then, you must apply each rule to the facts. The response will give you a snippet of the reasoning, but the first and second snippets could be on defenses while the third and fourth snippets are on the elements. Do not get tripped up. Only one of the answer choices is correct. Look at each one in isolation to determine if it is an accurate conclusion with accurate reasoning. Similarly, questions asking for the "best claim" or "best defense" will also have only one successful claim or defense.

Use these strategies to analyze Torts questions:

* Questions where the type of claim is identified that ask what the plaintiff will need to prove: Only one answer choice will supply the correct level of proof, and others will overstate or understate the required proof.
* Actual Causation: There can be more than one cause in fact. The defendant need only be a substantial factor in causing the plaintiff's damages.
* Legal Causation: Try ignoring every actor except the defendant and the plaintiff—were the plaintiff's injuries within the risk created by the defendant's act? If yes, proximate cause is established.
* Intervening causes only relieve the defendant of liability if the results of the intervening causes are unforeseeable.
* Plaintiff is free to pick his defendant.
* Negligence "shortcut"—If the defendant's conduct is reasonable, the defendant cannot be negligent.

Truth is a defense for defamation, but is not a defense to any of the invasion of privacy torts. Everything a defendant states may well be true, but she is still liable because she disclosed private facts or intruded on the plaintiff's seclusion.

Do not ignore Torts questions in your MBE practice because you think they may be "easier" than the other topics. The differences between the answer responses are actually quite subtle. Only practice followed by autopsying your answers will get you to the level of competency you need.

---

1. Some of these strategies are from Steven L. Emanuel, *Strategies & Tactics for the MBE* 333-41 (5th ed. 2013).

III. ESSAY PRACTICE QUESTION[2]

Susan, a student at University, lived in a University dormitory. Access to Susan's dormitory was restricted to dormitory residents and guests who entered the dormitory with a resident. Entry to the dormitory was controlled by key cards. Dormitory key cards opened all doors except for a rear entrance, used only for deliveries, that was secured with a deadbolt lock.

On November 30, at 2:00 am, Ann, a University graduate, entered the dormitory through the rear entrance. Ann was able to enter because the deadbolt lock had broken during a delivery four days before Ann's entry and had not been repaired. Ann attacked Susan, who was studying alone in the dormitory's library.

Jim, another resident of Susan's dormitory, passed the library shortly after Ann had attacked Susan. The door was open, and Jim saw Susan lying on the floor, groaning. Jim told Susan, "I'll go for help right now." Jim then closed the library door and went to the University security office. However, the security office was closed, and Jim took no other steps to help Susan. About half an hour after Jim closed the library door; Susan got up and walked to the University hospital, where she received immediate treatment for minor physical injuries.

One day after Ann's attack, Susan began to experience mental and physical symptoms (e.g., insomnia, anxiety, rapid breathing, nausea, muscle tension, and sweating). Susan's doctor had concluded that these symptoms are due to post-traumatic stress disorder (PTSD). According to the doctor, Susan's PTSD was caused by trauma she suffered one month before Ann's attack when Susan was robbed at gunpoint. In the doctor's opinion, although Susan had no symptoms of PTSD until after Ann's attack, Ann's attack triggered PTSD symptoms because Susan was suffering from PTSD caused by the earlier robbery. The symptoms became so severe that Susan had to withdraw from school. She now sees a psychologist weekly.

Since the attack, Susan has learned that Ann suffers from schizophrenia, a serious mental illness. From August to November, Ann had been receiving weekly outpatient psychiatric treatment from her Psychiatrist. Her Psychiatrist's records show that on November 20, Ann told her Psychiatrist that she "was going to make sure" that former University classmates who were "cheaters" got "what was coming to them for getting the good grades I should have received." Ann's Psychiatrist did not report these threats to anyone because Ann had no history of violent behavior. Ann's Psychiatrist also did not believe that Ann would take any action based on her statements.

At the time of the attack, Susan knew Ann only slightly because they had been in one class together the previous semester. Susan received an A in that class.

Susan is seeking damages for the injuries she suffered as a result of Ann's attack and has sued University, Jim, and Ann's Psychiatrist.

1. May Susan recover damages for physical injuries she suffered in Ann's attack from
   a. University? Explain.
   b. Jim? Explain.
   c. Ann's Psychiatrist? Explain.
2. Assuming that any party is found liable to Susan, may she also recover damages from that party for the PTSD symptoms she is experiencing? Explain.

2. The Multistate Bar Examination ("MBE®") questions, the Multistate Essay Examination ("MEE®") questions, and excerpts from the Multistate Performance Tests ("MPT®") have been reprinted by permission from the NCBE®. Copyright © by the National Conference of Bar Examiners. All rights reserved.

IV. SCORE SHEET

Stated	Implied	
		Point One(a) (30%)
_____	_____	**Conclusion:** University owed a duty of care to Susan, a resident of a dormitory controlled and maintained by University, to take reasonable precautions to protect Susan from foreseeable criminal activity.
_____	_____	University's failure to fix the broken lock or take other precautions against unauthorized entry into Susan's dorm violated that duty.
_____	_____	It was also the cause in fact and proximate cause of Susan's physical injuries.
_____	_____	**Rule:** A college does not stand in a *parens patriae* relationship with its students.
_____	_____	Modern courts have found that landlords, including landlords like University, have a duty to take reasonable precautions to protect tenants against foreseeable attacks.
_____	_____	The University might also have owed a duty of care to Susan because she was an invitee.
_____	_____	**Application:** Here,
_____	_____	Duty: Criminal activity was foreseeable.
_____	_____	Apartment buildings and college dormitories almost invariably have locked entrances to protect against intrusion by criminals.
_____	_____	Indeed, recognizing this risk, University had taken steps to ensure that nonresidents could not enter the dormitory.
_____	_____	Breach: The lock had broken four days before Ann's entry.
_____	_____	University employees had ample time to discover the break.
_____	_____	Even if repairs were impossible within the relevant time period, University could have taken other steps to prevent the door from being opened from the outside.
_____	_____	Actual Causation: Susan would not have been injured but for the University's failure to act.
_____	_____	Proximate Causation: Such precautions were warranted given the foreseeability that unauthorized persons could enter the dormitory to engage in criminal acts.
_____	_____	This risk prompted University to issue key cards to the dormitory residents.
_____	_____	**Conclusion:** A jury could find that University's failure to repair the broken lock or to take other steps to secure the door through which Ann entered the dormitory represented a breach of its duty of care.
_____	_____	Because Ann's entrance into Susan's dorm was made possible by University's failure to secure the damaged door, a jury could find that University's failure to repair the lock was the cause in fact and proximate cause of Susan's physical injuries.
		Point One(b) (25%)
_____	_____	**Conclusion:** Susan cannot recover damages from Jim.
_____	_____	**Rule:** There is no general duty to come to the aid of another.
_____	_____	A duty arises if the parties have a special relationship.
_____	_____	A duty also arises when an actor "takes charge of another who is helpless adequately to aid or protect himself."

continued on next page

Stated	Implied	
_____	_____	The actor is then liable when a) "the failure of the actor to exercise reasonable care to secure the safety of the other while within the actor's charge, or
_____	_____	b) the actor's discontinuing aid or protection,
_____	_____	if by doing so he leaves the other in a worse position than when the actor took charge of him."
_____	_____	If an actor assumes a duty, the victim must rely to her detriment on the actor's promise to obtain assistance or the victim was left in a worse position.
_____	_____	**Application:** Here,
_____	_____	The evidence does not show that Susan relied to her detriment or that Susan was in a worse position after Jim took charge.
_____	_____	Jim's failure to follow up his unsuccessful attempt to report Susan's injuries to the University security office with other action was arguably negligent.
_____	_____	Moreover, Jim's closing the library door made it less likely that anyone else would come to Susan's aid.
_____	_____	However, there is no evidence that Susan actually suffered any harm as a result of Jim's conduct. Susan obtained medical assistance herself only half an hour after Jim left her, and there is no evidence that her minor physical injuries or PTSD symptoms were aggravated by delayed treatment.
_____	_____	**Conclusion:** Thus, because there is no evidence that Jim caused or exacerbated Susan's injuries, Susan cannot recover damages from Jim.
		Point One(c) (30%)
_____	_____	**Rule:** A psychotherapist has a duty to warn a reasonably identifiable individual against whom her patient has made credible threats but has no duty to warn any individual who is a member of an indeterminate class against whom the patient has made threats.
_____	_____	Recovery is permitted either (a) when the therapist believed that the patient posed a real risk to the specified victim or (b) when the therapist negligently failed to take the threat seriously.
_____	_____	The duty is confined to intended victims who are readily ascertainable and subject to a serious threat of physical violence.
_____	_____	That a psychiatrist does not find the threats credible would not be a defense if the evidence showed that a reasonable therapist would have taken the threats seriously.
_____	_____	**Application:** Here,
_____	_____	Ann's Psychiatrist had a therapeutic relationship with Ann because Ann saw Psychiatrist weekly for several months.
_____	_____	That relationship imposed on Psychiatrist a duty to warn Ann's ascertainable intended victims if Ann made serious threats of physical violence against them.
_____	_____	Psychiatrist's decision not to warn anyone was likely reasonable based on Ann's lack of any history of violent behavior and the ambiguity of her vague threat to ensure that cheaters "get what is coming to them," which is not a clear threat of serious injury.
_____	_____	More importantly, Ann's threats were general; she did not specify any ascertainable victims.
_____	_____	**Conclusion:** Thus, a jury could not find that Psychiatrist is liable to Susan.

continued on next page

Stated	Implied	
_____	_____	**Point Two (15%)**
_____	_____	**Conclusion:** University is responsible for damages related to Susan's injuries because a tort defendant takes his victim as he finds him.
_____	_____	**Rule:** A tort defendant takes his victim as he finds him.
_____	_____	The victim with an "eggshell skull" who suffers injuries greatly in excess of those that a normal victim would suffer is entitled to recover for the full extent of his injuries.
_____	_____	Most of the "eggshell skull" cases involve unusual physical consequences of an underlying precondition.
_____	_____	However, with proper proof, the plaintiff may also recover damages for mental symptoms such as anxiety or insomnia.
_____	_____	Some courts have sometimes been reluctant to award tort plaintiffs damages for mental distress unaccompanied by any physical injuries
_____	_____	**Application:** Here,
_____	_____	Although Susan sustained only minor physical injuries from Ann's attack, Susan suffered a preexisting condition, PTSD.
_____	_____	Susan's PTSD symptoms that emerged after Ann's attack were attributable to her preexisting PTSD.

V. MBE PRACTICE QUESTIONS[3]

Question 1

An assistant to a famous writer surreptitiously observed the writer as the writer typed her private password into her personal computer in order to access her email. On several subsequent occasions in the writer's absence, the assistant read the writer's email messages and printed out selections from them.

The assistant later quit his job and earned a considerable amount of money by leaking information to the media that he had learned from reading the writer's email messages. All of the information published about the writer as a result of the assistant's conduct was true and concerned matters of public interest.

The writer's secretary had seen the assistant reading the writer's emails and printing out selections, and she has told the writer what she saw. The writer now wishes to sue the assistant for damages. At trial, the writer can show that the media leaks could have come only from someone reading her email on her personal computer.

Can the writer recover damages from the assistant?

(A) No, because the assistant was an invitee on the premises.
(B) No, because the published information resulting from the assistant's conduct was true and concerned matters of public interest.

---

3. *Id.*

(C) Yes, because the assistant invaded the writer's privacy.

(D) Yes, because the published information resulting from the assistant's conduct constituted publication of private facts concerning the writer.

Question 2

A man sued his neighbor for defamation based on the following facts:

The neighbor told a friend that the man had set fire to a house in the neighborhood. The friend, who knew the man well, did not believe the neighbor's allegation, which was in fact false. The friend told the man about the neighbor's allegation. The man was very upset by the allegation, but neither the man nor the neighbor nor the friend communicated the allegation to anyone else.

Should the man prevail in his lawsuit?

(A) No, because the friend did not believe what the neighbor had said.

(B) No, because the man cannot prove that he suffered pecuniary loss.

(C) Yes, because the man was very upset at hearing what the neighbor had said.

(D) Yes, because the neighbor communicated to the friend the false accusation that the man had committed a serious crime.

Question 3

A manufacturing plant emitted a faint noise even though the owner had installed state-of-the-art sound dampeners. The plant operated only on weekdays and only during daylight hours. A homeowner who lived near the plant worked a night shift and could not sleep when he arrived home because of the noise from the plant. The other residents in the area did not notice the noise.

Does the homeowner have a viable nuisance claim against the owner of the plant?

(A) No, because the homeowner is unusually sensitive to noise during the day.

(B) No, because the plant operates only during the day.

(C) Yes, because the noise is heard beyond the boundaries of the plant.

(D) Yes, because the operation of the plant interferes with the homeowner's quiet use and enjoyment of his property.

Question 4

Toxic materials being transported by truck from a manufacturer's plant to a warehouse leaked from the truck onto the street a few miles from the plant. A driver lost control of his car when he hit the puddle of spilled toxic materials on the street, and he was injured when his car hit a stop sign.

In an action for damages by the driver against the manufacturer based on strict liability, is the driver likely to prevail?

(A) No, because the driver's loss of control was an intervening cause.

(B) No, because the driver's injury did not result from the toxicity of the materials.

(C) Yes, because the manufacturer is strictly liable for leaks of its toxic materials.

(D) Yes, because the leak occurred near the manufacturer's plant.

Question 5

A man and his friend, who were both adults, went to a party. The man and the friend had many drinks at the party and became legally intoxicated. They decided to play a game of chance called "Russian roulette" using a gun loaded with one bullet. As part of the game, the man pointed the gun at the friend and, on her command, pulled the trigger. The man shot the friend in the shoulder.

The friend has brought a negligence action against the man. Traditional defenses based on plaintiff's conduct apply. What is likely to be the dispositive issue in this case?

(A) Whether the game constituted a joint venture.
(B) Whether the friend could validly consent to the game.
(C) Whether the friend was also negligent.
(D) Whether the man was legally intoxicated when he began playing the game.

Question 6

A woman signed up for a bowling class. Before allowing the woman to bowl, the instructor required her to sign a waiver explicitly stating that she assumed all risk of injuries that she might suffer in connection with the class, including injuries due to negligence or any other fault. After she signed the waiver, the woman was injured when the instructor negligently dropped a bowling ball on the woman's foot.

The woman brought a negligence action against the instructor. The instructor has filed a motion for summary judgment based on the waiver.

What is the woman's best argument in opposition to the instructor's motion?

(A) Bowling is an inherently dangerous activity.
(B) In circumstances like these, it is against public policy to enforce agreements that insulate people from the consequences of their own negligence.
(C) It was unreasonable to require the woman to sign the waiver before she was allowed to bowl.
(D) When she signed the form, the woman could not foresee that the instructor would drop a bowling ball on her foot.

Question 7

A pedestrian was crossing a street in a crosswalk when a woman walking just ahead of him was hit by a truck. The pedestrian, who had jumped out of the way of the truck, administered CPR to the woman, who was a stranger. The woman bled profusely, and the pedestrian was covered in blood. The woman died in the ambulance on the way to the hospital. The pedestrian became very depressed immediately after the incident and developed physical symptoms as a result of his emotional distress.

The pedestrian has brought an action against the driver of the truck for negligent infliction of emotional distress. In her defense, the driver asserts that she should not be held liable, because the pedestrian's emotional distress and resulting physical symptoms are not compensable.

What is the strongest argument that the pedestrian can make in response to the driver's defense?

(A) The pedestrian saw the driver hit the woman.
(B) The pedestrian was acting as a Good Samaritan.
(C) The pedestrian was covered in the woman's blood and developed physical symptoms as a result of his emotional distress.
(D) The pedestrian was in the zone of danger.

Question 8

Upon the recommendation of her child's pediatrician, a mother purchased a vaporizer for her child, who had been suffering from respiratory congestion. The vaporizer consisted of a gallon-size glass jar, which held water to be heated until it became steam, and a metal heating unit into which the jar fit. The jar was covered by a plastic cap with an opening to allow the steam to escape. At the time the vaporizer was manufactured and sold, there was no safer alternative design.

The booklet that accompanied the vaporizer read: "This product is safe, spill proof, and practically foolproof. It shuts off automatically when the water is gone." The booklet had a picture of a vaporizer sending steam over a baby's crib.

The mother used the vaporizer whenever the child was suffering from congestion. She placed the vaporizer on the floor near the child's bed.

One night, the child got out of bed to get a drink of water and tripped over the cord of the vaporizer as she crossed the room. The top of the vaporizer separated from the base, and boiling water from the jar spilled on the child when the vaporizer tipped over. The child suffered serious burns as a consequence.

The child's representative brought an action for damages against the manufacturer of the vaporizer. The manufacturer moved to dismiss after the representative presented the evidence above.

Should the manufacturer's motion be granted?

(A) No, because a jury could find that the manufacturer expressly represented that the vaporizer was spill proof.
(B) No, because the vaporizer caused a serious injury to the child.
(C) Yes, because it should have been obvious to the mother that the water in the jar would become boiling hot.
(D) Yes, because there was no safer alternative design.

Question 9

A man was admitted to a hospital after complaining of persistent severe headaches. While he was there, hospital staff failed to diagnose his condition, and he was discharged. Two days later, the man died of a massive brain hemorrhage due to a congenital defect in an artery.

The man's wife has brought a wrongful death action against the hospital. The wife offers expert testimony that the man would have had a "reasonable chance" (not greater than 50%) of surviving the hemorrhage if he had been given appropriate medical care at the hospital.

In what type of jurisdiction would the wife's suit most likely be successful?

(A) A jurisdiction that applies traditional common law rules concerning burden of proof.
(B) A jurisdiction that allows recovery based on strict liability.
(C) A jurisdiction that allows recovery for the loss of the chance of survival.
(D) A jurisdiction that recognizes loss of spousal consortium.

Question 10

A mother purchased an expensive television from an appliance store for her adult son. Two years after the purchase, a fire started in the son's living room in the middle of the night. The fire department concluded that the fire had started in the television. No other facts are known.

The son sued the appliance store for negligence. The store has moved for summary judgment. Should the court grant the store's motion?

(A) No, because televisions do not catch fire in the absence of negligence.
(B) No, because the store sold the television.
(C) Yes, because the son is not in privity with the store.
(D) Yes, because there is no evidence of negligence on the part of the store.

Question 11

A shopper was riding on an up escalator in a department store when the escalator stopped abruptly. The shopper lost her balance and fell down the escalator steps, sustaining injuries. Although the escalator had been regularly maintained by an independent contractor, the store's obligation to provide safe conditions for its invitees was nondelegable. The shopper has brought an action against the store for damages, and the above facts are the only facts in evidence.

The store has moved for a directed verdict. Should the court grant the motion?

(A) No, because the finder of fact could infer that the escalator malfunction was due to negligence.
(B) No, because the store is strictly liable for the shopper's injuries.
(C) Yes, because an independent contractor maintained the escalator.
(D) Yes, because the shopper has not produced evidence of negligence.

Question 12

A 14-year-old teenager of low intelligence received her parents' permission to drive their car. She had had very little experience driving a car and did not have a driver's license. Although she did the best she could, she lost control of the car and hit a pedestrian.

The pedestrian has brought a negligence action against the teenager. Is the pedestrian likely to prevail?

(A) No, because only the teenager's parents are subject to liability.
(B) No, because the teenager was acting reasonably for a 14-year-old of low intelligence and little driving experience.
(C) Yes, because the teenager was engaging in an adult activity.
(D) Yes, because the teenager was not old enough to obtain a driver's license.

Question 13

A firstborn child was examined as an infant by a doctor who was a specialist in the diagnosis of speech and hearing impairments. Although the doctor should have concluded that the infant was totally deaf due to a hereditary condition, the doctor negligently concluded that the infant's hearing was normal. After the diagnosis, but before they learned that the infant was in fact deaf, the parents conceived a second child who also suffered total deafness due to the hereditary condition.

The parents claim that they would not have conceived the second child had they known of the high probability of the hereditary condition. They have sought the advice of their attorney regarding which negligence action against the doctor is most likely to succeed.

What sort of action against the doctor should the attorney recommend?

(A) A medical malpractice action seeking damages on the second child's behalf for expenses due to his deafness, on the ground that the doctor's negligence caused him to be born deaf.
(B) A wrongful birth action by the parents for expenses they have incurred due to the second child's deafness, on the ground that but for the doctor's negligence, they would not have conceived the second child.
(C) A wrongful life action by the parents for expenses for the entire period of the second child's life, on the ground that but for the doctor's negligence, the second child would not have been born.
(D) A wrongful life action on the second child's behalf for expenses for the entire period of his life, on the ground that but for the doctor's negligence, he would not have been born.

Question 14

A boater, caught in a sudden storm and reasonably fearing that her boat would capsize, drove the boat up to a pier, exited the boat, and tied the boat to the pier. The pier was clearly marked with "NO TRESPASSING" signs. The owner of the pier ran up to the boater and told her that the boat could not remain tied to the pier. The boater offered to pay the owner for the use of the pier. Regardless, over the boater's protest, the owner untied the boat and pushed it away from the pier. The boat was lost at sea.

Is the boater likely to prevail in an action against the owner to recover the value of the boat?

(A) No, because the owner told the boater that she could not tie the boat to the pier.
(B) No, because there was a possibility that the boat would not be damaged by the storm.
(C) Yes, because the boater offered to pay the owner for the use of the pier.
(D) Yes, because the boater was privileged to enter the owner's property to save her boat.

Question 15

Unaware that a lawyer was in the county courthouse library late on a Friday afternoon, when it was unusual for anyone to be using the library, a clerk locked the library door and left. The lawyer found herself locked in when she tried to leave the library at 7 p.m. It was midnight before the lawyer's family could find out where she was and get her out. The lawyer was very annoyed by her detention but was not otherwise harmed by it.

Does the lawyer have a viable claim for false imprisonment against the clerk?

(A) No, because it was unusual for anyone to be using the library late on a Friday afternoon.
(B) No, because the clerk did not intend to confine the lawyer.

(C) Yes, because the clerk should have checked to make sure no one was in the library before the clerk locked the door.

(D) Yes, because the lawyer was aware of being confined.

Question 16

A man tied his dog to a bike rack in front of a store and left the dog there while he went inside to shop. The dog was usually friendly and placid.

A five-year-old child started to tease the dog by pulling gently on its ears and tail. When the man emerged from the store and saw what the child was doing to the dog, he became extremely upset.

Does the man have a viable claim against the child for trespass to chattels?

(A) No, because the child did not injure the dog.

(B) No, because the child was too young to form the requisite intent.

(C) Yes, because the child touched the dog without the man's consent.

(D) Yes, because the child's acts caused the man extreme distress.

Question 17

A mother and her six-year-old child were on a walk when the mother stopped to talk with an elderly neighbor. Because the child resented having his mother's attention diverted by the neighbor, the child angrily threw himself against the neighbor and knocked her to the ground. The neighbor suffered a broken wrist as a result of the fall.

In an action for battery by the neighbor against the child, what is the strongest argument for liability?

(A) The child intended to throw himself against the neighbor.

(B) The child was old enough to appreciate that causing a fall could inflict serious injury.

(C) The child was old enough to appreciate the riskiness of his conduct.

(D) The child was not justified in his anger.

VI. MBE PRACTICE ANALYSIS[4]

Question 1

An assistant to a famous writer surreptitiously observed the writer as the writer typed her private password into her personal computer in order to access her email. On several subsequent occasions in the writer's absence, the assistant read the writer's email messages and printed out selections from them.

The assistant later quit his job and earned a considerable amount of money by leaking information to the media that he had learned from reading the writer's email messages. All of the information published about the writer as a result of the assistant's conduct was true and concerned matters of public interest.

The writer's secretary had seen the assistant reading the writer's emails and printing out selections, and she has told the writer what she saw. The writer now

---

4. *Id.*

wishes to sue the assistant for damages. At trial, the writer can show that the media leaks could have come only from someone reading her email on her personal computer.

Can the writer recover damages from the assistant?

(A) No, because the assistant was an invitee on the premises.
Incorrect. The assistant exceeded the scope of any invitation, whether through his employment as an assistant or through the invitation to work on the premises. The writer did not leave the emails exposed so that others might see them. An invitation to enter premises does not normally include permission to access personal email, especially when the email is password-protected.

(B) No, because the published information resulting from the assistant's conduct was true and concerned matters of public interest.
Incorrect. Truth is a common law defense to defamation but not to invasion of privacy. In some circumstances, the First Amendment or a common law defense based on the public interest in the material disclosed can provide a defense to an action for disclosure of private matters. However, even if these defenses were applicable to the disclosure aspect of this case, they would not provide a defense to the privacy action based on intrusion. News-gathering does not provide general immunity from tort law.

(C) Yes, because the assistant invaded the writer's privacy.
Correct. By accessing the writer's email, the assistant was intruding upon her privacy. "Intrusion upon seclusion" is one category of the tort of invasion of privacy that is recognized in many states. The assistant did not have permission to access the emails, and the writer did not leave the emails exposed so that others might see them.

(D) Yes, because the published information resulting from the assistant's conduct constituted publication of private facts concerning the writer.
Incorrect. The appropriate privacy action here would be for "intrusion" rather than for "public disclosure of embarrassing private facts." Publication is irrelevant to whether a cause of action for intrusion has been established. By accessing the writer's email, the assistant was intruding upon her privacy. "Intrusion upon seclusion" is one category of the tort of invasion of privacy that is recognized in many states. The assistant did not have permission to access the emails, and the writer did not leave the emails exposed so that others might see them.

Question 2

A man sued his neighbor for defamation based on the following facts:

The neighbor told a friend that the man had set fire to a house in the neighborhood. The friend, who knew the man well, did not believe the neighbor's allegation, which was in fact false. The friend told the man about the neighbor's allegation. The man was very upset by the allegation, but neither the man nor the neighbor nor the friend communicated the allegation to anyone else.

Should the man prevail in his lawsuit?

(A) No, because the friend did not believe what the neighbor had said.
Incorrect. A successful defamation action does not depend on whether a third party actually believed the defamatory statement. It is enough that the defamatory statement was communicated to a third party.

(B) No, because the man cannot prove that he suffered pecuniary loss.
Incorrect. The statement was spoken rather than written, so the rules of slander apply. Often an action in slander requires that pecuniary loss be shown, but there is no such requirement where the statement accuses the plaintiff of engaging in serious criminal conduct. Arson is a crime of moral turpitude, so the neighbor's statement falls within the exception.

(C) Yes, because the man was very upset at hearing what the neighbor had said.
Incorrect. Proof of emotional distress is not required to establish a cause of action for defamation, whether the action is in libel or slander. The man should prevail, but it is because the defamatory statement was communicated to a third party. Here, the statement was spoken rather than written, so the rules of slander apply. Often an action in slander requires that pecuniary loss be shown, but there is no such requirement where the statement accuses the plaintiff of engaging in serious criminal conduct. Arson is a crime of moral turpitude, so the neighbor's statement falls within the exception, and special harm need not be shown.

(D) Yes, because the neighbor communicated to the friend the false accusation that the man had committed a serious crime.
Correct. The core of a defamation action is the communication of a defamatory statement about the plaintiff to a third party. Here, the statement was spoken rather than written, so the rules of slander apply. Often an action in slander requires that pecuniary loss be shown, but there is no such requirement where the statement accuses the plaintiff of engaging in serious criminal conduct. Arson is a crime of moral turpitude, so the neighbor's statement falls within the exception, and special harm need not be shown.

Question 3

A manufacturing plant emitted a faint noise even though the owner had installed state-of-the-art sound dampeners. The plant operated only on weekdays and only during daylight hours. A homeowner who lived near the plant worked a night shift and could not sleep when he arrived home because of the noise from the plant. The other residents in the area did not notice the noise.

Does the homeowner have a viable nuisance claim against the owner of the plant?

(A) No, because the homeowner is unusually sensitive to noise during the day.
Correct. A landowner is liable for nuisance only when his invasion of another's use and enjoyment is both substantial and unreasonable. Under the norms of the area, the plant owner is not imposing an unreasonable degree of noise upon his neighbors. An unusually noise-sensitive neighbor will not be permitted to block the plant owner's use of his own land.

(B) No, because the plant operates only during the day.
Incorrect. If the noise were too loud given the normal expectations of residents in the area, it could still constitute a nuisance even if limited to daylight hours. The homeowner does not have a valid nuisance claim, but it is because he is unusually sensitive to noise during the day.

(C) Yes, because the noise is heard beyond the boundaries of the plant.
Incorrect. Recovery in nuisance requires evidence of substantial and unreasonable interference with the plaintiff's use and enjoyment of his own land. Merely showing

that a noise can be heard beyond the boundaries of the defendant's land is not enough to establish a nuisance, especially when the noise can be heard only by an unusually noise-sensitive person.

(D) Yes, because the operation of the plant interferes with the homeowner's quiet use and enjoyment of his property.
Incorrect. It is not enough to demonstrate interference with quiet use and enjoyment. The interference also must be shown to be both substantial and unreasonable. The noise emitted by the plant interferes only with one unusually noise-sensitive neighbor, so it is unlikely to be found to be unreasonable.

Question 4

Toxic materials being transported by truck from a manufacturer's plant to a warehouse leaked from the truck onto the street a few miles from the plant. A driver lost control of his car when he hit the puddle of spilled toxic materials on the street, and he was injured when his car hit a stop sign.

In an action for damages by the driver against the manufacturer based on strict liability, is the driver likely to prevail?

(A) No, because the driver's loss of control was an intervening cause.
Incorrect. The driver's loss of control was not intentional, nor was it either unforeseeable or unusual. For that reason, it should raise no proximate cause problem.

(B) No, because the driver's injury did not result from the toxicity of the materials.
Correct. Strict liability in this situation would be based on the abnormally dangerous nature of the toxic materials. But a successful strict liability action requires that the risk that materializes be the same risk that led courts to label the activity "abnormally dangerous" in the first place. Here, the toxicity of the materials did not contribute to the driver's injury, so his only cause of action would be in negligence.

(C) Yes, because the manufacturer is strictly liable for leaks of its toxic materials.
Incorrect. Strict liability in this situation would be based on the abnormally dangerous nature of the toxic materials. But a successful strict liability action requires that the risk that materializes be the same risk that led courts to label the activity "abnormally dangerous" in the first place. Here, the toxicity of the materials did not contribute to the driver's injury, so his only cause of action would be in negligence.

(D) Yes, because the leak occurred near the manufacturer's plant.
Incorrect. The manufacturer would be strictly liable for injuries caused by its toxic materials regardless of where the leak occurred, so long as the manufacturer could be said to be responsible for the leak. However, in this situation the toxicity of the materials did not contribute to the driver's injury, so his only cause of action would be in negligence.

Question 5

A man and his friend, who were both adults, went to a party. The man and the friend had many drinks at the party and became legally intoxicated. They decided to play a game of chance called "Russian roulette" using a gun loaded with one bullet. As part of the game, the man pointed the gun at the friend and, on her command, pulled the trigger. The man shot the friend in the shoulder.

The friend has brought a negligence action against the man. Traditional defenses based on plaintiff's conduct apply. What is likely to be the dispositive issue in this case?

(A) Whether the game constituted a joint venture.

Incorrect. The fact that the man and the friend might have been engaged in a joint venture would be relevant if the action were being brought by a third party who was not part of the venture but who had been injured as a consequence of their activities. It is irrelevant to a suit among participants in a joint venture unless it indicates an assumption of risk.

(B) Whether the friend could validly consent to the game.

Incorrect. It is likely that consent to this activity would be routinely found to be against public policy, although the consequences of such a determination would vary from state to state. But consent is a defense more appropriately raised in an intentional tort case, not a case for negligence. There is no indication that the friend consented to any negligence, and in any case she was too intoxicated to give a valid consent.

(C) Whether the friend was also negligent.

Correct. Contributory negligence is an appropriate defense to a negligence action, and here both parties seem to have been acting unreasonably in exactly the same way. Whether the argument is put in the form of the friend's carelessness in engaging in the activity or in her unreasonable assumption of risk, many states would now evaluate the defense under comparative negligence principles.

(D) Whether the man was legally intoxicated when he began playing the game.

Incorrect. The man's intoxication would not insulate him from liability to those he injured while in that state. He would still be held to the "reasonably prudent person" standard.

Question 6

A woman signed up for a bowling class. Before allowing the woman to bowl, the instructor required her to sign a waiver explicitly stating that she assumed all risk of injuries that she might suffer in connection with the class, including injuries due to negligence or any other fault. After she signed the waiver, the woman was injured when the instructor negligently dropped a bowling ball on the woman's foot.

The woman brought a negligence action against the instructor. The instructor has filed a motion for summary judgment based on the waiver.

What is the woman's best argument in opposition to the instructor's motion?

(A) Bowling is an inherently dangerous activity.

Incorrect. Bowling is not inherently dangerous; virtually no one is seriously injured while bowling. Even if bowling were inherently dangerous, that characterization would support an argument for permitting recreational participants who appreciate the risks of the activity to assume the risks by signing a waiver rather than constituting a reason for ignoring the waiver.

(B) In circumstances like these, it is against public policy to enforce agreements that insulate people from the consequences of their own negligence.

Correct. Waivers are most easily justified when an activity poses inherent risks that are familiar to the participants and cannot be entirely eliminated without removing the pleasure from the activity. The risk that materialized here is not inherent to bowling but could arise whenever someone is careless while holding a heavy object. A court might find that it is against public policy to permit individuals or businesses to insulate themselves from the deterrent incentives provided by the threat of negligence liability. For that reason, the court might find that the waiver did not present the woman with a fair choice and could hold the waiver ineffective.

(C) It was unreasonable to require the woman to sign the waiver before she was allowed to bowl.

Incorrect. Although the court might find that the waiver did not present the woman with a fair choice and therefore hold the waiver to be no bar when the harm was due to the instructor's negligence, asking the woman to sign the waiver was not in itself negligent or unreasonable. For example, the waiver might have barred recovery against the instructor if the woman were injured by the negligence of another class participant, or the court might have decided that the waiver was not inconsistent with public policy given the recreational nature of the activity.

(D) When she signed the form, the woman could not foresee that the instructor would drop a bowling ball on her foot.

Incorrect. Pre-injury waivers are often enforced despite the fact that the precise injury that materializes is virtually never foreseen with a high level of specificity at the time of the signing of the waiver. The problem here is that the risk that materialized was not inherent to the enjoyment of bowling.

Question 7

A pedestrian was crossing a street in a crosswalk when a woman walking just ahead of him was hit by a truck. The pedestrian, who had jumped out of the way of the truck, administered CPR to the woman, who was a stranger. The woman bled profusely, and the pedestrian was covered in blood. The woman died in the ambulance on the way to the hospital. The pedestrian became very depressed immediately after the incident and developed physical symptoms as a result of his emotional distress.

The pedestrian has brought an action against the driver of the truck for negligent infliction of emotional distress. In her defense, the driver asserts that she should not be held liable, because the pedestrian's emotional distress and resulting physical symptoms are not compensable.

What is the strongest argument that the pedestrian can make in response to the driver's defense?

(A) The pedestrian saw the driver hit the woman.

Incorrect. Most states allow plaintiffs to recover damages for the emotional distress of seeing another person injured or killed by a negligent driver, but they usually require that there be a close relationship between the plaintiff and the injured person before recovery is allowed.

(B) The pedestrian was acting as a Good Samaritan.

Incorrect. Normally, the fact that someone chooses to come to the aid of another neither insulates that person from liability for his or her own negligence nor provides that person with a cause of action for the pure emotional distress suffered as a consequence of providing the aid.

(C) The pedestrian was covered in the woman's blood and developed physical symptoms as a result of his emotional distress.

Incorrect. The negligent driver did not herself touch or impact the pedestrian, so the fact that the pedestrian became covered in blood and ultimately suffered physical symptoms as a result of emotional distress is not alone sufficient to support a claim for damages.

(D) The pedestrian was in the zone of danger.
Correct. Because the pedestrian was in the path of the truck, he was under a direct physical threat from the driver's negligence. He could recover for the emotional distress that he suffered as a result of his fear for his own safety, and many courts would also allow him to recover for all other emotional distress that he suffered in connection with the event.

Question 8

Upon the recommendation of her child's pediatrician, a mother purchased a vaporizer for her child, who had been suffering from respiratory congestion. The vaporizer consisted of a gallon-size glass jar, which held water to be heated until it became steam, and a metal heating unit into which the jar fit. The jar was covered by a plastic cap with an opening to allow the steam to escape. At the time the vaporizer was manufactured and sold, there was no safer alternative design.

The booklet that accompanied the vaporizer read: "This product is safe, spill-proof, and practically foolproof. It shuts off automatically when the water is gone." The booklet had a picture of a vaporizer sending steam over a baby's crib.

The mother used the vaporizer whenever the child was suffering from congestion. She placed the vaporizer on the floor near the child's bed.

One night, the child got out of bed to get a drink of water and tripped over the cord of the vaporizer as she crossed the room. The top of the vaporizer separated from the base, and boiling water from the jar spilled on the child when the vaporizer tipped over. The child suffered serious burns as a consequence.

The child's representative brought an action for damages against the manufacturer of the vaporizer. The manufacturer moved to dismiss after the representative presented the evidence above.

Should the manufacturer's motion be granted?

(A) No, because a jury could find that the manufacturer expressly represented that the vaporizer was spill proof.
Correct. The vaporizer may not have been "defective," in that there was no reasonable alternative design, but the express promise by the manufacturer that it was "safe" and "spill-proof," especially when combined with the manufacturer's picture suggesting that it was safe to place the vaporizer near a child's bed, could be the basis of recovery on the ground of misrepresentation.

(B) No, because the vaporizer caused a serious injury to the child.
Incorrect. The fact that a product poses a danger to a user or a bystander will not support the manufacturer's liability in the absence of negligence, defect, or misrepresentation. The manufacturer's motion should not be granted, but it is because the express promise by the manufacturer that the vaporizer was "safe" and "spill-proof," especially when combined with the manufacturer's picture suggesting that it was safe to place the vaporizer near a child's bed, could be the basis of recovery on the ground of misrepresentation.

(C) Yes, because it should have been obvious to the mother that the water in the jar would become boiling hot.

Incorrect. The mother could be found to have reasonably relied upon the manufacturer's express promise that the vaporizer was "safe" and "spill-proof," especially when those words were combined with the manufacturer's picture suggesting that it was safe to place the vaporizer near a child's bed. The mother could have believed that the boiling water posed no danger if it could not be spilled. She would have an action against the manufacturer for misrepresentation.

(D) Yes, because there was no safer alternative design.

Incorrect. The fact finder may conclude that the vaporizer could not be found to be "defective" because there was no reasonable alternative design, but the manufacturer's express promise that the vaporizer was "safe" and "spill-proof," combined with the manufacturer's picture suggesting that it was safe to place the vaporizer near a child's bed, could still be the basis of recovery on the ground of misrepresentation.

Question 9

A man was admitted to a hospital after complaining of persistent severe headaches. While he was there, hospital staff failed to diagnose his condition, and he was discharged. Two days later, the man died of a massive brain hemorrhage due to a congenital defect in an artery.

The man's wife has brought a wrongful death action against the hospital. The wife offers expert testimony that the man would have had a "reasonable chance" (not greater than 50%) of surviving the hemorrhage if he had been given appropriate medical care at the hospital.

In what type of jurisdiction would the wife's suit most likely be successful?

(A) A jurisdiction that applies traditional common law rules concerning burden of proof.

Incorrect. If traditional common law rules concerning burden of proof were applied, the wife would be required to prove that reasonable action on the part of the hospital (presumably a correct diagnosis) would, more likely than not, have led to the man's survival. Here, however, the wife cannot establish that the chances of the man's survival would have been greater than 50% even if he had been given appropriate medical care. Therefore, the wife could not carry her burden of proof on the issue of cause in fact in such a jurisdiction.

(B) A jurisdiction that allows recovery based on strict liability.

Incorrect. Cause in fact is a necessary element of a plaintiff's case in strict liability as well as in negligence. Under either theory, the wife must establish that reasonable action on the part of the hospital (presumably a correct diagnosis) would, more likely than not, have led to the man's survival. Here, however, the wife cannot establish that the chances of the man's survival were greater than 50% even if he had been given appropriate medical care. Therefore, the wife could not carry her burden of proof on the issue of cause in fact in such a jurisdiction.

(C) A jurisdiction that allows recovery for the loss of the chance of survival.

Correct. Jurisdictions that allow recovery for the loss of the chance of survival have created an exception to the traditional common law rules for establishing cause in fact. Under the traditional rules, the wife would be required to prove that reasonable action on the part of the hospital (presumably a correct diagnosis) would, more likely than not, have led to the man's survival. Here, the wife cannot establish that the chances of the man's survival would have been greater than 50% even if he had been given appropriate medical care. A jurisdiction that allows recovery for loss of the chance of survival, however, would allow the wife to recover for the reduction in her husband's chance of surviving that was caused by the failure to properly diagnose.

(D) A jurisdiction that recognizes loss of spousal consortium.
Incorrect. Cause in fact is a necessary element of a plaintiff's case for loss of spousal consortium, as well as in cases in which a plaintiff is suing for personal injury. In a loss of consortium action, the wife must establish that the hospital's negligence was the cause of her husband's death. Traditional rules of proof regarding causation would require that the wife prove that reasonable action on the part of the hospital (presumably a correct diagnosis) would, more likely than not, have led to her husband's survival. Here, the wife cannot establish that the chances of her husband's survival would have been greater than 50% even if he had been given appropriate medical care. Therefore, the wife could not carry her burden of proof on the issue of cause in fact in such a jurisdiction and she could not recover for loss of spousal consortium.

Question 10

A mother purchased an expensive television from an appliance store for her adult son. Two years after the purchase, a fire started in the son's living room in the middle of the night. The fire department concluded that the fire had started in the television. No other facts are known.

The son sued the appliance store for negligence. The store has moved for summary judgment. Should the court grant the store's motion?

(A) No, because televisions do not catch fire in the absence of negligence.
Incorrect. Even if it were true that televisions do not catch fire in the absence of negligence, the fact that this television did is insufficient to establish that the store acted negligently. This is not an appropriate case for res ipsa loquitur, because the manufacturer, rather than the store, may have been negligent or the negligence may have occurred after the sale (for example, during a repair or while the television was being used by the son). Because the son cannot establish the store's negligence, the court should grant the store's motion.

(B) No, because the store sold the television.
Incorrect. The son sued the store for negligence, not for strict liability. To recover on a negligence claim, the son must establish that the store itself was negligent. If the son had sued under strict liability, he would have had to establish that the television was defective at the time it was sold to his mother. Because the son cannot establish the store's negligence, the court should grant the store's motion.

(C) Yes, because the son is not in privity with the store.
Incorrect. A lack of privity is not a barrier to negligence claims based on malfunctioning products. Anyone foreseeably put at risk by a defective product and actually injured by the product's defective condition can sue for negligence. The court should grant the store's motion, but it is because the son cannot establish that the store was the negligent actor.

(D) Yes, because there is no evidence of negligence on the part of the store.
Correct. The son is suing in negligence, not in strict liability. To make out a prima facie case in negligence, the son must introduce evidence that the store was negligent.

However, the son has not pointed to any negligent action or omission by the store. This is not an appropriate case for res ipsa loquitur, because the manufacturer, rather than the store, may have been negligent or the negligence may have occurred after the sale (for example, during a repair or while the television was being used by the son).

Question 11

A shopper was riding on an up escalator in a department store when the escalator stopped abruptly. The shopper lost her balance and fell down the escalator steps, sustaining injuries. Although the escalator had been regularly maintained by an independent contractor, the store's obligation to provide safe conditions for its invitees was nondelegable. The shopper has brought an action against the store for damages, and the above facts are the only facts in evidence.

The store has moved for a directed verdict. Should the court grant the motion?

(A) No, because the finder of fact could infer that the escalator malfunction was due to negligence.

Correct. There is enough evidence here to support an inference of negligence on the part of the store. A jury could find that the malfunction was due to the negligent installation, maintenance, or operation of the escalator; the store would be responsible for all these possible causes under the nondelegable duty doctrine.

(B) No, because the store is strictly liable for the shopper's injuries.

Incorrect. Landowners and occupiers are not strictly liable even for injuries to their business invitees. The court should not grant the motion, but it is because the fact finder could infer negligence on the part of the store.

(C) Yes, because an independent contractor maintained the escalator.

Incorrect. Even if the malfunction were due to the negligence of the independent contractor, the store would also be responsible under the nondelegable duty doctrine. These facts illustrate a common situation in which that doctrine is applied: the defendant owns a building and invites the public to enter the building for the defendant's financial benefit. There is enough evidence here to support an inference of negligence on the part of the store. A jury could find that the malfunction was due to the negligent installation, maintenance, or operation of the escalator; the store would be responsible for all these possible causes under the nondelegable duty doctrine.

(D) Yes, because the shopper has not produced evidence of negligence.

Incorrect. There is enough evidence here to support an inference of negligence on the part of the store. A jury could find that the malfunction was due to the negligent installation, maintenance, or operation of the escalator; the store would be responsible for all these possible causes under the nondelegable duty doctrine.

Question 12

A 14-year-old teenager of low intelligence received her parents' permission to drive their car. She had had very little experience driving a car and did not have a driver's license. Although she did the best she could, she lost control of the car and hit a pedestrian.

The pedestrian has brought a negligence action against the teenager. Is the pedestrian likely to prevail?

(A) No, because only the teenager's parents are subject to liability.

Incorrect. The parents and the teenager may both be liable. The teenager was engaging in a dangerous adult activity, so she will be held to the adult standard of care and can be sued for the injuries caused by her negligent driving.

(B) No, because the teenager was acting reasonably for a 14-year-old of low intelligence and little driving experience.

Incorrect. The teenager was engaging in a dangerous adult activity, so she will be held to the adult standard of care. No adjustment will be made to that standard to reflect her low intelligence and lack of experience. Her lack of intelligence and her inexperience put others at risk, and she will be held to the standard of a reasonably prudent driver even if she is not capable of reasonable prudence.

(C) Yes, because the teenager was engaging in an adult activity.

Correct. The teenager was engaging in a dangerous adult activity, so she will be held to the adult standard of care. No adjustment will be made to that standard to reflect her low intelligence and lack of experience. Her lack of intelligence and her inexperience put others at risk, and she will be held to the standard of a reasonably prudent driver even if she is not capable of reasonable prudence.

(D) Yes, because the teenager was not old enough to obtain a driver's license.

Incorrect. In the absence of a statute setting a different standard, the teenager's failure to obtain a license ordinarily would not be evidence that she was actually negligent at the time of the accident. The plaintiff would have to prove actual negligence, which should be easy given that the teenager lost control of the car and given the fact that the teenager will be held to an adult standard of care because she was engaging in an adult activity.

Question 13

A firstborn child was examined as an infant by a doctor who was a specialist in the diagnosis of speech and hearing impairments. Although the doctor should have concluded that the infant was totally deaf due to a hereditary condition, the doctor negligently concluded that the infant's hearing was normal. After the diagnosis, but before they learned that the infant was in fact deaf, the parents conceived a second child who also suffered total deafness due to the hereditary condition.

The parents claim that they would not have conceived the second child had they known of the high probability of the hereditary condition. They have sought the advice of their attorney regarding which negligence action against the doctor is most likely to succeed.

What sort of action against the doctor should the attorney recommend?

(A) A medical malpractice action seeking damages on the second child's behalf for expenses due to his deafness, on the ground that the doctor's negligence caused him to be born deaf.

Incorrect. The parents assert that they would not have conceived a second child had the doctor properly diagnosed the first child's deafness. Under that theory, the second child would never have been born had the doctor acted properly. Most courts are unwilling to say that it is worse to be born deaf than to never be born at all. Where that approach is taken, the second child has suffered no injury under this theory.

(B) A wrongful birth action by the parents for expenses they have incurred due to the second child's deafness, on the ground that but for the doctor's negligence, they would not have conceived the second child.

Correct. This cause of action will be permitted in many states. The parents sought an accurate assessment of their first child, which the doctor failed to provide. Unaware of the hereditary condition, the parents conceived a second child and incurred unexpected expenses that could have been avoided had the doctor acted properly.

(C) A wrongful life action by the parents for expenses for the entire period of the second child's life, on the ground that but for the doctor's negligence, the second child would not have been born.

Incorrect. A wrongful life action would be brought by a child who would not have been born. An action by the parents based on advice that would have avoided a conception of a child is a wrongful birth action. Also, most courts would not permit the parents to recover all of the expenses for the second child's life even in a proper action, but only those additional expenses attributable to the child's disability.

(D) A wrongful life action on the second child's behalf for expenses for the entire period of his life, on the ground that but for the doctor's negligence, he would not have been born.

Incorrect. Most states reject this claim, and of the few states that do permit it, some would limit recovery to the special damages attributable to the disability. The parents' wrongful birth action is more likely to be successful in almost all jurisdictions.

Question 14

A boater, caught in a sudden storm and reasonably fearing that her boat would capsize, drove the boat up to a pier, exited the boat, and tied the boat to the pier. The pier was clearly marked with "NO TRESPASSING" signs. The owner of the pier ran up to the boater and told her that the boat could not remain tied to the pier. The boater offered to pay the owner for the use of the pier. Regardless, over the boater's protest, the owner untied the boat and pushed it away from the pier. The boat was lost at sea.

Is the boater likely to prevail in an action against the owner to recover the value of the boat?

(A) No, because the owner told the boater that she could not tie the boat to the pier.

Incorrect. The boater was privileged to trespass on the owner's property under the doctrine of private necessity, because the boater's property was at risk. Because the boater's intrusion onto the pier was privileged, the owner had no right to exclude her or her boat from the pier. In telling the boater that she could not tie the boat to the pier, the owner was asserting a right that he did not possess. When the owner untied the boat, he committed an unprivileged trespass upon the boater's property, so the owner must pay for the loss of the boat.

(B) No, because there was a possibility that the boat would not be damaged by the storm.

Incorrect. The boater was privileged to trespass on the owner's property under the doctrine of private necessity, because her property was at risk. In order to establish that privilege, the boater need not establish that harm to the boat was inevitable, but only that her actions were reasonable given the circumstances. Because the boater's intrusion onto the pier was privileged, the owner had no right to exclude her or her boat from the pier. When the owner untied the boat, he committed an unprivileged trespass upon the boater's property, so the owner must pay for the loss of the boat.

(C) Yes, because the boater offered to pay the owner for the use of the pier.

Incorrect. The boater is likely to prevail, but it is because the boater was privileged to trespass on the owner's property under the doctrine of private necessity. Because the boater's property was at risk, her intrusion onto the pier was privileged, and the owner had no right to exclude her or her boat from the pier. Whether or not the boater offered to pay the owner is irrelevant to the privilege of private necessity. When the owner untied the boat, he committed an unprivileged trespass upon the boater's property, so the owner must pay for the loss of the boat.

(D) Yes, because the boater was privileged to enter the owner's property to save her boat.

Correct. The boater was privileged to trespass on the owner's property under the doctrine of private necessity, because the boater's property was at risk. Because the boater's intrusion onto the pier was privileged, the owner had no right to exclude her or her boat from the pier. When the owner untied the boat, he committed an unprivileged trespass upon the boater's property, so the owner must pay for the loss of the boat.

Question 15

Unaware that a lawyer was in the county courthouse library late on a Friday afternoon, when it was unusual for anyone to be using the library, a clerk locked the library door and left. The lawyer found herself locked in when she tried to leave the library at 7 p.m. It was midnight before the lawyer's family could find out where she was and get her out. The lawyer was very annoyed by her detention but was not otherwise harmed by it.

Does the lawyer have a viable claim for false imprisonment against the clerk?

(A) No, because it was unusual for anyone to be using the library late on a Friday afternoon.

Incorrect. The fact that it was unusual for anyone to be using the library at the time the clerk locked the door might lead a fact finder to conclude that the clerk was not negligent in failing to detect the lawyer. However, because false imprisonment is an intentional tort, the reasonableness of the clerk's conduct is irrelevant. If the clerk had intended to lock the lawyer in the library, the lawyer would have a claim for false imprisonment even if it was unusual for anyone to be using the library at the time. Under these facts, however, the clerk did not intend to lock the lawyer in the library, so the lawyer does not have a viable claim for false imprisonment.

(B) No, because the clerk did not intend to confine the lawyer.

Correct. Intent to confine the claimant (or to commit some other intentional tort) is essential to establishing liability for false imprisonment. There is no evidence that the clerk had such an intent.

(C) Yes, because the clerk should have checked to make sure no one was in the library before the clerk locked the door.

Incorrect. Whether a reasonable person in the clerk's position would have checked before locking the door is irrelevant to a claim for false imprisonment. False imprisonment is an intentional tort requiring intent to confine the claimant (or to commit some other intentional tort). What a reasonable person would have done is relevant to a negligence claim, but not to a false imprisonment claim.

(D) Yes, because the lawyer was aware of being confined.
Incorrect. In cases involving false imprisonment, courts often hold that the plaintiff must have been aware of the confinement at the time of the imprisonment or else must have sustained actual harm. It is also essential, however, that the defendant have had an intent to confine the plaintiff (or to commit some other intentional tort). If the clerk had had such an intent, the lawyer's awareness that she was confined might have completed the prima facie case, but the clerk had no such intent.

Question 16

A man tied his dog to a bike rack in front of a store and left the dog there while he went inside to shop. The dog was usually friendly and placid.

A five-year-old child started to tease the dog by pulling gently on its ears and tail. When the man emerged from the store and saw what the child was doing to the dog, he became extremely upset.

Does the man have a viable claim against the child for trespass to chattels?

(A) No, because the child did not injure the dog.
Correct. Trespass to chattels requires that the plaintiff show actual harm to or deprivation of the use of the chattel for a substantial time. Here the child's acts caused emotional distress to the man, but the acts did not result in harm to the man's material interest in the dog.

(B) No, because the child was too young to form the requisite intent.
Incorrect. Even a small child can commit an intentional tort, such as trespass to chattels, so long as the child is old enough to form an intent to touch. But trespass to chattels requires that the plaintiff show actual harm to or deprivation of the use of the chattel for a substantial time. Here the child's acts caused emotional distress to the man, but the acts did not result in harm to the man's material interest in the dog.

(C) Yes, because the child touched the dog without the man's consent.
Incorrect. Trespass to chattels requires that the plaintiff show actual harm to or deprivation of the use of the chattel for a substantial time. Here the child's acts caused emotional distress to the man (because they were without his consent), but the acts did not result in harm to the man's material interest in the dog.

(D) Yes, because the child's acts caused the man extreme distress.
Incorrect. Trespass to chattels requires that the plaintiff show actual harm to or deprivation of the use of the chattel for a substantial time. Here the child's acts caused emotional distress to the man, but the acts did not result in harm to the man's material interest in the dog.

Question 17

A mother and her six-year-old child were on a walk when the mother stopped to talk with an elderly neighbor. Because the child resented having his mother's attention diverted by the neighbor, the child angrily threw himself against the neighbor and knocked her to the ground. The neighbor suffered a broken wrist as a result of the fall.

In an action for battery by the neighbor against the child, what is the strongest argument for liability?

(A) The child intended to throw himself against the neighbor.

Correct. To recover on a claim for battery, it is sufficient for the neighbor to show that the child intended to touch the neighbor in a way that would be considered harmful or offensive, even though the child may have been too young to understand that what he was doing was wrong or to appreciate that the neighbor might be unusually vulnerable to injury.

(B) The child was old enough to appreciate that causing a fall could inflict serious injury.

Incorrect. Proof of intent to cause injury or knowledge that injury may result is not necessary to recover on a claim of battery. Instead, it is sufficient that the child intended to touch the neighbor in a way that would be considered harmful or offensive, even though the child may have been too young to understand that what he was doing was wrong or to appreciate that the neighbor might be unusually vulnerable to injury.

(C) The child was old enough to appreciate the riskiness of his conduct.

Incorrect. Whether the child was old enough to appreciate the riskiness of his conduct is irrelevant to the neighbor's battery claim. It is sufficient that the child intended to touch the neighbor in a way that would be considered harmful or offensive, even though the child may have been too young to understand that what he was doing was wrong. Whether a child is old enough to appreciate a given risk would be relevant in a negligence action, but not in an action for battery.

(D) The child was not justified in his anger.

Incorrect. It is sufficient that the child intended to touch the neighbor in a way that would be considered harmful or offensive, whether or not the child was justifiably angry. The motive for a defendant's actions may be relevant to an affirmative defense in some situations, but even justified anger is not a defense to an intentional tort.

CHAPTER 16

Mapping Business Topics

I. AGENCY/PARTNERSHIP

Although the NCBE considers Agency and Partnership one topic, consider them as separate topics for your preparation. Usually, your question will center on one or the other.

A. Agency

1. Mind Map
Your mind map for Agency consists of two questions:

* Who is suing whom?
* Tort or Contract?

Asking just those two questions covers almost all of Agency. Agency involves only three types of people—an agent, a principal, and a third party. By first identifying the parties involved, you immediately narrow the possible rules. Is it the principal suing the agent? Is it a third party suing the principal? Is it the third party suing the agent? What frequently happens in agency essay questions is that the issues look at different setups. The first issue may be third party v. principal while the second issue is principal v. agent. Identifying the parties starts your analysis on the correct path.

The second question is whether the party is being sued in tort or contract. That differentiation then helps you lay out the specific rules that apply to each conflict.

For example, in order to hold a principal liable to a third party for an agent's actions in contract, the agent must have authority to enter the agreement. That authority comes from actual authority, apparent authority, or ratification. And, voilá! The rules are quickly recalled and off you go! If instead the answers to the two questions set up whether a principal is liable to a third party for an agent's tort, your analysis would be based on *respondeat superior* or the rules for liability for an independent contractor's tort.

The only two issues not covered with the two-question mind map are determining whether the **agency relationship** exists in the first place and determining whether the servant is an **independent contractor or an employee**. The employer

First Question to Ask

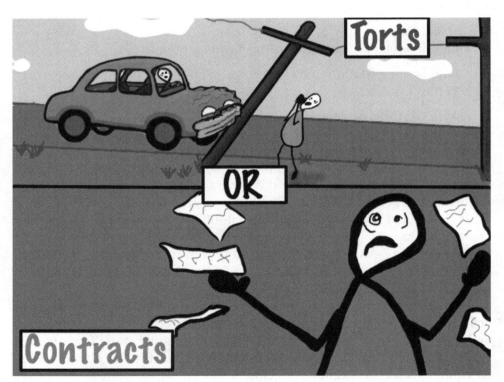

Second Question to Ask

versus independent contractor distinction is relevant only for determining tort liability. The rules for both issues are relatively straightforward:

- Creating an agency relationship: One person, a principal, assents to another person, an agent, to act on the principal's behalf. The agent must also assent to act.
- Independent contractor or employee?

* The employer has no right to control the details of the performance of the independent contractor. Factors considered include:
  * Distinct occupation or business
  * Work customarily done under a principal's supervision
  * Skill required in the agent's occupation
  * Who supplies the tools and place of performance
  * Length of time the agent is engaged by the principal
  * Whether agent is paid by the job or by the hour
  * Intent of the parties
  * Whether the principal is in business
* The employer has the right to control the details of the conduct of its employee as to the result and the means to the result.

Tort Liability
* Third party v. principal:
  * Agent is **employee**.
    * ***Respondeat superior:*** Doctrine imposes vicarious liability upon a principal for the torts his agent commits in the **scope of employment**.
      * Agent performs tasks assigned by the employer or engages in a course of conduct subject to employer's control.
      * Serves employer's purposes.
      * Employer is not liable if the employee substantially deviates from the authorized route (frolic).
        * Employee can return to the scope of the employment after a frolic.
      * Employer is still liable for slight deviations (detour).
    * Employer's liability is in addition to the agent's liability.
    * Employer and employee are jointly and severally liable.
    * Strict liability doctrine, so no defenses.
  * Agent is **independent contractor**:
    * General rule: No liability.
    * Exceptions:
      * Inherently dangerous activities: nature and circumstances of the work to be performed are such that injury to others will probably result unless precautions are taken.
      * Nondelegable duty.
      * Loaned agent.
      * Negligent selection of contractor.
* Third party v. agent:
  * Individuals are always liable for their own torts.
* Principal v. agent:
  * Agents are liable for breach of their duties to the principal (COLA).
    * Duty of **C**are.
    * Duty of **O**bedience.
    * Duty of **L**oyalty.
      * No self-dealing.
      * May not usurp a business opportunity belonging to the principal.
      * Duty not to compete.
      * No dual agency.
    * Duty to **A**ccount.
* Agent v. principal:
  * Individuals are always liable for their own torts.

Contract Liability

- Third party v. principal:
  - An agent acting within the scope of his **authority** may bind his principal in contract.
- Types of authority:
  - **Actual:** Manifestation of the principal to the agent that the agent acts for the benefit of the principal in a particular way and that the principal agrees to be bound by the agent's actions.
    - Express: Principal directly requests the agent to act.
    - Implied:
      - Authority to accomplish the principal's express request; or
      - Things the agent believes the principal wishes him to do based on his reasonable understanding of the principal's expressed request.
  - **Apparent:** The agent is "cloaked" with authority.
    - Third party reasonably believes the agent has authority to act on behalf of the principal, and
    - Belief is based on the principal's representations made to the third party.
  - **Ratification:** Principal grants retroactive authority for his agent's earlier unauthorized actions.
    - Ratified act must be one that the principal could have authorized at the time of the act.
    - Once ratified, an act has the same effect as if it were originally done with authority.

EXAM TIP
Apparent authority is a favorite of the bar examiners. Always address any cloaking of authority!

In your answer, be sure to address each type of authority—giving the rule for each type of authority and applying each rule to the facts. Do not stop even if you find authority out of the gate. Analyze each type to gather all the low-hanging fruit points. These work best as separate CRACs.

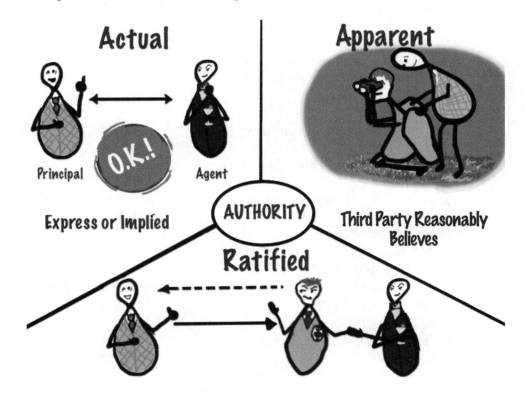

Types of Authority

Contract Liability (cont.)

- Third party v. agent:
  - Disclosed v. undisclosed principal:
    - Fully disclosed principal: Agent is not liable in contract.
    - Undisclosed principal: Agent is personally liable in contract.
    - Partially disclosed principal: Agent is personally liable in contract.
      - When the third party learns the identity of the principal, the third party must elect to go after either the agent or principal, but not both.
  - Breach of warranty of authority: Agent acts beyond her authority on behalf of a principal. Agent is personally liable.
- Principal v. agent: Contract liability based on the terms of their contract.
  - Would be highly unusual to be a test area as examiners would have to give you the contract terms.
- Agent v. principal: Contractual duties owed to agents.
  - Compensate—per the agency contract.
  - Indemnify—for reasonably incurred legal liabilities.

AGENCY CHART			
Is this a principal-agent relationship? Rule:			
	Tort		**Contract**

Third Party v. Principal	Independent Contractor
	• Employer has no right to control performance.
		Employee
		• Employer has right to control performance.
		Factors?
			Authority:
			• Actual
			  • Express
			  • Implied
			• Apparent
			• Ratification
			Same rules if principal seeks to hold a third party to a contract.

	No liability unless: • Inherently dangerous activities • Loaned agents • Nondelegable duty • Negligent selection of contractor	*Respondeat superior:* Scope of employment	
Third Party v. Agent	Individuals are liable for their own torts.		Undisclosed principal or Breach of warranty of authority

Principal v. Agent	• Care
	• Obedience
	• Loyalty
	  • Not to compete
	  • Not to be a dual agent
	• Account
			Terms of their contract
			(Probably never tested as they would have to give you the contract, but tort questions are tested.)

Agent v. Principal	Individuals are liable for their own torts.		Compensate Indemnify Reimburse Cooperate

- Reimburse—for reasonably incurred expenses.
- Cooperate:
  - Principal may not interfere with the agent's performance.
  - Principal must affirmatively aid where reasonably required to do so.

Organizing your memorization materials around the two-question mind map works on either a graphical map or a simple chart. Take this chart and add more detail to the rules.

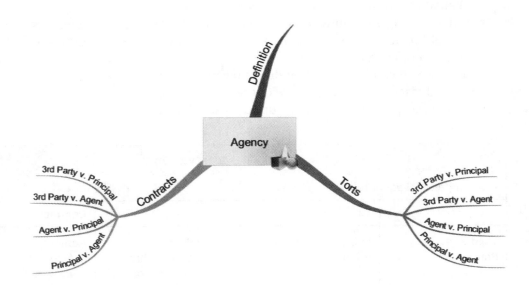

2. Essay Practice Question[1]

Hanson's Fruitcakes (Hanson's) is the largest producer of fruitcakes in the world. The company was founded 150 years ago and uses an original secret recipe closely guarded by the company.

Because of a significant drop in the demand for fruitcakes, Hanson's decided to expand its product line to include other baked goods that will not compete with its fruitcakes.

Because Hanson's has limited experience producing baked goods other than fruitcakes, it decided to hire Taster as a consultant. The contract between Hanson's and Taster provided as follows:

(1) Taster would travel for six months tasting baked goods at "high-end" bakeries. Taster was expressly authorized, on behalf of Hanson's, to buy the recipes of any baked goods he thought Hanson's could produce successfully. Taster was expressly prohibited from committing Hanson's to pay more than $5,000 cash for any one recipe, because market research confirmed that baked-goods recipes typically sold for prices between $3,000 and $6,000.

(2) Hanson's would disclose to Taster the secret recipe for Hanson's fruitcake so that Taster would not inadvertently agree to buy any baked-goods recipes that were substantially similar to the fruitcake. Taster is required to keep Hanson's recipe secret from everyone.

Hanson's president announced the company's plans to expand its product line at the annual baking industry trade show attended by everyone in the baking industry. At the trade show, Hanson's president stated: "Hanson's is breaking new ground in the baking industry by hiring a consultant, Taster. Taster will be entering into contracts to buy recipes from other bakers on Hanson's behalf." Hanson's president did not disclose the precise terms of the Hanson's Taster contract.

Purporting to act on behalf of Hanson's, over the next four months Taster entered into contracts to buy the following recipes:

(1) Boysenberry-granola muffins for $4,000 from Monumental Muffins,
(2) Almond-pecan tarts for $6,000 from Bakers Bonanza, and
(3) Chocolate truffle cake from Parisian Delights in exchange for a copy of Hanson's secret fruitcake recipe.

Purporting to act on behalf of Hanson's, Taster also entered into a contract with Iron cast Enterprises to buy a sophisticated baking oven for $5,000.

Is Hanson's legally bound to any of the four contracts made by Taster? Explain.

---

1. The Multistate Bar Examination ("MBE®") questions, the Multistate Essay Examination ("MEE®") questions, and excerpts from the Multistate Performance Tests ("MPT®") have been reprinted by permission from the NCBE®. Copyright© by the National Conference of Bar Examiners. All rights reserved.

3. Agency Score Sheet

Stated	Implied	
		1. Monumental Muffins' muffin recipe contract
_____	_____	**Conclusion/Issue:** Because Taster had actual authority to enter into the Monumental Muffins' recipe contract, Hanson's is bound.
_____	_____	**Rule:** Under agency law principles,
_____	_____	Agency is a fiduciary relationship.
_____	_____	It arises when a principal manifests assent to an agent that the agent shall act on the principal's behalf.
_____	_____	An agent has actual authority when he takes action designated or implied in the principal's manifestation and the acts necessary or incidental to achieving the principal's objectives.
_____	_____	**Application:** Here,
_____	_____	The contract gave Taster the power and ability to enter into contracts on Hanson's behalf—as long as it was for recipes and did not exceed $5,000.
		Taster contracted to buy a recipe and did not exceed the monetary limit.
_____	_____	**Conclusion:** Therefore,
_____	_____	Hanson's will be bound because Taster had actual authority to enter into this contract.
		2. Bakers Bonanza's tart recipe contract
_____	_____	**Conclusion/Issue:** Hanson's is legally bound to this contract because Taster had apparent authority to enter into it.
_____	_____	**Rule:** An agent has apparent authority when a third party reasonably believes the agent has authority to act on behalf of the principal.
_____	_____	This belief must be traceable to the manifestations of the principal.
_____	_____	Apparent authority can occur with or without actual authority.
_____	_____	**Application:** Here,
_____	_____	Taster did not have the actual authority to enter this contract because the price exceeded the limitations placed on him by Hanson's.
_____	_____	But at the industry trade show, Hanson's president announced that Taster would be buying recipes on behalf of Hanson.
_____	_____	Based on that statement, Bakers Bonanza could reasonably believe that Taster had actual authority.
_____	_____	Moreover, the price fell in the typical price range for these recipes.
_____	_____	**Conclusion:** Therefore,
_____	_____	Taster had apparent authority to enter into the contract and Hanson's is bound.
		3. Parisian Delights' chocolate truffle cake recipe contract
_____	_____	**Conclusion/Issue:** Hanson's is not bound because Taster did not have authority to enter into this contract.
_____	_____	**Rule:** A third party has a duty to make further inquiry if facts suggest that it might be unreasonable for that third party to believe that a purported agent has authority.
_____	_____	**Application:** Here,

continued on next page

Stated	Implied	
_____	_____	Taster's contract with Hanson's does not allow him to exchange Hanson's fruitcake recipe for another recipe.
_____	_____	Also, while baked-goods recipes usually sell within a particular price range, there is no indication that non-cash consideration is a regular practice.
_____	_____	Moreover, Parisian Delights likely would have known that Hanson's fruitcake recipe was secret and that Hanson's did not authorize its disclosure.
_____	_____	Parisian Delights could have determined that Taster lacked the authority simply by asking if Taster had the authority to exchange the recipe.
_____	_____	**Conclusion:** Therefore,
_____	_____	Taster did not have authority and Hanson's will not be bound by this contract.
_____	_____	**4. Contract with Iron cast Enterprises for the oven**
_____	_____	**Conclusion/Issue:** Hanson's is not liable to Iron cast Enterprises because Taster did not have authority to enter this contract.
_____	_____	**Rule:** Certain acts may fall within express grant of authority.
_____	_____	Others, in absence of an express grant, might be within an agent's authority as acts that are necessary or incidental to achieving the objectives of the principal.
_____	_____	**Application:** Here,
_____	_____	Taster does not have actual authority because his contract with Hanson's limits his contracting power to recipes and not ovens.
_____	_____	The purchase of the oven was not an act that was necessary to achieving the objectives of Hanson's.
_____	_____	Taster does not have apparent authority because there is no reason for Iron cast to believe that Taster had the authority to buy the oven.
_____	_____	**Conclusion:** Therefore,
_____	_____	Taster did not have apparent or actual authority and Hanson's will not be bound by this contract.

B. Partnership

1. Mind Map

Think about Partnership as a living entity. It has a beginning, a life in the middle, and an end. Thus, the mind map follows that life:

- Creation
- Working life
- Dissociation/dissolution
- Winding up/termination

Creation. Partnership questions may tell you "Bob and Sam had a valid partnership agreement to . . . ." That one sentence tells you loads. First, it is a partnership question. Second, because it already states there is a valid partnership agreement, you will not have *any* issues regarding **creation**! You can leap frog over this part of your mind map.

Instead, if the problem states that Bob and Sam started a business, you will need to consider both partnership and corporations. The rest of the fact pattern and the call of the question will let you know if the question is partnership or corporations. The facts will lead you down either the partnership path or the corporations path. Corporations' questions will require some facts that address filing Articles of Incorporation or facts that reference the name of the business as including "Inc." If those facts are missing, then it is a partnership question. This type of problem automatically requires you to go through **creation** of a partnership.

First define a partnership: an association of two or more persons to carry on as co-owners a business for profit. Then, address the aspects of general partnership creation. Apply to your facts. You have two possible results. First, the parties agreed to work together on a handshake, shared profits, yet put nothing in writing. That would be a general partnership. Secondly, the parties agreed to work together, shared profits, and put everything in writing. That would also be a general partnership. But then another issue arises. Is this a limited partnership? Address the additional requirements for a limited partnership and apply to your facts.

Reach your conclusion: no partnership, general partnership, or limited partnership:

- **General partnership:** an association of two or more persons to carry on as co-owners a business for profit.
  - No writing required.
  - No statutory formalities required.
  - Types:
    - For a specific undertaking.
    - For a term.
    - At will.
  - Key test: intent of the parties, no matter what it is called.
  - Sharing of profits is *prima facie* evidence of a partnership.
- **Limited partnership:**
  - Types of partners:
    - General partners: manage the business and are personally liable without limitation for partnership obligations.

- Limited partners: contribute capital and share in profits, but take no part in the control or management of the business, and whose liability is limited to their contributions.
- Formation:
  - Filing a certificate of limited partnership with the Secretary of State.
  - Must have at least one general partner and at least one limited partner.

Working life. Once a partnership is created, the business of the partnership begins. This part of your mind map deals with issues such as who can bind the partnership in contract, who receives remuneration, the partnership's liability in torts to third parties, and whether the partnership or the individual partners are liable for any judgment. In addition, a frequent question concerns what happens when a new partner joins the partnership, both in relation to liability for contracts and for torts. Issues within the working life branch include:

- Partners' powers:
  - Every partner is an agent of the partnership for the purpose of its business.
  - Authority:
    - Express.
    - Apparent: based on the nature and course of business.
    - Restrictions: Third party must know about restrictions on authority or the partnership will be bound.
      - Partner who acted without authority may be liable for breach of the partnership agreement.
- Remuneration: Partners are not entitled unless specified in the partnership agreement.
- Liability:

Creating a Partnership

- All partners are jointly and severally liable for all obligations of the partnership.
- Each partner is individually liable for the entire amount of the partnership's obligation.
- Partner is entitled to indemnification by the partnership for any payments he makes on the partnership's behalf.
- Partner may seek contribution from other partners if he pays more than his share of liability.
- Retiring partner remains liable on all obligations incurred before retirement.
- Incoming partner is not personally liable for any partnership obligation incurred prior to her admission as a partner.

Dissociation and Dissolution. Now, one of the partners wants out of the partnership. This triggers the last two parts of the mind map. **Dissociation** refers generally to a partner's separation from the partnership including death, withdrawal, bankruptcy, or expulsion. The partnership is technically still alive at that point as the law wants businesses to continue.

Once a partner wants out, the next question is whether he has a right to dissociate. Generally, a partner always has a right to dissociate. That does not mean, however, that he may not be liable to the partnership for wrongful dissociation.

After a partner dissociates from the partnership, the next issue is whether the partnership is dissolved. Usually on the bar exam, very few partners are involved—sometimes only two. On the exam partnerships tend to be on a hand-shake and thus more frequently dissolve. Thus, the dissociation of a partner inevitably means a race immediately to **dissolution** of the partnership. The partnership continues after dissolution only for the purposes of winding up the business.

Winding up. Every dissolved partnership must go through **winding up** before the partnership is **terminated**. Winding up includes reducing the partnership assets to cash and then distributing that cash to the entitled parties.

There may be an issue as to whether a specific asset is actually partnership property or whether it is the individual partner's property:

- Partnership property:
  - Originally brought in—part of capital of partnership.
    - May contrarily contend in agreement.
  - Subsequently acquired.
  - Purchased with partnership funds.
- Partner's individual property:
  - Intent evidenced that any property originally brought in was not to be partnership property.
  - Partners have a contrary intention from the applicable law.

Once that is decided, the assets are sold and the cash distributed in a specific order:

- Costs of the sale
- Outside creditors
- Inside creditors
- Capital contributions
- Profits

Issues arise when assets are insufficient to cover the partnership's obligations. Partners must contribute the amount necessary to cover liabilities. If a

Key:
1 = Cost of Sale
2 = Outside Creditor
3 = Inside Creditor
4 = Capital
5 = Profit

Winding Up –
Profits

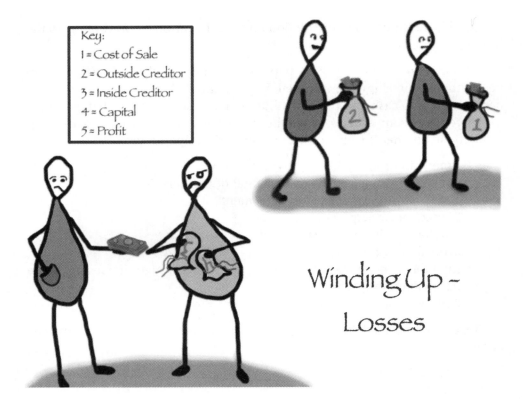

partner fails to contribute, the other partners must make up the difference and then seek contribution from that partner.

Watch for "advances" given by a partner to keep a failing business afloat. These are not capital contributions, but an inside creditor loan. If the cash comes up short and doesn't cover everything, add up the loans and capital contributions. Subtract from the available cash. Then divide the losses equally between the partners. If math is not your strong suit, then describe what

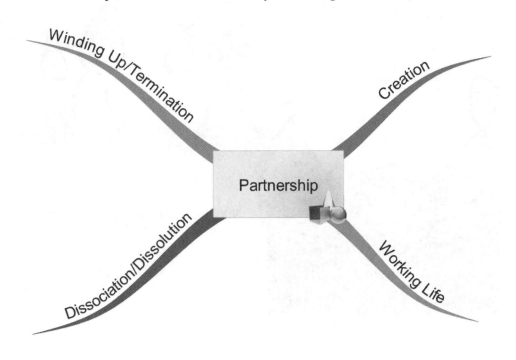

needs to be done and make an attempt. Don't worry if you get the math right. You will get the points for having described the process accurately.

2. Essay Practice Question[2]

Six months ago, Andy, Ben, and Carol executed a document entitled "Metropolitan Limited Partnership Agreement" (the Agreement). Under the terms of the Agreement, Andy, Ben, and Carol were to be "limited partners" in the "Metropolitan Limited Partnership" (MLP). The Agreement provided that each would contribute $500,000 to the venture, which they each did.

The Agreement also provided that Warren would be the "general partner" of MLP, but Warren never signed the Agreement.

The Agreement further provided that the venture would buy undeveloped land and hold it for development. The land was purchased, and a deed for the land naming "Metropolitan Limited Partnership" as grantee was executed, delivered, and recorded. In the MLP name, Andy, Ben, and Carol also hired a marketing company, Marketing, to develop a campaign to resell the land as "Metropolitan Estates."

Two months after the Agreement was executed by Andy, Ben, and Carol, Marketing sued MLP, and Andy, Ben, and Carol individually, for nonpayment of amounts due to Marketing for services it had provided to MLP. MLP is unable to pay Marketing because the land, its only asset, has substantially depreciated due to an economic downturn.

Immediately after Marketing filed suit, Andy, Ben, and Carol filed a Certificate of Limited Partnership in the name of Metropolitan Limited Partnership in the appropriate state office.

Two weeks after the Certificate of Limited Partnership was filed, Zack went onto the land owned in the name of Metropolitan Limited Partnership and fell down an uncovered well. Zack died as a result of injuries suffered in the fall. Zack's estate has filed a wrongful death action against Andy, Ben, and Carol individually.

1. What type of entity is the Metropolitan Limited Partnership? Explain.
2. Can Marketing recover from Andy, Ben, and Carol personally for the amounts it is owed by Metropolitan Limited Partnership? What steps must it follow if it tries to do so? Explain.
3. If Zack's estate is entitled to damages, can it recover from Andy, Ben, and Carol personally for the wrongful death claim? What steps must it follow if it tries to do so? Explain.

---

2. *Id.*

3. Partnership Score Sheet

Stated	Implied	
		1. Type of entity
_____	_____	**Conclusion/Issue:** Even though labeled a limited partnership, MLP is actually a general partnership because the statutory requirements to form a valid limited partnership were not met.
_____	_____	**Rule:** Under the Uniform Limited Partnership Act,
_____	_____	A limited partnership must include a general partner who has signed the certificate of limited partnership.
_____	_____	The certificate must be filed with the Secretary of State.
_____	_____	If a limited partnership is not created because these requirements are not met, the venture may be a general partnership instead.
_____	_____	Under the Uniform Partnership Act, the association of two or more persons to carry on as co-owners of a business for profit forms a partnership.
_____	_____	Formation does not depend on the subjective intent of the persons involved. Thus, if the intended limited partnership fails, a general partnership may have been formed.
_____	_____	A partnership cannot be established solely by common property or part ownership.
_____	_____	**Application:** Here,
_____	_____	Warren never signed the actual agreement, although he was designated as a general partner.
_____	_____	When Andy, Ben, and Carol finally filed the certificate with the state (which they did not do initially), it was still missing Warren's signature.
_____	_____	But they acted as co-owners of a business for profit and, even though they intended to form something else, they inadvertently formed a general partnership.
_____	_____	If they had only purchased property and nothing more, they would likely not have formed a general partnership.
_____	_____	Instead, they hired a marketing company to help resell the land, which exceeds mere co-ownership
_____	_____	**Conclusion:** Therefore,
_____	_____	While a limited partnership was never formed, they inadvertently formed a general partnership instead.
		2. Marketing's recovery
_____	_____	**Conclusion/Issue:** As general partners, Andy, Ben, and Carol are personally liable for the partnership debts, but Marketing must take several steps in order to collect from them personally.
_____	_____	**Rule:** Partners in a general partnership are jointly and severally liable for all partnership obligations unless otherwise agreed.
_____	_____	A claimant typically cannot pursue an action against the separate assets of a partner unless the partnership assets fail to satisfy the claimant's judgment.
_____	_____	A judgment against a partnership is not a judgment against a partner and cannot be satisfied out of the partner's separate assets unless there is also a judgment against that partner.

continued on next page

Stated	Implied	
_____	_____	But a judgment against a partner personally can be sought at the same time as the judgment against the partnership.
_____	_____	Thus the claimant must first obtain a judgment against the partners individually and a judgment against the partnership. After the claimant has first levied execution against the partnership's assets, the claimant can proceed against the individual partners' assets.
_____	_____	**Application:** Here,
_____	_____	There is no statutory provision or portion of the agreement that indicates they are not jointly and severally liable.
_____	_____	**Conclusion:** Therefore,
_____	_____	If Marketing follows those steps, it can recover from the partners personally.
_____	_____	*3. Recovery for Zack's estate* **Conclusion/Issue:** All three are personally liable for the wrongful death claim because a limited partnership was never formed and they are jointly and severally liable as general partners.
_____	_____	**Rule/Application:** General partners are jointly and severally liable—which means that Andy, Ben, and Carol are liable for the wrongful death claim even though the claim arose after they had filed the Certificate of Limited Partnership.
_____	_____	They are not protected by the Certificate of Limited Partnership that they had filed with the state before the claim arose because no limited partnership was created.
_____	_____	The certificate did not create a limited partnership because it lacked a general partner.
_____	_____	**Conclusion:** Therefore,
_____	_____	All are jointly and severally liable and Zack's estate must follow the discussed procedures in order to recover.

II. CORPORATIONS

A. Mind Map

Like a partnership, think of a corporation as a living entity with a beginning, a life in the middle, and an end. Unlike a partnership, a corporation usually involves more people and has more formalities and structure in its formation. As such, the people involved have more responsibilities and distinctions than just general partner or limited partner. As a result, our mind map becomes a bit more complicated. Most of the bar exam questions will deal with small, closely-held corporations. The branches of your mind map are:

- Formation
- Directors, officers, and shareholders' rights and responsibilities
- Issuance of stock
- Fundamental corporate change
- Federal securities law

Formation. First, look to see if there is a promoter liability issue. Promoters act on behalf of the corporation prior to its formation. Then, understand what is required to form a corporation, which includes understanding the difference between a *de facto* corporation and a *de jure* corporation. Alternative forms of corporations may be tested including closely-held corporations, professional corporations, and limited liability companies. Formation issues can include:

- Commencement: Corporate entity begins at the filing of the Articles of Incorporation with the Secretary of State's office.
- **Promoter liability:**
  - Promoter: person who causes a corporation to be formed, organized, and financed.
    - Usually they become shareholders, officers, and directors of the new corporation.
  - Promoters are personally liable on pre-incorporation contracts entered on the corporation's behalf as its agent.
    - Contract can specifically disclaim a promoter's personal liability.
    - Personal liability continues until a novation—the corporation adopts the contract and all parties agree that the promoter will be discharged from the contract.
  - Corporation is not liable on any pre-incorporation agreements unless it assumes liability by its own act after the Articles of Incorporation are filed.
    - Can be express or implied.
- Defective incorporation:
  - **De jure corporation:** organized in compliance with the statute but failed to comply with a statutory provision.
  - **De facto corporation:** statutory compliance is insufficient for *de jure* status. Formed if:
    - Good-faith, colorable attempt to comply; and
    - Corporate principals, in good faith, acted as if they were a corporation.

- **Corporation by Estoppel:**
  - Creditor who has always dealt with the principals as if they were a corporation is estopped from later alleging that the corporation is defective.
  - Defendant who has held himself out as a corporation cannot avoid liability by claiming there is no corporation.

Directors, Officers, and Shareholders' Rights and Responsibilities. Three types of people are involved in corporations. Individuals can be directors, officers, or shareholders. Indeed, an individual could be all three. Keep track of which role the individual was playing when taking a specific action. Ask yourself—which hat was the individual wearing at that time?

Points to remember about shareholders, directors, and officers:

- **Shareholders:**
  - No personal liability for the corporation's debts.
    - Exception: Challenger can **pierce the corporate veil**.
      - Court disregards corporate entity and holds shareholders liable.
      - Challenger goes against the corporation and corporate assets first and then goes against the shareholders and their assets.
      - Grounds:
        - Alter ego:
          - Corporation has no existence of its own.
          - Corporate form used fraudulently for improper purpose.
          - Injury or unjust loss resulted.
        - Inadequate capitalization:
          - Not sufficient alone if corporate formalities observed.
        - Failure to comply with corporate formalities:

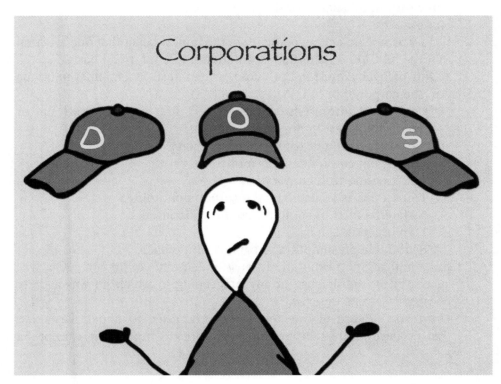

Director, Officer, or
Shareholder?

- Only those active in corporate management are held liable.
  - Corporate veil more likely pierced for a tort action.
- Shareholders are personally liable for any tort they commit, such as fraud.
- Meetings:
  - Annual.
  - Special: requires written notice stating the place, date, hour, and purpose of the meeting no less than 10 and no more than 60 days prior to the meeting.
    - Notice may be waived in writing before or after the meeting.
  - Quorum: majority of the shares entitled to vote.
- **Voting agreements**: contracts to ensure shareholders will vote in concert with regard to issues designated by the agreement:
  - Often used to ensure election of certain directors.
- **Voting trusts**: involves the transfer of legal title to a trustee who votes the shares according to the trust terms.
- **Shareholder derivative suit**: Shareholder sues on behalf of the corporation to redress a wrong when the corporation fails to enforce its right.
  - Must be a shareholder at the time of the transaction.
  - Must make a demand upon the corporation unless futile.
- Majority shareholders owe fiduciary duty to refrain from exercising control to obtain a benefit not shared proportionately with minority shareholders.

- **Directors:**
  - Directors manage the corporation.
  - Directors are protected from liability by the **Business Judgment Rule**: rebuttable presumption that directors are honest, well-meaning, and acting through informed decisions.
  - Directors are fiduciaries of the corporation.
  - Duties:
    - Duty of care: to act in good faith in the honest belief that one is acting in the best interests of the corporation on an informed basis.
    - Duty of loyalty: must not promote own interests in a manner injurious to the corporation.
      - **Conflict of interest** is inherent when director has a personal or financial interest in the transaction:
        - Business dealings with the corporation.
        - Usurping corporate opportunity.
        - Competing with corporation.
      - Transaction is voidable by the corporation unless:
        - Material facts of conflict were fully disclosed, or
        - Transaction is fair.
      - Rebuttable presumption of conflict of interest.
  - Indemnification: Corporation must indemnify a director who was successful in the defense of any proceeding to which he was a party because he was a director.
  - *Ultra Vires*: Board of directors is not permitted to undertake action that is beyond the corporation's authority. Corporation cannot be

> **EXAM TIP**
>
> Be careful concerning notice of director and shareholder meetings. Attendance at a meeting constitutes waiver of a notice defect. "Attendance" does not require physical presence, but includes using a device where the person can hear everyone.

obliged to undertake a contract or activity that is beyond the scope of its powers.
- **Officers:**
  - Same duties as directors.
  - Agents of the corporation.
  - Hired by the directors and can be removed by the directors.

Issuance of Stock. Every corporation must authorize and issue at least one class of common stock and may authorize one or more classes of preferred stock:

- Any unissued stock may be issued by the vote of the shareholders or by the vote of the directors.
- Judgment of board of directors is conclusive as to the value of consideration received for shares.
- Shareholders' **preemptive rights:** right of existing shareholders to acquire unissued shares in the corporation in proportion to their holdings of the original shares when the corporation seeks to issue additional stock:
  - Not automatic.
  - Must be in Articles of Incorporation.
- **Dividends:** A distribution by a corporation to its shareholders of cash or property of the corporation:
  - Shareholder has no inherent right to be paid a dividend.
  - Board of directors has discretion to decide whether and when to declare a dividend.
- Voting: Unless the Articles of Incorporation state otherwise, each share is entitled to one vote.

Fundamental Corporate Change. A significant number of bar exam questions focus on fundamental corporate change. First, define when a fundamental corporate change is attempted: sale of all or substantially all of the corporation's assets. Then, go through every step to be sure all procedures were followed:

- Notice to directors to hold meeting.
- Board enters resolution to hold a special meeting of shareholders.
- Notice of special meeting is sent to shareholders. This notice has specific requirements:
  - Written.
  - States place, date, hour, and purpose of meeting.
  - No less than 10 and no more than 60 days prior to the meeting.
  - Notice can be waived.
- Approval by a majority of all shares entitled to vote and by a majority of each voting group adversely affected by the change.
- Possibility of dissenting shareholders' **right of appraisal**: Shareholder who objects to the action is entitled to an appraisal and payment for his stock.
  - Dissenting shareholder must file a written objection to the proposed action before the shareholders' vote.
  - Dissenter must not vote his shares in favor of the proposed action.
  - If corporation and dissenter fail to agree as to the value of the stock, the court makes a determination of value.
- File notice with the state.

Be especially careful about meetings. Usually it is a closely-held corporation in which some of the directors/shareholders meet and push through a change. Be sure to identify whether they are meeting as directors or shareholders. There may be only one meeting. Thus, going through each step of what is necessary for a fundamental corporate change will garner mega points.

Federal Securities Law. Occasionally, questions will have issues regarding federal securities law. Include in your mind map the elements of a section 10(b) action of the Securities Exchange Act of 1934 and a section 16(b) action regarding short-swing trading profits:

- Section 10(b) action of the Securities Exchange Act of 1934 (applies to all corporations):
  - Available causes of action:
    - Against those who made misrepresentations in connection with the purchase of securities
    - Against those who traded in the stock while under a duty either to disclose or to abstain from trading until the inside information is disclosed
  - Elements:
    - A misrepresentation of a material fact
    - Knowledge by the defendant of the misrepresentation or reckless disregard of the truth
    - Scienter (intent to deceive, manipulate, or defraud)
    - Reliance of the plaintiff
    - Damages

- Section 16(b) action: recovery of short-swing profits (applies only to publicly traded companies):
  - Prevent unfair use of information and internal manipulation of price
  - Profit recoverable
  - Requires two transactions in stock
  - Strict liability offense
  - Damages

B. Essay Practice Question[3]

Macy took steps to incorporate Cyam Construction Corp. He sent the Articles of Incorporation to the Secretary of State as required. Prior to receiving back the Articles from the Secretary of State, Macy sought to set up contracts for the corporation.

A sales representative of Modern Homes entered into a contract to supply building and construction materials for Macy's enterprise. Macy signed the contract "Cyam Construction Corp./Joe Macy, President," and the corporation was listed as the buyer. A week later, the Articles of Incorporation for Cyam Construction Corp. were approved.

Under the Articles, the corporation was authorized to issue 2,000 shares of common stock, par value of $5 per share. The corporation issued 500 shares to Macy and 200 shares to his friends, Crandall and Peterson.

At the first meeting, Macy, Crandall, and Peterson were elected directors. Macy was also elected President and Treasurer. Crandall was elected Secretary.

Shortly after the first meeting, Macy, without obtaining approval of the board of directors, issued 400 shares of stock to Jackson for a used truck.

Cyam subsequently fell upon hard times and did not pay Modern Homes. Modern Homes brought an action against Macy, personally, to recover the amount owed. At the same time, Jackson sought to recover the truck on the ground that the stock transferred to him was void since the Board did not approve it and it violated the preemptive rights of the original shareholders.

Before these two disputes could be resolved, Cyam Construction Corp. sold all of its assets, including construction progress and the truck, to Omar Builders. Discuss:

1. Can Modern Homes recover the amount owed from Macy?
2. Can Modern Homes recover the amount owed from Omar Builders?
3. Can Jackson recover his truck?

Give reasons.

---

3. *Id.*

C. Corporations Score Sheet

Stated	Implied	
		1. Can Modern Homes recover the amount owed from Macy?
		Conclusion: Modern Homes can probably recover the amount owed on the contract from Macy.
		Issue: At issue is the liability of one entering into a contract in the name of a corporation before the corporation exists.
		Rule: By statute,
		If a person enters into a contract in the name of the corporation before the corporation is incorporated, that person will be personally liable on the contract.
		Incorporation occurs when the Secretary of State approves the corporation's Articles of Incorporation for filing.
		Application: Here,
		Macy entered into the contract before the Articles were approved and he can be held personally liable on the contract.
		Exception/Rule: However, personal liability does not exist after a novation.
		Novation—corporation agrees to replace promoter under contract and third party agrees to release promoters.
		Application: Here,
		No indication that Modern Homes would release Macy. Thus, no novation was made.
		Conclusion: Therefore,
		Modern Homes can likely recover from Macy.
		2. Can Modern Homes recover the amount owed from Omar Builders?
		Conclusion: Modern Homes cannot recover from Omar Builders.
		Issue: At issue is the liability of the purchaser of the assets of a corporation.
		Rule: Generally, a corporation that purchases the assets of another corporation is not liable for the debts and liabilities of the seller.
		Exceptions: 1. the successor agrees to assume the liabilities; 2. the transaction amounts to a merger or consolidation; 3. the buyer is a mere continuation of the seller, or 4. the transaction was fraudulently entered to allow the seller to escape its liabilities.
		Application: Here,
		There was no agreement, no merger or consolidation, no continuance of business of the seller, and no continuity in ownership interests between the two corporations; and no facts indicate fraudulent intent.
		Conclusion: Therefore,
		Omar Builders is not liable for Cyam Construction's liabilities.
		3. Can Jackson recover his truck?
		Conclusion: Jackson cannot recover his truck.
		Issue: At issue is whether the stock issued to Jackson is void.

continued on next page

Stated	Implied	
_____	_____	**Rule:** Stock can be issued by the board of directors for such consideration as the board deems appropriate.
_____	_____	The board's good faith valuation of property exchanged for stock is conclusive, absent fraud.
_____	_____	Usually third parties cannot raise the doctrine of *ultra vires*—to recover property from a corporation when they have already benefitted from the *ultra vires* act.
_____	_____	**Application:** Here,
_____	_____	Since the board did not authorize the issuance nor determine the value of the truck, the issuance was improper—*ultra vires*.
_____	_____	Nevertheless, Jackson will not be able to recover his truck because a third party is generally estopped from raising the doctrine of *ultra vires* to recover property from a corporation when the third party has already obtained the benefit of the *ultra vires* act.
_____	_____	**Rule:** Shareholders also do not have preemptive rights by operation of law if the Articles of Incorporation are silent. Articles of Incorporation must include preemptive rights.
_____	_____	But, preemptive rights do not apply to stock issued in exchange for property.
_____	_____	**Application:** Here,
_____	_____	Jackson's claim that the sale violated the original shareholders' preemptive rights will fail.
_____	_____	**Conclusion:** Therefore,
_____	_____	Jackson will be unable to recover his truck.

CHAPTER **17**

Mapping Decedents' Estates and Trusts

The NCBE combines the topics of Decedents' Estates, Trusts, and Future Interests. Future Interests are studied as part of Property for the MBE. That mind map is in Chapter 14.

I. DECEDENTS' ESTATES

A. Mind Map

A will is a document that takes effect on the death of the testator. If properly executed, a will disposes of the person's property, but need not do so. The mind map for Decedents' Estates considers the life of a will in the sense of studying its creation and then studying later events such as changes in the testator's intent, changes in the property owned by the testator, or changes in beneficiaries. Lastly, the mind map considers intestate succession that applies not only to circumstances where there is no will, but also where the will is not properly executed and no substitute will exists. Intestate succession also applies when changes in beneficiaries result in no named person receiving the residue of the will.

- Validity
- Revocation
- Bequests
- Beneficiaries
- Intestate succession

Many topics have the same first step: is _____ valid? You have already seen this step in Contracts, Partnership, and Corporations. Now, you will see it in Decedents' Estates, Trusts, and Family Law. Here, the examiners want to know if the will was **valid**, that is, was it properly executed by an individual with capacity. Start your analysis with the requirements of execution. If the facts state Testator executed a valid will or give another indicia of validity, then skip this step. There would be no points for that analysis. The graders would decide that you could not spot the true issues, and you would waste time that should have been spent on the true issues.

Each state has its own statutes for **will execution**. If the statutory requirements are not met, the will is void and not just voidable. That is, the will cannot be admitted to probate at all even if no one objects. The most common formalities include:

- Will must be in writing: Most states recognize a holographic will—that is, a will entirely in the testator's handwriting and no attesting witnesses.
- Testator's signature: may be by any mark. Testator can direct another person to sign for him in his presence.
- Two attesting witnesses.
- Testator must sign or acknowledge a previous signature in each witness's presence.
- Witnesses sign in testator's presence.

Some states' additional requirements include:

- Testator's signature must be at end of will.
- Testator much publish the will—declare to the witnesses that this document is intended to be the testator's will.
- Witnesses must sign in the presence of each other.

If the testator's writing was in contemplation of a future writing, then the writing is not a valid will, even if holographic. For example, the testator writes a letter to her attorney spelling out her bequests and beneficiaries and asks the attorney to change or prepare her will. If the testator dies before the new will is executed, the court will not accept the letter as a holographic will.

A **codicil** is a later testamentary instrument that amends or alters the prior will. A codicil must be executed in the same manner as a will. Some states will accept an amendment through incorporation by reference such as a list of personal property if the will manifests intent to incorporate the document.

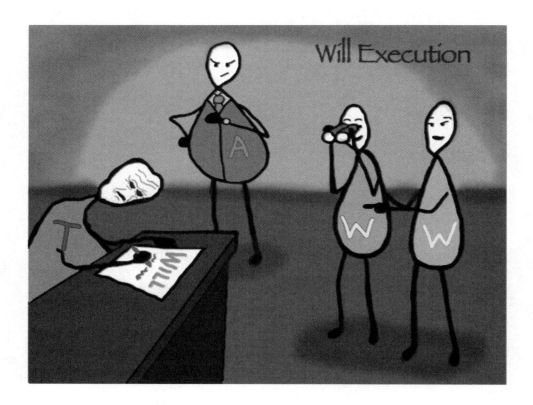

Will contests focus on a defective execution, a testator's lack of capacity, or a revocation. Lack of capacity arises with issues of mental capacity, undue influence, and fraud. **Mental capacity** to execute a will is a lower standard than capacity required to contract. Mental capacity requires:

* Testator must be 18 years old or older at date of execution of will;
* Testator understands the nature of the act;
* Testator understands the nature and extent of his property;
* Beneficiaries are the natural objects of his bounty; and
* Testator understands the nature of the disposition he is making.

A will contest based on the will being obtained through the **exercise of undue influence** requires:

* Influence exerted on testator;
* Effect of influence overpowers the testator's mind and free will; and
* Product of influence was a will not being executed but for the influence.

Look for situations where a presumption of undue influence arises such as the existence of a confidential or fiduciary relationship between the testator and the beneficiary; the beneficiary participated in some way in procuring or drafting the will; and the will's provisions appear to be unnatural and favor the beneficiary who allegedly exercised undue influence.

Fraud could be fraud in the factum or fraud in the inducement. Fraud in the factum would involve a misrepresentation as to the nature of the contents of the will. Fraud in the inducement would be a misrepresentation as to facts which would influence the testator's motivation to make a will in the first place.

A **no-contest clause** attempts to disqualify anyone contesting the will from taking under it. Most states hold that the clause is ineffectual if the person affected had reasonable cause to contest the will. The no-contest clause will be enforceable if the will contest is unsuccessful and no probable cause existed.

Several considerations arise when analyzing **revocation** of a will:

* Types of revocation:
  * Methods:
    * Operation of law:
      * Testator divorces after making a will—all provisions in favor of the ex-spouse become ineffective for all purposes, unless the provisions were intended to survive the divorce.
      * Surviving spouse married testator after testator executed the will. Surviving spouse entitled to the value of the share she would have received if the testator had died intestate.
    * Written instrument: executing a subsequent will or codicil.
    * Physical Act: burning, tearing, canceling, obliterating, or destroying the will or any part of it.
  * Partial revocation is allowed under the Uniform Probate Code.
  * Dependent relative revocation: Testator revokes an old will with the intention that a newly executed will replaces it. If new will is not made or is invalid, some jurisdictions will admit the revoked will to probate. Need evidence of testator's intent.
* Presumptions.
* Revival after revocation.

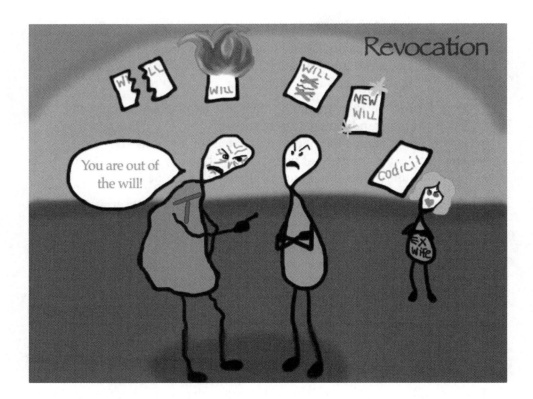

Dependent relative revocation appears frequently as part of an essay question. This is an equity doctrine where a court may disregard a revocation. Look for dependent relative revocation when the testator revokes based on a mistake of law or fact where the testator would have made a different bequest but for the mistaken belief.

Presumptions arise when the will is found after a testator's death, but is mutilated. There must be some extrinsic evidence to show testator's intent. A prior will is **revived** upon undergoing all formalities of making a will or by codicil. Otherwise the previous will is revived only if it is evident from the circumstances of the revocation of the subsequent will or the testator's contemporary declarations that the testator intended the previous will to take effect as executed.

Issues with **beneficiaries** arise when a beneficiary dies prior to the testator or when a child of the testator is not included as a beneficiary. When a beneficiary dies prior to the testator, that person's gift **lapses**, or fails. It does not automatically pass to that person's heirs, but falls into the residue. For example, a wife predeceases her husband. She has a child from a prior relationship. Husband then dies. Husband's gift to wife under the will does not pass to the stepchild and instead becomes part of the residue. If the gift was the residue, there is generally no residue of residue. Modern statutes provide that the residuary beneficiaries who survive the testator take the deceased beneficiary's share of the residuary estate.

Most states have an **anti-lapse statute**. This statute operates to save the gift when the predeceased beneficiary was in a specified degree of relationship to the testator and left descendents. Some states require the beneficiary to be a descendent of the testator and the beneficiaries' descendent to also be the descendent of the testator. Thus, a step-child would not receive the gift. The

Uniform Probate Code extends the statute's application to the testator's step-child, a grandparent, or a descendant of the testator's grandparent.

If a beneficiary participates in any fashion in the willful and unlawful killing of the testator, that beneficiary receives nothing under a will according to **Slayer Act** statutes.

If a testator fails to provide in his will for any of his children born or adopted after the execution of the will, the **omitted after-born** or after-adopted child may receive a share of the decedent's estate unless the omission was intentional or the testator has provided for the child outside of the will.

A **simultaneous death** occurs when two or more persons, one of whom is the beneficiary of the other, die under circumstances where there is insufficient evidence to determine which party survived the other. Under the Uniform Probate Code, a person who cannot be established to have survived the decedent by 120 hours is deemed to have predeceased the decedent.

A person may **disclaim** an interest in property under a will. In order to be effective, a disclaimer must:

* Be in writing or other record;
* Declare the disclaimer;
* Describe the interest or power disclaimed;
* Be signed by the disclaiming party; and
* Be delivered or filed.

Bequests under a will are subject to ademption, satisfaction, advancement, and a spouse's elective share. The first step to determine a beneficiary's right to specific property is to classify the type of bequest:

* **Specific bequest** or specific devise: gift of a specific article or other property, which is identified and distinguished from all other things of the same kind and is satisfied only by delivery of the particular thing.
  * Use of the word "my"—"my car" versus "a car."
* **General legacy**: payable out of the general assets of the decedent's estate and not in any separated or distinguished fund from other things of the same kind.
* **Demonstrative bequest**: bequest of a certain sum to be paid out of a particular fund.
  * "100 shares of stock" v. "my 100 shares of stock," which would be a specific bequest.
  * Beneficiary is entitled to value of the 100 shares of stock out of the general estate if the particular fund is not in existence at the testator's death.

The doctrine of **ademption** applies to specific bequests that are not in the testator's estate at the time of death. The gift is considered "adeemed" and other property is not substituted. Ademption does not apply to general or demonstrative legacies. Modern statutes have modified the common law doctrine with various exceptions including casualty insurance proceeds, comdemnation awards, and property sold by a guardian such that the property is not adeemed.

Satisfaction occurs when a gift has been satisfied by an *inter vivos* transfer from the testator to the beneficiary subsequent to the will's execution. The testator must provide for the satisfaction in the will or a contemporaneous writing or the devisee acknowledges in writing. An **advancement** is a lifetime gift made to an heir with the intent that the gift be applied against the heir's share of the estate. Lifetime gifts are presumed not to be an advancement unless intended as such.

Surviving spouses are protected from disinheritance by **elective share** statutes. These statutes give the spouse an election to take a statutory share in lieu of taking under the will. Under most statutes, the amount is one-third of the net probate estate if the decedent is survived by issue and one-half if the decedent is not survived by descendants.

If no will exists or a will is found invalid, then the decedent's property passes under the state's **intestate succession** statutes. If there are no surviving descendants, the spouse takes the entire estate. A surviving spouse takes one-third or one-half of the estate if there are surviving descendants. The descendants take the remainder of the estate.

Two different schemes are used by states:

* Majority rule—per capita with representation
* Modern trend—per capita at each generational level

Under a per capita with representation scheme, the property is divided into equal shares at the first generational level with living heirs. Each person at that level takes a share. If they are deceased, their share passes to their issue by right of representation. That is, their share is divided between their own children. Under this scheme, the grandchildren receive different amounts based on whether they have siblings.

Under a per capita at each generational level, the first split is the same. But instead of an heir's children dividing only that share, all takers with deceased parents at that generational level divide the shares equally. Under this scheme, the grandchildren take equal shares.

Per Capita with Representation

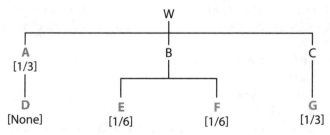

The survivors are **bold**. All others are dead.

Per Capita at Each Generational Level

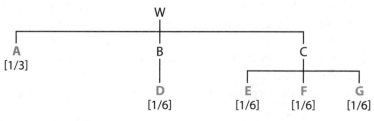

The survivors are **bold**. All others are dead.

Parents, siblings, and other collateral kin never inherit if the decedent is survived by children or more remote descendants such as grandchildren and great-grandchildren. If there is no spouse or descendants, then parents take the estate followed by siblings and then their descendants.

When faced with an intestate succession question, best to make your own generational graph to be sure not to confuse who is who.

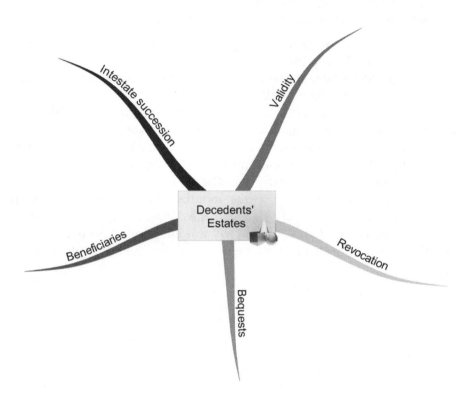

B. Essay Practice Question[1]

In 2004, Testator duly executed a will providing as follows:

1. I give my 100 shares of XYZ common stock to my cousin Andy.
2. I give my home at 4 Cypress Garden to my cousin Ben.
3. I give my automobile to my friend Carrie.
4. I give $10,000 to my friend Donna.
5. I give the residue of my estate to my friend Ed.

In 2006, Testator sold her home at 4 Cypress Garden and, with the entire sales proceeds, purchased a condominium as her new home.

In 2007, Testator traded the white automobile that she owned when her will was executed for a blue automobile.

In 2008, Testator died. At the time of her death, Testator owned 200 shares of XYZ common stock, having acquired an additional 100 shares as the result of a dividend paid by XYZ to its shareholders in its own stock. Testator also owned the condominium, the blue automobile, and a $50,000 bank account.

Testator was survived by Andy, Ben, Carrie, Donna, and Ed. She was also survived by Donna's daughter. Three months after Testator died, Donna made a valid disclaimer of any rights to the $10,000 bequest to which she might otherwise be entitled. Testator's will was admitted to probate.

To whom should Testator's probate estate be distributed? Explain.

C. Decedents' Estates Score Sheet

Stated	Implied	
_____	_____	**Conclusion on stock:** Andy is entitled to the 200 shares of XYZ stock Testator owned at the time of death unless the jurisdiction does not follow the modern approach.
_____	_____	**Rule:** Historically, a bequest of stock owned by a testator when the testator's will was signed excluded subsequently acquired shares of the same stock acquired by the testator as the result of a stock dividend.
_____	_____	If the testator had wanted the legatee to take the later-acquired shares, the testator could have changed the will to take those additionally acquired shares into account.
_____	_____	A contrary rule applied to shares acquired as a result of a stock split.
_____	_____	Today, stock dividends are typically treated like stock splits because, in each case, nothing of value has been distributed by the corporation to the shareholder.
_____	_____	Additional shares of the same company, when acquired by stock split or stock dividend, are, from the shareholder's economic perspective, merely a change in form, not substance.
_____	_____	**Application/Conclusion:** Here,
_____	_____	Under the UPC or a like statute, Andy would be entitled to all 200 shares of XYZ stock owned by Testator at her death.
_____	_____	**Conclusion on Home:** In most states, the bequest of the home to Ben adeems.
_____	_____	However, in some states Ben would be entitled to the substitute home.
_____	_____	**Rule:** Under common law, an ademption occurs when the subject matter of specific devise is not found in the probate estate at the time of the testator's death.
_____	_____	**Application:** Here,
_____	_____	Testator specifically bequeathed to Ben Testator's home located at 4 Cypress Garden.
_____	_____	Since Testator did not own that home when she died, the bequest adeems.
_____	_____	**Conclusion:** As a result, the condo passes to Ed, the residuary legatee.
_____	_____	**Minority Rule:** Under UPC §2-606(a)(5) or a like statute, however, Ben would be entitled to Testator's condominium.
_____	_____	This section provides that the devisee of specifically devised real estate is entitled to any "real property . . . owned by the testator at death which the testator acquired as a replacement for specifically devised real property. . . ."
_____	_____	**Application:** Here, Testator purchased the condominium as a replacement home for the home that was specifically devised to Ben.
_____	_____	The "replacement property" concept appears to have little support in case law although supported by the Restatement if the result is consistent with the testator's intent.
_____	_____	**Conclusion on automobile:** Carrie is entitled to the blue automobile.
_____	_____	**Rule:** A bequest of generically described property (e.g., my automobile) applies to property that meets the generic description at the testator's death.
_____	_____	**Application/Conclusion:** Thus, the bequest of the automobile is unlike the bequest of the home in that the home was described in a non-generic manner. (Note: This is still a specific bequest because of the inclusion of "my." However, this is not an ademption problem because Testator did not refer to a specific automobile when executing

continued on next page

Stated	Implied	
		her will. Also, an examinee might analyze this under the doctrine of independent significance and get to the same result.)
_____	_____	**Conclusion:** The $10,000 bequest to Donna fails because of Donna's disclaimer and because Donna is not the type of legatee typically described in an anti-lapse statute. The bequest passes to Ed, the residuary legatee.
_____	_____	If Donna had not disclaimed the $10,000 legacy, it would have passed to her under the provisions of Testator's will.
_____	_____	However, she did disclaim the bequest.
_____	_____	**Rule:** Under the typical disclaimer statute, if a legatee disclaims a general bequest, the bequest passes as if the disclaimant had predeceased the testator.
_____	_____	When a disclaimant is deemed to have predeceased the testator, the question arises whether the bequest to that disclaimant passes to her issue.
_____	_____	**Application:** The answer here depends upon the application of the anti-lapse statute.
_____	_____	**Conclusion:** The typical anti-lapse statute would not apply here because Donna was a friend, not a relative, of Testator.
_____	_____	If the anti-lapse statute is inapplicable, then the $10,000 passes to Ed as the residuary legatee.

II. TRUSTS

A. Mind Map

A trust is a fiduciary relationship where the trustee holds legal title to property with a duty to manage, invest, safeguard, and administer the trust assets and income for the benefit of designated beneficiaries, who hold equitable title. Although shorter than other mind maps, the trusts mind map focuses on the three main issues that arise in essay questions:

- Creation
- Classification
- Trustee's powers and duties

Just like Decedents' Estates, your inquiry begins with whether or not this is a valid trust. If the facts indicate in any manner that the grantee executed a valid trust, then you can skip this first step of **creation**. Otherwise, go through each element of creating a valid trust:

- Settlor's capacity: Analyze similar to a testator's capacity to form a will.
- Intent: Present intent to create a trust now, not in the future. No particular words required, not even "trust"; just a manifestation of intent to create a trust.
- Trustee: Must have mental capacity to administer the trust. Cannot be a minor or a mentally incompetent person. Corporations are allowed to be trustees. State statutes may impose additional requirements on corporations as trustees. A settlor can create a trust naming herself as trustee.
- Res—trust property: Settlor places title to the trust property and delivers to the trustee by

- an *inter vivos* transfer, or
- a testamentary trust (Testator can direct the executor of his will to distribute property to a trustee).
- Identifiable beneficiary: Except for charitable trusts, trust must have definite or ascertainable beneficiaries. Beneficiaries are equitable owners of trust property.
- Proper purpose: virtually any purpose except an illegal purpose, a purpose that violates the Rule Against Perpetuities, or a purpose contrary to public policy.
- Statute of Frauds and Statute of Wills, if necessary.

A trust terminates automatically at the end of the trust term. A trust also terminates when all the purposes of the trust have been accomplished.

Modification of a trust depends upon which party seeks the modification:

- Settlor: can revoke or amend a trust unless the terms state it is **irrevocable**.
- Beneficiaries:
  - Modification conflicts with a material purpose of the trust: settlor's consent is required.
  - Modification does not conflict with a material purpose of the trust: settlor's consent is not required.
  - If all the beneficiaries do not agree, a court may modify or terminate a trust when
    - the trust could have been modified if all beneficiaries had consented, and
    - the interests of any nonconsenting beneficiaries will be adequately protected.
- Trustee: can terminate a trust when the property's value is less than $50,000 and the amount is insufficient to justify the cost of administration.

Two special trust provisions warrant notice. Both **spendthrift provisions** and **discretionary provisions** appear on essay questions. A beneficiary's equitable interest in the property is freely transferable. A frequent scenario is one in which a beneficiary's creditor seeks to reach the property in appropriate proceedings. A creditor can only reach the beneficiary's interest and not the trust property itself. In order to avoid this scenario, a settlor may include a spendthrift provision in the trust.

A **spendthrift provision** means that the beneficiary cannot voluntarily or involuntarily transfer his interests. This provision does not apply if the income has already been paid to the beneficiary. Once in the beneficiary's hands, it is no longer protected by the trust's provisions and is fully owned by the beneficiary. Creditors can then reach the beneficiary's income from the trust. A spendthrift clause does not protect against a claim by the government or a claim for child support or spousal maintenance or for necessary supplies or services rendered to a beneficiary. A settlor is not allowed to create its own spendthrift trust to avoid creditors' claims. Note that a trustee's creditor cannot reach trust property as the trust "owns" the property, not the trustee.

A trust may contain **discretionary provisions**. These vest additional power in the trustee to decide when to distribute income of the trust. If the beneficiary's interest stems from a discretionary provision, then the beneficiary has no "right" to income until the trustee distributes the income. The trustee's decision is subject to an abuse of discretion review.

Trusts may be **classified** as an express trust, a charitable trust, a constructive trust, or a resulting trust:

- Express trusts arise from the intention of the property owner:
  - Private express trusts: comprise most of the trusts established by individuals.
  - Charitable trusts: resemble private express trusts but have some significant, distinguishing characteristics.
- Implied trusts arise by operation of law:
  - Resulting trusts: places property in the hands of rightful owners when circumstances require it, even though there has not been any wrongdoing on anyone's part.
  - Constructive trusts: deprive a wrongdoer from retaining improperly obtained property.

An **express trust** may be created by:

- An *inter vivos* trust created by a declaration of trust by the property owner, stating the trustee holds the property as trustee in trust.
- An *inter vivos* trust created by transfer of property during settlor's lifetime.
- A testamentary trust created by a will. In addition, "pour over" provisions in a will are allowed. Pour over provisions direct the transfer of property into a trust established either by the testator during his lifetime or by another person rather than creating a brand-new trust.

Spendthrift Clause

Charitable trusts have distinctive rules because of their substantial benefit to society. Charitable trusts are liberally construed to effectuate the purpose of the settlor:

- Indefinite beneficiaries:
  - But—trust cannot be restricted to a small group of people even if the benefits are payable for charitable purposes like education or health.
- Charitable purpose:
  - Categories:
    - Relief of poverty
    - Advancement of education
    - Advancement of religion
    - Promotion of health
    - Performance of governmental and municipal purposes (parks and recreation)
    - Other purposes beneficial to the community
  - Purpose can be broad.
  - Objective must be to benefit the public, although settlor can have a selfish reason such as reducing personal tax burden.
- Rule Against Perpetuities: limited application to charitable trusts.
  - Trust may have a perpetual existence.
  - If preceded by a noncharitable estate, the charitable interest must vest within the period of time proscribed by the RAP.
- *Cy pres* **doctrine** applies: When designated charity is not in existence at settlor's death, the court may redirect the trust to a purpose as near as possible to the charitable endeavor designated by the settlor.
- Termination: If the charitable trust cannot be performed as intended and the requirements for *cy pres* are not met, the charitable trust terminates and a resulting trust in favor of the settlor's estate results.

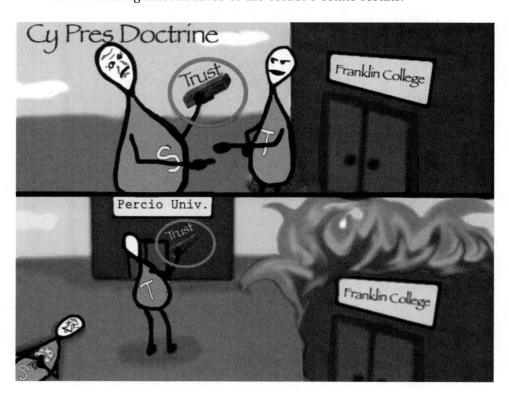

Constructive trusts are an equitable remedy in cases involving wrongful conduct and unjust enrichment. The trustee's duty is to convey the property to the person who owned it but for the wrongful conduct. A constructive trust may arise from theft, conversion, fraud, duress, or other situations requiring an equitable remedy such as breach of fiduciary duty.

A **resulting trust** arises upon the failure of an express trust, from a purchase money resulting trust or from an incomplete disposition of trust assets. The beneficiary is the one responsible for supplying the trust property, and the trustee holds title, but did not give consideration for the trust property.

The examiners frequently focus on the **trustee's powers and duties**. A trustee's powers originate in the terms of the trust together with the powers appropriate to achieve the proper investment, management, and distribution of the trust property.

A **trustee's powers** include to:

* settle or abandon trust claims;
* exercise all rights and powers an unmarried individual has over his own property;
* borrow money;
* sell or lease trust assets;
* apportion trust income; and
* incur reasonable expenses necessary to maintain trust property.

Matters within the trustee's discretion are not subject to attack unless she has abused her discretion in undertaking the conduct in question. If the trustee has absolute discretion, then her actions are improper only if undertaken in bad faith.

A trustee has specific fiduciary **duties**:

* Duty of loyalty and good faith:
  * No self-dealing, unless trust permits specific acts
  * No personal benefit other than official compensation
  * No apparent conflict of interest
  * Keep trust assets segregated from personal assets
* Duty to preserve trust property and make it productive:
  * Objective standard of care unless superior skills warrant a higher standard of care
  * Prudent investor rule governs:
    * Trustee is permitted to invest trust assets as would a prudent investor, considering both the interests of life beneficiaries and remaindermen. Thus, the trustee must consider both the investment's ability to produce a reasonable rate of income and the safety of the principal.
    * Trustee must seek to diversify the investments.
    * Standard is reasonable care, skill, and caution.
    * Some states maintain a "legal list" approach of approved types of investments.
  * Duty to dispose of wasting or non-productive assets
  * Duty to maintain accounting of transactions
  * Duty to enforce claims and defend trust from attack

Assets and expenses received by the trustee must be allocated to either principal or income of the trust. Why? One beneficiary may have a life interest in the trust principal, while another beneficiary is to receive the income from the trust. Income is usually attributed to income, while assets are principal. The problem arises with receipts of a mixed nature. Likewise, certain expenses benefit both the principal and income.

Because a trustee stands in a fiduciary relationship with the beneficiaries, trustees incur **liability** to the beneficiaries when duties are breached. When addressing an issue of whether a trustee violated a duty, ask first whether the trustee was authorized to perform the act. Then, ask whether the trustee performed to the required standard of care. Remedies available include compelling the trustee to convey property back to the trust, recovering profits made by the trustee, returning appreciation or profits from commingled funds, punitive damages, and removal as trustee.

Trustees may incur liability to third parties through performance of their duties. In certain situations, a trustee can obtain indemnification from the trust. The trustee cannot then be personally at fault. A trustee is entitled to indemnification where the tort was a normal incident to an activity in which the trustee was properly engaged on behalf of the trust, the tort is based on strict liability, or liability is based upon *respondeat superior* principles and the trustee did not make an improper delegation of discretionary functions to an agent or violate his duty to exercise reasonable care in the selection and supervision of the agent. A trustee is not personally liable on a contract properly entered into in the trustee's fiduciary capacity in the course of administering the trust if the trustee in the contract disclosed the fiduciary capacity.

Trusts may be an area that you did not take in law school, and you may not have had personal experience in the area. Parts of trusts law are extremely complicated. Those parts are in that 25% that you do not need to push yourself to know. Keep to the mind map and you can pass a Trusts essay.

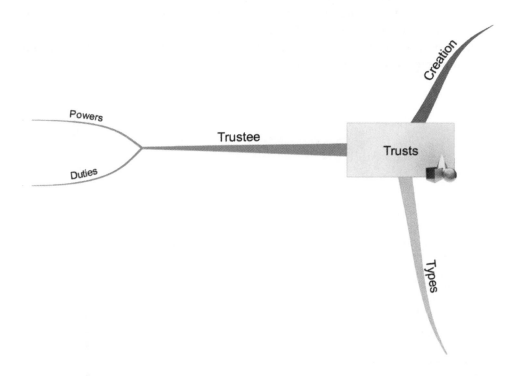

B. Essay Practice Question[2]

Prior to his death, Settlor created a valid irrevocable trust and named Trustee as trustee. The trust instrument specified that:

1. Trustee shall distribute trust income to Trustee's adult children, David and Edna, in such amounts as Trustee, in Trustee's absolute and uncontrolled discretion, shall determine.
2. Trustee may distribute all trust income to either David or Edna.
3. Trustee shall have the power to sell any trust property.
4. This trust shall terminate in 10 years and, upon its termination, Trustee shall distribute 60% of trust property to David and Edna, in equal shares.
5. In view of my long-standing interest in the area of education, Trustee shall distribute all remaining trust property to my alma mater, Business College.

During the last year of the trust, Trustee paid all trust income to David. Trustee's decision was motivated solely by her personal disagreement with Edna's political opinions.

During the same year, Trustee decided to sell certain trust assets. Solely to avoid paying a 6% sales commission that would have reduced the trust's sales proceeds, Trustee, in her personal capacity, purchased these assets for their undisputed fair market value. After the sale, the assets unexpectedly increased in value. Trustee recently sold these assets to a bona fide purchaser for a significant profit and retained the profit for herself.

The trust has terminated, and Trustee has discovered that Business College no longer exists. Trustee seeks judicial approval to distribute Business College's share of the trust to Settlor's estate.

1. Did Trustee breach any fiduciary duty by paying all trust income to David during the last year of the trust? Explain.
2. Must Trustee return to the trust the profit she retained from assets she purchased from the trust? Explain.
3. Should a court authorize Trustee to distribute trust property that was payable to Business College to Settlor's estate? Explain.

---

2. *Id.*

C. Trusts Score Sheet

Stated	Implied	
		Issue 1
_____	_____	**Rule:** Even when a trustee has absolute and uncontrolled discretion, she may be held liable for actions representing an abuse of discretion.
_____	_____	A failure to distribute trust income based entirely on a personal motive constitutes an abuse of discretion.
_____	_____	A trustee has a fiduciary duty to carry out the terms of the trust established by the settlor; failure to do so constitutes a breach of trust.
_____	_____	**Application:** Here,
_____	_____	The trust instrument conferred upon Trustee absolute and uncontrolled discretion to make income distributions, including distribution of all trust income to only one beneficiary.
_____	_____	**Conclusion:** Trustee's distribution thus appears to be consistent with the terms of the trust.
_____	_____	**Rule:** A court will not ordinarily question a trustee's exercise of a discretionary power, particularly when the trustee is granted absolute and uncontrolled discretion. However, even when a trustee is granted absolute and uncontrolled discretion, her actions may be reviewed for abuse of discretion.
_____	_____	Application of this standard will insulate the trustee with respect to decisions about which reasonable individuals might disagree.
_____	_____	But when the trustee's decision is based exclusively on personal reasons unrelated to the settlor's goals, the trustee's decision may be overturned.
_____	_____	**Application:** Here,
_____	_____	Trustee withheld all income from Edna solely because of her personal disagreement with Edna's political opinions.
_____	_____	Such vindictiveness probably represents an abuse of discretion.
_____	_____	**Conclusion:** It is likely that a court would hold that Trustee's decision not to pay Edna any trust income during the last year of the trust was an abuse of discretion and therefore a breach of the duty to carry out the terms of the trust.
		Issue 2
_____	_____	**Conclusion:** Trustee breached her duty of loyalty by purchasing trust property in her personal capacity. Trustee must return the profits to the trust.
_____	_____	**Rule:** Trustees have a duty of loyalty to trust beneficiaries.
_____	_____	The duty of loyalty includes the duty not to engage in self-dealing, such as purchasing property from the trust without court approval.
_____	_____	The prohibition on self-dealing applies even if the purchase price is fair and reasonable.
_____	_____	**Application:** Here,
_____	_____	Trustee clearly breached her duty of loyalty to the trust beneficiaries by buying trust assets in her personal capacity.
_____	_____	Under the no-further-inquiry rule, the reasonableness of Trustee's action and her goal to save the trust the sales commission are irrelevant.

continued on next page

Stated	Implied	
		Conclusion: Therefore, Trustee is liable to the trust beneficiaries for all profits resulting from the breach.
_____ _____ _____ _____ _____ _____ _____ _____ _____	_____ _____ _____ _____ _____ _____ _____ _____ _____	*Issue 3* **Conclusion:** The court should find that Settlor had a general charitable intent. Therefore, the trust property should not be returned to Settlor's estate. Instead, the court should exercise its *cy pres* power and order that the property be distributed to a charity that falls within the general charitable purposes expressed in the trust. **Rule:** Although a settlor or the settlor's estate is generally entitled to the return of any trust property that cannot be distributed in accordance with the terms of the trust, an exception applies to charitable trust dispositions that reflect a general charitable intention. In such a case, a court should exercise its *cy pres* power and direct distribution of the failed disposition to another charity. Until recently, it was necessary to demonstrate that the settlor had a general charitable intention before the *cy pres* doctrine could be applied. However, the latest Restatement of Trusts adopts the position that there should be a presumption that the settlor had a general charitable intention. **Application:** Under either approach, a court should find that Settlor had a general charitable intention given that the trust instrument itself specified that the gift to Business College derived from Settlor's "long-standing interest in the area of education." **Conclusion:** Because Settlor had a general charitable intention to benefit education, Settlor's estate is not entitled to a return of any portion of the trust property. Instead, a court should exercise its *cy pres* power and direct distribution to another educational institution.

CHAPTER 18

Mapping Family Law

I. MIND MAP

Family law covers all parts of the relationship between spouses—before and after divorce—and between parents and children. Family law contains principles of contract law and property law, with a side of torts, evidence, and criminal law. The issues can range from a property dispute between unmarried cohabitants to determining which court has jurisdiction over a child's custody in a divorce. The starting point is establishing a marriage, but the end is not divorce, as issues arise between the parties years later. Family law covers:

- Marriage
    - Establishing marriage
        - Procedural requirements of formal marriage
        - Common law marriage
        - Limitations on marriage
    - Annulment
    - Antenuptial agreements
- Divorce
    - Child Custody
    - Visitation
    - Money issues
        - Child support
        - Maintenance
        - Property division
- Parents and children
    - Establishing parenthood
    - Nonmarital children
    - Termination of parental rights
    - Adoption

Issues regarding **marriage** focus on establishing marriage and antenuptial agreements, also called pre-nuptial agreements. The legal effects of the marital relationship are not heavily tested. This includes interspousal immunity, liability for debts, necessaries of a needy spouse, domestic violence, and postnuptial property agreements.

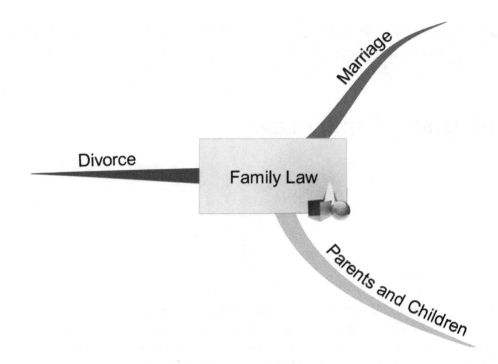

Establishing marriage includes addressing the procedural requirements, common law marriage, and the limitations on marriage:

- Procedural requirements of formal marriage:
  - License
  - Solemnization: ceremony performed by an authorized official
- Common law marriage:
  - Only a minority of states recognize
  - Issue still relevant for recognition by another state
    - Second state must recognize a valid marriage from another state
    - Basis—Full Faith and Credit Clause of the Constitution
  - Requirements—state-specific:
    - Consent
    - Cohabitation
    - Holding out as husband and wife
    - Legal capacity
- Limitations on marriage:
  - Age: parental consent required if under 18. State may require court approval if under 16 and prohibit marriage under 14.
  - Not closely-related
  - Capacity:
    - Mental capacity: must understand the nature of the marriage contract
    - Lack of consent: intoxication
    - Fraud
  - Gender: Recent legislation in many states has abolished the opposite gender requirement.
  - Prior marriage still in force

A **putative spouse** is one who entered into a ceremonial marriage and had a good faith belief in the validity of the marriage. They later discover that the

DISTINGUISHING INFORMAL RELATIONSHIPS		
Type of Relationship	**State of Mind**	**Effect**
Common law marriage	Entered with present ability and intent	Creates full marital rights
Putative spouse	Believes they are legally married because there was a ceremony, but unaware of impediment to marriage	May have equitable spousal inheritance rights, but rights of property division and support are same as annulment
Unmarried partners	Know they are not married	May have statutory, contractual, or equitable rights that vary by state

marriage is void or voidable. In some states, a putative spouse acquires the rights conferred upon a legal spouse, including inheritance, property rights, and right to maintenance. In other states, the court will use equitable remedies.

Unmarried partners have no legally recognized status unless they meet the requirements for common law marriage or putative spouses. Most states will recognize express and implied contracts between the partners concerning support and property, as long as there is consideration other than their sexual relationship. States will also utilize equitable remedies such as *quantum meruit.*

If the validity of a marriage is in doubt in any context from probate to divorce, a party may seek a judgment declaring the marriage invalid. This process is seeking an **annulment**. Most states distinguish between marriages that are void and marriages that are voidable. A void marriage has no legal effect. A voidable marriage is valid unless an aggrieved party obtains an annulment or ratifies the marriage. If one of the parties of a voidable marriage dies, the marriage's validity cannot be attacked by any person—a third party lacks standing to challenge the marriage.

VOID v. VOIDABLE MARRIAGES	
Grounds	**Result**
Bigamy	Void
Same-gender	Void
Closely-related (incest)	Void
Under age	Voidable
Impotence	Voidable
Temporary incapacity (intoxication, duress, fraud)	Voidable
Mental incompetence	Voidable

Antenuptial agreements, often called pre-nuptial agreements, are contracts. The consideration is the entry into marriage. The statute of frauds applies. The validity requirements are state-specific. Most states have adopted standards regarding basic contract formation, procedural fairness, and substantively fair terms. Particularly look at procedural fairness. Was execution of the agreement voluntary or under duress? Was there full financial disclosure?

Only **divorce** terminates a legal marriage. Remember, an annulment is a declaration that a marriage is invalid. No common law divorce exists. Parties to a common law marriage must seek a divorce decree from a court. Divorce or dissolution issues focus on four categories:

* Procedure
* Child custody
* Visitation
* Money issues
  * Child support
  * Maintenance
  * Property division

Most states only have **no-fault grounds** for divorce—the marriage is irretrievably broken. Some states have retained fault grounds, such as adultery and desertion. A court has **jurisdiction** to enter a divorce decree if one of the parties is domiciled in that jurisdiction. Personal jurisdiction is not required as a divorce is considered an *in rem* action. Spousal support, child support, and property rights require personal jurisdiction over both parties. Thus, a court can grant a divorce, but not decide any other issues without personal jurisdiction.

Jurisdiction for child custody and visitation is governed by the Uniform Child Custody Jurisdiction and Enforcement Act ("UCCJEA"). The UCCJEA focuses on the home state of the child—the state in which the child lived with a parent for at

Children and Money

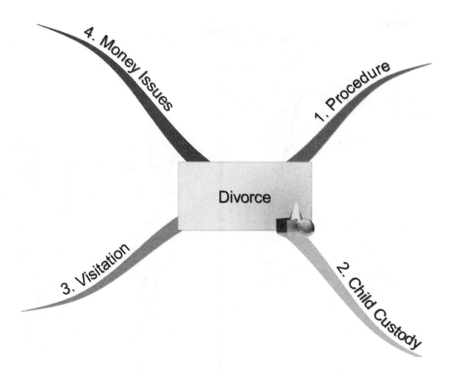

least six consecutive months prior to the commencement of the proceeding. The home state maintains jurisdiction not only to grant the original order, but also to modify it. Thus, even though the child has moved to another state, the home state maintains jurisdiction.

When faced with a family law issue involving any type of divorce, the next issue to address is **child custody**. A court's decree regarding custody affects all other issues. Custody can mean legal custody, which is decision-making power, or physical custody, where the child resides. If both parents are granted custody, it can be joint legal custody (parents share decision-making, but child resides with one parent) or joint physical custody (parents share decision-making and child divides time between each parent's home, although does not need to be equal time) or both. Some states have a preference for joint custody. Others do not award it unless the parents expressly agree.

Child custody is determined by the **best interest of the child** standard. Courts consider several factors in determining the child's best interest:

- Wishes of the parents and child
- Interaction and interrelationship of the child with parents, siblings, and others
- Child's adjustment to home, school, and community
- The mental and physical health of the individuals involved

A child's preference is generally not considered until over the age of 12. The judge would then question the child in chambers. A preference may be given to a primary caregiver—the one most involved in the child's day-to-day life. Preference may also be given to the "friendly parent"; that is, the parent willing to cooperate and facilitate the child's relationship with the other parent.

Child custody awards are always modifiable. The standard is a substantial and material change in circumstances such that the child's best interests would be better served by a change in custody. Custody modifications usually require a certain amount of time to elapse. On the exam, an applicant may go

Original or Modification?

Months or Years Later...

down the wrong path if they do not realize the issues involved a modification instead of the original order. Watch for language such as "four years later." That's a signal that it probably involves a modification.

Relocation issues are the most difficult custody modification issues. One parent wishes to relocate to another state to better their situation and the situation for the child. Yet it will mean a separation from the other parent and will make it more difficult to maintain frequent, in-person contact. Courts will use a balancing test as to the impact on visitation versus the benefits of the move. The overall trend is to be lenient to the needs of the parent with whom the child primarily lives. If the motivation to move is vindictive, the court will generally not permit the child to move.

Visitation or parenting plans are granted to the **noncustodial parent** unless visitation is detrimental to the best interests of the child. While a court may limit visitation if a parent engages in actions that amount to misconduct that might injure the child, absolute denial of visitation is rare. Failure to pay child support does not entitle the custodial parent the right to deny visitation to the noncustodial parent.

State statutes vary widely in granting visitation to **third parties**, such as grandparents. The best interest standard still applies and usually may not override the wishes of a fit parent. Usually, these statutes are limited to situations when the grandparents' child has died or the child's parents have divorced. Some statutes are broader and include siblings, stepparents, or a parent's former same-sex partner. Other statutes are broader still and allow visitation when the family is intact; that is, there has been no death or divorce. These statutes are constitutionally limited. As long as a parent is fit, that parent's determination as to the appropriateness of third-party visitation must be given "special weight." The judge may not override a fit parent's decision to deny a third-party visitation, even if she feels visitation would be in the best interests of the child.

Therefore, with both custody and visitation issues, keep in mind that fit parents' wishes regarding their children are not overridden in favor of third parties. Be leery of concluding that a third party should have custody over a fit parent. For example, a stepfather has raised the child with the biological mother, but never adopted the child. The stepfather has no right to visitation in a divorce unless a statute provides for stepparent visitation.

Money issues are child support, spousal maintenance, and property division. Both parents equally share a duty to support their child. The amount of any **child support** award is based on both parents' income and determined by state guidelines. The guidelines use a formula based upon both parents' income and considers the age of the child and how many children are supported. Because of this formula, you will never need to determine an actual monetary amount for child support. The formula sets a presumptive amount. This can be rebutted with a showing that a variation is in order. Remember, denial of visitation cannot be used as a punishment for failure to pay child support.

Child support is modifiable based upon a substantial change in circumstances. Most states have presumptions set in their guidelines for increases. Child support terminates upon the child's death or emancipation (usually 18 years of age).

A frequent issue with child support deals with parents who have lost income. If it is a voluntary reduction in pay, the court will impute income to the parent. What would the parent be making if employed in a job suitable to the parent's experience and education? This same concept will arise in determining the income of a homemaker.

Spousal **maintenance**, formerly called alimony, is awarded to ensure an adequate income stream for spouses whose economic dependency has resulted from the marital relationship. Different types of maintenance can be awarded:

- Periodic maintenance: a certain amount of money paid at set intervals, usually monthly. Obligation ends at the recipient's death, remarriage, or a court-ordered modification.
- Lump sum maintenance: fixed amount of money, although may be paid in installments. The award is not modifiable.
- Rehabilitative maintenance: awarded for a limited period of time to support the recipient in receiving education or training to be employable and self-supporting.
- Reimbursement maintenance: awarded if the recipient spouse made contributions in the marriage to the other spouse's education, training, or increased earning capacity.

The amount is based on factors including:

- standard of living established during the marriage,
- duration of marriage,
- age and health of both parties,
- financial resources of both parties,
- contribution of each party to the marriage,
- time needed to obtain education or training to enable either party to find appropriate employment, and
- ability of payor spouse to meet hers needs while paying support.

Maintenance terminates upon the spouse's death or remarriage. Modification requires a substantial and continuing change in circumstances. Some states will consider cohabitation as a factor in a modification.

For **property division**, the court follows three steps: classify the property, value the assets, and divide the property. First, the court classifies the property as either separate property or marital property:

- Separate property: all property owned before the marriage, property acquired after the dissolution, and property acquired by gift or inheritance during the marriage.
- Marital property: earnings from both parties and appreciation of marital property. Property acquired after the marriage is presumed to be marital property.

One issue that arises is mixed property. Mixed property includes commingled property, transmuted separate property, and improvement of separate property. Commingled property is when separate property becomes marital property because it is inextricably mingled with marital property or with the separate property of the other spouse. If the property can be traced back to its origins, it retains its nature as separate property.

Mixed property also includes transmuted property. If separate property is treated in a way that evidences an intention for the property to be marital property, it is transmuted into marital property. Separate property can be improved with marital funds. The property maintains its nature as separate property, but the marital estate is reimbursed for the value added to the separate property.

Specific property interests that arise:

- Marital residence:
  - Difficulties arise if the house was purchased prior to the marriage but marital funds were used to pay off the mortgage or build equity.

- Difficulties also arise if a spouse's separate funds are used to make improvements or build equity; then, a gift to the marital estate is presumed but can be rebutted.
- If a spouse's labor increases the value of the other spouse's separate property, the increase is marital.
- **Source of funds** rule is used to apportion the value of the property between separate and marital efforts and funds.
- Appreciation in the value of the property is apportioned in the same manner.
- Pensions:
  - Subject to equitable distribution if accumulated during the marriage.
  - Vested or nonvested.
  - Premarital and post-separation increases or contributions are usually not deemed marital property.
  - A **qualified domestic relations order (QDRO)** recognizes the right of the alternate payee to receive all or a portion of the retirement benefits that would otherwise be payable to the spouse.
- Stock options: presumed to be marital property.
- Professional degrees and licenses:
  - Most states hold they are not a property interest subject to equitable distribution.
  - May be considered in the division of other marital property or in a maintenance or reimbursement award.
- Professional practice and goodwill:
  - A professional practice or corporation is subject to disposition as a marital asset.
  - Enterprise goodwill—transferable with the business.
  - Personal goodwill—generated solely by the reputation and professional expertise of the owner-spouse and not divisible.

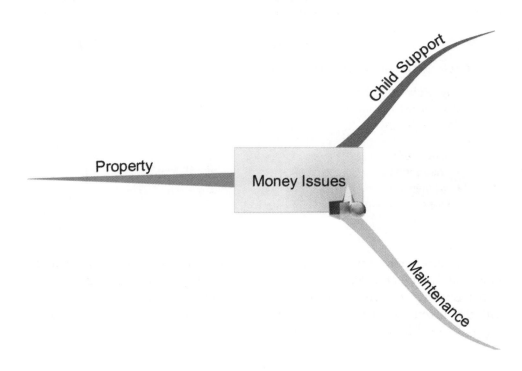

Valuation of assets is usually not tested. Valuation disputes require expert witnesses to appraise the property. Instead, the examiners will give you a dollar amount. States take one of three different approaches to **property division:**

- Community property approach: All property acquired during marriage is deemed owned one-half by each spouse. Each keeps separate property and the remainder is divided.
- Equitable division of all property approach: All property owned, whether marital or separate, is divided between each spouse.
- Equitable division of all marital property approach: Spouses keep separate property that includes property owned prior to the marriage, gifts, or inheritance and the remainder is divided.

Under the equitable division approaches, courts look to factors to decide how to divide. Note that the division does not have to be equal, but equitable. Courts consider:

- Age, education, and earning capacity
- Duration of marriage
- Standard of living enjoyed during marriage
- Present income
- Source of funds for acquisition of property
- Health
- Assets, debt, and liabilities of parties
- Parties' needs
- Child custody
- Contribution as a homemaker
- Evidence of dissipation

The court's order dividing property is a final judgment and is not modifiable. For example, if the parties omitted property from the division, the party would not seek modification of the divorce degree but would have to follow the civil procedure rules for reopening a judgment.

Analysis Order for Divorce Issues

- Jurisdiction over each issue
- Original order or modification?
- Child custody
- Visitation
- Money issues
  - Child support
  - Maintenance
  - Property division

The issues involved with **parents and children** include establishing parenthood, nonmarital children, termination of parental rights, and adoption.

Establishing maternity usually is fairly straightforward for obvious reasons. With the advent of surrogacy and assisted reproduction methods, motherhood may now need to be established through adjudication.

Establishing paternity is more complicated:

* Presumption of marital paternity: A child born and conceived by a woman while she is married is presumed to be the child of her husband.
  * Presumption is rebuttable by clear and convincing evidence.
  * Many states allow DNA evidence within a few years of the child's birth.
* Putative fathers: an alleged father when the child has a presumed father:
  * State statutes dictate time limits on when an unmarried father can establish his paternity.
  * Time limits are imposed to resolve the issue without subjecting the child to a long period of unsettled circumstances.
  * Additional presumptions under the Uniform Parentage Act:
    * Parents married after the child's birth and the man voluntarily asserted his paternity.
    * Parents resided in the same household for the first two years of the child's life and the man openly held out the child as his own.

Suits to establish paternity may be brought by the mother, the child, or the state. The statute of limitations encompasses the child's minority.

A **"nonmarital child"** is a child born to an unmarried woman. Nonmarital children have the same right to support and government benefits as marital children. A nonmarital child has the same right of inheritance from its mother as a marital child. The state may require that paternity has been proven during the life of the alleged father in order to inherit from him.

Termination of parental rights occurs through emancipation of the child, voluntary relinquishment of parental rights, and involuntary termination of parental rights:

* Emancipation
  * Age of majority set by statute
  * Financial independence and maturity are considerations
  * Minor who marries before the age of majority
* Voluntary relinquishment of parental rights
* Involuntary relinquishment of parental rights
  * Due process concerns
    * Notice
    * Hearing
  * Considerations
    * Abandonment
    * Neglect
    * Abuse

Adoption questions involve jurisdiction, consent, and the consequences of adopting a child. The UCCJEA excludes adoption from its provisions. Thus, each state's statutes govern jurisdiction within the state. The biological parents must consent to the adoption by the adopting parents. Consent is not required if the biological parents' rights have been terminated or they have abandoned the child, which is defined by state statute. A committed father is entitled to due process, if he chooses to protest the adoption. Some states have statutes that grant fathers a veto right in any possible adoption. After the adoption, the adoptive parents have all the legal rights and responsibilities with their child as if they were the biological parents.

II. ESSAY PRACTICE QUESTION[1]

Fifteen years ago, Mom and Dad were married in State A, where both were domiciled.

Fourteen years ago, Mom gave birth to Daughter in State A. Dad is Daughter's biological father.

Four years ago, Dad died in State A. After Dad's death, Mom relied heavily on Dad's parents, Grandparents. Mom and Daughter moved to an apartment near Grandparents in State A. Thereafter, Grandparents visited Mom's home at least once a week. Daughter was also a frequent visitor at Grandparents' home. Grandparents also helped Mom to support Daughter financially.

Four months ago, Mom married Stepdad and moved with Daughter to Stepdad's home in State B, 500 miles from Mom's former residence in State A. Stepdad believes that Grandparents discouraged Mom's marriage to him, and he asked Mom not to invite Grandparents to visit. Mom agreed to Stepdad's request. However, she allowed Daughter to visit Grandparents in State A during a school vacation.

One week ago, Grandparents sent Daughter a bus ticket. Without revealing her plans to Mom, Daughter used the ticket to go to Grandparents' home in State A. When she arrived at Grandparents' home, Daughter telephoned Mom and said, "I hate State B, I dislike Stepdad, and I want to live with Grandparents in State A until you leave Stepdad and return to State A, too."

On the same day that Mom received this telephone call, she was served with a summons to appear in a State A court proceeding, brought by Grandparents, in which Grandparents seek custody of Daughter. Grandparents' petition was brought pursuant to a State A statute that authorizes the award of child custody to a grandparent when the court finds that (1) the "child has been abandoned or one of the child's parents has died" and (2) an award of custody to the petitioner grandparent "serves the child's best interests."

Both State A and State B have enacted the Uniform Child Custody Jurisdiction and Enforcement Act (UCCJEA).

Mom has sought advice from your law firm. She asks the following questions:

1. Does State A have jurisdiction to award custody of Daughter to Grandparents? Explain.
2. On the merits, may a court deny Grandparents' custody petition if Daughter testifies that she wants to live with Grandparents? Explain.
3. Is the State A statute authorizing the award of custody to Grandparents constitutional? Explain.

---

1. The Multistate Bar Examination ("MBE®") questions, the Multistate Essay Examination ("MEE®") questions, and excerpts from the Multistate Performance Tests ("MPT®") have been reprinted by permission from the NCBE®. Copyright© by the National Conference of Bar Examiners. All rights reserved.

III. SCORE SHEET

Stated	Implied	
_____	_____	**Point One (40%)** **Conclusion:** State A has jurisdiction because no state is Daughter's "home state"; Daughter and Mom both have significant connections with State A, and substantial evidence is available in State A regarding Daughter's care.
_____	_____	**Rule:** Under the Uniform Child Custody Jurisdiction and Enforcement Act, a state has jurisdiction to make an initial child-custody determination if "this State is the home state of the child on the date of the commencement of the proceeding, or was the home State of the child within six months before the commencement of the proceeding and the child is absent from this State but a parent or a person acting as a parent continues to live in this State" and no other state's courts would have jurisdiction under the above standard or other courts having jurisdiction have declined to exercise it.
_____	_____	A "home state" is the state in which the child "lived with a parent or a person acting as a parent for at least six consecutive months immediately before the commencement of a child-custody proceeding."
_____	_____	Under the UCCJEA, when—and only when—a court of another state does not have jurisdiction as the home-state rule, a court may exercise jurisdiction over a child-custody determination if
_____	_____	the child . . . and at least one parent . . . have a significant connection with this State other than mere physical presence; and
_____	_____	substantial evidence is available in this State concerning the child's care, protection, training, and personal relationships.
_____	_____	**Application:** Here,
_____	_____	Daughter and Mom moved to State B only four months before the State A custody petition was filed in State A, so State B is not Daughter's home state.
_____	_____	State A was the home state of Daughter within six months of the proceeding commenced in State A.
_____	_____	However, State A may not have home-state jurisdiction because neither statutory condition has been met: a parent (Mom) does not continue to live in State A, and the child is not absent from State A.
_____	_____	However, State A court would have jurisdiction because Daughter and Mom both have a significant connection with State A and substantial evidence relating to Daughter's care is available in State A: Mom was married in State A, gave birth to Daughter there, and lived there with Daughter from the time of her birth until four months ago.
_____	_____	Daughter is currently in State A, and so are Grandparents. Other evidence related to Daughter's schooling, friendships, and other personal relationships is also available in State A.
_____	_____	**Conclusion on State A:** State A has jurisdiction.
_____	_____	**Conclusion:** State B may also have jurisdiction: Daughter and Mom both have a significant connection with State B as it is where they both lived until Daughter's recent return to State A and substantial evidence from Mom, Stepdad, Daughter's school, etc., is available in State B.

continued on next page

Stated	Implied	
_____	_____	**Rule:** However, under the UCCJEA, a court "may not exercise its jurisdiction . . . if . . . a proceeding concerning the custody of the child has been commenced in a court of another State having jurisdiction substantially in conformity with this [Act]. . . ."
_____	_____	**Conclusion on State B:** Thus, State B could not exercise jurisdiction because a petition has been filed in State A.
_____	_____	**Rule:** The federal Parental Kidnapping Prevention Act (PKPA) sets out child-custody jurisdictional standards much like those contained in the UCCJEA.
_____	_____	Under the PKPA, a State A court would have jurisdiction because no state is Daughter's home state, "the child and at least one contestant[] have a significant connection with . . . State [A] other than mere physical presence . . . and there is available in such State substantial evidence concerning the child's present or future care. . . ."
_____	_____	Like the UCCJEA, the PKPA provides that where a court of another state is exercising jurisdiction that complies with the federal standard, another court shall not exercise jurisdiction.
_____	_____	**Application/Conclusion:** Thus, State A has jurisdiction over the custody action initiated by Grandparents.
		Point Two (25%)
_____	_____	**Conclusion:** Although the wishes of an older child are relevant to a custody determination and are typically given great weight, they are not determinative; a court may thus deny Grandparents' custody petition over the express opposition of Daughter.
_____	_____	**Rule:** In all states, the views of a child who is mature enough to form and express a preference are relevant to a custody determination.
_____	_____	The wishes of older children like Daughter are typically given substantial weight.
_____	_____	However, the child's wishes "are not treated equally in every case": Sometimes the child's wishes are given controlling effect, while at other times the wishes are disregarded altogether.
_____	_____	The circumstances include the comparative effect of objective factors affecting its welfare generally, the natural right of the child's parent to have its custody (frequently invoked successfully, at least in the absence of the parent's long-term abandonment of the child to another's custody): the child's age and judgment capacity; the basis for and strength of its preference, generally; the treatment extended to the child by the contestants for its custody; and the wrongful inducement of the child's wishes.
_____	_____	In a handful of states, the court must defer to the wishes of an older child when choosing between fit parents.
_____	_____	Even if State A has such a statute, it would not be applicable here, as the custody contest is between a fit parent and a nonparent.
_____	_____	**Conclusion:** Thus, although the wishes of Daughter are relevant in an action regarding her custody, a court may disregard those wishes and deny Grandparents' custody petition.
		Point Three (35%)
_____	_____	**Conclusion:** Because the State A statute gives "no special weight" to a parent's determination of her child's best interests, the statute is unconstitutional.
_____	_____	Grandparent visitation statutes require that special weight be given to a parent's determination of the child's best interests.

continued on next page

Stated	Implied	
_____	_____	A fit parent is presumed to act in the best interests of the child.
_____	_____	**Application:** Here,
_____	_____	The State A grandparent-custody statute is almost certainly unconstitutional.
_____	_____	The State A statute does not require the court to give any special weight to a parent's determination of her child's best interest; in fact, it does not appear to require the court to give *any* weight to a parent's determination of a child's best interest.
_____	_____	Moreover, the State A statute permits a much larger intrusion upon parental prerogatives in that it authorizes a court to award a nonparent *custody*, not just *visitation*.
_____	_____	Although the State A statute does restrict nonparent custody petitions to grandparents and additionally requires that the child have been abandoned or have had a parent who has died, this should not alter the constitutional analysis.
_____	_____	The State A statute is unconstitutional.

CHAPTER 19

Mapping Secured Transactions

The Uniform Commercial Code (UCC) is intimidating at first glance. Fortunately, Article 9 Secured Transactions lends itself well to mind mapping. If followed, this system results in at least 75% of the issues and rules involved.

I. MIND MAP

First, always begin your answer with "Under Article 9 of the Uniform Commercial Code, . . ." You do not need to remember UCC section numbers.

Secured Transactions (ST) focuses on creditors. A **secured transaction** is created when a debtor seeks a loan and the entity giving the loan takes a special property interest—a **security interest**—in a specific piece of the debtor's property—the **collateral**—to insure repayment of the loan. Debtors have few rights under Article 9. In a secured transaction question, debtors always don't pay their debts. Occasionally an issue that relates to the debtor's interests arises when the sale of the collateral does not follow UCC requirements. When you see only one creditor, think default.

For the most part, the issues on ST essay questions relate to which creditor has priority over the collateral in order to sell it and apply the proceeds to its loan. Thus, the issues center on the creation of the secured interest and how a creditor has priority over other creditors.

Keys to a High ST Score

- More than one creditor → almost always!
- Debtor doesn't pay → always!
- Go through each analytical step with each creditor for each piece of collateral, keeping in mind each loan that creditor made.
- Determine each creditor's status.
- Only then can you apply the correct priority rule.

Our mind map then focuses on laying out the analytical steps you must address for each creditor for each piece of collateral, keeping in mind each loan that creditor made to that debtor:

- Classify collateral
- Attachment
  - Creation of security interest
  - Debtor has rights in the collateral
  - Creditor gave value
- Perfection
- Priority
- Default

The first two steps of your analysis, classification and attachment, deal with whether the creditor has actually created a security interest. If a creditor has not created a security interest, they are at the end of the line when that collateral is sold. Creditors always want to be secured and want to be first in line. The first step then is to classify the **collateral**. This step is first because some later rules vary depending upon the classification. These classifications include:

- Consumer goods
- Business use:
  - Inventory: goods that are used up or sold
  - Farm products: crops, livestock, etc.
  - Equipment: machinery, office equipment
- Intangibles: negotiable instruments, investment property, deposit accounts
- Chattel paper: written promise to pay and security interest in goods
- Fixtures: personal property adhered to real property
- Proceeds

In addition, a creditor can include property the debtor has yet to own if it includes an **after-acquired property clause**.

The same type of personal property is not always the same type of collateral. For example, an office desk is business equipment when used in a business's office. But the same desk is inventory at the office supply store and a consumer good if a customer takes it home for personal use.

The next step, **attachment**, is one some applicants skip over instead of garnering all the low-hanging fruit points they can get by meticulously going through each step of attachment with each creditor on each collateral for each loan. Indeed, attachment is a key concept for scoring well. Attaching a security interest to collateral gives the creditor rights against the debtor on that collateral.

The concept of attachment starts with creating the security interest itself and then affixing the security interest to the collateral.

A mnemonic to remember the creation of a security interest is **CAP**. A creditor can create a security interest by having **control** of an intangible, by having an authenticated security **agreement** creating the security interest, or by taking **possession** of the collateral.

But the security interest just created is worthless if it is not affixed to specific collateral. To affix the security interest to the collateral, the debtor must also

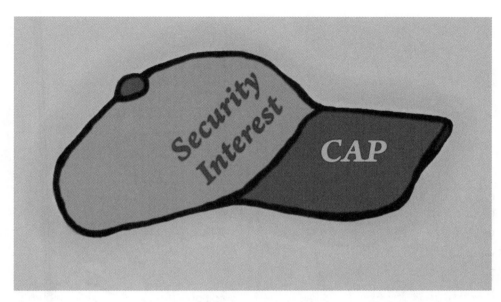

Creating a Security Interest

have rights in the collateral and the creditor must give value. If the security interest never attaches to the collateral, then the creditor remains unsecured and the creditor cannot claim that specific property to sell.

Use the mneumonic ARV to remember the requirements to attach a security interest to collateral:

ARV
- **A**uthenticated security agreement/possession/control
  - **C**ontrol: used for intangibles
  - **A**uthenticated security **a**greement
  - **P**ossession
- Debtor has **R**ights in the collateral.
- Secured party gives **V**alue in exchange for a security interest.

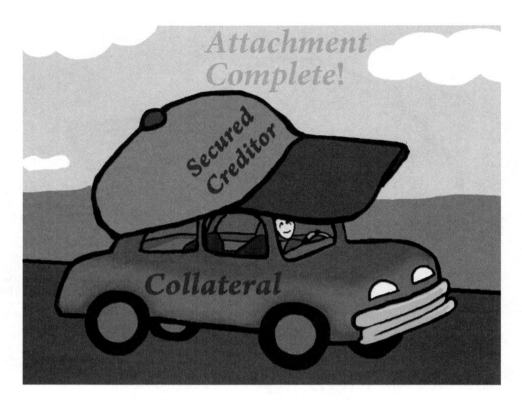

Once the security interest has attached to the collateral, the secured creditor must tell the rest of the world that it has a security interest in this specific collateral in order to claim priority over other creditors. This notice is called **perfection**. The security interest must be perfected in the specific collateral.

Methods of perfection:

- File financing statement
- Automatic
- Temporary
- Possession
- Control

Not all five types of perfection apply to all types of collateral. For example, possession cannot work on intangibles as there is nothing to possess. Have you noticed that possession and control keep popping up? Possession or control of collateral not only creates a security interest, but it also operates as perfection.

The most common way to perfect a security interest is to file a **financing statement** with the Secretary of State's office where the collateral is located. This gives actual notice to those who look at the financing statement and constructive notice to all others.

> **Perfection or control of collateral are a triple threat! They operate to:**
>
> - create a security interest,
> - satisfy one step of attachment, and
> - perfect the security interest.

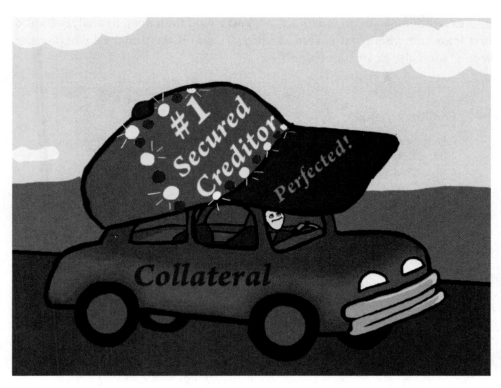

Perfection of a Security Interest

Automatic perfection arises with a special kind of secured interest called a **Purchase Money Security Interest** (PMSI). A PMSI is created when:

- Seller sells goods to a buyer on credit
  OR
- Lender lends the purchaser money to buy specific goods

This security interest is given special status because the lender or seller has directly given value for a particular purchase. PMSI creditors who properly perfect are given priority over all other perfected secured creditors—a super-priority.

If the PMSI is for the purchase of consumer goods, perfection is automatic. The creditor doesn't need to do anything except for two situations: for motor vehicles, where the security interest must be noted on the vehicle's title, and for fixtures that require filing in the Recorder of Deeds office.

Not all PMSIs have automatic perfection. If the PMSI purchase is collateral other than consumer goods, the security interest is **temporarily perfected** for 20 days. If the creditor files a financing statement within the 20 days, its priority relates back and continues. If they perfect over 20 days, they lose their PMSI status, although they still are a perfected secured creditor. If they don't perfect, they are an unperfected secured creditor.

Remember to go through classification, attachment, and perfection with each creditor for each piece of collateral and each loan. Determine each creditor's status on each collateral. For example, Bank has a security interest in Machine One and gives a loan of $100,000. Debtor then acquires Machine Two. Does Bank's security interest cover Machine Two? Let's say it does, and then Bank gives a second loan to debtor for $50,000. Does the security interest apply to the second loan? Then, our second creditor is Finance. Finance gave Debtor a loan of $75,000 to purchase Machine Two. The call of the question is who has priority over Machine Two. You would need to analyze Finance's

EXAM TIP

PMSI issues are ripe for picking! Remember, only security interests in consumer goods have automatic perfection. Everything else requires the creditor to perfect within 20 days. If they don't, they lose super-priority. If you classify the collateral first and remember this distinction, you will have it nailed.

interest with one loan on one machine. You would then need to analyze Bank's first loan and whether it covers Machine Two and then analyze whether the second loan also covers Machine Two.

Creditor's Status

- Perfected secured party
- Unperfected secured party
- Unsecured party

Use this chart while doing practice essays to get used to analyzing creditors' interests separately and to analyze each collateral and loan for each creditor separately.

Once you have identified each creditor as a perfected secured creditor, an unperfected secured creditor, or an unsecured creditor, you need to apply the correct **priority** rule to the conflicting interests. Be sure to keep track of the dates each event occurs. Constructing a timeline can help.

Priority Rules for Creditors

PMSI Perfected Secured Creditor = **Wins over all other creditors**
Perfected Secured Creditor v. Perfected Secured Creditor = **First to File or Perfect**
Perfected Secured Creditor v. Unperfected Secured Creditor = **Perfected Secured Creditor**
Unperfected Secured Creditor v. Unperfected Secured Creditor = **First to Attach**
Secured creditor (whether or not perfected) v. Unsecured Creditor = **Secured Creditor**

Pay particular attention to the rule for a dispute between two perfected secured creditors. The rule is the **first to file or perfect**. "Perfect" means the creditor has already created the security interest, attached the security interest, *and* perfected its interest. "File" means they have filed a financing statement. The creditor need do nothing else at first. It's like calling "dibs" to hold your place in line. The creditor who just files is holding its place in line. It keeps its place in line as long as it completes the requirements of creating and attaching its security interest. Its interest then relates back to the original filing date. Thus, even if a second creditor comes along and perfects fulfilling all three steps first, the first creditor has priority.

THIS RULE IS THE NUMBER ONE BAR TRAP! This rule is tested frequently and absolutely must be understood and recognized on an essay.

A note concerning two other types of entities that may usurp a secured party's place in line: buyers and lien creditors. The general rule is that a secured interest stays attached to the collateral despite a sale to a buyer. There are three primary exceptions: when the creditor consents, when the buyer is in the ordinary course of business, and when a buyer purchases a consumer good from another consumer (garage sale exception).

EXAM TIP

1ST to Perfect v. 1st to Attach
While perfection of a security interest relates back to the date of the filing, attachment does not occur until the last event and does not relate back.

			Creditor #1			Creditor #2		
			Original	Proceeds?	After-Acquired?	Original	Proceeds?	After-Acquired?
	Classify Collateral	1. Tangible (CIFE) **C**onsumer Goods **I**nventory **F**arm Products **E**quipment 2. Intangible 3. Proceeds						
Decides If S E C U R E D	Attachment (**ARV**)	**A**uthenticated Security Agreement (Can be by **P**ossession, **A**greement, or **C**ontrol) **PAC**						
		Debtor has **R**ights in collateral						
		Creditor has given **V**alue						
	Perfection	Filed Financing Statement **OR**						
		Possession **OR**						
		Control						
		Possible **PMSI**? (Automatic if consumer goods; 20 days temporary perfection if not)						

SECURED TRANSACTIONS ANALYSIS CHART
Is creditor secured and perfected for this property with this loan?

A buyer in the ordinary course of business (BIOC) purchases the goods from a seller who sells goods as part of their regular business. A buyer of consumer goods who, in a resale, purchases consumer goods with an automatically perfected PMSI takes free of the creditor's security interest. If, however, the creditor does file, then the security interest remains attached.

Buyers

Discount store shopping = BIOC
Car purchase from car dealer = BIOC (but if purchase on credit, buyer has given creditor its own security interest)
Car purchase from neighbor = Not BIOC (unless neighbor in car selling business]
Garage sale purchase = Not BIOC, but possible buyer of consumer goods

---

A lien creditor is not a secured creditor. The lien creditor acquires a lien on the collateral through a court judgment. If the lien creditor has levied on the collateral before a security interest is perfected, then the lien creditor has priority except for a PMSI creditor.

The last step of your analysis is to look for any issues related to **default**. Default is defined by the security agreement between the parties. Thus, whether a default has occurred will be given to you. Upon default, the creditor can take two steps. It usually does both, although depending upon the collateral and the amount of the remaining debt it may decide to take only one of the steps.

- Creditor can sue upon the debt
  OR
- Take possession of the property

Possession can occur by an action for replevin or by self-help repossession. Yes, the repo man. Self-help repossession is allowed as long as there is no breach of the peace. Do not rely on any reality television show for defining breach of the peace! If in doubt, give the reasoning on both sides.

After default, the debtor has a right to redeem the debt. The debtor must pay the entire debt plus attorney fees. They are then entitled to keep the collateral.

Any sale of the collateral upon default must be commercially reasonable.

- Is a public or private sale required or allowed?
- Has notice been given to all parties?
  - Notice not required if:
    - property can be sold on a recognized market, such as the stock market, or
    - the collateral is perishable (that is, the collateral's value is threatened to decline prior to sale; think of a truck full of lettuce to get the picture).
- Has secured party made an effort to get the best price?

Following the sale, the proceeds are distributed in a set order. If the sale proceeds don't cover the debt and costs, the debtor is still liable for the remainder—a deficiency judgment. If the creditor does not follow the proper procedure after default, it may forfeit the right to receive a deficiency judgment. The distribution order is:

- Costs of sale
- First secured party's debt
- Any other secured party's debt in priority order
- Surplus to debtor (very rare)

Five tricky issues arise in secured transactions questions. The file or perfect rule is the most common. PMSI issues are second. The remaining traps are after-acquired property, future advances, and proceeds. Understand the rules for these five issues and the fact patterns that trigger the issues and you are well on your way to a high score on a secured transactions essay.

Beware of Bar Traps

- File OR Perfect
- Purchase Money Security Interest
- After-acquired property
- Proceeds
- Future advances

After-acquired property clauses are one of the reasons that you *must* analyze each creditor's interest by analyzing attachment and perfection. After-acquired property issues arise when a creditor's initial security agreement includes a clause that covers future acquisitions of property. The security interest attaches the moment the debtor acquires an interest in the new collateral. An after-acquired property clause is not needed for inventory or

After-Acquired Property

Future Advances

proceeds. After-acquired property clauses are tricky because typically a second or third creditor pops up between the first creditor's first acquisition of the security interest and the debtor's acquisition of the second collateral. If you lay the groundwork of attachment and perfection, you garner most of the points for the question, even if you are incorrect on who would ultimately prevail.

Likewise, a **future advance** clause refers to events that happen after the initial security agreement. Here, the creditor loans additional money and the original security interest secures the loan. The second loan is covered only if the original security agreement includes a future advances clause. Look for it when the debtor gets additional money from the same creditor. The same tricky circumstances arise as with after-acquired property—a second creditor jumps in and loans money to the debtor. If the first creditor did not include a future advance clause, then it must get a new security agreement from the debtor. This security agreement will relate back to the original filing. Just keep track of attachment and perfection of each piece of collateral and each loan and you'll get the points.

The last tricky issue regards **proceeds**. Proceeds occur when the original collateral is sold. Whatever the debtor receives from the sale is proceeds, including cash, negotiable instruments, and chattel paper. Proceeds are temporarily perfected for 20 days. That perfection continues if the proceeds are identifiable cash proceeds or the financing statement for the proceeds would be filed in the same office as the original collateral. If it's in a different office, then another filing (possession or control) must occur.

Follow the mind map, analyze each creditor separately on each piece of collateral and on each loan, and you will garner most of the points available on a secured transaction question.

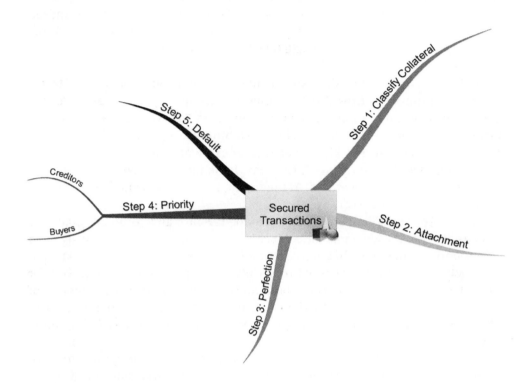

II. ESSAY PRACTICE QUESTION[1]

Debtor manufactures widgets. On May 3, Lender loaned Debtor $100,000 for general operating expenses. That same day, Lender filed a valid financing statement signed by Debtor, in the proper U.C.C. filing offices. The financing statement covered all widget machines owned by Debtor, "including after-acquired widget machines." On that date, May 3, Debtor owned just one widget machine, Machine No.1, which was worth $50,000. No security agreement was signed at that time.

On May 13, a second lender, Bank, loaned Debtor an additional $100,000 for general operating expenses. On the same day, Debtor signed a valid security agreement that granted Bank a security interest in "all widget machines, now owned or hereafter acquired by Debtor." Debtor also signed a valid financing statement, which covered all widget machines owned by Debtor, "including after-acquired widget machines." That day, Bank filed the financing statement in the proper U.C.C. filing offices. At that point, Debtor still owned just one widget machine, Machine No.1.

On May 16, a third lender, Credit Co, loaned Debtor an additional $50,000 to purchase a second widget machine, Machine No.2. On that day, Debtor signed a valid security agreement that granted Credit Co a security interest in Machine No.2. Debtor used the proceeds of Credit Co's loan to purchase Machine No.2 for $50,000 on the next day, May 17. Debtor, however, did not receive possession of Machine No.2 until May 28. On May 31, Credit Co filed a valid financing statement that covered Machine No.2, signed by Debtor, in the proper U.C.C. filing offices.

Meanwhile, on May 29, Lender discovered that it had forgotten to have Debtor sign a security agreement for the May 3 loan. Later that day, May 29, Lender got Debtor to sign a security agreement in which Debtor granted to Lender a security interest in all of Debtor's widget machines, "including after-acquired widget machines." On that date, May 29, Debtor owned both widget machines, Machine No.1 and Machine No.2, each of which was worth $50,000.

Debtor subsequently defaulted on all three loans. Shortly after the default, but before any of Debtor's creditors took steps to repossess the widget machines, Debtor sold Machine No.2 to Widget Co., another widget manufacturer, for $25,000. Widget Co. purchased the machine in good faith and had no actual knowledge that Machine No.2 was covered by a security interest.

1. As between Lender and Bank, whose security interest has first priority as to Machine No.1? Explain.
2. As among Lender, Bank, and Credit Co, whose security interest has first priority as to Machine No.2? Explain.
3. Can the secured party with priority recover Machine No.2 from the purchaser, Widget Co.? Explain.

---

1. The Multistate Bar Examination ("MBE®") questions, the Multistate Essay Examination ("MEE®") questions, and excerpts from the Multistate Performance Tests ("MPT®") have been reprinted by permission from the NCBE®. Copyright© by the National Conference of Bar Examiners. All rights reserved.

III. SCORE SHEET

Stated	Implied	
		Issue #1 Overall Conclusion/Issue—Machine 1
_____	_____	As between Lender and Bank, Lender has priority in Machine No. 1.
_____	_____	At issue is the priority between two perfected security interests in the same collateral.
_____	_____	Article 9 governs security interests and provides rules for priority of security interests.
		Creation/Attachment/Perfection of Creditors' Security Interests
_____	_____	Both Lender and Bank have perfected security interests.
		Conclusion
_____	_____	Security interest must attach.
		Rule—Attachment
_____	_____	Attachment requires a security agreement describing the collateral and granting a security interest in the collateral (or possession or control of the collateral), the creditor must give value, and the debtor has rights in the collateral.
		Application/Conclusion—Attachment
_____	_____	Debtor clearly had rights in the machine here, since it owns the machine.
_____	_____	Lender and Bank each gave value in exchange for their security interests ($100,000 loans).
_____	_____	Thus, Lender's security interest attached on May 29, when occurred the last event necessary for attachment (getting debtor to sign a written security agreement).
_____	_____	Bank's security interest attached on May 13, the date Bank accomplished all steps necessary for attachment of its security agreement.
		Rule—Perfection
_____	_____	A security interest may be perfected by filing, in an appropriate place, a financing statement describing the collateral that is authorized by the debtor in an authenticated record.
		Application/Conclusion—Perfection
_____	_____	Here, Lender filed a financing statement on May 3, and Bank filed a financing statement on May 13.
_____	_____	Debtor's later signature on the security agreement authorized the filing (the later authorization ratified the financing statement from the moment of filing).
		Conclusion—Classification of Creditors' Security Interests
_____	_____	Both Bank and Lender have perfected security interests in Machine No. 1.
		Rule—Priority
_____	_____	The basic priority rule for competing security interests where both are perfected is that the first interest for which a financing statement is filed or the first interest to be perfected, whichever is first, has priority.
		Application/Conclusion—Priority
_____	_____	Since both Bank and Lender have perfected security interests in the same collateral and Lender filed before Bank filed or perfected, Lender has priority in Machine No. 1.
_____	_____	Does not matter that Bank's security interest was perfected first, because the first to file or perfect has priority, whichever comes first.

continued on next page

Stated	Implied	
_____	_____	**Issue 2** *Overall Conclusion/Issue—Machine 2*
		Credit Co has first priority in Machine No. 2.
_____	_____	At issue is whether Credit Co has the super-priority of a purchase money security interest ("PMSI").
		Rule
_____	_____	A security interest in after-acquired property has the same priority as the security interest in the original collateral.
		Lender's classification
_____	_____	Here, Lender has a perfected security interest in Machine No. 2 since Lender's security interest and financing statement included an after-acquired property clause granting Lender a security interest in any widget machines that Debtor may acquire in the future.
		Bank's classification
_____	_____	Bank similarly reserved a security interest in after-acquired widget machines and has a perfected security interest in Machine No. 2.
		Credit Co's classification
		Conclusion
_____	_____	Credit Co has a PMSI in Machine No. 2 and its security interest was perfected within 20 days after Debtor received possession of the machine.
		Rule—PMSI defined
_____	_____	A PMSI arises where a creditor advances funds which are used by the debtor to purchase the collateral.
		Application—PMSI
_____	_____	Here, Credit Co gave Debtor $50,000 to purchase Machine No. 2 and Debtor used the money to purchase that machine.
		Application—Attachment of PMSI (rule does not need to be repeated)
_____	_____	Moreover, Credit Co's security interest attached to the machine since Credit Co gave value (the $50,000 loan), Debtor has an interest in the machine (owns the machine), and Debtor signed a security agreement granting Credit Co a security interest in the machine.
		Application—Perfection of PMSI (rule does not need to be repeated)
_____	_____	Credit Co also perfected its security interest by filing an authorized financing statement in the appropriate filing office on May 31.
		Rule—Priority with PMSI
_____	_____	Article 9 provides that a PMSI in non-inventory collateral will have priority over other perfected security interests in the same collateral as long as the security interest is perfected within 20 days after the debtor receives possession of the collateral.
		Application/Conclusion—Priority with PMSI
_____	_____	Since the filing took place just three days after Debtor received possession of the machine, Credit Co qualifies for the PMSI super-priority and has first priority on Machine No. 2.
		Issue 3 Conclusion/Issue
_____	_____	The secured party with priority can recover Machine No. 2 from Widget Co.

continued on next page

Stated	Implied	
_____	_____	At issue is whether a buyer of goods outside the ordinary course of business takes the goods subject to a perfected security interest in the goods.
		General rule
_____	_____	A perfected security interest in collateral is *not* defeated by a sale of the collateral to a third party; the third party takes the collateral subject to the perfected security interest and the secured party will have the right to recover the collateral from the third-party purchaser on the debtor's default.
_____	_____	True, even if the third party purchased the collateral in good faith and without actual knowledge of the perfected security interest, because perfection is deemed to provide sufficient constructive notice of the security interest.
		Exception
_____	_____	If the buyer purchases the goods in the regular course of business (i.e., from someone in the business of selling goods of the kind), then the buyer takes free of any security interest formed by the seller.
		Application of Exception
_____	_____	Nothing in the facts indicates that the sale by Debtor was in the regular course of business.
_____	_____	Exception does not apply. The security interest stays attached to Machine No. 2 and the secured party with priority may recover.

CHAPTER 20

Mapping Conflict of Laws

Conflict of Laws is no longer a stand-alone topic; that is, you will not have a question that only involves Conflict of Laws. Instead, Conflict of Laws issues will be embedded into other MEE topic areas. The most frequent inclusion is in Federal Civil Procedure, Contracts, Family Law, and Wills. The Conflicts portion of a question may well be over 50% of the points allowed. Thus, spend some time on Conflicts, but not as much time as you would on other topics that stand alone.

I. MIND MAP

Conflict of Laws centers around two main issues:

- Recognition of another state's judgment
- Choice of law in an on-going suit

A. Recognition of Another State's Judgment

Whether a judgment in one state is recognized by another state is governed by the **Full Faith and Credit Clause** of the Constitution: "Full faith and credit shall be given in each state to the public acts, records, and judicial proceedings of every state."[1] A federal statute provides that this clause is extended to federal courts requiring recognition of judgments between state and federal courts and between federal courts. Three considerations arise:

- Requirements met?
- Any defenses?
- Effects of recognition

Analyze **each requirement** of the Full Faith and Credit Clause separately:

- There must be proper jurisdiction:
  - Subject-matter and personal jurisdiction.
  - If jurisdiction was fully and fairly litigated in the original action, the defendant cannot have that determination re-litigated in the recognizing state.

---

1. U.S. Const. art. IV, §1.

- Why? The litigated issue of jurisdiction has already been determined. That determination is subject to full faith and credit itself.
- Judgment must be on the merits:
  - Must involve the substance of the plaintiff's claim.
  - Includes default judgments.
- Judgment must be final: No further action by the rendering court is needed to resolve the litigation.

Defenses to full faith and credit include penal judgments, extrinsic fraud, and inconsistent judgments. The public policy exception is no longer recognized. Thus, even if the first action in the rendering state could not have been brought under the recognizing state's law as it was against that state's public policy, the recognizing state is required to enforce it.

The **effects** of applying full faith and credit are *res judicata* and enforcement of the judgment. *Res judicata* operates the same in the recognizing state as it does in the rendering state. Because both parties and those in privity with those parties are bound, the recognizing court can enforce the judgment against them. Parties in privity include beneficiaries, holders of future interests, successors in interest, and all persons represented in a class action.

A special note about **family law** judgments. Full Faith and Credit applies to divorce judgments as long as one of the spouses is domiciled in the rendering state. Domicile is determined by physical presence and intent to be domiciled.

Meanwhile, **child custody** is governed by reciprocal statutes adopted by all 50 states. The Uniform Child Custody Jurisdiction and Enforcement Act determines which state is the "home state" of the child and all other states must give full faith and credit to that judgment. The home state retains jurisdiction and no other court may modify that order unless the rendering court has no remaining significant connection with the child or any parties in the dispute.

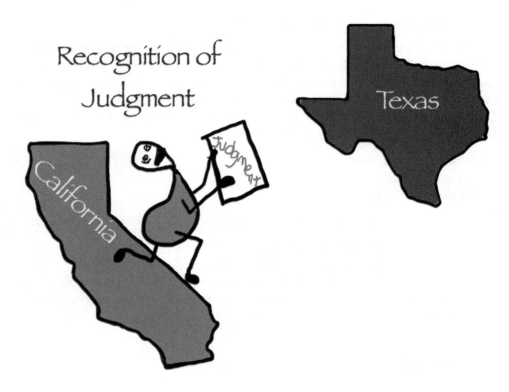

Full Faith and Credit

B. Choice of Law

Deciding what law applies to an ongoing case when two or more potential jurisdictions' laws apply is determined by the choice of law approach used by the forum trying the case. Questions may ask you to analyze the issue under each approach or to analyze under a single approach. The approaches to focus upon are:

- Vested-Rights Approach of the First Restatement:
  - Traditional approach.
  - Forum state must apply the law of the state in which the rights of the parties "vest"—where the act or relationship giving rise to the cause of action occurred or was created.
  - Forum applies its own procedural rules, although applying a foreign state's substantive law.
    - Particularly relevant for statute of limitations.
      - Traditional approach viewed as procedural.
      - More modern approach views as substantive.
  - Characterization as procedural or substantive determined by the forum state's law.
- Most Significant-Relationship Approach of the Second Restatement:
  - Modern approach.
  - All circumstances considered to determine which state has the most significant relationship to each issue raised.
  - *Depeçage*: choice of law depends upon the issue involved:
    - Different factors for different topics of law.
    - Different law may apply in one cause of action as determined by each issue.
  - Public policy considerations.
    - the needs of the interstate and international systems to further harmony and facilitate commerce;
    - the relevant policies of the forum;
    - the relevant policies of other interested states;
    - protection of justified expectations;
    - the basic policies underlying the particular field of law;
    - certainty, predictability, and uniformity of result; and
    - the ease in the determination and application of the law to be applied.

Special rules may exist under each approach for specific topics.

1. Torts

The vested-rights approach looks to the law of the place of the wrong. In essence, the place where the last event giving rise to the injury occurred.

The significant-relationship approach looks at which state has the most significant relationship to both the occurrence and the parties. Factors considered include:

- place of the injury;
- place where the conduct causing the injury occurred;

* the domicile, residence, nationality, place of incorporation, and place of business of the parties; and
* the place where the relationship between the parties is centered.

2. Contracts

If the parties choose to include a clause that expressly sets forth the governing law, a court will apply that law. If the contract does not specify which law applies, the traditional approach would look to the place where the contract was made or performed.

Displeased with the often mechanical application of the traditional approach, the modern approach considers:

* the place of contracting;
* the place of negotiation of the contract;
* the place of performance;
* the location of the subject matter of the contract; and
* the domicile, residence, nationality, place of incorporation, and place of business of the parties.

3. Property

If the issue is the interpretation of a real estate contract, then the contract choice-of-law rules apply. If the cause of action focuses on a property interest, then the first step is to characterize the property as immovable or movable:

* Immovable: closely connected with or related to land:
  * Law of the *situs* governs.
  * Includes mortgages, validity of a deed, capacity of a grantor, and liens.
* Movable: all other property interests, including personal property:
  * Law of the *situs* at the time of the relevant transaction governs.
  * Security interests and sale of goods governed by the Uniform Commercial Code.
  * Intangible: law of the representative instrument governs. If no instrument, then the law of the place of transfer.

4. Corporations

Look to the law of the state of incorporation regarding issues of the existence of a corporation and issues related to its structure, including the authority and liability of directors and the rights of shareholders.

5. Family Law

Choice of law in an action that must determine the validity of a marriage can range from a probate action, a property dispute, or a dissolution of marriage. A marriage is generally valid if the state where celebrated considers it a valid marriage. An exception is if the marriage violates a prohibitory rule of the domicile of one of the parties. Choice of law relating to the grounds for divorce is governed by the plaintiff's domicile. Remember, a divorce may be entered even if there is no personal service or domicile of the other party as the divorce itself needs only subject-matter jurisdiction. The other party may attack a finding of domicile of the procuring party. For a judgment to pay money or transfer property, personal jurisdiction is required.

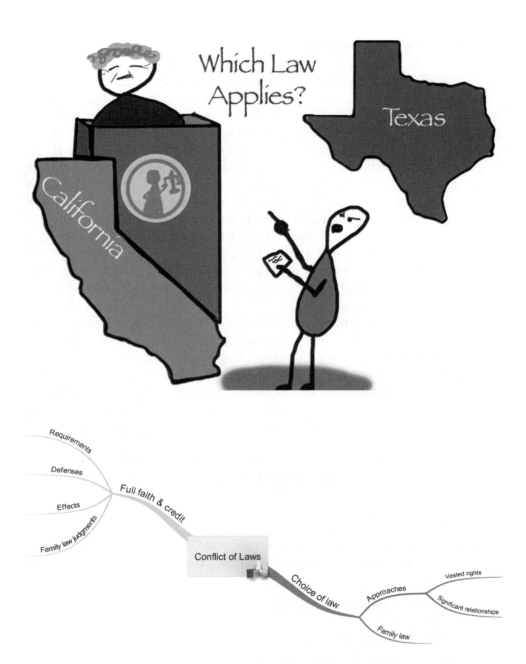

II. ESSAY PRACTICE QUESTION[2]

Note: This question combines Conflict of Laws with Family Law

Dave and Meg lived in State A. Three years ago, they began dating. Two years ago, Meg became pregnant with their child. Shortly thereafter, Dave and Meg discussed marriage. Dave told Meg, "Perhaps we should get married if we're going to have a child." Meg told Dave, "I am committed to marrying you, but I want a real wedding, and we can't afford that now." Meg proposed that Dave move in with her so that "we can save money to get married." Dave agreed and began living in Meg's rented apartment. Meg did not tell her landlord about Dave. She did tell her family and friends that "Dave, my fiancé, has moved in."

Fifteen months ago, Meg gave birth to Child. Meg and Dave agreed that Child's birth certificate would identify Dave as Child's father. Meg and Dave sent birth announcements to friends and relatives noting the birth of "our son, Child." After Child's birth, Meg quit work. Dave took on a second job in order to support Meg and Child.

Five months ago, Meg took Child and abruptly left Dave. Dave hired a private investigator to find Meg and Child. The investigator recently discovered that they are living in State B with Husband, whom Meg married three months ago. The investigator also discovered that Meg and Husband have filed a petition to terminate Dave's parental rights and authorize Husband's adoption of Child.

State B permits a mother or a married father to veto the adoption of his or her child unless he or she "has willfully refused to support said child for a period of one or more years."

State B permits an unmarried father to veto the adoption of his child only if he (a) "has consistently supported such child" and (b) "has maintained a residential relationship with such child for at least 9 of the 12 months immediately preceding the filing of an adoption petition."

State B does not have a putative father registry.

State A recognizes common law marriage. State B does not. Both State A and State B have adopted the Uniform Child Custody Jurisdiction and Enforcement Act (UCCJEA).

1. Will State B recognize a common law marriage contracted in State A? Explain.
2. Did Dave and Meg enter into a common law marriage in State A? Explain.
3. Assuming that Dave is an unmarried father, can State B constitutionally grant Meg and Husband's adoption petition over Dave's opposition? Explain.
4. Does the UCCJEA permit State B to terminate Dave's parental rights or issue an order awarding custody of Child to Meg? Explain.

---

2. The Multistate Bar Examination ("MBE®") questions, the Multistate Essay Examination ("MEE®") questions, and excerpts from the Multistate Performance Tests ("MPT®") have been reprinted by permission from the NCBE®. Copyright© by the National Conference of Bar Examiners. All rights reserved.

III. SCORE SHEET

Stated	Implied	
		Issue 1: Conclusion on Conflicts of Law issue:
_____	_____	A common law marriage that is valid where contracted is also valid in a state that does not permit common law marriage.
_____	_____	**Rule:** Under accepted conflict-of-laws principles,
_____	_____	A marriage valid under the law of the place in which it was contracted is valid elsewhere unless it violates a strong public policy of the state which has the most significant relationship with the spouses and the marriage.
_____	_____	If a man and woman were domiciled in a state that permits common law marriage and their conduct met the requirements of that state's law for establishing such a marriage, recognition of the marriage does not violate a strong public policy.
_____	_____	A common law marriage, once established, is the equivalent of a ceremonial marriage.
_____	_____	**Application/Conclusion:** Thus, if Dave and Meg entered into a valid common law marriage in State A, it would be recognized by a State B court.
		Issue 2: Conclusion on common law marriage issue:
_____	_____	Dave and Meg did not enter into a common law marriage.
_____	_____	**Rule:** Under family law,
_____	_____	To establish a common law marriage, the proponent must show:
_____	_____	(1) capacity to enter a marital contract,
_____	_____	(2) a present agreement that the two parties are married,
_____	_____	(3) cohabitation, and
_____	_____	(4) "holding out" a marital relationship to the community.
_____	_____	**Application:** Here,
_____	_____	The evidence clearly establishes capacity and cohabitation. It also suggests an agreement to *become* married.
_____	_____	However, a common law marriage requires a *present* marriage agreement.
_____	_____	If Dave and Meg made any marriage agreement, it was an agreement to be married *in the future*:
_____	_____	Meg told Dave that she was "committed to marrying him," but "wanted a real wedding, and we can't afford that now;" Meg also proposed that Dave move in with her so that "we can save money to get married."
_____	_____	There is also no evidence that Dave and Meg held themselves out as a married couple. Although Meg said to friends and family that Dave was her fiancé, a fiancé is an intended spouse, not a current marriage partner.
_____	_____	**Conclusion:** Thus, Dave and Meg did not enter into a valid common law marriage, and Dave would be categorized as an unmarried father under State B's adoption-consent statute.
		Issue 3: Conclusion on constitutionality:
_____	_____	State B is constitutionally prohibited from permitting the child's adoption without his consent.

continued on next page

Stated	Implied	
_____	_____	**Rule:** An unwed father must demonstrate a full commitment to the responsibilities of parenthood by participating in the rearing of his child.
_____	_____	Then, his interest in personal contact with his child acquires substantial protection under the Fourteenth Amendment Due Process Clause.
_____	_____	**Application:** Here,
_____	_____	Dave is a committed father who consistently held himself out as a parent, who resided with his child and who provided support for his child and the child's mother.
_____	_____	**Conclusion on commitment:** Thus, Dave has a strong argument that State B is constitutionally precluded from permitting his child's adoption without his consent.
_____	_____	**Rule on constitutionality:** A committed father is entitled to a hearing to demonstrate his parental fitness before his parental rights may be terminated.
_____	_____	Rule conflict as to whether an unmarried father has a right to veto an adoption by another man.
_____	_____	**Application:** Dave has demonstrated the kind of commitment that should trigger protection under the Fourteenth Amendment.
_____	_____	Dave held himself out as Child's father; he consented to be identified as Child's father on Child's birth certificate and sent birth announcements identifying himself as Child's father.
_____	_____	Dave lived with Child and Child's mother and provided support to them.
_____	_____	After Child's birth, Dave was the only family breadwinner and held down two jobs in order to provide for Meg and Child.
_____	_____	He also had volunteered to marry Meg and thus would have been a marital father had Meg agreed. Dave is also blameless for his failure to satisfy the statutory veto requirements; Dave would have lived with Child and Meg for the relevant nine-month period but for Meg's abrupt and unannounced departure from their home.
_____	_____	**Conclusion on constitutionality of adoption-consent statute:** It is likely that Dave would prevail.
_____	_____	**Rule:** Adoption-consent statutes that would deny a veto right to a father who has done everything in his power to establish a full relationship with his child are unconstitutional as applied in such a case.
_____	_____	Under federal law, a voluntary acknowledgment of paternity is binding if unchallenged by the named father within 60 days.
_____	_____	State B does not provide unmarried fathers with a putative father registry, and Dave thus had no way of obtaining notice of an adoption proceeding.
_____	_____	**Application:** Here, Dave established his paternity by voluntarily acknowledging Child and causing his name to be placed on Child's birth certificate.
_____	_____	**Conclusion:** Thus, State B's adoption consent statute appears to be unconstitutional as applied to Dave, a committed parent who has fully participated in the rearing of his child.
_____	_____	***Issue 4: Conclusion on Choice of Law for child custody:***
_____	_____	Because State A has been Child's home state within the past six months and Dave, a parent continues to live in State A, State B does not have jurisdiction to terminate Dave's parental rights or to make an initial child-custody determination respecting Child.
_____	_____	Under the Uniform Child Custody Jurisdiction and Enforcement Act, a child's "home state" has exclusive jurisdiction to issue an initial custody decree.

continued on next page

Stated	Implied	
_____	_____	A "home state" is a state where the child has lived with "a parent, or a person acting as a parent, for at least six consecutive months immediately before the commencement of a child-custody proceeding."
_____	_____	A "child-custody proceeding" includes a proceeding for termination of parental rights.
_____	_____	A home state continues to have exclusive jurisdiction to issue an initial custody order even if the child is absent from the state when a custody petition is brought, so long as no more than six months has elapsed since the child's departure from the jurisdiction and a parent or person acting as a parent continues to live in the home state.
_____	_____	Physical presence of, or personal jurisdiction over, a party or a child is not necessary to make a child-custody determination.
_____	_____	**Application:** Here, Meg took Child from the family home in State A only five months ago, and Dave still lives in State A.
_____	_____	**Conclusion:** Thus, State A has exclusive jurisdiction to issue an initial custody decree and also to terminate parental rights. State B lacks jurisdiction to do either.
		(Note: The UCCJEA does not apply to adoption proceedings, but termination of a parent's rights is typically a precondition for an adoption. Thus, as a practicality, the UCCJEA should preclude a State B court from granting petition for Husband's adoption of Child.)